Writing History in Late Imperial Russia

Library of Modern Russia

Advisory Board:

Jeffrey Brooks, Professor at Johns Hopkins University, USA
Michael David-Fox, Professor at Georgetown University, USA
Lucien Frary, Associate Professor at Rider University, USA
James Harris, Senior Lecturer at the University of Leeds, UK
Robert Hornsby, Lecturer at the University of Leeds, UK
Ekaterina Pravilova, Professor of History at Princeton University, USA
Geoffrey Swain, Emeritus Professor of Central and East European Studies at the University of Glasgow, UK
Vera Tolz-Zilitinkevic, Sir William Mather Professor of Russian Studies at the University of Manchester, UK
Vladislav Zubok, Professor of International History at the London School of Economics, UK

Building on Bloomsbury Academic's established record of publishing Russian studies titles, the *Library of Modern Russia* will showcase the work of emerging and established writers who are setting new agendas in the field.

At a time when potentially dangerous misconceptions and misunderstandings about Russia abound, titles in the series will shed fresh light and nuance on Russian history. Volumes will take the idea of 'Russia' in its broadest cultural sense and cover the entirety of the multi-ethnic lands that made up imperial Russia and the Soviet Union. Ranging in chronological scope from the Romanovs to today, the books will:

- Reconsider Russia's history from a variety of inter-disciplinary perspectives.
- Explore Russia in its various international contexts, rather than as exceptional or in isolation.
- Examine the complex, divisive and ever-shifting notions of 'Russia'.
- Contribute to a deeper understanding of Russia's rich social and cultural history.
- Critically reassess the Soviet period and its legacy today.
- Interrogate the traditional periodizations of the post-Stalin Soviet Union.
- Unearth continuities, or otherwise, among the tsarist, Soviet and post-Soviet periods.
- Reappraise Russia's complex relationship with eastern Europe, both historically and today.
- Analyse the politics of history and memory in post-Soviet Russia.
- Promote new archival revelations and innovative research methodologies.
- Foster a community of scholars and readers devoted to a sharper understanding of the Russian experience, past and present.

Books in the series will join our list in being marketed globally, including at conferences – such as the BASEES and ASEEES conventions. Each will be subjected to a rigorous peer-review process and will be published in hardback and, simultaneously, as an e-book. We also anticipate a second release in paperback for the general reader and student markets.

For more information, or to submit a proposal for inclusion in the series, please contact: Rhodri Mogford, Publisher, History (Rhodri.Mogford@bloomsbury.com).

New and forthcoming:

Fascism in Manchuria: The Soviet-China Encounter in the 1930s, Susanne Hohler

The Idea of Russia: The Life and Work of Dmitry Likhachev, Vladislav Zubok

The Tsar's Armenians: A Minority in Late Imperial Russia, Onur Onol

Myth Making in the Soviet Union and Modern Russia: Remembering World War II in Brezhnev's Hero City, Vicky Davis

Building Stalinism: The Moscow Canal and the Creation of Soviet Space, Cynthia Ruder

Russia in the Time of Cholera: Disease and the Environment under Romanovs and Soviets, John Davis

Soviet Americana: A Cultural History of Russian and Ukrainian Americanists, Sergei Zhuk

Stalin's Economic Advisors: The Varga Institute and the Making of Soviet Foreign Policy, Ken Roh

Ideology and the Arts in the Soviet Union: The Establishment of Censorship and Control, Steven Richmond

Nomads and Soviet Rule: Central Asia under Lenin and Stalin, Alun Thomas

The Russian State and the People: Power, Corruption and the Individual in Putin's Russia, Geir Hønneland et al. (eds)

The Communist Party in the Russian Civil War: A Political History, Gayle Lonergan

Criminal Subculture in the Gulag: Prisoner Society in the Stalinist Labour Camps, Mark Vincent

Power and Politics in Modern Chechnya: Ramzan Kadyrov and the New Digital Authoritarianism, Karena Avedissian

Russian Pilgrimage to the Holy Land: Piety and Travel from the Middle Ages to the Revolution, Nikolaos Chrissidis

The Fate of the Bolshevik Revolution, Lara Douds, James Harris, and Peter Whitehead (eds)

Writing History in Late Imperial Russia, Frances Nethercott

Translating England into Russian, Elena Goodwin

Writing History in Late Imperial Russia

Scholarship and the Literary Canon

Frances Nethercott

BLOOMSBURY ACADEMIC
LONDON • NEW YORK • OXFORD • NEW DELHI • SYDNEY

BLOOMSBURY ACADEMIC
Bloomsbury Publishing Plc
50 Bedford Square, London, WC1B 3DP, UK
1385 Broadway, New York, NY 10018, USA
29 Earlsfort Terrace, Dublin 2, Ireland

BLOOMSBURY, BLOOMSBURY ACADEMIC and the Diana logo
are trademarks of Bloomsbury Publishing Plc

First published in Great Britain 2020
Paperback edition published 2021

Copyright © Frances Nethercott, 2020

Frances Nethercott has asserted her right under the Copyright, Designs and
Patents Act, 1988, to be identified as Author of this work.

For legal purposes the Acknowledgements on p. x constitute
an extension of this copyright page.

Cover design by Tjaša Krivec
Cover image: Illustration for the Fairy tale of Ivan Tsarevich, the Firebird, and the
Gray Wolf, 1902. Artist: Bilibin, Ivan Yakovlevich (© Heritage Image Partnership
Ltd/Alamy Stock Photo)

All rights reserved. No part of this publication may be reproduced
or transmitted in any form or by any means, electronic or mechanical,
including photocopying, recording, or any information storage or retrieval
system, without prior permission in writing from the publishers.

Bloomsbury Publishing Plc does not have any control over, or responsibility for,
any third-party websites referred to or in this book. All internet addresses given
in this book were correct at the time of going to press. The author and publisher
regret any inconvenience caused if addresses have changed or sites have ceased
to exist, but can accept no responsibility for any such changes.

A catalogue record for this book is available from the British Library.

A catalog record for this book is available from the Library of Congress.

ISBN: HB: 978-1-3501-3040-1
PB: 978-1-3502-4533-4
ePDF: 978-1-3501-3041-8
eBook: 978-1-3501-3042-5

Typeset by Integra Software Services Pvt. Ltd.

To find out more about our authors and books visit www.bloomsbury.com
and sign up for our newsletters.

For Constance Blackwell
in memory

Contents

Acknowledgements		x
Introduction		1
1	Between State Patronage and Oversight: Developments in History as a University Discipline	21
2	The Scholar-Artist: Master Historians and their Literary Muses	35
3	Style: The Literary Cadences of Russian Historical Narrative	57
4	The Historian's Literary Toolbox: Portraiture	77
5	Literary Evidence: Realist Aesthetics and Historical Enquiry	99
6	Place: Excursion History and the Question of Literary Sites	117
7	The Historian's Literary Compass: Modern Poets and Novelists	139
8	Historical and Literary Historical Scholarship: A Hybrid Science?	165
Epilogue: The Forgotten Legacy		187
Notes		192
Select Bibliography		264
Index		275

Acknowledgements

I would like to thank the following institutions for their generous financial support, which greatly assisted me during the course of researching and writing this book: the Institute for Advanced Studies, Princeton, the Leverhulme Trust and the Institute for Historical Research (Scouloudi Award). I am also grateful to my home university, St Andrews, for providing optimal research conditions in the form of regular sabbaticals and for encouraging research-led teaching: students can be among the best 'sounding boards' for trialling new ideas.

People make a difference. There are several I would like to thank, some, sadly now deceased: Morton White, Oleg Grabar and Irving Lavin whom I encountered during my stay in Princeton when I first began thinking about Russian historical culture. Although not specialists in the field, their insights into so many issues, and the conversations I had with them, almost on a daily basis, were indirect, yet powerful sources of inspiration to think about things. My thanks, too, go to Lionel Gossman, Avishai Margalit and Jonathan Israel, Vera Kaplan and Aleksandr Dobrokhotov for their constructive criticism and suggestions. I am also very grateful to the insightful comments provided by the anonymous reviewer of the first draft of this book and for spotting things, which I had not seen. As for the laborious process of editing, I must give due thanks to Laura Reeves for her patience and gentle nudging. I am also extremely grateful to the staff of the Slavic Reference Service, University of Illinois, Urbana-Champaign: their help in tracking down references has been second to none.

Some of the materials in the book were first published as articles: a few short sections in Chapter 6 about 'excursion history' were originally published in a special issue of the *Revue des études slaves* (2017) examining developments in the human sciences in the aftermath of the October Revolution. I would like to thank Astrid Mazabraud for her careful editing and suggestions and Catherine Depretto for taking on my proposal in the first place. Pierre Gonneau is due thanks for editing and translating another short piece that I wrote about Kliuchevskii 'and his literary muses' as part of a larger, international project on the writing and rewriting of Russian history across four centuries. All of them, whether knowingly or unknowingly, have ensured that I bring this book to completion.

St Andrews, May 2019

Introduction

'For the historian (…) it is a great find when he encounters the artist'.[1] To the outside observer, Vasilii Kliuchevskii's vindication of the historian's felicitous encounter with the world of creative imagination, cited here from his 'Pushkin Speech' in 1880, might seem peculiarly at odds with the climate of positivism and rigorous science-based approaches to the past that otherwise characterized the discipline of history across Continental Europe during the closing decades of the nineteenth century. Yet, for his Russian audience, the remark spoke to an axiomatic truth about the broader formative significance of the literary world in the nation's intellectual and cultural tradition: fiction, many believed, was a powerful tool for raising historical awareness. But, why exactly did Kliuchevskii and others think this, and what forms did the 'encounter' between the historian and the artist actually take? Was the appeal of creative fiction merely a form of late-nineteenth-century outreach, a tool to raise the profile of the discipline, or did the world of literary imagination actually have a place in research agendas and endeavours to enhance historical understanding?

It is, of course, widely accepted that, until the late eighteenth century, history, across Europe, was a branch of literature, and in this respect Russian historical writing was no exception. Conceived as the modern successor to the epic, what counted, as Lionel Gossman put it, was 'an ability to filter and select material shaped by literary tradition and popular imagination, and thereby build upon the reader's expectations as to what was generally regarded as "true"'.[2] The success of a historian was thus largely dependent on his narrative flair. However, once history entered the university as a subject to be taught and researched, its ties with literary imagination gradually loosened. Commentators generally trace the origins of the split between literature and history to the emergence of German idealist philosophy in the early nineteenth century, and suggest that the rise of historical pedagogy across Continental Western Europe during the latter part of the century (notably the institutionalization of the seminar in European universities) completed this process.[3] With this came a clear demarcation between popular history and the 'high erudition of historical science' as historians began writing for dedicated audiences – peers, pupils and general public.[4] In Russia, too, the consolidation of a scholarly historical discourse derived from neighbouring disciplines of sociology, economics, neo-idealist philosophy and law went hand in hand with the production of some specialist research and theories of history that were intended for the academic community both at home and abroad: the works of Legal

Marxists, economic historians and Russian advocates of neo-Kantianism are all clear examples of an ambition to harness the tools of social science and philosophy for historical study.[5] The formation of scholarly communities and the growth of specialist journals as platforms for advancing historical debate also supported this trend of writing for dedicated audiences. Still, notwithstanding the obvious parallels between west European and Russian historiography, there are grounds to suggest that, in Russia, creative literature remained integral to the historian's quest to establish objective truths about the national and west European past and that the reasons for this were as much narrowly institutional – namely, a proximity between literary and historical scholarship that lasted well into the final years of imperial rule – as they were broadly cultural. The relationship between the academic community and the state, a culture of learning in informal settings such as the home seminar and privileged master–pupil relations, the role of certain 'master historians' as embodiments of 'true' as opposed to 'pure' scholarship and their commitment to the idea of public service through enlightenment all affected the nature and forms of historical knowledge. Master historians, or so-called scholar-artists (*uchenye khudozhniki*), in particular, expressed a lasting affinity with the intelligentsia tradition, Russia's men of letters who, in the absence of appropriate platforms to advance political and intellectual debate, used fiction and literary criticism as tools not only for social comment and moral injunction, but also for broader reflections on the meaning of history or, indeed, for uncovering the contemporary cultural and political resonances of specific episodes in the national past. With these domestic factors in mind, then, one may begin to appreciate why political and socio-economic historians, such as Kliuchevskii, responded to the social, cultural and psychological resonances of creative literature and readily drew on the national and west European canon as a valuable resource. As I shall argue, not only did works of fiction, lyric poetry and even the lives of artists themselves (national and foreign) provide supporting evidence, but as historical documents in their own right they also constituted rich source materials in studies of collective mentalities and the social tissue of everyday life. It is this largely overlooked aspect concerning the 'literary interface' of Russian historical enquiry in the late imperial era that forms the topic of this present study.[6]

The institutional context

Students of history had a strong grounding in philology.[7] In and of itself there is nothing especially remarkable about this; modelled on the approach championed in the 1820s and 1830s by the German scholar, Leopold von Ranke, to transform history into a more systematic or 'scientific' (*wissenchaftliche*) discipline, emphasis on close textual analysis, establishing the authenticity of a source, was – indeed, still is – an important feature of historical study. However, in Russia, the philological axis of historical enquiry was, in large part, strengthened through a series of ministerial decrees regarding the organization of university instruction in the humanities. The 1804 University Charter, which established chairs in 'World History, Statistics and Geography' (*Vsemirnaia istoriia, statistika i geografiia*) and 'History, Statistics and Geography of the Russian (*Rossiiskoe*) State' alongside chairs in Greek and Latin,

Russian Language, Rhetoric and Poetics in the newly created Humanities Department (*Otdel slovesnykh nauk*) established a template for the institutional proximity between history and 'literary studies' (*slovesnost'*) which would prove to be resistant to (and, in a sense out of kilter with) theoretical and methodological developments in historical enquiry itself.[8] But it was really as a consequence of an extensive reorganization of the faculties and the creation of chairs of Russian History and Russian Language and Literature (*slovesnost'*) in the 1830s that instruction in the humanities forged such strong ties – methodologically and substantively – between the two subjects. Well into the so-called golden age of Russian historical scholarship/science (*nauka*) coinciding with the final decades of tsarist rule, history and literature continued to be perceived as a single entity.[9] *Slovesnost'* (Language and Literature) was taught in the Historical–Philological Faculty (renamed as such as part of the 1864 Ministerial Decree) as a cycle of courses for students majoring in History or Literature/Philology. For example, in the 1880s, the syllabus covered Philosophy, Classical Philology, Sanskrit and Comparative Grammar, Russian Language and Literature, Slavic Philology, World History, Russian History, Church History, Theory and History of Art and Romano-Germanic Philology (Modern Languages and Literature).[10] Granted, literary scholarship had a strong historical orientation, and definitions of both historical and literary scholarship, particularly in the pre-reform era, were inchoate and provisional in nature. But the gradual process of specialization within humanities curricula in the latter part of the nineteenth century did little to erode the ties across disciplines; on the contrary, they were strengthened as evidenced in the research agendas of the principal historians whose work is discussed in this book.

In his study of the development of literary scholarship in late imperial Russia, Andy Byford identifies a number of key trends and methodological paradigms, elements of which, I argue, also shaped the profile of historical studies during the same period.[11] Beginning in the 1830s and 1840s, the ethos of romantic nationalism privileged analysis of traditional folk songs and popular Slavic mythology, a trend which found an echo in the work of contemporary historians, particularly those sympathetic to the idea of *samobytnost'* (Volksgeist) fostered in Slavophile and ethnic national discourses.[12] From the 1860s on, as literary studies became anchored in a broad system of 'historical–philological sciences', the prominent literary scholars, Aleksandr N. Afanas'ev (1826–71) and Alexander N. Veselovskii (1838–1906), developed a strong cultural historical and comparative approach to the study of literary production. This, again, found clear parallels with, if not offering a model to, work conducted by their historian peers.[13] By the end of the century, interconnections between the two fields had become, if anything, even more pronounced. At the height of the counter-reform era (1880s and 1890s), heavy handed restrictions on humanities curricula and extensive reorganization of the syllabus – including a temporary ban on instruction in modern European history – resulted in a continuous use of and reference to a common body of topics, sources and methods (positivist and inductive) among historians and literary scholars: authorized emphasis on the study of medieval chronicles, ancient languages and culture, the production of 'literary monuments' (*pamiatniki literatury*), bio-bibliographies and, in Byford's words, 'the meticulous historical and philological processing of textual materials'.[14]

If the state dictated the terms and scope of historical enquiry, usually in response to tensions in the current political climate, it arguably also created possibilities and unforeseen applications.[15] Mandatory training in philological techniques for the criticism of historical documents generated a number of original research agendas, some of which, paradoxically, resonated with, even preempted, Continental European trends in the first half of the twentieth century. The career of Ivan Grevs (1860–1941) and his circle of medievalists at the University of St Petersburg is often cited as an incidental precursor of the French *Annales*.[16] In their work on the medieval world they treated 'historical' documents such as chronicles or the lives of saints as 'literary artefacts'. Studying the verbal tissue of these documents, and offering a broader contextualization, a number of Grevs' closest pupils – including Lev Karsavin (1882–1952), Georgii Fedotov (1886–1951), Olga Dobiash-Rozhdestvenskaia (1874–1939) and, in parallel, the Odessa-based medievalist Petr Bitsilli (1879–1953) – reconstructed the experiences and worldviews of medieval man.[17] Grevs also pioneered 'excursion history' (visual perception of the past), which his pupil and life-long friend, Nikolai Antsiferov (1889–1958), developed during the Stalinist era, placing at its core the study of 'literary monuments', in particular the Russian classics, Pushkin and Dostoevskii. That Antsiferov and other contemporaries facing rapid victimization in the new Bolshevik regime as 'bourgeois historians' were able to re-channel their training as historians into literary studies with relative ease clearly speaks to the hybrid character of historical scholarship in which they had been trained as students in the run-up to war and revolution: at the root of Antsiferov's literary critical work lay the same methodological principles and approaches he had applied as a historian, namely, close analysis of the verbal tissue of a literary work of art combined with a cultural-anthropologically driven account of the writer's worldview.[18]

This brief overview of what I call the historian's 'nostalgia for fiction' presents a rich seam of enquiry into historiographical developments in late imperial Russia. It is, however, a topic that has been largely neglected by students of Russian society and culture. If social historians have traditionally been more concerned with the dynamics of power that existed between the professoriate as 'epistemic' authorities and the political authority of the state, studies of developments in humanities scholarship tend, with few exceptions, to privilege institutional frameworks and to associate distinctive methodological paradigms with individual 'schools'.[19] If anything, their findings have reproduced a pattern of classification that originated in some of the early Russian historiographical surveys dating from the 1880s and 1890s, and which went mostly unchallenged in the Soviet era both within the Soviet Union and in émigré studies intended for a west European and North American readership.[20] Typically, Moscow University has been regarded as a foyer for the development of theories of history and the so-called juridical or 'state' school of historiography, whereas St Petersburg/Leningrad has been linked with the advancement of source-based analyses. Accordingly, surveys of the discipline and its main representatives tend to single out the work of the Moscow Professor, Timofei Granovskii (1813–55), specialist in early modern Europe and a 'Russian Ranke' of sorts, and his immediate contemporary, M. S. Kutorga (1809–96), chair of Ancient History in St Petersburg, for spearheading these two distinctive trends, namely, Hegelian-style grand schemes of history versus source analysis. Granovskii's pupils included the founders of the 'juridical-statist' approach to the national past – Sergei Solov'ev (1820–79), Konstantin Kavelin (1818–85) and Boris Chicherin (1828–1904) – as well as the intellectual historian and specialist in modern European history, Vladimir I. Ger'e (1837–1919). Kutorga's name is linked in the literature with the emergence of Medieval and Byzantine studies, which dominated historical-philological research at the University of St Petersburg in the late imperial period. His pupil, the Byzantinist, Vasilii G. Vasilevskii (1838–99), whose teaching career began in 1870 (and with whom Grevs studied), was pivotal in establishing the international prestige of this school.

Although the designation of schools was ostensibly intended to signal interests in specific fields of inquiry or subject matter, it was a practice that was also politically and ideologically charged.[21] There is considerable literature on the ideological-cum-political climate (and rivalry) associated with Russia's two main universities during the nineteenth century. In this scheme, Moscow is generally perceived as the home to liberal thought, whereas scholarly production in St Petersburg, which fell under close government scrutiny, tended, on the surface, to be more 'conservative'. The Leningrad scholar, Sigizmund Valk, for example, spoke of a causal link between the geographical proximity to government structures and the spirit of intellectual enquiry, arguing that it was largely for this reason that Moscow was able to promote the social function of knowledge in the 'liberal' sense of personal empowerment, whereas St Petersburg academics did not venture beyond the less turbulent (and politically conservative) waters of 'science for science's sake'.[22] Any challenges to the status quo incurred government reprisals in the form of university closures and the temporary dismissal of members of staff on the grounds of their suspected sympathies for student unrest – the case, notably, of Ivan Grevs and Nikolai Kareev, following student-led riots in 1899.[23]

It has really only been in the decades since the collapse of the Soviet Union that scholars have been able to test the viability of the 'two schools' theory. Wladimir Bérélowitch has suggested that the term 'school' itself is open to interpretation, if not redundant, since it applies as much to broader institutional affiliations as it does to a system of individual or group loyalties 'institutionalized' through the practice of *pokrovitel'stvo*, namely the sponsoring (patronage) of talented students in preparation for a professorship. If anything, he argues, the label works best as a geographical qualifier, rather than as shorthand for 'methodology'.[24] Bérélowitch's views are supported by the publication of archival-based research, edited correspondence, personal memoirs and diaries. These materials bring to view the ways in which individual historians reflected on their discipline and evidence not so much institutional differences as what Byford describes as 'paradigmatic continuities and overlaps of professional worldview that were extremely important to this academic community'.[25] It was, in fact, common practice for historians (and academics in general) to teach in several institutions at the same time (the university, Higher Courses for Women, gymnasium, the Theological Academy) or to be trained in one institution before taking up a post in another. The career of Nikolai Kareev (1850–1931), a noted theorist of history, yet whose doctoral dissertation on the history of the French Revolution drew on extensive archival work, is just one example of these professional peregrinations facilitating greater overlap and methodological continuities across institutions. Having studied under Ger'e in Moscow, Kareev initially taught at Warsaw University before receiving his appointment as professor of modern European history at St Petersburg University in 1892. In sum, Russia's scholarly universe was far more complicated than the notion of 'schools' allows, and, indeed, in the strongly ideological climate of the closing years of Tsarist rule, a historian's political affiliation, which need not correspond to his or her expressions of intellectual or personal loyalties, only served to complicate this picture even further.[26]

As a way of circumventing the issue of institutional affiliations and its repercussions on the profile of historical research, the present study foregrounds the figure of the historian, a line of enquiry that, in recent years, has been taken up by a number of Russian scholars interested in the formation and social significance of historical culture in an autocratic state.[27] This approach requires study of the circumstances (upbringing, formative influences, peer relations, friendships, together with the broader intellectual and cultural conventions of the age) that helped shape a given historian's view of the discipline, his specialist fields of interest within it, and also, importantly, his self-ascribed role as a scholar and public enlightener writing for a variety of audiences – from pupils, peers, the wider reading public or, indeed, the tsar as the 'patron of knowledge'.[28] Whether explicit or assumed, such relations and attendant expectations not only had an impact on the formulation of historical knowledge (and possibly the nature of historical enquiry itself), but also informed the way historians perceived their role as 'producers of knowledge'.[29] Indeed, the historians whose careers form the main subject of this book not only were conscious of the place of biography and of the historian's personal qualities in scientific endeavour, but repeatedly drew attention to it, as did their readers: Kliuchevskii's modest beginnings and provincial background, for example, undoubtedly informed his reflections as a historian and the topics he privileged in his work; what ensured Karamzin's *History* a place in the canon was that it was 'not only the work of a great writer, but the feat of an *honnête homme*'. Without such qualities, Pushkin believed, Karamzin's achievements would be worthless.[30] Accounting, then, for figure of the historian as a scholar, intellectual-cum-moral role model and public enlightener (or *Kulturtrager*, to borrow George Fischer's term in his classic study of Russian Liberalism) combines consideration of the historians' biographies, of the cultural and political contexts in which Russian historical literature was produced and issues of professional identity together with the public role of historical studies.

The historian-*nastavnik*

Since the age of Peter the Great, the 'ethos of service' understood as an expression of loyalty to the tsar through an engagement with public enlightenment was a component of most professions.[31] As state employees, university professors derived their status and privileges from the bureaucratic system, but their epistemic and moral authority was built upon relations with colleagues and pupils (in the various forums of peer review, the learned society, research seminar) and, more broadly, in relation to society (*obshchestvo*) through the channel of public lectures and the production of generalist historical literature.[32] This meant that the ethos of service could be, and indeed was, open to interpretation. As an expression of loyalty to the discipline, 'service' entailed 'academic professionalization' and the advancement of 'disinterested' knowledge. However, caught as he was between two potentially competing poles of interest – the public and officialdom – the historian's enlightenment mission could be, and indeed was, conceived as a means to empower society through knowledge. Inversely, it could become an effective channel for promoting official discourses about the nation. Individual historians negotiated these social, bureaucratic and professional expectations in a variety of ways. Broadly speaking, if some historians tended to regard historical knowledge as a means of social control and produced – whether for professional advantage or because of personal conviction – narratives of the past 'on command' in order to instil a sense of patriotism or to foster collective myths, for those committed to the advancement of knowledge qua knowledge at stake was a question of historical understanding or 'truth'. Accordingly, they conceived the gains of historical knowledge primarily as a tool for the moral, aesthetic and intellectual empowerment of the individual. Adapting the platforms assigned to them (seminar, lecture, textbook, essay) to fulfil their enlightenment pledge, professional historians exhibited a vocational attitude traditionally regarded as the province of the intelligentsia, Russia's more famous champions of social and moral justice. Typically, these men of letters formulated their ideas in the informal settings of the salon, unauthorized circles or as part of a journal's editorial board, using *publitsistika*, fiction and literary criticism as the principal channels for their dissemination.[33]

In the history of the intelligentsia, the existence of these non-institutionalized forums for the pursuit of knowledge underscored distinctions frequently made by contemporaries between formal and authentic education (*obrazovanie* versus *vospitanie*), together with the importance they placed in the role of the teacher (*vospitatel'*) as both a moral and intellectual guide.[34] Similarly, in the university context, formal pedestrian training was often contrasted with 'true' education. Affording a sense of community (*soobshchestvo*), 'true education' was centred on the figure of the historian as an epistemic and moral authority. 'True' scholarship, as opposed to the aridity of 'pure' scholarship, depended on the master's ability to invest scientific endeavour with both personal–moral and social significance. Without doubt, the original template for the Russian scholarly ideal was the figure of Granovskii: 'Many of his former pupils', Aleksandr Stankevich, his first biographer, wrote, 'thought of Granovskii as a "*nastavnik*" whose influence defined the character of their activities and moral conviction'.[35] As an aspirational quality for Russian academics, this image of the *nastavnik* stood in sharp contrast with prescriptions for learning that one might come across in contemporary west European literature. Friedrich Schleiermacher, for example, famously posited that the task of the university was 'to awaken the idea of scholarship in noble-minded youths already equipped with knowledge of many kinds, to help them to a mastery of it in the particular field of knowledge to which they wish to devote themselves, so that it becomes second nature for them to view everything from the perspective of scholarship, and to see every individual thing not in isolation, but in its closest scholarly connections, relating it constantly to the unity and entirety of knowledge, so that in all their thought they learn to become aware of the principles of scholarship, and thus themselves acquire the ability to carry out research, to make discoveries, and to present these, gradually working things out in themselves. This is the business of a university'.[36] Missing from this description was a relational component based on a moral bond between 'master' and 'pupil', which, in Russia, became standard in assessments of a master's career. For example, in an obituary tribute to the early modernist, Petr Kudriavtsev (1816–58), his successor, Stepan Eshevskii, characterized the *nastavnik* in terms of the loyalty he inspired: Kudriavtsev had understood the importance of a 'morally-based relationship with the audience', and it was the deep affection that he inspired among his public that made him 'a *nastavnik* in the fullest sense of the term, enabling him to channel his message, namely that "scholarship alone means little," that the political education of society is as vital as purely scientific activity, that the heart is as important for understanding the historical process as any rationally devised set of logical premises'.[37] In sum, esteemed by their pupils and peers as true mentors and 'authentic teachers' (*uchiteli zhizni*), both for the way they promoted fact-based historical knowledge as a tool for addressing questions of immediate social, political and moral relevance and for the courage they showed in the face of government scrutiny and victimization, these elected role models acquired status as embodiments of the 'power of thought' (*sila mysli*).[38] High on the list of 'burning questions' they tackled using the tools of historical knowledge were serfdom and the vexed issue of Russia's relations with the West.

The significance attached to 'true' scholarship and its repercussions for reflections on methodological developments and the social role of knowledge feeds into the leading hypotheses of this book concerning the literary dimensions of Russian historiography. I argue that the rejection of what was, perhaps, stereotypically conceived as 'narrow science' (often associated with west European practices) goes some way to explaining the durability of the literary impulse in historical narrative and explanation. Moreover, these ascriptions of 'true scholarship' not only were an integral part of the *nastavnik*'s identity, but also formed part of his self-elected successors' right of inheritance across generations. For this reason, I have opted to examine ideas concerning developments within the discipline, methodological 'continuities' and 'differences' in light of privileged mentor–pupil relations. I explore these with reference to the intellectual biographies of a select number of historians as well as with an eye to broader cultural conventions, namely the sensibilities and corresponding lexicon – whether romantic or realist – of the age in which they lived. Such conventions clearly 'conditioned' the ways historians gave expression to personal sentiment, values and to their professional code of conduct. In other words, if biographical data throw light on a given historian's temperament, convictions and experiences, the 'sensibilities of the epoch' were equally important for articulating the terms of his 'professional vocation'. Built on formative experiences, crafted from the conventions of the age, the persona of the historian was, I suggest, integral to the production of knowledge.[39]

This book covers three generations of historians, each witness to fluctuations in degrees of (permitted) academic freedom and censure as part of the cycle of government reform, counter-reform and revolution mentioned earlier. The first generation, born in the 1810s, began teaching in the 1830s and experienced first hand both the positive and negative implications for their discipline of Nicholas I's programme of 'controlled modernization'. The principal figures of this generation include Timofei Granovskii (1813–55); his immediate successor to the chair of European history, Petr Kudriavtsev (1816–58); and the historian of ancient Rome, Stepan Eshevskii (1829–65). All three died young. Among their contemporaries, specializing in Russian and Ukrainian history, were Mikhail Pogodin (1800–75), first chair of Russian History (Moscow University), which was established in 1835 as part of a new university charter, and Nikolai Kostomarov (1817–85), professor at St Petersburg and Kiev, whose career spanned the ages of romanticism and realism. The second generation was born in the decade 1830–40s and began teaching in the age of reform. Initially benefitting from a brief period of relaxed censorship, this generation also experienced the rapid erosion of academic freedom during the 1870s as part of a government response to acts of terror orchestrated by an incipient revolutionary movement. Besides Vasilii Kliuchevskii (1841–1911), prominent historians, whose careers coincided with these pendulum swings in government measures, include Konstantin Bestuzhev–Riumin (1829–97) and Vasilii Vasilevskii (1838–99). The third generation, born during the reign of Alexander II, entered higher education as the Minister of Education, Dmitrii Tolstoi (1866–80), began instituting his 'classical' reform measures.[40] Devised in the (vain) belief that these measures might help curtail terrorism, Tolstoi's curriculum placed the accent firmly on the study of ancient culture and rote learning of ancient Greek and Latin grammar. The teaching careers of this last generation, which included Ivan Grevs and the literary specialist, Semon Vengerov (1855–1920), coincided with the closing decades of imperial rule, while those of their pupils, who reached maturity as scholars when Russia was entering its decisive phase of revolutionary upheaval, responded to expectations of the new Bolshevik regime in a variety of ways – from endorsement, compromise, accommodation to disavowal.

Within this framework, my discussion of the historian-*nastavnik* privileges three historians: Timofei Granovskii, Vasilii Kliuchevskii and Ivan Grevs. Reconstructing their formal and informal training as historians, accounting for the literature (historical and fictional) that shaped their early interest in the subject and the importance of intellectual mentors, both within and outside the university context, and/or the discipline, will serve as a point of entry to the main topic of this book concerning the various ways, and with what consequences, creative literature informed Russian historical enquiry. All three men were celebrated in commemorative texts for their achievements in advancing historical knowledge. Similar in temperament, Granovskii and Grevs embodied a fusion of professional and personal charisma that their pupils and peers referred to repeatedly in texts dedicated to them. If such expressions of devotion were largely absent from posthumous assessments of Kliuchevskii, who did not cultivate close ties with his university colleagues, but, instead, found interlocutors among artists and writers, his legacy nevertheless generated a body of work that perpetuated an image of him as the exemplary 'scholar-artist'.

Representations of the historian-*nastavnik* were in part susceptible to shifting intellectual and cultural paradigms; the romantic sensibilities of the 1830s and 1840s and the age of realism that followed obviously coloured the ways historians gave expression to their respective visions of history as well as the ways in which they perceived their roles as producers of knowledge, whether writing for peers, pupils or the wider public. Equally, though, a number of attributes remained constant across generations. Of these, reference to narrative skills played a prominent role in the construction of the ideal historian. Contemporaries frequently drew attention to the historian's use of imagery, metaphor and rhetoric, regarding it as integral to the task of instilling a fact-based historical awareness among students and wider public. It was, for example, Granovskii's celebrated talents in this regard that earned him the soubriquet of 'the Pushkin of history', while Kliuchevskii's multi-volume *Course of Russian History* (based on lectures he delivered during the 1880s and 1890s) was received as a literary masterpiece on a par with the genius of Tolstoi.[41]

Which literary muse?

Historians' memoirs, diaries and correspondence, their notes and jottings on literary themes or recently published novels attest to a familiarity with the pantheon of literary masterpieces. Granovskii, Grevs and Kliuchevskii all read Sir Walter Scott, Shakespeare, Byron, Goethe, the classics of Greek and Roman antiquity and, of course, Russia's modern and contemporary literary chef d'oeuvres. Of these, Pushkin, Turgenev, Gogol, Tolstoi and Lermontov rank among the names most often cited both for their formative influence and for their lasting inspiration. Pushkin, Gogol and Tolstoi, we know, wrote historical fiction, which, if largely credited to the example of Sir Walter Scott, also drew on a native tradition popularized by a host of practitioners, including Mikhail Zagoskin (his *Iurii Miloslavskii*, 1829), Ivan Lazhechnikov, Faddei Bulgarin, Ol'ga Shishkina, Rafail Zotov and various anonymous hacks.[42] There is little doubt that historians would have read these as children and young adolescents. Yet, if this extremely popular genre opened up past worlds to the reader, beyond their ability to captivate impressionable young minds by artistically reconstructing past events they did not, in my understanding, remain an enduring source or resource for historical enquiry. This is partly because one of the devices commonly used in these novels was to draw (the illusion of) a clear distinction between fictional invention, usually the remit of the narrator, and historical verisimilitude tasked to the author who might furnish the novel with extensive footnotes and/or historical commentary. Acting as a sort of adjudicator, the author might also interrupt the narrator's tale to address the reader directly cautioning him/her of the factual inaccuracy just provided by the first-person narrator. To this point, as Dan Ungurianu has argued with reference to Bulgarin's *Dmitrii the Pretender*, a trait of historical fiction dating from the 1820s and 1830s was a view of history as empirical truth which the authors endeavoured to reconstruct: phrases such as 'the author confesses to these anachronisms' or 'the exact chronology of events was not followed' similarly equate 'history' with a reconstruction of events.[43] For historians, however, whether the factual information provided in these novels was accurate or not was irrelevant. Rather, what counted, and what made a work of historical fiction, and fiction more generally, a valuable resource for the historian was the way in which the author managed to capture the spirit behind the facts. Among literary critics, one of the first to defend the artist's 'right' to poetic licence was, as Ungurianu claims, Vissarion Belinskii in 1835: 'In the higher meaning of the word,' he wrote, historical truth 'consists not in the accurate rendering of facts, but in the accurate portrayal of the development of human spirit during this or that epoch'.[44] Belinskii's observation allows us to appreciate why only certain writers who experimented with this genre became favourites among historians: Pushkin (*The Captain's Daughter*) and, of course, Tolstoi (*War and Peace*), who chose to ignore the opposition between artistic and factual truths, which originally lay at the core of the Romantic historical novel. In other words, in answer to Zagoskin's or Bulgarin's constant reminders of where fiction begins and history ends, in later examples of the historical novel corresponding to the rise of literary realism this dichotomy by and large disappeared. Paradoxically, then, it was the requirement in these novels that the reader suspend disbelief, which made them viable material for the historian.

How did borrowings from the literary world sit with the consolidation of a specialist historiographical lexicon with its hallmark terms 'progress', 'development', 'purposefulness' derived from neighbouring fields of philosophy and the natural sciences? My argument that the demands of a rigorous 'science-based' historical enquiry never entirely succeeded in dislodging the narrative conventions more typically associated with imaginative literature in part takes its cue from Andrew Wachtel's study of 'intergeneric dialogue'. It is a 'hybrid genre' trait which he ascribes to the writings of certain novelists and poets who evinced, as he put it, a 'heightened Russian concern for history':

> For almost 200 years, – Wachtel writes – Russian writers of belles lettres have not only produced fiction, drama, and narrative poetry on historical material, but they have also turned to what they consider to be nonfictional genres, particularly history and the philosophy of history. Rather than assert the primacy of poetic experience [...] they produced complementary texts on the same historical subject, at least one claiming to be nonfictional and one claiming to be 'poetic'. This has allowed them to exploit the differences in tone, approach, and authority that by convention have separated imaginative literature and history.[45]

The upshot of this 'refusal on the part of Russian authors and readers to recognize any one discourse type as most appropriate for the writing of history' was a situation 'in which various genres, each possessing its own authoritative viewpoint, could, through their interaction, dialogize the presentation of historical material'.[46] Whether they produced both a fictional and nonfictional account of a single event (the case of Pushkin and Karamzin, and Nikolai Gogol), whether they switched back and forth between a fictionalized narrative and historical explanation within the body of a single work, as Tolstoi did so brilliantly in *War and Peace*, the aim – and result – was, Wachtel argues, to dissolve the overly rigid distinctions between history and imaginative literature.[47] In sum, Wachtel argues, the Russian 'failure' to adopt the split between history and imaginative literature that gradually became canonized in Western Europe in the first half of the nineteenth century was quite fortuitous insofar as it allowed for the appearance of a multi-generic tradition that would have been unthinkable in Europe.[48]

Wachtel's account of 'intergeneric dialogue' may usefully be applied to the work of university-based historians in the sense that they, too, used a variety of platforms – textbook histories, lectures, 'historical letters', public speeches, journalistic articles, aphorisms, polemic – and in some instances fiction (Kostomarov, Pogodin, Kudriavtsev) without necessarily prioritizing one 'genre' over the other as they endeavoured to reconstruct and reflect on the past. The historian's pedagogical skills, imaginative character analysis and storytelling came together especially well in the construction of 'historical portraits' which constituted an important axis in popularizing knowledge of the Russian past. This is particularly true of Kliuchevskii whose psychologically probing accounts of men and women – both historical personalities and fictional protagonists – in 'the flow of history' furnished original evidence for probing states of mind and the problem of collective identity against a background of social transformation during the eighteenth and early nineteenth centuries.[49] Encapsulating and articulating the spirit of the age in which they lived, Kliuchevskii's masterfully drawn cameos belong to the national canon of 'epochal personalities' (to borrow a term from Lidiia Ginzburg) alongside Pushkin's 'superfluous man', Lermontov's demonic hero, Turgenev's nihilist or Goncharov's portrayal of sloth in the figure of Oblomov. The socio-psychological portraits he crafted, particularly his portrayal of the changing mores of the Russian nobility, just mentioned, effectively integrated the provinces of literary invention and historical enquiry, namely the personalizing, subjective view of the novelist/poet and the (putatively) distanced, more inclusive perspective of the historian.

Poetry, fiction and chronicles became objects of historical enquiry in their own right for the insights they yield into aspects of mentality and everyday life.[50] Here, the work of the medievalist, Ivan Grevs, and his circle of pupils at the University of St Petersburg is especially significant. For their studies in cultural history, with its marked emphasis on (religious) mentality, and 'excursion history', the literary document was key and used in quite imaginative ways: whereas their textual-based analyses of the medieval world treated 'historical' documents, such as medieval chronicles and hagiography as 'literary artefacts', in excursion history, which explored the cultural historical resonances of place in literary production and intellectual biography, literary texts were treated as historical evidence informing social psychology.[51]

History and Literature in Russian and west European historiography

Among some of the more thought-provoking studies concerning the relation between history and literature, and the question of professionalization in the west European historiographical tradition are Hayden White's seminal *Metahistory: The Historical Imagination in Nineteenth-Century Europe* (1973) and Lionel Gossman's collection of essays on French nineteenth-century historiography, *Between History and Literature* (1990).[52] Although different in scope and aims, both authors acknowledge that by mid-century the 'linguistic protocol' (White's term) of the historian's 'explanatory/

interpretative strategies' attested a break with 'the idea of mimesis and the central importance of rhetoric' that had previously been the common ground of fictional and historical narrative.[53] Thereafter, regardless of whether a given historian enriched his narrative with literary tropes, privileged a 'scientific lexicon', or sought to reconcile what White calls the 'two cultures' of history and literature 'in common service to the goals of civilized society', the advent of the scientific (Positivist) paradigm 'created an irrevocable breach with the "free" (Romantic) arts that preceded it'.[54] This breach, however, 'was not attended by the sort of conceptual revolution that has accompanied such transformations in other fields, such as physics, chemistry, and biology'. What White meant by this was that, if during the course of the nineteenth century, history became the object of professionalized enquiry, its theoretical basis as a discipline remained unclear; the deep 'structural content' of nineteenth-century historical writing continued to be 'generally poetic, and specifically linguistic', its narrative 'emplotted' and its explanatory argumentation imitated literary conventions.[55] In light of this, he questioned the value of 'colour-coding' nineteenth-century historiographical trends as, for example, Romantic, Liberal, Conservative or Positivist as if these were substantively distinct from one another:

> Historians of the nineteenth century stressed the notion that, whatever a true historical account might consist of, it could not be constructed out of purely 'artistic' principles on the one hand or in the interest of producing the kind of laws in which the physical sciences dealt on the other. [...] The main line of historiographical work in the nineteenth century stressed the historian's dependence upon principles that were scientific, philosophical, and artistic, all at the same time. [...] Its science was 'empirical' and 'inductive', its philosophy was 'realistic', and its art was 'mimetic', or imitative, rather than expressive or projective.[56]

In other words, if White conceded that Positivistic, Idealistic and Romantic historiography was written, indeed flourished, as, he says, 'the work of Comte, Buckle, and Taine; Heinrich Leo, Strauss, and Feuerbach; Chateaubriand, Carlyle, Froude, and Trevelyan are enough to suggest', these trends did not preclude the underlying issues concerning the defining principles of 'true' history as a hybrid of 'art' and 'science'.

It is possible to track analogous 'surface' developments in Russian historical writing as well as the more complex 'subterranean' issues, which White describes. Like their early and mid-century counterparts in France – namely, Augustin Thierry and Jules Michelet – Russian historians were gifted narrative craftsmen. Sensitive to new methodologies developing abroad during the 1840s and 1850s, they assimilated the terms and theoretical positions of historicism and sociology and began producing works of historical theory intended for a specialist readership of peers. In the process, the Russian historian's professional arsenal became virtually indistinguishable from that of Western peers. Also – although, it must be stressed, for quite different reasons – the progression, in Russia, from Romantic historiography to the Positivist paradigm was neither linear, nor smooth, and so it is tempting to argue, as White does, that these labels are, in a sense, redundant. Certainly, the romantic sensibilities of the 1830s and 1840s and the mood of realism corresponding to the age of reform (1860s and beyond) describe a generation gap, and this goes some way to explaining the shift in perceptions of the historian (as well as the historian's self-perception as a scholar) from a 'backward-looking prophet' to 'artisan'. But, at the same time, the dominant historiographical paradigms of the two eras were also 'challenged' in paradoxical, unexpected ways as these same historians gave expression to their visions of the discipline they represented. In her authoritative biography of Granovskii, Priscilla Roosevelt makes the following valid point: 'Though raised in the romantic era, and a romantic by temperament, Granovskii, as an historian, emphasized the rationality of the historical process, the ennobling influence of reason on human existence and the centrality of the intellect to human progress'.[57] Granovskii's endeavours, from the late 1840s, to anchor the discipline in premises derived from the natural sciences signalled a renunciation of his romantic literary muse. Yet his arguments were largely dismissed by his peers as heresy and in conflict with his temperament as a beguiling, charismatic human being.[58] If they accepted his contention that a philosophical qua scientific understanding of the historical process was needed in order to engage with the substance of history, they nevertheless insisted that it was Granovskii's 'poetic feeling', his love of 'the poetry in history' which gave his account of history its form.

Kliuchevskii wanted to distance history from the natural sciences. As I noted in my opening comments, Kliuchevskii's career coincided with a period dominated by the 'scientific' positivist paradigm in history and realism in creative literature. In the introduction to his course of lectures, he gave a definition (admittedly, rather tortuous) of historical sociology. Yet, in the few instances where he spoke about the discipline (e.g. in his lectures dedicated to historiography, unpublished jottings or in reviews of works by contemporaries), he repeatedly appealed to the artistic qualities of history. For him, the study of history was an art, not a science – a view that became particularly pronounced as he started work on the publication of his lectures in the late 1890s: 'Determining what had happened and describing that accurately and lucidly were a scholar's goal. Trying to find laws behind history, even in the record of one nation, was illusory'.[59] As I argue in this book, Kliuchevskii's paradoxical qualification of the limits of the scientific paradigm owed much to his formative influences as a student at Moscow University in the early 1860s. If he openly acknowledged his indebtedness to the historian, Sergei Solov'ev, for his schooling in the subject, he accredited his intellectual inheritance to two masters in the department of literature: Afanasii Shchapov and, especially, Fedor Buslaev.[60]

In many respects, then, reflections by Russian historians on developments within the discipline, no matter how inchoate or refined, resonated with debates across borders concerning the relation of history to science and/or art, together with the fundamental (if intractable) problem of establishing the distinctive narrative and explanatory contours of the discipline. Like their west European contemporaries and elders, Granovskii and Kliuchevskii articulated their conceptions of history with reference to – or in reaction against – the intellectual paradigms and sensibilities, which dominated their age. The issues they raised also turned around the core concerns of establishing and rendering the truth about the past.[61] However, in view of the role of the Russian state as patron and watchdog of scholarship, it seems reasonable to suggest that the stand historians took on these issues was also conditioned by domestic socio-political strategies and their impact on university instruction. Thus, Granovskii's belief that history should be profiled as a modern science (whether framed by Hegelian or natural scientific precepts) may be read as a negative response to the (enforced) coupling of history with philology as part of the educational reform measures orchestrated by the Minister of Education, Sergei Uvarov. Or, again, that Grevs, writing in the 1890s, framed his definition of history with reference to classical philology may be interpreted as implicit (or possibly, resigned) acknowledgement of the real impact that the rulings of the counter-reform had had on instruction in the subject as an officially designated historical–philological science.[62] Politics and culture also played into the way master historians perceived their role as scholars and public enlighteners. As self-designated guardians of 'science', Russian professors paradoxically resisted the notion of 'science for science's sake', 'cabinet science' or 'pure' disinterested science which many (stereotypically, perhaps) associated with the work of German scholars. Rather, their self-ascribed mission was to serve the 'common good', and it was public recognition of their role as moral and intellectual authorities that made this task possible. In this connection, the 'voice' of the historian, a sense of his presence, was key: publications that grew out of lectures and public addresses often retained elements of direct discourse – rhetoric, irony, metaphor or strong visual imagery. The upshot is that in parallel with the professionalization of historical discourse built on a specialist, largely imported lexicon, historians continued to construct their narratives and interpretation according to the same hybrid characteristics of 'intergeneric dialogue' that Wachtel ascribes to the writer of fiction, who, 'as a divinatory of historical truth', attempted to provide historical knowledge and the presentation of it with something approaching the cherished value of fiction.[63] For the historian addressing a wider, less informed audience, fiction was a powerful pedagogical tool for making the past 'present'. The seamless way in which he managed to do so was widely regarded as one of the chief markers in his status as a 'master historian'.

In sum, then, the literary impulse prompts us to reflect on historical culture and praxis in late imperial Russia and on the circumstances both intrinsic and extrinsic to the discipline that shaped it. General censorship measures, specific restrictions placed on the syllabus on government orders, the profile of formal education and informal instruction, narrative conventions in a given period and the practice of writing for a variety of audiences – all these factors account for the literary impulse in Russian historical writing and help us appreciate why, for example, Granovskii's and Kliuchevskii's writings were regarded as cultural monuments on a par with contemporary classics in the literary canon or why Grevs chose to use poetry as a source in an economic history of ancient Rome.

The literary impulse frames the scope of the book; it is not an account charting the genealogy of Russian historiography. There are many books of this kind by Western scholars, as well as some Russian classics, which, still today, retain their value as benchmark studies in the field.[64] If anything, my topic sits with research conducted in the last few decades concerning 'national styles' of scientific thought in which sociologists of knowledge have explored the impact of local contexts on the production and form of scientific knowledge.[65] I would only stress that it is not my intention to argue that the 'literary impulse' was unique to Russia; rather, by taking into account the 'local context' I hope to nuance our understanding of Russia's contribution to historical scholarship and of her intellectual dialogue with Western peers. This seam of enquiry may, moreover, be a useful tool for re-examining traditions, trends and revived legacies in Russian historical writing in post-Soviet historiography, notably those focusing on the individual, culture and everyday life, and which, according to some scholars, represent a revival of, or a return to, historical enquiry of the Thaw era.[66] My findings, by contrast, provide grounds to argue that the study of culture, mentality and an interest in agency was a feature of late imperial and early Soviet history. If largely ignored in surveys of Russian historiography which, instead, tend to focus on the impersonal forces of history (viz., socio-economic or political structures and progress as the salient characteristics of positivism and Marxist historiography), an enduring interest in the 'human factor' among historians informed a discrete tradition that arguably merits attention in contemporary analyses of Russian intellectual culture.[67]

The book opens with an account of the domestic political and institutional conditions together with the broader, European-wide literary conventions and philosophical theories, which helped shape the development of history as a discipline during the late imperial era. Specifically, Chapter 1 presents an overview of the contexts of learning, from the formal, institutionalized platforms of lecture, seminar and publication to the semi-formal and informal settings of research circle, master–pupil relations, home upbringing, mentors and friendships. Accounting for the various settings in which historians developed and exchanged ideas not only brings to view the problematic relations that existed between the academic community and the government, but also allows us to appreciate that within the professoriate itself there were differences of opinion regarding the socio-cultural and political role of historical knowledge. The study of these sites of learning also serves as a point of entry for an analysis of the role, perception and self-perception of certain master historians as intellectual and moral authorities. This last aspect forms the main topic of Chapter 2, which identifies a number of 'mentors' and scholars together with (where relevant) the small scholarly communities they forged. It sets out their respective views of the meaning of history in terms of its educational and moral function, their sense of purpose as historians and the ways in which their pupils fixed images of them as inspirational models to emulate.

The artistry of historical writing is taken up in the next two chapters. If Russian historians readily assimilated terminology associated with the succession of intellectual discourses in Continental Europe, from German idealism to the social science-based approaches that characterized most historical analyses in the late nineteenth century, the growth of a distinctive, largely imported historiographical lexicon never entirely dislodged other potential narrative forms. For this reason, accounting for stylistic conventions and the individual inflections embedded within historical discourse is a useful tool for re-examining traditions, trends and revived legacies in historical writing. I argue that, while verbal artistry undoubtedly played an important role in the project to popularize historical knowledge in Russia, it was also integral to attempts at establishing the defining features of the discipline itself. With this in mind, Chapter 3 addresses the literary inflections of the historian's explanatory narrative in light of the literary conventions of the age in which he was working. It opens with a brief account of Russia's first modern historian, Nikolai Karamzin (1766–1826), celebrated author of a twelve-volume *History of the Russian State*. Published between 1816 and 1829 – just as the split between history and literature was being codified across Continental Europe – Karamzin provided Russia with a work that could be read as both.[68] His *History* is therefore indispensable for appreciating the lasting presence of the literary impulse in the canon of national historiography. My main focus, however, is on Granovskii and Kliuchevskii where the discussion is framed by an account of their responses to one of the vexed questions concerning the status of history: is it a science or an art? Originating in debate among German and French scholars (Hegel, Humboldt, Augustin Thierry and Michelet) during the first quarter of the nineteenth century, Russian engagement with this question was, I argue, somewhat paradoxical, again, attesting to the impact of the local context, viz., government intervention in the humanities syllabus.

Chapter 4 explores the use of literary tropes in the construction of historical portraits. Portraiture constituted a major strand of nineteenth-century historical writing. Whether designed to foreground salient character traits of universal significance in political leadership (from violence to reason and compromise), as Granovskii did in a series of public lectures, or, inversely, to depict historical figures (the tsars) as representative types, a technique that Kliuchevskii mastered so brilliantly, this exercise in portraiture offered considerable scope to dissolve the overly rigid distinctions between history and imaginative literature. In the closing section of this chapter, and as a bridge to the following chapter, I introduce Ivan Grevs' biographical method (economic biography), a tool he developed for exploring not just the broad scheme of economic and political change in ancient Rome as it transitioned to Empire, but importantly its impact on daily life and culture, and the moral world of individuals.

Chapter 5 examines the ways historians, active in the second half of the nineteenth century and early twentieth century, worked with poetry and prose as supporting historical evidence. The broad assumptions of realist aesthetics as a model to imitate and an authentic representation of reality informed the ways Kliuchevskii and Grevs handled creative literature. Both men recognized that fiction contained evidence of everyday life and served as a valuable resource for grasping the intangible realms of human motivation, tastes and attitudes. Grevs justified his inclusion of Horace's lyric poetry in his study of farm management during the late Roman era on the grounds of the paucity of economic and legal sources. But it was also his belief that the 'social–psychological' observations harnessed in the artist's impressions complete our understanding of this period in Roman history by accounting for the ways in which economic change impacted social mood and a subjective sense of change. If, like Grevs, Kliuchevskii accepted the close correlation between fiction and fact, his handling of literary material was, as I have mentioned, not limited to its value as a source to complement economic and legal data or, indeed, as evidence for a specific theme. Rather, in tracing the historical origins of some of the nation's most famous fictional protagonists (most notably, Pushkin's *Evgenii Onegin* and Fonvizin's *Nedorosl'*), he managed to dissolve the boundaries between the real and the imaginary to produce a series of socio-psychological and historically identifiable types of his own invention.

Chapter 6 focuses in more depth on the career of Ivan Grevs after 1900 as he turned his attention to the study of 'excursion history', a multi-faceted – topographical, architectural, aesthetic and philological – approach to locations and the people (principally creative and spiritual thinkers) who inhabited them. Excursion history (or 'excursionism' 'monumental history' or *gradovedenie*', as it was called interchangeably) also functioned as a portal to the literary dimension of historical enquiry, both in Grevs' own writings dating from the outbreak of the First World War and the 1920s, but especially in the work of one of his closest pupils, Nikolai Antsiferov (1889–1958), who played a pivotal role in advancing literary excursionism as part of a Narkompros-funded (Commissariat of Enlightenment) project to transform secondary and higher education in the years following the October Revolution. Like Grevs, Antsiferov invested considerable energy in devising a typology of excursions and in refining a methodology for the humanities branch of the discipline. However, it was the accent he placed on artistic intuition as a vital component of the historian's task to uncover deeper, rationally unfathomable truths about man's emotional affinity with his habitat that established a place for literary topography within the excursionist project. Antsiferov's popular and scholarly studies of national literary sites, in particular those associated with the writings of Puskhin and Dostoevskii relative to the city of St Petersburg, were both a successful adaptation of and a faithful tribute to Grev's experiments with the methodology that he had originally devised for his study of Horace's villa in the province of Rome.

Turning the literary world into an object of historical and historical–philosophical enquiry was also a feature of late-imperial-era historiography which obscured the borders between history and its sister disciplines. With this in mind, Chapter 7 examines a selection of writings by historians on the nation's modern literary pantheon: Pushkin, Lev Tolstoi, Lermontov and Turgenev. If, in their essays, monographs and commemorative public addresses, they performed as historians in the sense that they tended to contextualize and generalize the personal experiences shaping the artist's 'historical sensitivities', the accent they placed on expressions of 'the human condition' – from grief to friendship and love – was, for its time, an unexpected departure from the established practices of historical enquiry. Kliuchevskii's exploration of the state of melancholy evoked in Lermontov's poetry, and Grevs' studies of love and friendship prompt reflection not only on the points of intersection between historical and literary critique, but also on the way this type of enquiry led historians to redefine or rethink the purpose and object of history itself.

My final chapter revisits some of the broader questions relating to developments in historical scholarship in terms of its ties to literary scholarship, namely, the rise of literary history as a sub-discipline during the closing decades of the nineteenth century and its impact on the career profile of the 'generalist' historian. It reconsiders the way folklore, songs and legends functioned as a resource for historians with a nationalist or cultural particularist agenda (the case of Nikolai Kostomarov) in the pre-reform era, before examining the way it was used to support theories of cultural production in a comparative perspective by historians of literature. Fedor Buslaev (1818–97), as the first professor in world literature, is a pivotal yet transitional figure in this regard, but it was his pupil, Aleksandr Veselovskii (1838–1906), who famously turned the romantic conception of poetry as the colour of national life on its head: poetry is the colour of national life, he conceded, but 'to understand the colour of life – that is, poetry – we must, I think, begin with the study of life itself; to smell the soil, we must stand on it'.[69] Veselovskii's contribution to the European-wide debate on the profile of literary studies as a recognized discipline prompted historian-peers to rethink the relationship between history and literature. Among the latter, one of the best-known attempts to classify the nature of this relationship was that of the historian-sociologist, Nikolai Kareev. And he did so not only by echoing his immediate Russian contemporary, but also by tackling some of controversial claims of the French historian and critic, Hippolyte Taine.

The book ends with a short epilogue, asking that we reconsider the standard narrative about the legacy of Russian historical scholarship in the Soviet and post-Soviet eras. It is often said that the collapse of the Communist regime witnessed a 'cultural turn' in historical enquiry as a much-needed antidote to several decades of ideologically driven accounts of socio-economic factors and law-governed progress. As I have mentioned, the question as to whether this 'turn' should more accurately be treated as the most recent in a series of cultural 'turns' dating back to the post-war era has also been raised by a number of west European and North American scholars. In this connection, the work of the 'revisionist' Moscow-Tartu school of semiotics, which emerged during the Thaw era as part of the wider processes of state authorized de-Stalinization, has received (and deservedly so) most attention. In part building on these analyses, the present study, however, concludes that the accent on culture and mentality, the importance attributed to 'historical biography' (of both real and fictional personalities) as a catalyst for grasping broader socio-political reality, was, in fact, a constant of Russian historical enquiry since its inclusion as a university-taught subject during the reign of Alexander I, coterminous with the succession of historiographical trends predicated on theories of progress in the political and socio-economic arenas. Highlighting this 'counter-current', then, will not only help resituate the current emphasis on the cultural paradigm in historical research, but, hopefully, offer considerable scope for redressing some of the imbalances in established views of Russia's imperial and Soviet historiographical legacy.

1

Between State Patronage and Oversight: Developments in History as a University Discipline

In many respects, the rise of the disciplines in Russia resembled patterns of development across Continental Europe, where, typically, states assumed the role of patron of knowledge in the formation of institutions dedicated to teaching and the advancement of research.[1] As the chief architect of modern Russian scholarship, Peter the Great called upon Western advisors, Gottfried Leibniz and Christian Wolff, to aid in the creation of an Academy of Sciences. Founded in 1724, the Academy initially focused on the natural and mathematical sciences, with history added to the list of subjects in the 1740s during the reign of Elizabeth Petrovna (1741–62). From its beginnings, the Academy's membership was made up of a large contingent of foreign, predominantly German, scholars, and the early profile of Russian historical scholarship was no exception. Among the 'founding fathers' of the discipline were Gerhard Friedrich Müller (1705–83) and August Ludwig Schlözer (1735–1809) whose work in the field established two distinct approaches: source compilation (Müller) and philological analysis (Schlözer). Albeit challenged or rivalled by indigenous and largely self-styled historians, such as Mikhail Lomonosov (1711–65) and Mikhail Shcherbatov (1733–90), this pattern of foreign dominance in Russian scholarship remained generally unchanged for the rest of the century.

It was really due to the consolidation of a rudimentary network of universities in European Russia during the early decades of the nineteenth century that the promotion of native expertise in humanities scholarship became at all possible. However, by the 1830s, the growing number of Russian-born teachers and professors also seemed to validate the rationale behind a state-sponsored initiative in educational reform to promote political and cultural nationalism.[2] In 1833, the Minister of Education, Sergei Uvarov, outlined proposals for a new university charter, which, he believed, was pivotal to the development and paced modernization of the Russian nation state. Formulated as three interrelated principles – autocracy, orthodoxy and nationhood (*narodnost'*) – Uvarov's proposals framed a programme of instruction in which far greater emphasis would be placed on the study of the nation's past as a means to highlight the specificity and endurance of Russia's political and cultural prowess as an empire.[3] In practice, the 'orthodoxy' requirement was met by the decision to make theology, Church history and

Church law compulsory subjects, while the creation of several new chairs of modern Russian Law and special chairs of Russian and Slavic Philology and History anchored the principle of nationality firmly at the centre of the humanities syllabus.

The ideological ramifications of national history hardly need stating. Narratives about the nation's past provided a convenient platform for authorizing accounts of Russian statehood while insisting on her unique path, distinct from patterns of development elsewhere. The first professors of Russian history and literature, Mikhail Pogodin (1800–75) and Stepan Shevyrev (1806–64) (appointed respectively to 'Ordinarius' in 1835 and 1847), advocated these principles of cultural originality (*samobytnost'*) and political greatness, evidenced, they claimed, in the early chronicles which highlighted the place of Byzantine Christianity and Slavic learning from the southwest. Committed to the idea of Holy Russia, they produced triumphalist historical narratives celebrating Russia's mission on the world stage and her future, thereby bolstering Uvarov's vision of Russia as a European power while downplaying her dependence on foreign (notably 'Western') influence.[4]

The 'Russian Question', as contemporaries called it, absorbed the intellectual life of the 1840s and became the main stage for a contest of opinions concerning the defining traits of the nation and her role in world politics. In the salons of Moscow and St Petersburg, competing accounts of collective identity set the terms of possibly the most famous debate in modern Russian history, the so-called Slavophile–Westernizer controversy. While the Slavophiles insisted on a native cultural distinctiveness built on Orthodox confession, a pronounced anti-individualism and political quietism, the arguments of their opponents were largely inspired by patterns of development in west European governance, social organization and law.[5] University-based historians took an active part in these debates, often siding with one or the other camp. Pogodin and Shevyrev co-opted the Slavophile notion of *samobytnost'* to expound on the moral character of the Russian people (unlike, as Shevyrev famously coined it, the 'putrid West'). In response, westernizing liberal historians harnessed elements of philosophical idealism to challenge both the theoretical foundations of Slavophilism and the doctrine of official nationality premised on the glorification of the political status quo.

'If parts live organically, then the whole does too.'[6] The terminology associated with the philosophy of Schelling, alluded to here, provided Timofei Granovskii with an apt analogy for exploring the history of European nations and peoples as an 'organic whole'. Much like Leopold von Ranke, his elected master under whom he had studied in Berlin (1836–39), Granovskii believed that the goal of history was the 'morally enlightened individual' and a society corresponding to the demands of such an individual. To his mind, this balance was assured once the laws and policies of a state and/or the idea of monarchical power were 'invested with the moral radiance of incorruptible justice'.[7] However, if one effect of the idealist philosophy that he embraced was to alert the Russian audience to their country's position as a 'world-historical nation' whose past was, indeed, intimately related to that of her European counterparts, another, as Priscilla Roosevelt has suggested, was to issue an indirect but clear warning regarding her present and future. Granovskii's assertion, for example, that Roman slaves and medieval serfs eventually undermined their respective economic structures of empire and feudal order was intended and, indeed, recognized by his audience as a thinly veiled critique of Nicholas I's reluctance to abolish the practice of serfdom at home.[8] 'History', he wrote,

> should, more than other sciences, take on board contemporary ideas. We cannot but look at the past from the point of view of the present. In the destiny of our fathers, we are above all seeking explanations about ourselves. Each generation turns to the past with its own set of questions; the diversity of historical schools and trends is testimony to the profound thoughts (*zadushevnye mysli*) and cares of the age.[9]

As the official hallmark of Nicholas I's reign, then, Uvarov's tri-part principle had far-reaching consequences for the historical discipline. But it also had some unintended ones, too: if, on one level, it placed considerable demands on historians that would test their professional and intellectual calibre as scholars and public enlighteners, and, as I discuss below, affect their status as members of a fledging scholarly community in its relations with the government, it is also true that the minister of education's extensive reorganization of the faculties and appointments of a young generation of professors specifically trained for the purpose in west European universities facilitated an important shift away from the old-style 'professor-encyclopaedist' towards greater subject specialization. The upshot was to generate new tasks for historical study.[10] Using current methodologies and philosophical systems originating in Western Europe, historians on both sides of the debate shifted their attention away from 'the picturing of the individual achievements of different heroes' (the case, for example, of Karamzin, author of the first 'modern' history of the Russian State) to what Alexander Kiesewetter later described as an engagement with the 'logical disclosure of universal reason in the successive appearance of historic peoples on the scene of world history'. Accordingly, the historian's attention became 'fixed on the discovery of the fundamental principles of national life and the study of those forms of state order in which these principles were expressed as they developed'.[11] In practice, as Kiesewetter argued, the impact of German idealism merged with the Russian question to produce two fairly distinct fields of historical enquiry: historians sympathetic to the idea that Russian (and more generally Slavic) culture rested on principles entirely opposed to those of civilization in Western Europe privileged 'the study of the inner content of national life, of national beliefs, of national creation, of national customs and of national economics'. In addition to Pogodin and Shevyrev, principal authors engaged with these questions included Iurii Samarin (1819–76), Ivan Zabelin (1820–1908), Nikolai Kostomarov (1817–85) and Mikhail Koialovich (1828–91). By contrast, the first generation of historian-Westernizers, writing in the 1830s and 1840s, focused predominantly on state formation, while their successors active in the age of reform and counter-reform turned their attention to the study of social and economic structures. Applauded by Western peers as significant contributions to the field, the analyses of medieval and modern Europe that they produced nevertheless continued, albeit tangentially, to fuel the debate on Russia's historic mission. The work of the medievalist, Pavel Vinogradov (1854–1925), for one, provides a telling illustration of the political and ideological registers of historical scholarship well into the late nineteenth century.

Specializing in Continental European and English feudal practices, which he studied through the lens of socio-economic relations combined with law, one of Vinogradov's most celebrated works was a social history of thirteenth-century England published in Russian and English in the early 1890s. In it, he challenged certain existing premises concerning the organization of the English village community under the manorial system. Vinogradov argued that although the growth of common law on its soil was a decisive factor in subordinating society to the feudal system of private law and management, older principles of communal activity, the logic of which stemmed from the open-field system, remained intact. The continuing practice of fielding strips of land scattered across the village territory necessitated what he called 'mutual guarantees/responsibilities', thereby exhibiting a communal mentality that stood in glaring contrast to the current acceptance of private rights throughout most of Western Europe.[12] 'Equal partnership among free members' ensured that fellow villagers received equal shares of the arable ploughed: 'It is', he wrote, 'evidently communal in its very essence. Every trait that makes it strange and inconvenient from the point of view of individualistic interests renders it highly appropriate to a state of things ruled by communal conceptions'.[13] The point that Vinogradov wanted to emphasize here was that if these primordial forms of social organization were long since lost in England's distant past and ultimately eclipsed by the rise of the manor and the legacy of Roman individualism in judicial affairs, 'at the present time in the East of Europe, the absence of perpetual enclosures and the intermixture of strips have continued to be normal practice. Despite differences in climate and soil conditions, and in spite of all the obvious inconveniences, nations have consistently adopted the open-field system'.[14]

In the preface to the English version of this study, Vinogradov explained the fascination with medieval English documents for the Russian scholar:

> I do not think that anybody is likely to maintain at the present day, that, for instance, a study of the formation and dissolution of the village community in the West would be meaningless for politicians and thinkers who have to concern themselves with life at present in village communities of the East [...]. Social history, study of the economic development of other nations, their class divisions, forms of cooperation hold for us Russians a very special interest.[15]

Vinogradov believed that research into the formation and dissolution of the village commune in the West was key to resolving the problems confronting the Russian government and society in the wake of the Emancipation Act: both its socio-political repercussions and its impact on culture and morality were relevant to the dramatic changes that Russia was currently experiencing.[16] At the same time, these experiences enhanced an understanding of the European 'other', allowing Russian scholars, as outside observers, to dismantle accepted 'national' canons of interpretation, in some instances lifting the veil from what otherwise appeared as intractable problems for their west European counterparts. Thus, in much the same way that Granovskii's audience had detected a thinly veiled critique of Nicholas I's Russia in his history of Western Europe, so too, Vinogradov's study of feudal England functioned as a mirror onto modern-day Russian socio-political reality caught between tradition and reform. Of course, between the two generations of historians there were significant substantive and methodological differences: the move away from the study of political institutions to aspects of society and the economy was accompanied by a decline in the historicist approach in favour of a comparative and inductive method as a tool to establish laws of development.[17] But it remains that Granovskii's and Vinogradov's findings relating to a distant west European past positioned them as both measured critics of Slavophile and National Conservative doctrines of Russian specificity, together with the Official National glorification of empire built on traditions of peasantry and orthodox beliefs.[18]

In recent scholarship there has been broad agreement that the Russian state's endorsement of enlightenment as a tool to modernize Russia was rewarded by significant advances in historical scholarship and the institutionalization of knowledge.[19] But it is equally the case that these advances encouraged a sense of scientific vocation within the professoriate, which, under circumstances of close government scrutiny, took the form of a civilizing mission more typically associated with the intelligentsia tradition. In other words, historical knowledge could function as a powerful critique of the political conjuncture.[20] During periods of reaction, in particular, 'westernizing' ideas about individual freedoms, rights and civic duties that the liberal professoriate upheld as part of their professional ethos were tested in clashes with the government, on occasion resulting in the dismissal or suspension of professors or, indeed, walkouts by members of the professoriate themselves in protest against government infringements on collegial liberty that many believed was rightfully theirs.[21] Vinogradov famously left Russia for England in 1901 after an initiative by a joint faculty–student committee at Moscow University to discuss student grievances foundered on account of the government's second thoughts on the matter. As I discuss below, at the root of these clashes regarding institutional organization and management were competing modern and classical views of higher learning: the pledge of the professoriate to advance specialist knowledge was repeatedly thwarted by the government's priority to provide humanities students with a 'general culture'.[22]

The academic community and the state

The tensions between science and ideology arising from Uvarov's educational reforms had lasting implications for the corporate identity of the professoriate in its relations with the Ministry of Education. Specialists in the history of education generally situate the underlying cause of a contest of interests between the academic community and the state in the co-existence on Russian soil of French and German university models. The Napoleonic model with its system of specialist *grandes écoles* provided a training ground for state service; by contrast, the German Humboltian–Schleiermacher inspired model was predicated on collegiate and scholarly autonomies, and, accordingly, conceived the university as a setting for the development of free, critical thought and for the advancement of scholarship.[23] While the tsarist reform of education at the beginning of the nineteenth century ostensibly rejected the French model for the German (indeed, privileged close ties with German universities by sending its best students there to complete their studies), its commitment to this model was, nevertheless, tempered by a domestic policy which required adequately trained, loyal civil servants to take up posts in ministerial departments. The decision, as part of the 1835 Charter, to curtail the powers of the university council thus set the terms of a relationship between the professoriate and the government that, for the remainder of the imperial era, would oscillate back and forth between cooperation and resistance in response to fluctuating levels of state-sanctioned liberalization or, inversely, strict, heavy-handed oversight (*nadzor*).[24] These alternating phases of cooperation and clashes between the professoriate and the Ministry of Education also modulated the character of state tutelage from that of patron to official caretaker of knowledge exercising direct control over the content of scholarship. As patron of science, the state encouraged the development of the discipline and created the conditions for the emergence of the 'scholar-historian'. Inversely, in its role as watchdog and censor, the state imposed measures requiring obedience from the historian as a state servitor that threatened to compromise his loyalty to the discipline as he conceived it.[25]

The late imperial era offers numerous instances of patronage combined with state control in the production of historical knowledge. They range from the 'soft touch' of commissioned histories, the appointment of an official state historiographer,[26] to more draconian measures, such as the suppression of politically suspect topics (namely, constitutionalism and ancient Greek as alleged bedrocks of republicanism), preliminary scrutiny of the content of lectures by a government-appointed censor, dismissal of professors and temporary closure of the universities in order to forestall social unrest.[27] Official reaction to the revolutionary upsurge in Western Europe and Poland during 1830–32, for example, had a direct impact on the university and on instruction in history in particular: rigid curricula were introduced, and professors received clear instructions from Count Benckendorff, head of Nicholas I's gendarmerie (its infamous 'third section'), concerning the 'tone' of historical narrative: 'Russia's past was marvellous, her present even greater, as far as her future is concerned it will exceed all expectations (…). Such is the point of view from which Russian history should be looked at and written'.[28] The potentially subversive message of world history also came under official scrutiny. Following the events of 1848 across Europe, the Ministry of Education outlined a new programme of instruction in the subject that required the historian to demolish the putative virtues of ancient republics and highlight the real values of the Roman Empire. Henceforth, world history was to be written from the Russian perspective and 'in the Russian spirit'. In practice, this meant greater emphasis on Byzantine history – a subject generally overlooked in world histories written by west European scholars.[29] Topics in ancient history, such as 'democracy', were taboo, while the works of Herodotus, Thucydides, Titus Livy and Tacitus were all outlawed as dangerous influences on young minds. It was at the height of censored learning that Granovskii was commissioned by the Ministry of Education to write a textbook in world history. As he tentatively introduced prohibited subjects of republicanism and democracy, it is clear from his comments, cited below, that in 1850s Russia, world history, like national history, had fallen under a brutally suspicious *nadzor*, its findings classified in terms of its usefulness or nefariousness to the task of public enlightenment in an 'official nationalist' key:

Whereas the development of western nations occurred in many respects not only independently of the monarchical principle, but even in defiance of it, at home autocracy has left its mark on all the main aspects of Russian life: we took Christianity from Vladimir, state unity from Ivan, education from Peter [...]. By placing such a purely Russian view at the core of this work the compiler of the proposed textbook in world history will provide a more reliable measure for evaluating political life in other nations. A comprehensive and clear outline of the history of ancient and modern republics is unlikely to present any major difficulties when, in advance, an explanation will be given of the geographical and historical circumstances under which such institutional structures are possible. In addition, it would be crucial to stress to the student that the fortunes of correctly constructed republican states depend on respect and the citizens' trust in that power that has supplanted the monarchical principle. [...]. Thus, the compiler of a Russian textbook, having established on merit the sanctity of the monarchical idea, and having demonstrated its benefits on home soil, will not be placed in a position of having to tempt young minds by such phenomena, only a distorted version of which we witness in practice.[30]

On the surface, the contrast between Nicholas I's attempts to stall scientific enquiry and the climate of liberalization promised in Alexander II's far-reaching programme of reform in the 1860s could hardly have been any greater. Hitherto untouched or taboo topics – serfdom, agrarian history, revolution (banned since the age of Catherine the Great) – now began to feature in social scientific and historical research agendas giving rise to a number of innovative studies on the west European past which, as Vinogradov's comments cited earlier suggest, clearly resonated with contemporary events at home.[31] The lifting of strict censorship also encouraged the publication of textbooks, transcripts of lectures and a range of periodicals, both specialized and generalist, as platforms for the dissemination of historical documents and interpretative articles.[32]

The recent emancipation of the serfs was, without doubt, the principal catalyst for the development of these new research agendas, particularly in branches of the social sciences. Using runs of statistics and materials collated by *zemstvo* organizations, a new generation of specialists produced innovative studies of the rural commune (*obschina*) and its place in the national economy. Focusing on patterns of economic development they also analysed the deeper sociological phenomena embedded in economic change.[33] The questions they posed, the methods they worked with and the findings they produced all filtered into historical scholarship. Kliuchevskii, for example, used the topic of serfdom and emancipation to frame his lecture course in Russian history; historians of the European medieval and early modern worlds, such as Vinogradov and Kareev, as well as Grevs in his work dating from the 1890s, all produced monographs on agrarian life.[34] In addition, more sustained contacts with the academic community abroad (including the founding of cross-national institutions) encouraged a more meaningful level of engagement with liberal principles, which had affected the intellectual climate in Western Europe since the middle of the century.[35] Understood as a broad church of intellectual and political ideas, these liberal principles denoted reformist thinking on matters of society, the economy and law.

Whereas the measures introduced during Alexander II's reign helped restore the government's role as benign patron, the University Charter of 1884, issued during the ministry of Ivan Delianov (1882–97) but already in preparation during the ministry of his predecessor, Dmitrii Tolstoi (1866–80), inaugurated a last-ditch return to a phase of 'militarization' that would remain more or less in force until the collapse of imperial rule in 1917.[36] Issued in the wake of Alexander II's assassination, it brutally reneged on the collegiate autonomy promised in the tsar-liberator's reform programme by placing faculty appointments, rectorships and student discipline under ministerial control. Universities were re-classified as 'teaching institutions' (*uchebnye uchrezhdeniia*), a measure, which, as Kassow notes, effectively downgraded them to mere 'training mills for the professions and the civil service'.[37] It was, moreover, not just a matter of lifting any ambiguity regarding the obligations of the teaching corps as state employees; by imposing curricula heavily circumscribed by the state-endorsed demands for a classics-biased education, the charter also eroded the growing diversity of specialist subjects offered within the faculty. Subjects that had been introduced in the 1863 Charter – comparative grammar in Indo-European languages, history of world literature, Church history, theory and history of art, and philosophy – were effectively turned into subsidiary disciplines.[38] Significantly, too, instruction in modern European history was temporarily suspended.[39]

In a diary entry dated 24 April 1906, Kliuchevskii reflected with characteristic acerbity on what, ultimately, turned out to be the lasting and damaging effects of the counter-reform both on the morale of the student population and on the collective identity of the academic corps: 'Count [Dmitri] Tolstoi and [Mikhail] Katkov generated a school of "police classicism" with the aim of turning students into mannequins, uniform in thought, morally and intellectually castrated servants of the tsar and country'.[40] In Kliuchevskii's eyes, Tolstoi had prioritized a classics-dominated syllabus for crudely pragmatic and political reasons: his principal goal was to produce a cohort of much-needed secondary school teachers; he also (vainly) hoped that close textual/philological analysis of predominantly ancient texts would re-channel the potentially subversive energies of student revolutionaries and help put a stop to the acts of terrorism that were being carried out by members of the radical wing of populism. But, while, as Kliuchevskii's remark suggests, Tolstoi enjoyed some success in numbing the brains and moral fibre of university undergraduates, the clashes between the professoriate and the government that had escalated in the wake of the 1884 Charter also described a dramatic climax in the relationship between the two parties in the run-up to war and revolution. A student strike in 1899 at St Petersburg University, in part triggered by the dismissal of Kareev and Grevs, along with the Marxist economic historian, Tugan-Baranovskii, for their 'liberal-democratic leanings' triggered a series of student disturbances culminating in the closure of the university between 1904 and 1906.[41] Underpinning this last round of confrontations were, as Kassow puts it, two goals that, in practice, were mutually exclusive. In Kassow's words, 'The faculty council wanted basis reform; the government wanted peace and quiet'.[42] Weakened by ten months of strike action across most sectors of the work force, the government introduced a number of conciliatory measures to enlist the support of the professoriate as the most proficient means to curb student unrest. However, as Kassow argues, concession made to the professoriate in the wake of the 1905 revolution (namely autonomy and right of collegial assembly) were motivated not by the promise of reform in the spirit of constitutional democracy, rather by utilitarian considerations, namely a view of academic disciplines 'in the spirit of *Wissenschaft als Grosbetrieb* that had characterised the 1884 charter'.[43] Thus, if the Temporary Regulations (27 August 1906) restored the electoral and judicial powers of the university council, it did not replace the 1884 statute as many professors hoped; rather, it complicated (if not exacerbated) the legal relationship between the professoriate and the government. New terms introduced by Petr Stolypin (prime minister, 1906–11), which included the requirement for all teaching staff to 'acknowledge their civil service status and sign a disclaimer denying membership in anti-government organizations (including the Kadet party)', illustrate this very well. As Kassow put it, 'Such measures epitomised a degree of humiliating state tutelage not experienced by the academic community since the reign of Nicholas I'.[44]

The impact on the corporate identity of the professoriate of heavy-handed ministerial intervention in the university administration and curricula and of the government's more dramatic acts of coercion and reprisal was, in a word, corrosive. It not only produced a conflict of loyalties among professors in terms of their role as state employees and public enlighteners (and scholars), but also exposed deep political divisions. The mass walkout by liberal Moscow professors in 1911 protesting the unfair dismissal of their rector and two pro-rectors (for failing to contain student meetings) is a case in point. Authorized by Stolypin's Minister of Education, Lev Kasso (a former university professor), it, sadly, vindicated what Grevs had earlier condemned as the 'corporate passivity and fecklessness' of colleagues whose public loyalties to the state effectively condoned the victimization of peers committed to scholarly endeavour and service to society. Grevs' main complaint was that government measures had produced a breed of 'professor-*chinovniki*'. Teaching in a climate of censorship therefore required a moral example; referencing Dante, he reiterated the poet-thinker's enjoinment that reason requires freedom.[45] In a sense, though, such fissures within the academic community between its 'willing accomplices' and liberal–democratic 'critics' may be understood as a consequence of the regime's oscillation between the French and German educational models. With opinions on the 'Russian question' sharply divided from the moment it entered Uvarov's modernizing agenda, by the closing decades of tsarist rule, an eroded corporate identity had made it virtually impossible to present a united front in negotiations with the government on university autonomy.

Institutionally, then, the consolidation of the discipline was almost entirely the product of state initiative, leaving the academic community susceptible to repeated bureaucratic intervention and sanctions. Used to enhance the power of the tsar and official ideology, the subordination, whether symbolic, ritualized or coerced, of the past to politics and ideology, became a permanent feature of institutionally endorsed historical practice and, arguably, has remained so to the present day. The national past, in particular, has been repeatedly co-opted as a tool to reinforce official discourses, from autocracy to empire and statehood in the nineteenth century, with some of the most extreme examples of historical manipulation dating from the Soviet era.

Parallel sites of learning

The problematic relations between the academic community and the state, together with tensions within the academic community itself, provide a point of entry for appreciating the strategies some professors adopted in order to circumvent the institutional expectations and strictures placed on them as the nation's educators. Beginning in the 1870s, a growing network of university-affiliated learned societies (and corresponding journals), the emergence of student-led study circles and the introduction of the seminar all attest, in Byford's words, a 'relocation of *nauka*' away from the lecture hall to a variety of parallel, informal and semi-formal platforms.[46] Providing an environment for the development and exchange of ideas, these alternative sites created the terms of the historian's professional identity as an individual scholar and helped foster a sense of privileged 'community' (*soobshchestvo*) in the shared pursuit of true learning as opposed to 'sectarian knowledge'. The establishment of the university seminar in the post-reform era and its transformation over time into a forum of collaborative research illustrate this point very well. Originally intended in the 1884 Charter as practical classes (in Greek and Latin translation and the exegesis of classical texts) to be taught by *privat docenty* as a complement to the professorial lecture, by the late 1900s the seminar had superseded the lecture as the privileged locus of scientific debate. However, as this time frame suggests, recognition of the symbolic importance of the seminar and study groups as a refuge for science and for harnessing a sense of group identity was slow to develop and largely dependent on the initiative of individual scholars, whose vision – and temperament – determined the success of the new format. As a rule, Byford writes, 'The demands of state-exam programmes meant that seminars continued to have an auxiliary function as "practical classes" entrusted primarily to the growing body of untenured junior lecturers until well after the turn of the century.'[47] But there were some notable exceptions: in St Petersburg, the Byzantinist, Vasilii Vasilevskii and the philologist, I. V. Iagich, were among the first professors to pioneer 'practical studies as a forum for in-depth reading and source interpretation with students'.[48] In 1889, Vasilevskii extended the possibilities of group discussion by co-founding a historical seminar at faculty level; its ambitious mission statement (drafted by Kareev) set out to 'unify the discipline' by 'bringing the histories of Western Europe, the ancient world, and Russia closer together, thereby providing a forum for theoretical reflections on historical methods'.[49]

In Moscow, among the first teachers to lead seminars, with varying degrees of success, were Vladimir Ger'e, a specialist in modern European history, Kliuchevskii and Vinogradov. If Kliuchevskii's tendency to be dogmatic in the seminar context did not, according to his former pupil and cofounder of the Kadet party, Pavel Miliukov, encourage student initiative, Vinogradov's example as a 'hands on' and problem-solving teacher was a key factor in transforming the seminar into a real forum for research.[50] As a junior member of faculty in the late 1870s, Vinogradov had been an active participant in a semi-formal peer group of young professors working in a variety of different disciplines. It included Maksim Kovalevskii, dean of Russian sociology; Vsevolod Miller, a linguist specializing in Sanskrit; the jurists, I. V. Ianzhul, S. A. Muromtsev and A. I. Chuprov, with N. I. Storozhenko and Aleksei Veselovskii from the department of literature: 'No single orientation characterized the entire group', but 'the empirical, comparative and multi-disciplinary approach to the history of culture, law and society' that they developed in this context clearly attests active intellectual involvement with contemporary west European scholarship, particularly in terms of the broader paradigm shift from the political sphere to social and economic questions that had been shaping historical enquiry there since the mid-century.[51]

These isolated experiments with the seminar model were initiated by a commitment to anchor 'science' or 'scholarship' (*nauka*) firmly within the university as an integral part of its profile as an institution. But, even though after 1900 there is every indication to suggest that this format had, at last, established its place within the framework of higher education, the reasons for this had relatively little to do with the seminar's formal legitimacy as such. Rather, in view of the rapid erosion of university autonomy granted in the October manifesto of 1905, emphasis on the seminar as a site of learning had become a way of registering the liberal professoriate's disappointment with the government's unwillingness to recognize the university as a place of disinterested scholarship. In the process, they lost sight of the seminar's potential as a foundation stone in university-based teaching and research; instead, it became an 'enclave of science' that was symbolically remote from its immediate institutional context.

It is really from this point on that, whether incorporated as part of the syllabus or, increasingly, assuming the form of informal (often cross-disciplinary) study group sessions in professors' homes, the seminar format acquired symbolic status as a refuge for shaping and safeguarding a distinct academic identity and professional ethos. As such, it bore some resemblance to the *kruzhok* phenomenon of the intelligentsia, which, as Barbara Walker has put it, 'flourished at the fluid interstices of the regular order of society and a state that in many ways sought to prevent intelligentsia activity from impinging upon a formally recognized sphere'.[52] Often bringing together students at different stages in their degree course, including postgraduates and, not infrequently, running for several consecutive academic sessions, seminars facilitated the growth of close-knit, integrated communities, the distinctive qualities of which were ultimately shaped by the inspiration, organizational skills and guidance of the seminar leader.[53] For example, in St Petersburg, Ivan Grevs and the noted Pushkin scholar, Semon Vengerov (1855–1920) extended the parameters of the seminar format by involving their pupils in the process of creating tools for further research.[54] Vengerov's highly popular Pushkin seminar was conceived as a laboratory of sorts to compile a dictionary of Pushkin's lexicon sensitive to contextual usages of a single word and its declensions. That Grevs also used his Dante seminar (from 1909) to build an interpretative dictionary (intended for internal use) of hallmark terms in the work of the Florentine master is one telling example of a cross-fertilization of ideas and methods between the medievalist and literary historian.[55] Like Vengerov, Grevs and his seminar group mapped out the various contexts affecting the meaning of a word, paying particular attention to the idiosyncratic inflections of the authorial voice.[56]

According to one of his closest pupils, Nikolai Antsiferov, Grevs' repeated attempts to establish alternative forums for collaborative study were driven by a belief that the cathedra had the effect of alienating the professor from his students.[57] Grevs himself openly acknowledged his indebtedness to his own mentor, Vasilevskii, for turning the seminar into a platform for historical-critical and historiographical discussions. But he also drew on his formative experience as a member of the short-lived Oldenburg circle', a 'student scientific–literary society' (*Studencheskoe nauchno-literaturnoe obshchestvo*) (1884–89). Dedicated to the advancement of knowledge, members of the circle believed that engagement with science was a powerful tool to combat terrorist activities, at that time rife among students. By the same token, the scholarly activities of the group, including a small library they put together, were clearly intended as a corrective or counter-balance to the generally arid teaching they felt was provided in the university curricula.[58] As undergraduates, the group members (which included the neo-Kantian historians, A. S. Lappo–Danilevskii, V. V. Vodovozov, A. A. Kaufman and N. D. Chechulin) already appreciated that professional integrity and true social responsibility could only be fostered in isolation from the pragmatic requirements and qualification-focused orientation of the degree structure. In 1886, a name change, from 'circle' to 'fraternity' (*bratstvo*), was intended to strengthen the bond among members (together with their wives). As Vera Kaplan writes in her authoritative study of Russian historical circles, the '*Priiutinskoe bratstvo*' was named after the landed estate, Priiutino, which the fraternity members dreamt of buying as the ideal setting within which to pursue their aspirations of living 'in accordance with the highest ethical principles through maintaining their friendly bonds'.[59] As I discuss in Chapter 2, it was essentially this conception of scholarship and community or fellowship (*soobshchestvo/bratstvo*) that Grevs would harness in his own role as tutor and life mentor (*nastavnik*).

By the end of the 1900s, a 'distinctive professional ethos', to borrow Christophe Charle's expression, had emerged through a process of expanding and resetting the established hierarchy of teaching formats within the university.[60] Whereas Granovskii and Kliuchevskii had acquired their authority as scholars and enlighteners through the medium of the lecture and public addresses delivered from the university lectern, after 1900, it was, rather, the seminar that played a pivotal role in establishing the reputation of certain elected historians as role models in the pursuit of knowledge. In a sense, the pragmatic and ideological expectations of the government merely acted as a catalyst for this process, which ultimately (and paradoxically) came full circle with a tradition of informal, yet 'authentic' learning that had originally flourished in the salons and friendship circles during the reign of Nicholas I. Periodic denial of academic freedom meant that historians endeavoured to harness the spirit of informal learning in their careers, and they did so by renegotiating the terms of 'formal' scholarship, understood (if not stereotyped) as arid, dehumanized science. Whether they attempted to incorporate this tradition within existing institutional structures by, for example, circumnavigating the authorized remit of a lecture course,[61] or through the creation of university-affiliated circles and journals as a platform for 'scholarly debate' (one of Granovskii's thwarted ambitions in the 1840s), or whether they resolved to protect its spirit by segregating it from the wider university to forge close-knit study groups in the professors' homes, at stake was a concern to cultivate 'true scholarship'. For both Granovskii and Grevs, writing some seventy years later, the existing university structures were 'so cut off from life', so 'alienating' that they were, by definition, inadequate to such a task.[62]

Most specialists in the history of Russian education agree that tsarist Russia produced great scholars and scientists whose research received international recognition, but that it failed to develop a stable university system or a satisfied academic profession. Contemporaries, themselves, were aware of this. Writing in the 1890s, the literary historian and *publitsist*, Alexander Pypin, noted that the government's suspicion of science had had detrimental effects on the nation's academic profile and, by extension, on a sense of national worth: 'The existence of our scholarship continues to be incidental, lacking solid foundation and lags behind Western *obrazovannost'*.'[63] *Nadzor* compromised or denied outright the possibility of academic freedom, which in turn affected a sense of professional corporate identity. But inversely, it arguably helped strengthen a sense of vocational identity in terms of a commitment to 'true scholarship'. In this connection, Kassow makes an important distinction between scientific and academic freedom. The fragility of academic freedom, which Kassow defines as university autonomy and recognition of the permanence of a professional identity 'that linked professors, across disciplines, in a relationship of shared responsibility for university governance and structural safeguards of academic freedom', contrasts with the pursuit by individual scholars and their immediate circle of peers and pupils of scientific freedom.[64] In other words, the tradition of censorship, which thwarted the scholar's authority as a member of an academic institution, served as a sine qua non of the historian's loyalty to his discipline. It also helped establish his authority as a *nastavnik*. Thanks to his example as a teacher and moral guide, the 'true scholar' bridged formal education (*obrazovanie*) and informal upbringing (*vospitanie*) in which the putative 'literary-centredness' of Russian culture figured so prominently and so consistently, irrespective of the paradigm shifts in methodology that university-trained historians otherwise followed.[65]

As I argue in the following chapters, the existence, throughout the late imperial period, of parallel – informal and semi-formal – sites of learning meant that the study of history never entirely vacated its common ground with *belles lettres*. In the wake of the Napoleonic Wars, the salons which, as I have mentioned, were frequented by a first generation of 'professional' historians, including Granovskii and Pogodin, generated hybrid modes of historical enquiry, from the epic poem, novella, essays, public addresses to epistolary exchanges as means to raise a sense of historical awareness across a wider reading public. By the close of the nineteenth century, historians returned to literary representations of the past as valuable evidence and source materials for analyses of collective mentality and daily life. If, then, from the age of romanticism to the climate of positivism that dominated research in the humanities and social sciences from roughly the 1860s, the relationship between historical enquiry and literary representation of the past altered, it nevertheless continued to play a significant, if unstated, role in the development of historical understanding.

2

The Scholar-Artist: Master Historians and their Literary Muses

In recent years, historians of science have developed the notion of 'scholarly selfhood' or 'persona' as a tool for examining the emergence of scholarly traditions and debate. Whether located in the past or present, inherited or invented, the takeaway point is that scholarly personae are more than 'individual performances of identity'; rather, they function as models created by successive generations to emulate.[1] As I discuss in this chapter, the ways in which individual Russian historians thought about their role as producers of knowledge formed an integral part of broader processes of consolidating the subject as a university-taught discipline. Importantly, the various terms or mechanisms of self-representation and reflections on what it meant to be a historian-scholar in a climate of government oversight became fixed by pupils and peers in commemorative publications, personal memoirs, anecdotal reminiscences, obituaries, even in verse.[2] In addition, historiographical surveys, which began to appear in the latter part of the century, also helped anchor the work of certain historians – and by extension their professional personae – as benchmarks within the canon of historical writing. The result was a body of work, which in many ways functioned as a set of broad guidelines for determining the essence of 'true' scholarship. Often articulated through the prism of privileged master–disciple relationships, these texts also assisted in the formation of a historically continuous 'republic of minds' across generations.

True historical scholarship was conceived as a fusion of intellectual achievement and moral/aesthetic culture, qualities that, typically, were traced to the mentor's childhood discoveries of art, poetry and history. Almost without exception, the historian's formative reading included the works of Francois Guizot, Augustin Thierry, Gibbon, Robertson, Hume, Karamzin, Michelet and the historical novels of Sir Walter Scott, which Russian readers first encountered in 1811 and in translation beginning in the 1820s.[3] The influence of the historian's peer group and interlocutors was also important: with temperament, tastes, political convictions, moral principles and, in some instances, physical appearance all regarded as integral to the task of elevating the role of historical knowledge and its impact in the public arena, assessments of the master's scholarly output thus tended to foreground its 'performative' function so as to create an organic bond of sorts between the historian as a producer of knowledge and his oeuvre. The posthumous canonization of Timofei Granovskii illustrates this very well. Friends and immediate successors repeatedly subordinated the terms of the pledge he made to build the discipline on Hegelian-inspired principles to his personal moral qualities and charisma.[4] It was, as Vladimir Ger'e put it, thanks to Granovskii's very person (*lichnost'*) that he justified his teaching.[5] 'The substance of Granovskii's message', Kiesewetter wrote,

> was channelled by, and made wholly dependent on, his personality. This is what Herzen meant when he said that Granovskii thought through history, felt through history, and propagandized by means of history. (…). Like no one else, Granovskii was for Russian society the symbol of scholarship, university education and humanism. He was the head of the Moscow Hegelians. But he attracted friends (who did not sympathize with Hegel's philosophy) by his personality, his sincere mildness, and the purity and honesty of his character and thought.[6]

To the modern-day reader, it may seem puzzling that Granovskii commanded so much respect as the ideal scholar because his written legacy was so meagre. He did not leave a magnum opus, and the bulk of his work, published posthumously, was made up of lectures, correspondence and various public addresses.[7] Yet, as records faithfully preserving the distinctive inflections of the master's voice, his gravitas, his rhetorical flourishes or irony, Granovskii's writings played a major role in the creation of an identikit portrait of the *nastavnik* and a template for a tradition of learning. Moreover, his early death generated a cult of memory, which, if it blurred distinctions between his legacy as a historian and the legendary status he acquired as a champion of social justice, created a model of professional practice to which successive generations of historians aspired. 'All of us', wrote Kliuchevskii, 'are, to a greater or lesser extent, students of Granovskii, and revere his pure memory; for it was Granovskii and none other who created for subsequent generations the prototype of the ideal professor. His name became a symbol of social resurrection, achieved by transforming scholarly concepts into living deeds'.[8] Irrespective, then, of changes in sensibilities – from romantic to realist – during the course of the nineteenth century, or indeed the temperament of individual scholars, the enduring image of the historian-*nastavnik* was one of a morally accountable protector of true scholarship. His voice and idiosyncrasies were embraced both as a precondition and as a measure of his achievements. This was as much the case for Kliuchevskii, whose dark moods occasionally found expression in the form of pithy, ironic axioms in his public addresses ('History is a brace of horrors', he once declared) as it was for Ivan Grevs, affectionately remembered by his closest pupils as 'padre sereno' in the more private sphere of the seminar.[9]

Portraits of the historian

The ideal professor: Timofei Granovskii

The life of Granovskii, and his untimely death at the age of forty-two, generated a vast commemorative and biographical literature. Crafted shortly after his death by figures such as Aleksandr Herzen, Petr Kudriavtsev, Granovskii's successor to the chair of World History, and the radical thinker, Nikolai Chernyshevskii, the dominant accent in these early tributes was placed on Granovskii, the man, a beguiling personality, a beautiful/noble soul (*prekrasnaia; blagorodnaia dusha*): 'It was not possible for any worthy person not to love Granovskii. Wherever he was, there could only be one feeling, the feeling of brotherhood'.[10] Afflicted by delicate health, suffering at the hands of rival professors (namely, Pogodin and Shevyrev as proponents of official nationality), Granovskii's dedication to scholarship was driven by an unshakeable belief that knowledge was a tool for sharpening one's moral conscience and sense of (civic) duty: 'Rigorous, systematic study was alien to him' (*Upornyi sistematicheskii trud byl emu ne po dushe*). Work (*rabota*) alone did not satisfy him: he was guided by the idea that 'all of the person (*chelovek*) should make itself felt in whatever he did.'[11] To this point, it is worth noting that Granovskii took up teaching duties in a period, the late 1830s, when the university exerted very little influence on educated society. His goal was to break down barriers, and he did this using the public lecture as a medium. In Kudriavtsev's opinion, such aspirations made Granovskii acutely sensitive to the spirit of the past, his findings more profound than mere rational comprehension. Unlike the pedestrian 'erudite' – a mere master of facts or specialist on a narrow topic – Granovskii couched 'the secret of living knowledge (*zhivoe znanie*)' in artistic forms: 'More than anyone else he had the gift of rendering scholarship in an artistic manner (*khudozhestvennaia obrabotka nauki*)'. Chernyshevskii made a similar comment, differentiating between pedantry and a pledge to place scholarship in service to public enlightenment: '[H]e was acutely aware of a greater need in our country for proponents of enlightenment (*dvigateli prosveshcheniia*), love and well being, for mediators (*posredniki*) between scholarship and ourselves (the public) rather than people dedicating all their energies to scholarly questions of secondary importance'.[12]

The views of Granovskii's immediate contemporaries were incorporated, sometimes verbatim, into biographical sketches written over the course of the next fives decades, their publication usually timed to coincide with various anniversaries of his death.[13] Building on original eyewitness accounts, and referencing each other's appraisals, successive generations of historians produced a single leading narrative, which, over time, transformed Granovskii's legacy into legend.[14] Moreover, the ethos of romanticism that had informed early evaluations did not jar with the otherwise dominant 'realist' sensibilities of historians whose careers coincided with the age of reform and counter-reform; rather, it found endorsement among them as a set of principles to emulate. This point was made in an anonymous review of Aleksandr Stankevich's biography, author of the first comprehensive account of Granovskii's life and work:

[T]here are grounds to hope that the biography of Granovskii will become a favourite book among Russian youth, that from it they will learn humaneness, deep respect for everything that is noble, and morally pure, that the young generation will come away from this book with an idealism which is normal for their stage in life yet which has been totally obscured in so much of our more contemporary literature.[15]

In sum, Granovskii's self-acclaimed successors willingly accepted the pathos of his views concerning the goal of history, namely, the 'morally enlightened individual' and a society corresponding to the demands of such an individual, as well as the role he attributed to the historian, bound, as he put it, by a 'lawful requirement' to exert a 'moral influence on his audience'.[16] Above all, though, it was his struggle to transform the public perception of the university as a remote ivory tower into a symbol of the 'political' power of culture that resonated with historians active at the end of the century who continued to champion the same, yet still largely unrealized, ambition: 'Granovskii was the first professor of history who, having placed the idea of science on his banner, expressed the hope that this science would interconnect with other branches of human knowledge (…), that science would have a bearing on life (…) as an educative and guiding hand for the student youth and society more broadly'.[17] His strengths, as Kareev noted with reference to Kudriavtsev's commentary, resided in his scepticism towards the 'pure' disinterested science of '*kabinet*' scholars and in his appeal that history be life's mentor (*nastavnitsa zhizni*), in short, that historical enquiry be understood as a means for bringing humanity closer to the realization of the ideas of truth and the good.[18] Both Kudriavtsev and Stankevich confirmed that he had always hoped that university science would be a tool for influencing society: 'The fact that this was not the case', Kareev concluded, 'wounded him deeply'.[19]

An element of victimization was a component of the *nastavnik*'s moral pedigree, which enhanced his legendary status. It is well known that Granovskii did not find a receptive audience among his immediate peers. Pogodin was instrumental in blocking (on two occasions) his election as dean of faculty, and when, in February 1845, Granovskii faced the non-authorization of his master's degree, his public viva triggered a student protest against the university officials, the first of its kind in Russia. Following the defence of his doctoral study on Abbot Suger of St Denis, in 1849, he received a summons to appear before Metropolitan Filaret for daring to suggest that the foundations of the monarchic principle were human in design, and not from God.[20] In the eyes of his admirers, these episodes confirmed his stature as 'a progressive combatant (*peredovoi boets*) for the finest principles of human life (…) namely, the immortal ideals of truth, the good, love and beauty'.[21]

The aestheticized self

'In essence', wrote Ch. Vetrinskii, 'Granovskii modelled the ideal historian on himself'.[22] If Granovskii's posthumous canonization created an idealized portrait of the true scholar driven by a vision of moral perfectibility and civic responsibility, it was Granovskii, the romantic, who, during his lifetime, provided its tones and hues. Foremost among these was empathy as the following example suggests: 'Judgement', he wrote, 'must be based on a true and honest examination of the matter. It is pronounced not with the aim of disturbing the slumber of the accused in his grave (*mogil'nyi son*), rather to reinforce (…) the moral feeling of the living, strengthen their shaky faith in the good and the truth'.[23] Granovskii's belief that the mark of a true historian consisted in an ability to bring to the past 'that living feeling of love for his neighbours, and to recognize a brother among communities of the distant past' articulated what Priscilla

Roosevelt has described as a 'culture of the feelings', an attachment of extraordinary importance to matters of the heart and a quasi-deification of art that he and many of his contemporaries shared.[24]

In her compelling study of the semiotics of behaviour, Irina Paperno has suggested that 'a deliberate and programmatic expansion of literary categories into real life was typical of [romanticism]: ordinary life patterned on the norms and rules governing artistic texts was meant to be experienced as an aesthetic form'.[25] Love and friendship, the life of the 'inner self', found expression in a vocabulary of metaphysics and ethics sourced in German romanticism and philosophical idealism, as well as French Christian socialism and the novels of the social romantics. (Paperno mentions Balzac, Hugo, Eugene Sue and, of special importance, George Sand.) Embodied in fictional protagonists, these ideal representations were woven into the real life stories of the men (and women) of the 1830s and 1840s, creating what she describes as 'a complex cultural fabric with no clear line between "literature"and "life"'.[26] This innovative work of Russian-born literary theorists that has grown out of the pioneering research led by Iurii Lotman in the post-Stalinist and Brezhnev eras provides a useful template for exploring the construction of the historian's persona. The concept of 'theatricality', for example, which Lotman first developed to describe the highly semioticized behaviour of the Westernized noblemen during the reign of Alexander I and its prescriptive source in romantic literature renders very well the code of self-representation in the debates that played out in the salon culture of the first half of the nineteenth century. Hallmark terms of historicism and philosophical idealism – 'stage', 'development' (*Entwicklung/razvitie*), 'organic', 'spontaneity', 'unenlightened', 'subjectivity', 'accident', 'illusion', 'true life', 'freedom', 'necessity', 'concreteness' – filtered into Russian intellectual discourse where they functioned not only as tools to conceptualize the historical process, but equally as metaphors in exchanges about the emotions and the quest for self-fulfilment.[27] The leitmotifs of philosophical idealism, as Lidiia Ginzburg notes, had tremendous appeal for the post-Decembrist generation. They became, she says, 'part of the intellectual conversation in the circles of the two capitals and part of the intimate exchange between lovers and close friends. Metaphysical notions became the idioms of everyday speech, part of the common language. As a result, abstract philosophical categories were, in complete earnestness and with striking naiveté, applied to daily life'.[28]

A great deal has been written about Granovskii's friendship with Nikolai Stankevich, whose circle marked a decisive moment in the scripting of 'the aestheticized self'. At the core of their animated discussions on aesthetics and ethical topics lay the question of man's purpose and destiny, his behaviour, feelings and moral responsibility. According to Lidiia Ginzburg, these reflections prompted the need 'to create an image of personality that would have broad historical meaning'. It was, she writes, an image that emerged 'from every conceivable form of social life'. Ginzburg singles out the cultivation of the letter as a privileged genre in the creation of the romantic personality; correspondents couched their personal sentiments in the language of metaphysics and religion. In addition, diaries, philosophical and literary models of, for example, the divinely inspired poet as an elect personality (after Schelling) or, inversely, the disenchanted young man whose indignation leads him to destroy the romantic 'chimeras' (Ivan Turgenev) all played a part in the construction of an 'epochal personality'.[29]

The stock of literary conventions and received ideas informing the worldview and behaviour of Russian intellectuals in the age of romanticism also governed perceptions of the historian-*nastavnik*. With his heightened sense of purpose, selfless dedication to 'scholarship' (*nauka*) and poetic temperament, Granovskii manifestly exemplified the romantic 'art of living' (*zhiznetvorchestvo*).[30] Stankevich's advice that he 'love history as poetry', and complement it with philosophy (Hegel and Schelling), provided the ground rules for his vision of the role of history and of the historian's mission.[31] In this connection, Granovskii's sympathetic portrait of the Danish-born professor of ancient history at Berlin University, Barthold Niebuhr (1776–1831) is a highly instructive illustration of the way in which an 'epochal personality' for historians was crafted. Challenging the standard view of his older contemporary as a sceptic and arid scholar, Granovskii set out to demonstrate 'how much poetry there is in his vision of history'(...) 'his speech is simple but it has clarity and strength'. Gifted with an unusual ability to be carried into the past by his imagination, it was as if he, himself, had lived through the struggles of all the great parties of Greece and Rome.[32]

'The biographical form', Granovskii stated, 'offers the possibility to explain the book by life and life by the book'.[33] Although an unfinished account, Granovskii's presentation of Niebuhr as a historian-poet contained all the key components of the romantic personality. Hewn from a romantic-literary block, Granovskii created a portrait of his older contemporary that could just as easily read as a self-portrait. The details of Niebuhr's early life and character that Granovskii selected – his aesthetic/poetic sensitivities, an unstructured home education and his dissatisfaction with the formal instruction he received at the university – all mirrored Granovskii's own formative experiences and temperament.[34] Nature had blessed Niebuhr 'with a surplus of imagination and creative fantasy (...). The author of "Roman history" was born an artist'.[35] Physically frail, but free spirited, and politically aware, sceptical of the academic environment he was exposed to as a student, 'he did not want an exclusively scholarly, academic career (*deiatel'nost'*), possibly because he saw all round him the arid, narrow existence of the professors at Kiel University'.[36] Similarly, Granovskii's interest in history had developed in spite of the university lectures he attended.[37] His discovery of Hegelian philosophy (thanks mainly to Nikolai Stankevich) and Rankean historicism in the mid-1830s, which provided him with the tools to seek the underlying meaning of events and their interconnections, represented a radical departure from the scepticism and the routine compilation of facts, that, to his mind, characterized the work of older Moscow professors. Friendships, elective affinities and the professional experiences both men acquired in government service prior to taking up their university posts nourished their views of history and the significance they each attached to an empathetic grasp of the past. Niebuhr's career as a financier and diplomat posted to Rome allowed him to witness

> with his own eyes the living movement of events; (...) his participation in the destinies of peoples was not merely a theoretical exercise. In this respect, he belongs to (*primykaet*) the school of English political historians, who in turn, have

much in common with the ancients. But Niebuhr has more of a poetic feeling; his creativity is "truer" than that of the English. His scholarship surpasses even that of Gibbon.[38]

The image of the historian–poet–prophet that Granovskii and his peers cultivated was, of course, a defining feature of historiography across Europe during the first half of the nineteenth century. Schooled in the principles of German idealism, and 'nurtured' in the spirit of romanticism, this generation perceived history as a sacred text to be faithfully interpreted through intuitive cognition or empathy (*ahnen, einfuhlen*) by the historian in his role as 'God's servitor'.[39] The emphasis Granovskii placed on imagination as a means to resurrect the past clearly emulated the broad cultural range he found in the writings of contemporary French masters. As Lionel Gossman argues in his study of Jules Michelet and Augustin Thierry, 'the romantic vision of history embraced the imagination for its true insight into the nature of historical reality, and it was this insight that made it possible to select, group, and interpret evidence'.[40] Coupled with a view of the historian as a 'backward looking prophet', whose self-ascribed task consisted in 'bringing the people to a full awareness of itself, by articulating its unconscious thoughts, historical writing was (…) conceived and practised (…) as an integral part of the historian's activity as a public figure, inseparable from either his general worldview or, indeed, his immediate more concrete political ideals and goals'.[41] It goes without saying, though, that, in France and Germany, the political climate did not systematically prohibit the historian from engaging in the public arena as an informed citizen, or, indeed, his active involvement in what Gossman terms 'present history'. Here, it was not uncommon for historians to combine their roles as professors with political engagement; whether as statesmen or pamphleteers, historians found a platform for political prognoses which, as Gossman argues, 'far from being an obstacle to understanding the past, was a condition of genuine historical insight'.[42] Donald Kelley makes a similar point, adding that the authority of historians in the public sphere was bolstered by 'the vast expansion of their institutional base and of the media of publicity and influence. Not only the publication of books but also university chairs, public education on lower levels, control of journals (…) all contributed to make history an industry as well as a pedagogical and political calling (…) in its own right'.[43] By contrast, for Granovskii and his liberal Russian peers, such an ambition was thwarted by government oversight and measures intended to silence them. The spirit of 'oriental despotism' associated with the reign of Nicholas I meant that the privilege of political or ideological commentary was granted only to historian-apologists for the status quo.

Pogodin: 'Patriarch' of Russian history[44]

Granovskii's immediate contemporary, and, in many respects, nemesis, was Mikhail Pogodin.[45] Together with Stepan Shevyrev, Pogodin became a leading spokesman for official nationality.[46] Described by Kliuchevskii as a brutal, self-serving upstart, 'an egregious, mercurial, obnoxious, aggressive entity', this son of a freed serf sought his principal addressee not in his immediate auditorium of students (with whom, according to Kliuchevskii, he was highly unpopular), rather 'society' and, above all, the

Ministry and the Tsar.[47] He was the archetypal 'court historian' and ideologue.[48] Still, he was also, like Granovskii, a typical product of the romantic era, embracing its moral and aesthetic precepts in his activities as teacher, *publitsist* and as the author of short stories in which he explored themes of unrequited love, emotional self-discovery and Byronic disenchantment.[49] These platforms were all essential to his self-promotion as an intellectual missionary.

Pogodin considered the university cathedra as a channel not to elaborate on scholarly findings and models of explanation, rather to impart his visions. According to his former pupil, Konstantin Bestuzhev-Riumin, professor of Russian history at St Petersburg University (1864–85), his goal was to 'enliven' (*odushevit'*) his audience through the beliefs and faith on which he had been nurtured as a child growing up in 'that simple Russian family', and which were strengthened by the cultural and political events of the age he witnessed. The patriotic war of 1812 and the message of Karamzin's multi-volume *History of the Russian State* ('history [...] is the sacred book of a nation') were pivotal in shaping Pogodin's zealous defence of Russia's greatness: 'The magnificence (*velichie*) of Russia was created by the entirety of her history, by the activity of her people. Respect for the past, for this history, for this people is a necessary condition for her future greatness'.[50] As an 'impassioned stalwart (*stoiatel'*) of Moscow and the Russian land', Pogodin's mission to instil a sense of national pride, moreover, fuelled an ambitious pan-Slavic project to establish Russia's hegemony among the Slavic-speaking peoples. Pogodin sourced his arguments for Russia as the first among sister nations in a national past characterized by moral resilience and courage. In sum, wrote Bestuzhev-Riumin: 'He taught us to love science, love and respect Russia, to cherish (*tsenit'*) all the heavy sacrifices which ancient Rus' had managed to endure for the sake of preserving an independent existence and creating the only stable/solid state in the stormy history of the Slavic states. He taught us to see ourselves as Russians, as members of one single Russian,–of one great Slavic family'.[51]

Pogodin formulated his views in a collection of 'historical aphorisms'. Intended to serve a pedagogical purpose (many of them read like essay questions or topics for seminar discussion), these adages illustrate very well the way the tropes of literary and philosophical romanticism were just as much a part of the historian's lexicon. For example: 'History should create a single whole out of the entire human race, one man, and present the biography of this man through all the stages of his growth'. Gifted with intuitive insights, the historian probes 'history's unfathomable mysteries' beyond the 'laws of necessity and freedom'; 'sometimes unbeknownst to him, the historian-poet relates events while it is the discerning reader who uncovers their harmonious, balanced (*stroinoe*) development, an embedded system or, at any rate, the beginnings of one'.[52] And in what undoubtedly became his 'signature aphorism' – 'the historian is the true crown of a nation, for through him it comes to know itself' – Pogodin positioned himself as Karamzin's most faithful pupil.[53]

Like his elected master, Pogodin propagated a view of history in terms of a 'moral-psychological aesthetic'.[54] Complementing Karamzin's 'heroic epopee of Russian valour and glory' with more poignant tones of suffering and endurance, his explicit aim was to deepen the feelings of love and pride among the Russian people for their past. However, if some former pupils, such as Bestuzhev-Riumin, were prepared to recognize Pogodin's success in this regard, others (Kliuchevskii, notably) considered it a major disservice to Russian historical scholarship[55]: in the eyes of his sharpest critics, Pogodin was wrong to resist the paradigm shift in historical writing that was taking place in the second half of the century (and which Granovskii had prefigured in his call to ally history with the natural sciences[56]). Pogodin's tendency to parade his feelings and pronounce inspired visions concerning Russia's past and future greatness were deemed inappropriate and out of touch with the new realist sensibilities, which, by the mid-century, were beginning to inform the historian's professional persona.[57] In other words, for historians active in the age of reform and counter-reform, Pogodin's indebtedness to Karamzin placed him in an intellectual time capsule.

Towards realism

The intellectual movement of the mid-nineteenth century dictated a new set of principles, which, on the surface at least, marked a radical departure from the world of romanticism. Empirically verifiable facts became the hallmark of social science; in literature, 'everyday Byronism' was supplanted by 'everyday positivism'. Turning the ordinary and mundane material existence into an inseparable part of the 'inner life of the spirit, "pennies," "groceries" and "the animal side of human nature" (bodily needs), thus became legitimate facts of culture'.[58] Reflections on the meaning and uses of history also evolved: the romantic ideas of Providence and God's plan gave way to an emphasis on verifiable fact and the inclusion of more readily quantifiable data, such as statistics and legal records, in order to explore past societies in light of the political and economic lessons one might glean from them. Accordingly, the accent on the force of ideas in history (Schelling, Hegel) was superseded by an inductive approach to the past generating a slew of theoretical studies on history, sociology and economics by talented young scholars – Pavel Miliukov, Pavel Vinogradov and Nikolai Kareev, among them – graduating from the university in the late 1870s and 1880s.[59]

In many respects, perceptions of the historian-*nastavnik* reflected these broader cultural changes. Cast as a rational, impartial truth seeker, a collector, verifier and interpreter of facts, the new model historian was now a clear-headed realist who eschewed the zealousness and romantic fervour of his predecessors. 'One ought not to be a historian', Kiesewetter wrote, 'unless one knows how to sort through the motley hurly-burly of life's events to discern the patterns that unify them. Without this gift one cannot become a historian but can only become a narrator, because merely experiencing the past in one's imagination is not the same as being able to understand it'.[60] As Kareev, the so-called pagan priest of history, put it: 'Dispassionateness (*bezpristrastie*]) is a moral and intellectual virtue'.[61] These new priorities did not, however, disturb deeper trans-generational continuities in the practice of claiming allegiance to a master; and, in his self-ascribed task as a public enlightener, the persona of the historian altered even less: 'Historians', Kliuchveskii wrote, 'are as important as rulers: they reflect the laws of history, influence other elements of society, and enable a people to understand itself by explaining its origins and development'.[62] Historians continued to harness the social and political relevance of historical knowledge as well as its subversive potential. Moreover, they recognized that for the historian's enlightenment message to be heard, his intellectual authority still required moral rectitude, and, importantly, that he still needed to be a craftsman of the word.[63] The historian's gifts as 'artist-narrator' thus remained an integral part of what was otherwise presented as a more rigorous professionalism. Indeed, as Irina Paperno has argued in her study about Chernyshevskii, the archetypal 'man of the sixties', the age of realism contained a residual romanticism, thereby affording direct links and continuities between them. '[A]lthough a man of the sixties saw himself as a new man who had shaken off the "old Adam" (…), it was', she rightly claims, 'in the intellectual atmosphere of the philosophical and literary circles of the 1840s, centred around Mikhail Bakunin, Nikolai Stankevich, Timofei Granovsky, Alexander Herzen, Nikolai Ogarev, and Vissarion Belinsky that the men of the sixties were reared'. It is therefore not surprising that romantic consciousness 'was a tangible (though at times vehemently denied) presence, a substratum of the consciousness of the realist'.[64]

Vasilii Kliuchevskii: The scholar-artist (*uchenyi-khudozhnik*)[65]

In a diary entry dated 25 February 1903, Kliuchevskii posed the following question: 'What is historical *zakonomernost'* (law governed development)?' His answer consisted of a reasoned dismissal of 'cause and effect' and of 'necessity' as reductionist categories that were ultimately irrelevant to historical enquiry: 'For the historian', he wrote:

> [W]hat matters is not the fact that one thing derives from that which precedes it, rather what it reveals, namely, those qualities manifested by the individual and society in the given circumstances […]. Bearing in mind that history is not a logical process, but a collective (*narodno*)–psychological one, and that its principal object of scientific study is the manifestation of forces and the characteristics of the human spirit that develop within society, we come closer to the heart of the matter if we reduce historical phenomena to two intermeshing components – that of mind-set (*nastroenie*) and movement (*dvizhenie*) […]. This continuous reciprocal change among components (one constantly summoning and summoned by the other) constitutes the historical process, rather like the movement of a rake thrown into a freely moving stream. Is there really a place here for causal links, and may we deem as causal the movements of the rake, that, momentarily, rises on the crest of a wave where we catch a glimpse of it, and then is submerged?[66]

As one of Imperial Russia's most celebrated historians, Kliuchevskii was primarily interested in, and known for, his work in socio-economic questions.[67] His studies of the boyar duma, the *zemskii sobor*, the origins of serfdom and *kholopstvo*, which he analysed through the prism of social and institutional structures rather than governmental instructions (*ukazy*), all attest a 'bottom-up' approach to the history of social estates. In part prompted by the host of theoretical and practical issues raised by the emancipation of the serfs, Kliuchevskii's interest in these questions and evident sympathies for the peasantry, as his biographers repeatedly point out, also had deeper roots in his childhood experiences. His familiarity with the peasant world, which he witnessed first hand as the son of a village priest growing up in the region of

Penza, his assiduous reading of predominantly left-wing thick journals (*Sovremennik, Otechestvennye zapiski, Russkii vestnik*) charting the impact of wider socio-political change on public awareness and the intellectual climate he encountered when he entered university on the eve of reform all confirmed an instinctual populism that is clearly discernible in his work as a historian.[68] Pavel Miliukov, one of Kliuchevskii's former pupils, remarked on its 'quintessentially Russian character'; Kliuchevskii's oeuvre, he wrote, 'evolved on the soil of Russia's social sphere (*vyroslo na pochve russkoi obshchestvennosti*) and was infused with 'the ideals of humanity'.[69] Writing in emigration, another former pupil, Georgii Fedotov, offered an explanation of what 'realism' and 'populism' meant for Kliuchevskii: 'Realism (...) meant anti-idealism, a return to the land (...) to the lower, natural spheres of life: matter, physiology, economics, ethnography (...)'. Populism, in the broad sense, was 'a kind of social transcription of this naturalism'.[70]

Kliuchevskii's early formal schooling in national history was less than satisfactory: at the Penza Theological Seminary, it consisted of a digest of loyalist interpretations excerpted from Karamzin's *History* and officially commissioned textbooks compiled by Pogodin and his counterpart in St Petersburg, Nikolai Ustrialov.[71] If these helped nurture Kliuchevskii's affection for the Russian people, they would, however, have virtually no bearing on the types of enquiry he would later pursue. Rather, as memoir accounts suggest, his formation as a historian was predominantly shaped by independent reading of historical, juridical and literary historical scholarships (the names of Granovskii; Kostomarov; the literary historian, Fedor Buslaev; and historians of law and political philosophers, Konstantin Kavelin and Boris Chicherin, are mentioned), together with critical discussions of the national question that he followed in the *publitsistika* during the 1840s and 1850s. Led by Solov'ev, Kostomarov, Pypin, Buslaev, Chernyshevskii and Chicherin, the debate articulated competing opinions of Russia's past, her culture and her place in Europe, views with which Kliuchevskii would, himself, later engage in open and implicit dialogue in his role as public enlightener.

Matriculating at Moscow University in 1861, Kliuchevskii encountered two major influences – Sergei Solov'ev (1820–79), chair of Russian history, and Fedor Buslaev (1818–97), professor of Literature and a leading representative of the Russian 'mythological school' inspired by the theories of Jacob Grimm that dominated literary studies between the 1840s and 1860s. If he was later to declare that 'I am Solov'ev's pupil, that is all that I can be proud of as a scholar', it was Buslaev's love of learning, his enduring search for truth, patriotism, generosity and tolerance that provided a model of scholarship worthy of emulation.[72] According to Robert Byrnes, author of a detailed monograph of Kliuchevskii's life and work, it was Buslaev's view of teaching as 'the most holy and greatest office a man could occupy' that Kliuchevskii appropriated as a benchmark in his own prescriptions for the discipline.[73] 'In order to be a good teacher, Kliuchevskii wrote, "you have to love what you teach, and love those whom you teach"; "the teacher is endowed with the word not to send thought to sleep (*usyplyat'*), rather, to awaken another one (*chuzhuiu*)'; 'We need to know the past, not because it is past, but because, in departing, it did not manage to take away with it all its traces (*posledstviia*)'; 'Without knowledge of history we must regard ourselves as contingencies (*sluchainosti*), not knowing how and why we came into the world;

[we are like] mechanical dolls which are not born, but fabricated, which do not die according to the laws of nature, of life, but are broken as a result of some childish capriciousness'.⁷⁴ As a 'man of the sixties', however, and certainly unlike Buslaev or, indeed, Granovskii, Kliuchevskii's aphorisms and diary entries on his profession contained none of the elevated metaphors of the romantics and offered little solace to the student of history: 'History is not a teacher', he wrote, 'but an "intendant" (*nadziratel'nitsa*), magistra vitae: it does not teach anything, rather it punishes for ignorance of lessons taught'.⁷⁵ Although never intended for publication, the substance of these jottings was, as attested by his pupils and readers, consistent with both the damning verdict Kliuchevskii returned on the state of historical knowledge in the Russia of his day and his unshakable belief that, despite government meddling in university affairs, the intrinsic value of historical study was not diminished: 'Politics ought to be no more and no less than applied history. It is currently no more than a denial of history, and no less than a distortion of it'.⁷⁶

Kliuchevskii took a wide range of courses with Buslaev: Byzantine and early Russian literature; Russian and Slavic poetry, folklore and oral history, philology; old German and Norwegian literature and folklore; and comparative literature.⁷⁷ The strong cultural–historical accent in Buslaev's research as well as a historical comparative approach to mythology attested in his later writings (and which, arguably, foreshadowed the work of Aleksandr Veselovskii and Semen Vengerov) marked a departure from the then dominant practice (1830s) of collating sources and providing critical commentary. At the heart of his teaching was the idea that 'poetry, and particularly primitive epic poetry, is the expression of the life of a people (*narodnaia zhizn'*)'.⁷⁸ In his lectures, Buslaev established interconnections between religious, socio-political and domestic conventions (*byt*), science and literature. Even though, in 1861, world literature did not yet figure as a separate course in the curriculum, he incorporated a comparative perspective, thanks to which Kliuchevskii came not only to admire, as Byrnes notes, the Norwegian Eddas and German folktales, but also to recognize that the lives of the Norwegian and German peoples of those times were much freer than those of the Russians. Buslaev's stress on the importance of studying the general (i.e. trends in world literature) in order to understand the particular (i.e. national history) helped his students grasp the notion that 'each society is an organism different from other societies, and that history and tradition had combined to make the Russian character different'.⁷⁹

Buslaev's studies in ancient Russian literature, folklore, icons, Church Slavonic and the history of the Russian language significantly broadened Kliuchevskii's cultural horizons. In particular, his insistence that a people's language and its literature (*narodnoe tvorchestvo*) were an essential part of its history was a point of principle that remained with Kliuchevskii throughout his career, steering his interests towards the study of popular cultural life, the economy and social conditions.⁸⁰

> Teaching us about the structure of language and its links with the day-to-day life of the people (*narodnyi byt*), he taught us how to read ancient texts (*pamiatniki*), decipher the meanings of words as they were used in a given period, situate the

source in question with other contemporary sources thereby affording insights into the way of life and mindset (*sklad*) of the period as a whole.[81]

Buslaev's discovery of residual popular, pagan motifs in hagiographical texts was especially significant for the 'secular' approach Kliuchevskii later adopted in his masters dissertation, *Ancient Russian Lives of Saints as a Historical Source* (*Drevnerusskie zhitia sviatykh kak istoricheskii istochnik*) (1871): 'I recall', he wrote, 'how I started to search for a reflection, not of ideals, or norms of an order newly established in Rus' [i.e. Christianity – FN] (…), rather of the milieu in which these norms were gradually and not always coherently apprehended'.[82] For Kliuchevskii, these hagiographical writings contained traces of an 'oral tradition', which, as a valuable record of a linguistic heritage (*iazykovoe nasledie*), encapsulated the poetic nature of the people, its fantasies and imagination. The implications of these findings for Kliuchevskii's contribution to Russian national history cannot be overemphasized: 'Much of the past', he wrote, 'is etched in language which time otherwise takes from human memory' (*Iazyk zapomnil mnogo stariny, sveiannoi vremenem s liudskoi pamiati*).[83] As I argue in Chapter 3, this conviction honed his sensitivity not only to the poetic spirit he uncovered in the ancient chronicles, but also to the tonality of modern poetry and prose that he avidly read and commented on in his mature writings, and which he used in his studies of post-Petrine society.

Kliuchevskii spent the last decade of his life converting his lectures into a five-volume *Course in Russian History* (1904–12).[84] Framed by the rise and abrogation of serfdom, the methodological principles he set out in his introduction announced a Comtean-derived 'historical sociology'. In practice, though, his approach and the guidance he offered to his students systemically privileged close philological analysis of written sources. Just as Buslaev had 'explained to us the significance of language as a historical source', Kliuchevskii, in turn, urged his pupils to be sensitive to the literary and imaginative content of a historical document.[85] Study of history, he reminded them, was an art, not a science: 'A scholar's goal is to determine what happened and describe that accurately and lucidly. Trying to find laws behind history, even in the record of one nation, is illusory'.[86] It was this attitude that arguably made him such 'a powerful painter of history'; his ability to revive its outlines in pictures of sculptural clarity was testament not to his expertise with methodological tools, rather to a profound, intuitive feeling he had for the past.[87] In the words of the medievalist Aleksandr Presniakov, this was, ultimately, what made him the exemplary 'scholar-artist' (*uchenyi-khudozhnik*).[88]

Judging by memoir accounts, Kliuchevskii seems to have resisted the cultivation of an inner circle of interlocutors with peers and pupils, if anything finding a kindred spirit among literati and members of the performing arts: the famous Russian opera singer, Fedor Shaliapin, for example, sought his advice in preparing for his role as Boris Godunov. Among pupils – a long list comprising Pavel Miliukov, Pavel Vinogradov, Aleksandr Kiesewetter, Aleksandr Lappo-Danilevskii, Sergei Platonov and Mikhail Bogoslovskii, Kliuchevskii's successor to the chair of Russian history – loyalty was tainted by what they recognized as his dark moods, emotional distance, impatience with seminar students and possibly an overly protective attitude towards the intellectual fiefdom he had established for himself as the indisputable master of Russian history. As Sigurd Shmidt put it, 'he was admired but not loved'.[89] Pavel Miliukov, for example, who began frequenting Kliuchevskii's lectures in 1879, fell out of favour with the 'master', as did the future Marxist historian-bureaucrat, Mikhail Pokrovskii, who dominated historical research in the 1920s, largely by outmanoeuvring potential rivals.[90] In other respects, though, Kliuchevskii certainly did match the identikit portrait of the *nastavnik*: he recognized the function of history as a form of consciousness raising and used his expertise to challenge, rather than uphold, the status quo in his public addresses. Committed to building a tradition in historical research, he positioned himself, as Solov'ev's pupil, within a cross-generational 'republic of minds'. Granted, Kliuchevskii's declaration of loyalty struck some of his peers and pupils as somewhat disingenuous given that he diminished the importance Solov'ev had attached to gens (*rodovoe bytie*) as a defining characteristic of the appanage period and rejected the Hegelian-inspired concept of statehood that had structured Solov'ev's view of the historical process.[91] Indeed, for Aleksandr Lappo-Danilevskii, a specialist in the early modern period and an advocate of neo-idealism, this second point of declared difference with the master, if anything, exposed inconsistencies within the pupil's work: '[He] deliberates on the peculiar configuration of "political, social and economic facts" without considering the underlying "ideas"'. For Lappo-Danilevskii, this omission jarred with the importance that Kliuchevskii obviously attached to the development of national self-awareness together with the formational process of what he called 'the historical person of the Russian people/nation', that is, a deeply romantic idea shared by philosophers and historians from Herder to Michelet.[92] Kliuchevskii did eventually modify his views, however: if he remained true to his belief that 'history looks not at man, but at society', he also recognized, as Lappo-Danilevskii paraphrased it, that 'labours of the mind and moral achievements will always remain the best builders of society, the most powerful driving forces of human development'.[93] These reservations aside, everyone who knew Kliuchevskii recognized and paid tribute to his remarkable ability to unify 'scientific method' and insight. This was the hallmark of his indisputable genius, assuring his right of succession to Granovskii as the 'ideal professor'.[94]

Both Kliuchevskii and Granovskii acquired their authority as *nastavniki* at the university lectern before packed auditoriums of students from all faculties and the wider educated public. The rise of the seminar in the closing decades of the nineteenth century introduced an enclosed context of institutionalized learning, which, by contrast, strengthened perceptions of the *nastavnik* in terms of exclusive master–pupil relations. These changes were reflected in the dedicatory and commemorative literature. While this body of writing still conformed to the canon in the sense that it constructed the historian's authority on the twin pillars of scholarship and his commitment to public enlightenment, it now tended to differentiate between the master's written legacy and a genuine inheritance acquired through privileged first-hand acquaintance over the course of several years in the context of the seminar and informal home circles: 'Only he who followed your courses and seminars knows that the answer to the question concerning the substance of your scholarly activity lies not in your published works, but in the conspectus of your unpublished courses, in the ideas recorded by students in their notebooks, and in the marginal comments you made in their essays'.[95] With the introduction of the seminar, then, came more nuanced conceptions of scholarship and correspondingly greater differentiation in the style, form and language of historical knowledge depending on whether the historian was addressing his peers, his pupils or the wider public.

Ivan Grevs: 'Padre Sereno' and latter-day romantic

In an obituary tribute to the Byzantinist, Vasilii Grigor'evich Vasilevskii (1838–99), whom he eventually succeeded as professor of Medieval History, Grevs summarized the essential characteristics of the model scholar:

> Every representative of the university corporation has to forge for himself a definite social ideal, which he should bring to bear in faculty and council meetings, as well as in his relations with students. Since the work of a professor is conducted through constant contact with people, upon whom he exerts a considerable influence, his success in fulfilling his task depends entirely on the strength of his moral character. This alone affords him authority in his dealings with colleagues or superiors, and ensures his command [...] in the lecture hall. The intellectual–moral expectations placed on the professor are thus highly complex, and it is only by integrating these that he may become a true *uchitel' nauki* and *uchitel' zhizni*, a social pedagogue (*obshchestvennyi pedagog*) in the widest sense.[96]

Vasilevskii's efforts to subordinate demands for social change to a view of progress 'dependent not on political manifestos, rather on the recognition of the value of scholarship' were driven by a belief in the 'power of thought' (*sila mysli*) as the sine qua non of a solid, stable movement towards the perfection of the human person and the social order.[97] Set against a background of social unrest in large part orchestrated by a growing populist-student movement, his appeal signified a reasoned approach to contain violence. And it was an appeal that clearly resonated with the young Grevs: during his postgraduate years, which coincided with the onset of counter-reform measures in the wake of Alexander II's assassination in 1881, he became, along with his friends, the Oldenburg brothers, one of the chief architects of a fraternity (*priiutinskoe bratstvo*) ('the Oldenburg Circle') whose worldview, namely, an emphasis on personal moral perfection, mutual aid and the diffusion of knowledge, was entirely consistent with Vasilevskii's example.[98] Demanding 'sincerity, intelligence, talent and fortitude, as well as an attitude of sympathy and regard for the young men and women he taught', the qualities Vasilevskii brought to bear in his endeavours to serve society through scholarship and thought were also, Grevs commented, vital for the formation of a 'school', 'and a school is the consolidation of his work (*delo*), a pledge to the succession of his ideas'.[99]

'As a fifth grader, I became interested in the medieval world as a whole, in the peculiarities of its inner life, probably because of my childhood reading of French books about knighthood, popular beliefs/legends (*predanie*), life in castles, troubadours, and tales by Sir Walter Scott'.[100] In his tribute to Vasilevskii, Grevs accredited his scholarly interest in the medieval West, and particularly Italy as his specialist field, to his fortuitous encounter with his mentor. Yet in later life, as he looked back over his career, Grevs re-scripted Vasilevskii's role as a formative influence by placing it in a longer trajectory of fascination with the medieval world dating back further to his childhood and early schooling in Voronezh *guberniia* and St Petersburg. 'My passionate attraction for Italy', he recorded in a memoir note dating from the mid-1920s, 'was first implanted in my heart by my reading of Turgenev's *Three Meetings*'.[101] Most of the history books ('stories for children') he read at home as a child, though, were about France: 'The French middle ages with its chivalrous (*zamkovymi*) mores, knights, troubadours, saints, monks, pilgrimages, crusades, the Inquisition and religious wars were already familiar to me in the Lutovina (Voronezh) period, as well as the Revolution and Napoleon. Then Italy began to lure me'.[102] In 1872, Grevs' mother took the children to the capital to prepare for entrance exams to the classical gymnasium. In addition to instruction in classical languages, he had lessons in modern French and German. His introduction to medieval history relied heavily on a core textbook, an anthology compiled by the historian of ancient Greece and West European Middle Ages, Mikhail Stasiulevich, and which comprised excerpts from works by the Russian founding fathers of medieval studies – Granovskii, Kudriavtsev and Eshevskii.[103] Another major influence on the young Grevs was Viktor Petrovich Ostrogorskii, Grevs' instructor in Russian literature.[104] Not only did he make his pupils sensitive to the artistic value of Russian literature, he also encouraged them to account for its social relevance, the ideas it brought to society as well as the flaws it castigated.[105] Again, Turgenev's novels were instrumental in this regard: already part of his childhood reading (his mother had read excerpts of a *Nest of Gentlefolk* with him), the classroom setting, where they studied *On the Eve* and *Fathers and Sons*, consolidated what would become a lifelong attachment to the author's writings and his world.

If in terms of his area of specialization – from the early Carolingian period to Dante and the history of Florence – Grevs' career profile differed from that of Vasilevskii, the pedagogical innovations and tools of historical enquiry that he later became known for should, on the contrary, be credited almost entirely to the formative influence of his professor-mentor.[106] Vasilevskii, who had completed his formation under Mommsen, was highly critical of the current state of instruction in history at the Russian gymnasium and university. As Grevs would do after him, he challenged the dominant paradigm of political narrative with its emphasis on institutions and 'great men' by insisting on the importance of culture as an integral part of historical enquiry as well as on the slow pace and complexity of historical change. Aware that, for the majority of students, the putative 'law-governed character' of history was, if not an inscrutable concept, an empty phrase, 'his innovative approach consisted in a "genetic" study of the inner integrality of history' and in a rejection of rigid periodization based on political change for 'a depiction of history as a genesis of societal phenomena and spiritual culture'.[107]

> Thanks to Vasilevskii, we heard for the first time about 'genetic research', about the inner (structural) integrality of history and the impossibility of breaking it down into parts. Thanks to him, we understood that Antiquity is residually present in the Middle Ages [...] and that the latter had roots in the former. This prompted us not only to reject the rigid scholastic framework with its compartmentalization of history, but also [...] by exchanging the static principle of chronological parts for a concept of flexibly changing phases of development, to challenge the very concept of 'the Middle Ages' itself.[108]

In addition, Vasilevskii's inclusion of historiography and modern historical science as an essential component of survey courses of the medieval and early modern past was, in Grevs' view, possibly one of his most significant contributions to the task of raising the intellectual level of, and interest in, historical study. And, last, but not least, the seminar format which Vasilevskii refined, placing at its core the close reading of a 'monument' of Byzantine or west European history combined with a contextualized and historiographical interpretation, represented, for its time, an innovative student-led approach that ultimately became the mainstay of Grevs' work on the culture and society of the medieval west, a field in which he acquired his own reputation as a '*nastavnik*'.

Appointed professor of World History in 1903, and elected dean of faculty at the Women's Higher Courses (the Bestuzhevskie) in 1906, Ivan Grevs acquired, in his own right, what Anton Sveshnikov has called the 'institutional capital' necessary to forge a community of scholars.[109] The small study group (*kabinet*) that he set up with some of his most gifted students at the university and the Bestuzhevskie provided him with a privileged site of learning for the construction of an interpretative narrative of the medieval world foregrounding the study of its culture, everyday practices and religious worldview.[110] With his students, Grevs analysed a wide range of sources, including poetry, letters, together with the personal impressions of legislators and intellectuals. But it was the way he managed to combine a focus on language, key categories and ideas with a broader contextualized enquiry involving the study of architecture, urban topography and visual art that, in the eyes of his pupils, made him a true scholar worthy of emulation.[111] 'I have to say I really like him,' wrote Georgii Fedotov,

> even though I was wary of finding in him a mixture of scholarly Olympianism and an exaggerated, 'effeminate' ('*damskaia*') rapture – I mean, I feared too much pathos in him. I am used to being disappointed. On the surface at least, he seems gentle, modest. He is measured – has an air of nobility about him in the classic sense. Which does not prevent him from triggering a thought, awakening the mind. In a word, as a teacher, he is ideal.[112]

'It is not enough to be an advocate of scholarship; equally important is an emotional stimulus in the form of love and sympathy towards the students'.[113] Throughout his career, Grevs was fully aware of the responsibilities he assumed as an *uchitel' nauki* (scientific pedagogue) and *uchitel' zhizni* (life mentor). 'In temperament', he wrote, 'I was more of a teacher than a scholar hidden away in his study. Although I had a strong interest in research, my passion for teaching meant that I always subordinated the former to the latter'.[114] Like Vasilevskii before him, Grevs also answered his students' need for a model of social leadership in university politics.[115] Having faced dismissal in 1899 for his liberal–oppositional sympathies (he was reinstated in 1902), he fought tirelessly for university autonomy, defended the Higher Women's Courses as an institution and campaigned for mass education, contributing articles on the subject in various specialist and non-specialist journals, such as *Pravo, Poliarnaia zvezda, Svoboda i kul'tura, Rech'* (*Law, Northern Star, Freedom and Culture, Speech*). In 1904–5, he participated in the All–Russian Congress of Professors, and represented the Historical–Philological Faculty as part of a Student–University Council Liaison Committee set up in the wake of the 1905 revolution to draft a new university statute. It was arguably partly because of these experiences that he initiated informal, yet structured field trips (excursion history) with his students as a way of breaking with the restrictive cadres of formal learning.[116] Significantly, the sense of community (*soobshchestvo*) that this learning format helped strengthen was also a way of recapturing the spirit of friendship he had cultivated, thanks to his encounter with the Oldenburg brothers in 1885. As Sveshnikov notes in his detailed study of the St Petersburg school of medievalists throughout his career Grevs was uncomfortable with the formal role of scientific advisor and constantly sought to establish a system of learning defined by an emotional and existential connection with his pupils, which only a small circle of like-minded friends could offer: his quest for genuine interlocutors and an elective affinity of minds (*rodstvo*) was, at his own admission, extremely important to him.[117]

There is a considerable amount of literature on Grevs' former students, some of whom, such as the religious philosopher, Lev Karsavin, or Georgii Fedotov, are perhaps better known to historians of Russia than the master himself. (The latter's émigré publication, *The Russian Religious Mind* (1946), for example, ranks as an important introduction for a Western audience to Russian medieval culture and thought.) Both Fedotov and Karsavin left Russia after the Revolution.[118] But even as their career paths ultimately took them some distance away from the training they had received as undergraduate students at St Petersburg in the pre-war years (in Karsavin's case leading to an irretrievable break in their relations), their work on problems of religious mentality in the early Middle Ages and the accent both men placed on the subjective experience of faith undoubtedly took inspiration from Grevs' example. Of the two, Fedotov's studies more evidently retained the hallmarks of Grevs' approach, in the sense that his concerns lay with the formation of culture accessed through source analysis with a view to uncovering the complex formation of culture.[119] Grevs' relationship with Karsavin, dating from the academic year 1907–8, was more troubled – mainly on professional grounds – and is a topic that has been extensively covered by others.[120] Still, one may argue that, despite surface differences between them, intellectually, their understanding of history had more in common than their quarrel might otherwise suggest. In Roger Markwick's summary of Karsavin's understanding of the historian's craft as a study of 'material being' and 'everyday life as a specific sphere of social life in a specific period' which required an ability to 'really penetrate into an alien culture and genuinely merge with it' there was, in fact, little that separated him from Grevs' methodology. Some of Karsavin's early letters to Grevs written during a research trip to Italy confirm his recognition that to understand a textual source you also need to be sensitive to the environment (church architecture, landscape, art) in which it was produced.[121] As I discuss later in this book, this was entirely consistent with the underlying principles of historical research that Grevs developed in his seminars after 1900 and in the course of group excursions to Italy. The irreconcilable point of difference between the two men, however, was fuelled by Karsavin's hostility to positivism and historicism, which he dismissed as a '*geneticheskoi metod*' reducing all the complexity of historical reality to formal causal connections, a filiation of ideas and institutions. For his part, Grevs welcomed Karsavin's view that it was important to understand not how things came about (i.e. an enquiry focused on causal connections), but 'how it was' (*kak bylo*), that is, to uncover an 'immanent truth' about states of being and worldview.[122] He paid tribute to his pupil's intuitive grasp of the subject, noting his ability to penetrate beyond the surface layer of documentation to capture the pulse of life and belief. But it was Karsavin's introduction of novel concepts – *'religioznost';* *'religiia mass'*, and, in particular, his hallmark idea of 'the average person' *'srednii chelovek'* ('an imagined entity, but [...] none the less profoundly real'[123]) – as tools to explore states of mind and representations of mass consciousness that struck Grevs as empty of meaning and as inapplicable to the study of real historical individuals. In particular, he balked at Karsavin's suggestion that St Francis of Assisi exemplified the 'average man': this simply made no sense to Grevs.[124]

Among his immediate contemporaries, Grevs' friendship with the symbolist poet and classical scholar, Viacheslav Ivanov (1866–1949), is particularly significant for the insights it yields into Grevs' early development as a historian. Generating a rich correspondence, predominantly written during the early 1890s when both men were preparing their doctoral dissertations and resumed in the wake of the October Revolution, their dialogue brings to view the way Grevs thought about history and scholarship; they also evidence the importance of creative literature, particularly in terms of the way it provided an emotional-cum-spiritual anchorage for him in later years when he came under scrutiny as an 'old professor' in the new Bolshevik state. The two men first met in 1891 at the Bibliothèque nationale while Grevs was preparing his dissertation on the topic of landownership in the imperial period of Roman history as part of a two-year research scholarship in Paris and North Italy. Ivanov had studied with Vinogradov and Theodore Mommsen in Berlin (Roman law and economics), and in 1892 moved to Rome to pursue studies in Roman archaeology. Their correspondence dating from this period is a rich intellectual exchange on ancient history, the classical world and poetry. Through his interlocutor, Grevs refined his views of the historian's task, defending the novel approach he adopted in his dissertation, namely the inclusion of Horace's poetry as a historical source in what was nominally a contribution to economic history. Their correspondence also attests the practical support that Ivanov gave his friend. He revised and corrected chapters that Grevs sent him and even translated a passage of a Horatian epistle for inclusion in the dissertation – his first verse publication, as Michael Wachtel points out in his review of their correspondence, published after the collapse of the Soviet Union.[125]

Although the two men continued to correspond throughout the 1890s, the relationship chilled: Grevs had introduced Ivan to Lidiia Dmitrievna Zinov'eva-Annibal, a meeting which later Ivanov described as a 'Dionysian thunderstorm', causing him to abandon his wife and small child for an all-encompassing new passion. It was something that Grevs could never quite come to terms with and may explain why the two rarely met once they had resettled in St Petersburg: Grevs did not frequent Ivanov's 'tower' (the famous Wednesday soirées which the poet hosted in his Petersburg flat overlooking the Tauride Palace), although he did attend meetings of the Religious–Philosophical Society (1907–17) where the two men may have had occasion to meet, and, as Wachtel points out, Ivanov did speak – 'apparently quite eloquently' – at a banquet in Grevs' honour in 1909.[126] That aside, fundamental differences in temperament and lifestyle, especially during the years of Ivanov's greatest fame, arguably made any meaningful exchange between them impossible: for Grevs, the professor-enlightener, classical Russian liberal and man of pre-symbolist culture whose favourite authors were Ivan Turgenev and Romain Rolland, the mystical-erotic 'Dionysian' and avant-garde climate in which Ivanov lived in those years were, no doubt, shocking and incomprehensible.

Personal ties and an epistolary dialogue were eventually resumed during the years of Revolution and Civil War. As Wachtel notes, the few letters from this period are fascinating and at times genuinely moving. Importantly, they bear witness to what Grevs himself described as his 'homecoming' to poetry.[127] In an autobiographical note, Grevs confirmed this renewed encounter with the world of literature and religious philosophical thought: 'Of the writers I have studied', he wrote, 'my teacher is Dante, and of the Russians – Turgenev and Vladimir Solov'ev'.[128] Drawn to Solov'ev's 'humanism', Grevs found in him a spiritual interlocutor as he endeavoured to cope with a seemingly insurmountable sense of bereavement following the death of his sixteen-year-old daughter in 1910. The pathos with which he refers to this in a letter to Ivanov dated 1918 is, at once, a telling account of his grief and an eloquent statement of the principles he lived by:

> Spiritually, I think I am moving forward. Over the past eight years this movement has come from a secret communion with the spirit of my deceased daughter, the light from whose eyes I feel with all its strength reaching down to me from another world; it comes from a love for those who are near and dear, and from the collaboration with students, which fills my soul.[129]

It is fair to say that the sentiment expressed here made Grevs a natural successor to Granovskii and the 'noble, melancholic, Kudriavtsev'. Described as 'an artist and beguiling (*uvlekaiushchii*)', 'the servitor of an ideal (*sliuzhitel' ideala*])', he was restoring the 'culture of feelings', in which the romantics had originally anchored the credentials of the *nastavnik*.[130] 'He moved our hearts with his unshakable faith in the absolute good and absolute truth. And if we, as former *bestuzhevskie*, having lived a long and not easy life (…) managed to preserve our faith in the ultimate triumph of this good, this truth, it is as the shoots of the seeds that were planted by Ivan Mikhailovich'.[131]

Grevs remained in Leningrad after the October Revolution, where he continued to hold regular meetings at his home with former students.[132] Following his expulsion from the university in 1923, and the dismantling, in 1924, of the interdisciplinary Excursion Institute that he had helped set up with Antsiferov just three years earlier, he returned to his intellectual masters and spiritual interlocutors: Dante and Turgenev.[133] As the editor of a popular-scientific series entitled *Images of Mankind* (*Obrazy chelovechestva*) for Brokgaus and Efron (1923–4), he wrote a biography of Dante, which, according to his former student, Dveshnikov, was designed to bring out the Florentine's relevance in the modern world. The book was never published, however, an augury, no doubt, of things to come: by the late 1920s, like so many 'old professors', Grevs had fallen victim to the regime. Placed under suspicion for purportedly expressing views in favour of monarchy and for participating in a religious–philosophical organization (*Voskresenie*), he was forced to give up his work in urban studies and for a brief period in 1930 was held under arrest as a suspect in the Academic affair.[134] Thereafter he managed to survive by doing technical translations, only resuming some degree of university teaching following the reinstatement of historical faculties in the 1930s. In 1934 he was invited to return to Leningrad University as a '*spets*' (specialist) to run a seminar in medieval history with research students on topics he had worked on in the pre-revolutionary period: the Roman colonate, Dino Compagni's chronicle of Florence, the life and work of Pierre Abelard.[135] For someone who had always seen his role as '*vospitatel*' in the intelligentsia tradition of vocational, informal, authentic learning, Grevs' newly acquired status as a '*spets*' was an instance of historical irony of which he must have undoubtedly been aware.

It is, of course, part of the very nature of commemorative literature to generate fairly predictable tributes to the master as an inspirational model of professional practice. Moreover, cultural conventions of a given epoch according to which the historian's persona was aestheticized make it difficult to disentangle the 'real' Granovskii or Kliuchevskii from representations of them as scholars. Whether there is any legitimate need to do so is another question, although there are moments of tension, or contrast, between the prevailing image of the historian's persona and his temperament as an individual which, as I discuss in the next chapter, surfaces in the form of an 'authorial voice' in historical narrative and explanation. Caveats aside, a case may be made to suggest that these otherwise standardized depictions did reflect, quite accurately, the views held by historian-*nastavniki* themselves. Regardless of the progression in methodological paradigms – from an emphasis on the force of ideas in history (Schelling and Hegel) to the more empirically grounded approaches of the late nineteenth century – historians remained remarkably consistent in their attitudes towards science qua scholarship (*nauka*). All the historians mentioned in this chapter – Karamzin, Granovskii, Kudriavtsev, Pogodin, Kliuchevskii, Grevs – saw themselves as public enlighteners. Whether as proselytizers of official ideology (Pogodin, Karamzin) or as liberal dissenters intent on empowering the individual through learning, they used the various platforms available to them, from seminar, lecture hall, research agenda to *publitistika* to fulfil their self-ascribed mission. It is tempting to suggest, then, that despite growth in specialization towards the end of the nineteenth century, Russian historians remained committed to the ideal of a 'general culture': historical knowledge was conceived as a tool for turning the Russian people into citizens.[136] 'History', Granovskii claimed,

> is a most popular science (….). [F]ortunately, narrow conceptions of the false qualities of science that destroys itself in the search for refined form (…) which we witness in the stifling atmosphere of German *kabinety*, is not characteristic of the Russian mind – that lover of light and space. Guild-like science, proud of its exclusivity cannot count on our sympathy.[137]

Possibly unfair, contradictory and certainly a stereotype, Granovskii's remark was in fact a pledge, which successive generations of historians after him shared, to transform the university from a training ground for government service into a platform for raising social and cultural awareness.[138] That historical knowledge was conceived as the principal tool for achieving this goal goes some way to explaining the absence of differentiated discourses between 'textbook history', lectures and the public addresses more usually associated with the development and institutionalization of the disciplines.[139] As his contemporaries noted, in Kliuchevskii's work there was a seamless link between his lecture courses on a given topic and his public addresses; his essays on Pushkin, Fonvizin and Lermontov worked in tandem with his lecture-based account of the Russian nobility and needed to be read as components of a single explanatory narrative.[140] As I discuss in the next chapter, what one might call a hybrid historical discourse that seemed to blur the lines between scholarship and popularization provides an entry point for an analysis of the literary inflections of historical narrative and explanation: the historian's choice of images, metaphor and intertextual devices all speak to a strong indigenous literary culture.

3

Style: The Literary Cadences of Russian Historical Narrative

'To become a professional historian', wrote Aleksandr Kiesewetter,

> you (...) require the ability to reconstruct events, that is, to envision for yourself and recreate in words the events of the past in all their specificity, in all their individual uniqueness, in all the succulence of their vivid colours for others. Without this gift of a concrete reconstruction of bygone times one cannot be a historian, one can only be a resonating dialectician.[1]

Well into the reform era, the terms of historical explanation continued to be sourced in the nation's strong literary tradition as well as with reference to some of the classics of Western literature. Style remained paramount: skilled use of imagery, metaphor, rhetoric and intertextual devices was widely recognized as the credentials of the 'master historian' whose authority as a producer of knowledge reached well beyond the precinct of the university. Among the standout figures in this regard, Vasilii Kliuchevskii undoubtedly merits special attention. His celebrated lecture courses on Russian history became an inspirational model of historical writing, applauded by fellow historians and former pupils for the way he managed to bridge the expectations of contemporary scholarship with an artistry of narration that seemingly defied the current 'cult of science'. It was in large part due to the literary form in which he carefully crafted his lectures that his *Course* achieved the status of a cultural monument[2]: in addition to his pupils and auditors at Moscow University, Kliuchevskii's lectures were read in the palaces of Grand Princes (where he tutored), in schools and seminaries. Officers and artists read it, the revolutionary intelligentsia read it (including Lenin in 1891): as Sigurd Shmidt notes, it was no coincidence that, in 1908, Kliuchevskii was awarded honorary academic status in the department of belles lettres.[3]

I shall return to the topic of Kliuchevskii's stylistic genius later in this chapter. To begin, however, a brief overview of eighteenth-century precursors and some account of Russia's first modern historian, Nikolai Karamzin, are indispensable for appreciating the lasting presence of the literary impulse in the canon of national historiography. In his role as official historiographer to the court of Alexander I, Karamzin 'did not turn his back on literature'; rather, as Iurii Lotman put it, 'he boldly stretched its boundaries'.[4]

Designing a template for historical narrative

Between the reigns of Catherine the Great and Nicholas I narrating the past evolved from the rhetorical and didactic strategies of enlightenment historiography to the aesthetic subjectivism associated with the romantic vision of history. Beginning with Mikhail Lomonosov's famous panegyric on the reign of Peter the Great (1755) and Mikhail Shcherbatov's 'Petition of the City of Moscow on Being Relegated to Oblivion' (1787) – a poignant personification of Moscow as a city abandoned, her past glories spurned by the transfer of the imperial court to St Petersburg – it was customary to foreground the persona of the narrator as a spectator, or eyewitness, who openly engages with the reader as he depicts a historical scene or tableau. By contrast, a dominant feature of both nineteenth-century fictional and historical writings was the 'covert', yet omniscient narrator, whose text 'is not presented as a model to be discussed, criticized (...) by the free and inquiring intellect', rather as a non-negotiable, binding truth.[5] In this regard, the undisputed master of a literary-framed historical narrative was, of course, Nikolai Karamzin (1766–1826) whose career as novelist, travel writer and historian charted the transition from the age of enlightenment to the romantic sensibilities of the opening decades of the nineteenth century.

'It is said', Karamzin wrote, 'that our history is less remarkable than that of others: I do not think so; what is needed are intellect, taste, talent; one may select, enliven, embellish: the reader will be amazed to see how out of Nestor, Nikon and others could come something powerful, impressive not only for Russians but for foreigners, too'.[6] Adopting the narrative stance of an imaginary eyewitness, Karamzin's reconstruction of the Kievan and Muscovite past took the form of a dramatic reenactment of historical events and personages (both heroes and villains). Yet he also retained some of the rhetorical strategies derived from enlightenment-style pragmatism: the strong political message driving his narrative, namely an explicit and wholeheartedly patriotic endorsement of Russia's autocratic tradition, was in many ways typical of the intellectual and cultural formations in the age of empire building under Catherine the Great. In other words, by extolling the achievements of the nation's tsars who had cemented the principles of autocracy, Karamzin's history functioned as a critique of arguments in support of constitutionalism and democracy, then spreading across the European continent in the aftermath of the French Revolution.[7] Granted, he recognized the authority of historical truth and, in his foreword (published in 1815), drew attention to the challenges involved in unearthing it: 'History is not poetry'. But it remains, as Derek Offord has argued, that he subordinated the raison d'être of historical writing to the implicit demands of an emergent nation: 'the feeling of "we," "our"', he wrote, 'enlivens the narrative; and whereas crude partiality, the result of weak reason, or a weak soul, is intolerable in a historian, love of country gives his brushstroke ardour and power and appeal. Where there is no love, there is no soul'.[8]

One cannot emphasize enough the importance of Karamzin in Russian historical culture. Hailed as the Columbus of modern history, the last chronicler and first historian (Pushkin), the Homer of history (Pogodin), his *History of the Russian State* quickly became a staple in the upbringing of virtually every member of the educated elite.⁹ For generations of creative writers, it was both a model of literary elegance and a source of plot material.¹⁰ Career historians, too, acknowledged the work's importance as a benchmark in the historical–literary canon. That said, if, for the post-reform generation of scholars, Karamzin's prescription for historical writing – that it should possess 'noble eloquence', 'taste and flair' – or his counsel to the historian that he 'select, animate and add colour' remained relevant to their mission to make knowledge of the past accessible to a growing, non-specialist readership, his political nationalism and restrictive view of the Russian nation did not: by the 1860s and 1870s, as historical research began privileging the study of socio-economic questions, peasant customs and daily life, Karamzin's tale of tsars and, in particular, his 'sense of history' were long out of date. As Kliuchevskii put it, he 'did not explain, or generalize, but described, moralized and admired, he sought to turn the history of Russia (…) into a heroic epic of Russian valour and glory. (…) This is his greatest achievement in the eyes of Russian society, and his major detriment to Russian historical science'.¹¹ Indeed, methodologically, Karamzin's pragmatic, instructional tone had already been superseded during the romantic era by the turn to 'disinterested historical truth' as (German) philosophers and historians such as Herder, Schlegel, Schelling or Niebuhr began developing a critical approach to the past. If they acknowledged the value of the historian's narrative skill as a technique to resurrect the past without any apparent mediation or intervention on his part, of greater importance, in their view, was an ability to couple this with a sense of chronological distance from the events presented in order to interpret their meaning.¹² All the same, it is striking that no matter how much truth there was in the criticism that Karamzin's patriotic ardour was detrimental to historical science, it was, as Jurij Striedter rightly notes, *History of the Russian State* 'and not the historical works of contemporary and near contemporary rivals such as Nikolai Polevoi (author of a pointedly titled *History of the Russian People* [*Istoriia russkogo naroda*]) and other Romantics, that served for decades as a source and pattern for Russian historical poetry'.¹³

The final volume of *History of the Russian State* was published posthumously in 1829. By that time, chairs in World History had been established in the universities of Moscow and St Petersburg marking the beginnings of an institutionalized framework for learning. This process, however, did not, as I have already mentioned, supplant informal sites of learning: on the contrary, salon culture, home to the literary and intellectual elite, played a prominent role in the assimilation of the new philosophical terminology and theories of histories arriving from Western Europe, and it would continue to do so throughout the 1830s and 1840s as university instruction fell under the close scrutiny of Nicholas I's third section.¹⁴ If anything, then, historians of Granovskii's generation harnessed the vocabulary of historicism, thanks largely to informal intellectual exchanges among friends. In addition, the salon helped foster an atmosphere of reciprocity and mutual enrichment, and, with that, a sense of common purpose. From artistic evocations of the past, learned historians, like men of letters, acquired, what Lidiia Lotman called the 'pathos of steadfast endeavour to broaden the sphere of observation and knowledge of the nation's cultural legacy'.¹⁵ As Buslaev recalled in his memoirs:

The state of reverie that describes the mood of the men of the forties [...] meant that it was impossible to be satisfied with uniquely scientific elaboration of facts of the distant past; they loved to recreate it with their imagination, to relive the past just as Walter Scott did in his historical novels, just like Victor Hugo in *Notre Dame de Paris*, or just like our own Pushkin in *Boris Godunov*. With such dream-like feeling Granovskii captivated his listeners during his lectures in world history.[16]

Issues of composition were thus high on the agenda, and the question of how best to represent historical events remained entirely open. In sum, for these men of the forties, a broad literary and philosophical culture was coterminous with the process of establishing the subject's 'scientific' perimeters as a taught discipline.

Historical writing and the romantic aestheticization of life

Among the dominant literary genres in the 1820s and 1830s were the Byronic long poem – described by Jurij Striedter as a mixture of epic, lyric and dramatic dialogue/soliloquy[17] – historical drama and, most importantly, the historical novel, which Russian readers typically associated with Sir Walter Scott as its undisputed master.[18] In various complementary ways each of these artistic genres imparted a sense of history as an unfolding present, which the reader was allowed to experience or somehow identify with. If, for example, in epic poetry the inclusion of a narrator as an intermediary between past and present gave scope for panoramic descriptions of landscapes or close-ups of situations and moods as a backdrop to the events driving the tale, the technique in historical drama of 'chronological telescoping and discontinuity', as Striedter calls it, effectively reset the actions of historical personages – whether they be perpetrators, witnesses or victims of a historical event – in a 'scenic' present.[19]

Offering possibly the greatest scope for making the historical past both dramatically present and temporally remote was the historical novel. As a model of imaginative reconstruction in which fictional and historical personages interact, it allowed the author to position himself as an adjudicator of sorts, whose explanatory interpolations afforded chronological distance and, thereby, a place for historical reflection. This broader horizon dovetailed with the more personal, memoir-like perspective of the narrator-eyewitness. Depicting major historical events as they unfold, the narrator relates their impact on the protagonist and his or her immediate world. For Pushkin, this was the hallmark of Scott's genius: 'The most wonderful thing about the novels of Walter Scott, (the "Scottish sorcerer" – as Pushkin called him) is that in them we come to know the past not with the *enflure* of French tragedy, not with the priggishness of sentimental novels, not with the dignity of history, but as if it were contemporary, quotidian'.[20] It was, in particular, this 'domestic' view of history privileging the destinies of the individuals (those small 'differentials' as Lev Tolstoi coined it) affected by great historical events that assured the popularity of the genre among readers. By making the historical past scenically and psychologically 'present', literary art enabled the reader to relate to the characters and their destinies. Brilliantly mastered in their own right by Karamzin (e.g. in his tale, *Martha the Posadnik*) and by Pushkin and Tolstoi, the success of the genre was testament to, as Striedter put it, 'how far every narration of history depends on translating events into a story'.[21]

University-based historians of Pushkin's generation similarly recognized the power of literary art as a tool for awakening an interest in the past among a wide readership. It was, for example, Pogodin's belief that history should be understood just as much by a literate peasant, a society lady or gymnasium pupil, yet should be irreproachable with regard to the critique of a strict academic 'judge'. Pogodin championed the importance of literary language, especially in terms of its sound qualities and cadences for historical writing.[22] In this regard, Zhukovskii and Pushkin stood out for him as exemplary models of contemporary poetry and blank verse (Pogodin mentioned Zhukovskii's translation of Schiller's *Jungfrau von Orleans* [*Orleanskaia deva*] and Pushkin's *Boris Godunov*), but it was, above all, in the novels and comedies of Gogol that he found his greatest inspiration for enlivening the tone or timbre of historical narrative. In a notebook entry, dated 1840, he wrote: 'Listened to Gogol: there you have it. History needs such living people'.[23] And in a letter, dated February 1848, addressed to the writer himself, Pogodin openly acknowledged his due: 'My "history" is deeply indebted to you, to your impressions, your writings, to the ideas that absorb you in *The Government Inspector* and *Dead Souls*'.[24]

Pogodin, Polevoi, Granovskii and Kudriavtsev all published works of fiction and poetry. Pogodin and Kudriavtsev both wrote a number of short stories, often in the form of 'prose articles' for journal publications, a genre which, by the late 1820s, had become popular as a medium for making a strong didactic point, typically to do with a contest between the romantic ideal of an aestheticized life and the lure of material wealth: if the latter promised social position, it ultimately compromised personal integrity.[25] Kudriavtsev, in fact, started out in the late 1830s as a fiction writer, whose short novels – *Katenka Pylaieva, Antonina, Dve strasti* (*Two Passions*) and *Fleita* (*The Flute*) – won him praise from the contemporary critic, Vissarion Belinskii. In 1841, he began writing literary and art reviews for the journals *Otechestvennye zapiski* and *Sovremennik* alongside further novellas (under the pen name A. Nestroev), including the melancholy *Tsvetok* (*Flower*), *Nedoumenie* (*Bewilderment* [1840]), *Zhivaia kartina* (*Live Picture*), *Poslednii vizit* (*The Final Visit* [1844]), *Oshibka* (*The Mistake* [1845]) and *Sboiev, Bez rassveta* (*Without Sunrise*), all of which were, again, lauded for their insight and psychological depth.[26] Pogodin's short stories, likewise, explored the opposing pulls of love and duty, although he was seemingly unable to resist a didactic urge. *Chernaia nemoch'* (1829) (*Gloomy Helplessness*), for example, describes the tormented struggle of Gavrilo Semenovich, an adolescent drawn equally by a thirst for knowledge (metaphysics, theology, history, poetry) and the material comforts which a career in trade and a financially advantageous marriage offered him. Unable to cope with the demands and expectations of either world, the young man finally disappears into the night having just abandoned his betrothed and her dowry of precious jewels and silks. His drowned body is recovered the following day. Several passages in this melodramatic tale (of little or no artistic merit it has to be said) confirm Pogodin's belief in the civilizing power of knowledge: the inclusion of poems by Zhukovskii and references to Herder, Lomonosov, Schelling, the Apostles, are all telling markers of his own intellectual and spiritual affinities. In another story, *Rusaia* kosa (*The Light-Brown Plait*), published in 1827, he worked the titles and names of authors of contemporary historical literature and philosophy into an otherwise standard tale of infatuated love: reading Karamzin's *History* with her beloved, the heart of the young heroine burns with the deepest feeling for 'Holy Russia and the blessed Russian nation'.[27]

'Nowadays', Kudriavtsev said of Granovskii, 'few have retained so much feeling for elegant form and purity of taste. Only rarely do we come across an exposition that is so strict and reserved in vocabulary yet, which is so expressive in relation to the content'.[28] According to his first biographer, Aleksandr Stankevich, Granovskii's first love as an adolescent was in fact poetry, and not history at all: his prize winning romantic elegy, 'The Sufferer', written when he was fourteen years old, and published in Count Shalikov's journal, *Damskii zhurnal* (1828), seemed to confirm his reputation and calling as a promising writer.[29] He also translated the novels of George Sand and James Fenimore Cooper, famous for his romantic glorification of brigands and savages, such as Hawkeye in *The Last of the Mohicans*.[30] And, throughout his life, he constantly read and reread the works of Russian poets, especially Pushkin, and would often recite from memory his favourite verses of Schiller and Goethe in the company of friends. That said, of all the University-based historians in this period, it was not Granovskii, who, as I have argued, aspired to place history on a scientific footing, rather his younger contemporary, Nikolai Kostomarov, professor of Russian history at Kiev and St Petersburg universities, whose writings stood out in the eyes of contemporaries as a model of creative historical genius, a masterful fusion of fact and invention. Poet, playwright, novelist, author of both archive-based historical research and popular historical biographies, Kostomarov was celebrated during his lifetime for the way his imaginative prose and poetry combined historical and legendary motifs, while his archival researched history of Kievan Rus' and Little Russia in the seventeenth century became infused with literary imagination.[31] Like Karamzin and Pushkin, Kostomarov exploited multiple narrative possibilities to invoke aspects of the national (Great and Little Russian) past. Building on anecdotes sourced from his close reading of the chronicles, Kostomarov made historical figures, such as the seventeenth-century Cossack hetman Bogdan Khmelnytskii present and real in much the same way that a novelist might draw his reader into a world of invented characters and situations through an act of suspended disbelief.[32] As his younger contemporary, Dmitrii Korsakov noted, for Kostomarov, history

> was not some sort of abstract philosophical ideal to be resolved, nor was it simply the gathering of chronicle or archival material [...]. Russian history was a contemporary reality emerging from the depth of the centuries. He lived through the events that he had uncovered in the sources in the very same way that he lived through contemporary political, social, and intellectual life.[33]

Kostomarov's career spanned well into the 1870s but, intellectually and culturally, he remained a product of the 1830s and 1840s, deeply influenced by the romantic ideas of the German philosopher, Herder, who saw poetry as the fruit of the genius of the common people and the vernacular language as the vehicle and repository of the national spirit. A defender of Ukrainian national interests, Kostomarov spoke of Little Russia as a nationality separate from, yet equal to, Great Russia, and in later life following the onset of blindness and poor health which effectively prevented him from conducting archival research or field work, he began producing more popular history, syntheses, historical novels and polemical articles in which he crystallized his views on Ukrainian ethnic identity.[34] Drawing on compilations by compatriots of indigenous subject matter, for example, Mykhaylo Maksymovych's collection of folksongs and Izmail Sreznevskii's tales of old Zaporozhia (Cossack territory in the sixteenth to eighteenth centuries), Kostomarov positioned himself as a defender of a linguistically and ethnically based concept of nationality. Such views, however, deeply troubled some of his Russian contemporaries. In 1874, Pogodin, for one, took up a vicious ad hominem polemic embittered by what he saw as Kostomarov's sarcastic depictions of Russia's legendary princes.[35] That aside, while the political and ideological ramifications of Kostomarov's opinions turned his intellectual legacy into an object of controversy, no one, it seems, challenged his narrative craftsmanship or his ability to popularize historical knowledge, gifts which Kliuchevskii most certainly admired as these comments found in his unpublished papers show:

> For Kostomarov, Russian history was like a museum filled with collections of both rare and common-or-garden objects. He would walk past the latter and stop in front of the former, lingering there to observe them carefully. A while later, the reading public would receive a wonderful monograph to delight in with little thought as to the material out of which the absorbing tale was constructed. In this way a series of historical images taken out of the historical past and inextricably bound with the author himself gradually came about. We say: 'it's Kostomarov's Ivan the terrible, Kostomarov's Bogdan Khmelnytskii, Kostomarov's Stenka Razin [...]. We say: 'let those 'patented' archivists shape out of archival dust the real Groznys, Bogdans, Razins – may their labour intensive, but lifeless moulds decorate archeological museums; what we need are living portraits, and Kostomarov gives us such portraits. Anything dramatic in our history, especially in the history of our southwestern regions, is recounted by Kostomarov, and told with the mastery of a storyteller who derives great pleasure from his own tale.[36]

Narrative and 'reflective' history

Kostomarov's artistry in recreating the past prompted comparisons with Michelet and, in particular, with Augustin Thierry whose discursive method of presenting history in picturesque and dramatic terms had established him as one of the most outstanding romantic historians in Continental Europe.[37] Both Thierry and Michelet embraced the imagination and inspired insights in their reconstructions of historical reality. Admired by their readers for the way they managed to 'retrieve from the partial remains of the past an image of man, and to resurrect the unique character of a bygone age', it was their ability to suspend the reader's disbelief rather than the tools of analysis acquired through formal training that were deemed essential to the art of selecting and interpreting evidence.³⁸ 'Historical personages and even historical ages', Thierry wrote,

> should come on stage, as it were, in the narrative. They should appear, so to speak, fully alive in it, and the reader should not have to leaf through a hundred or more pages to find out what their true character was. The method of writing history that tends to isolate facts from that which gives them colour and their individual physiognomy is a false art, and it is not possible for an historian first to narrate well without depicting, then to depict well without narrating. Those who have adopted this method have almost invariably subordinated historical narrative, which is the essential part of history, to commentaries that follow up and are supposed to provide the key to the narrative.³⁹

Thierry's prescription for historical writing, cited here in Gossman's comprehensive study of French romantic historiography, was, in one respect, a clear vindication of artistic imagination as an indispensable component of the historian's craft. Like so many of his contemporaries across Europe, Thierry was, at his own admission, inspired by the novels of Sir Walter Scott. But equally, Thierry stressed, the historian needed to combine his depiction of the past as an unfolding present with retrospective narration. Thus, on the one hand, the historian resembles the imaginative artist-seer, who 'dares to descend into himself and to recall the tumult and passion that characterizes historical existence'. On the other hand, unlike the creative artist, the historian's insight, Thierry insisted, was necessarily impartial and reflective, conscious of the distance between past and present. In other words, the historian had to 'unite in himself (…) experience and reflection'.⁴⁰

The demands placed on the historian to tackle the distance between present and past, alluded to here in Thierry's prescription, registered a problem of reflective history, which, since the opening decades of the nineteenth century had been addressed in the context of German idealism. What exactly, though, did this entail? The ethos of reflective history, as well as the challenges it presented to the practicing historian, are very well summarized by Hayden White: 'Reflective histories (…) are written not only out of an apprehension of the passage of time but also in the full awareness of the distance between the historian and his object of study, which distance the historian consciously tries to close.' Specifically referencing Hegel's theory of historical writing as a verbal art, White reminds us that the historian is tasked to capture an inner truth, 'and the various theoretical devices that different historians use to close the gap which separates them from the past, to enter into that past, and to grasp its essence or content account for the various species of reflective history which this kind of history produces'.⁴¹

Among historians in Germany, Leopold von Ranke's view concerning the principles of historical enquiry was confirmation of this shift to reflective history. His conviction that history is purposeful, progressive and governed by discernible laws and, in particular, his famous command to study the past '*wie est eigentlich gewesen*' (as it really was⁴²) announced an engagement with the inner 'essential' truth of the past, both as Hegel conceived it in his lectures on the philosophy of history and, possibly more importantly, as Wilhelm von Humboldt defined it in relation to poetics in his seminal text, *On the*

Historian's Task (1821). For Humboldt, the quest for 'inner truth' dictated that the historian, like the poet, had to be 'active and creative'. Like the poet, the historian uses his imagination in order to 'reveal the truth of an event by presentation, by filling in and connecting the disjointed fragments of direct observation'. But, unlike the poet, the historian might not use 'pure fantasy'. He must instead call upon a uniquely historical mode of comprehension in the form of what Humboldt called a 'connective ability'. As the product of the historian's application of the 'laws of necessity', it was this 'connective ability' that Humboldt regarded as key to divining the meaning of the whole historical process (the purpose of history). A 'poetic' approach to history, then, meant an empathetic grasp yielding an essential inner truth about the past, as opposed to a creative invention of it.

In view of the privileged position of poetry in the contemporary literary canon, it is perhaps no surprise that the German idealists developed views on the distinctive nature and tasks of history with reference to the creative process. Yet, in practice, the philosophical conceptualization of the meaning of history framing the new historiography and the distinctions it urged between historical and artistic 'modes of comprehension' were ultimately too nuanced for the historian to mark a definitive break with the principal presuppositions of literary romanticism. The work of Ranke is a case in point. Again, to paraphrase Hayden White, Ranke's interest in the individual event in its uniqueness and concreteness, his conception of historical explanation as narration and his concern to enter into the inner world of the actors of the historical drama so as to see them as they saw themselves and thereby reconstruct the worlds which they faced in their time and their place were all signs of residual, and indelible, romantic impulses.[43] As I argue below, much the same observation applies to Granovskii as he set out to establish new ground rules for the discipline in the 1840s and early 1850s.

The Granovskii paradox: style versus conception of history

As a pupil of German idealism and historiography, Granovskii inherited the notion of 'empathy' framing a poetic approach to the past. But he also wrestled with his romantic inheritance as he set out to turn the emotional and spiritual understanding acquired through poetic insight from a *form* of historical knowledge into an *object* of historical enquiry in its own right. Granovskii's writings dating as far back as the 1840s clearly attest his endeavours to enhance the scholarly profile of historical enquiry. Indeed, he was quite specific about his aims when he announced a plan to launch a new scientific journal with Redkin, Korsh and Kriukov, colleagues in the faculty of law: to be excluded from the table of contents would be the novella and verse.[44] His essay on Niebuhr, discussed in the previous chapter, also contains a clear indication of this paradigm switch:

> Like many remarkable men of his age, Niebuhr had much in common with the romantics. But the clarity of his visions of history made him infinitely greater than they. […] The task of the thinking historian is, first, to point out the boundary separating pure history from the poetic, then to evaluate the latter. It [poetry] has its own truth. Besides the fact that it reflects, more purely and directly, the character of people as yet unchanged by outside influences, it contains indications (*ukazanie*) of events, and frequently reveals their inner meaning.[45]

And, again, Granovskii made much the same point regarding the distinction between 'poetic truth' and 'historical fact' in a review essay, published in 1854, on literary representations of the celebrated eleventh-century Castilian nobleman and military leader, El Cid. For the historian, he argued, the constant reinventions of El Cid over time (from the twelfth-century 'Poem of the Cid' to Corneille) were instructive of 'changes in literary conventions, and, more broadly, of shifts in social and political expectations'; only in this sense did they retain value as historical documents. Distancing himself from the work of Schlözer and his followers in Russia (Pogodin, notably) for the faith they placed in the reliability of sagas and chronicles, Granovskii signalled the task of the historian: 'let the people believe in these tales: for them they constitute history and poetry; they may be taken on by history if stripped of fantasy, though they should not be used as hard fact. They have a sense of their own, their own independent worth and significance'.[46]

If the distinction Granovskii advanced between poetic and historical understanding in these two essays stemmed from a personal re-evaluation of his intellectual and cultural lineage in romanticism, his public address of 1852 in which he outlined the tasks of history was intended (if received with a degree of suspicion) as confirmation of his new allegiance to positivism. Announcing law and natural science as the building blocks of historical thought, Granovskii even went as far as to call for a reorganization of the university faculties in order to sever the institutional ties linking history and philology.[47] Yet, as Priscilla Roosevelt notes, 'as an historian, Granovskii would remain in many respects a poet, primarily committed to, and affected by, the development and the fate of the individual'.[48] Despite his efforts to establish the scientific credentials of historical enquiry, Granovskii's style of narration as explanation and his concern with inner truth were indelibly romantic. His peers and pupils were all too aware of this and thus tended to judge his efforts to extricate history from both its literary roots and philosophical idealism as contra natura, an unwarranted disavowal of his beliefs, temperament and artistry as a historian.[49] In their eyes, the master historian was, first and foremost, the Pushkin of history, a brilliant, inspired narrator whose ability, like the poet, to convey impressions of the past with such clarity and economy of style was testament to the power of the literary impulse in history: 'The elegance and form of his lectures were a result of his poetic temperament (*poeticheskii stroi ego dushi*) (…) with which he was blessed by nature, and without which it was not possible, at his own admission, to be a great historian'.[50]

Kliuchevskii: The Tolstoi of history

'Among great Russian artists', Bogoslovskii wrote,

> Kliuchevskii belongs to the current that flourished in the second half of the nineteenth century, with its celebrated paintings by Repin and, which, in literature, found its greatest manifestation in Tolstoi. Like these great representatives of Russian art, Kliuchevskii was an artist–realist (…). He has no gods or earthly

heroes; one finds only people, more or less gifted, genius, saintly, but all in real life circumstances.[51]

For sure, one of the first things that readers have always noted about Kliuchevskii was his imaginative ability to convey what Marc Raeff calls 'the living texture of a people's past'.[52] Unlike his immediate predecessor and teacher, Sergei Solov'ev, who, as the author of the second major work of historical synthesis after Karamzin, eschewed literary embellishment in historical narrative, Kliuchevskii restored 'the artistic configuration of real facts'.[53] Scholarship, teaching and artistry were the materials, out of which Kliuchevskii's *Russia* was built.[54] Universally admired for his laconic style (a Mephistophelean scepticism, as Kiesewetter put it[55]), charged metaphors, pithy aphorisms, vivid imagery and the seamless way in which he managed to combine the idioms and colloquialisms of peasant oral tradition to which he had been exposed as a child growing up in the Penza region with the cadences of literary prose, Kliuchevskii's seminal *Course of Russian History* secured its place among 'the finest monuments of Russian literary art'.[56] In one memorable phrase he could sum up entire eras of the national past: *gosudarstvo pukhlo, a narod khirel* (the state became bloated, while the nation shrivelled up); 'individual freedom became obligatory and was maintained by the knout'.[57] If his short imaginative similes, use of irony, oxymoron, indirect speech and unexpected associations worked pedagogically as a mnemonic device helping the reader to grasp the essence of the institutions and the intricate processes of the past, they also all worked to brilliant comic effect. For example, he likened Nikon, the seventeenth-century Patriarch, whose reforms produced one of Russia's first religious dissenters – the Old Believers – to a sail 'that feels itself only in a gale, and when the wind falls flaps about, a wretched rag on the mast'. An early passage in his account of Catherine the Great's personality clearly demonstrates Kliuchevskii's playful wit and is worth quoting in full:

> Here, medieval German feudalism was wearing itself out and was down to its last dynastic regalia and genealogical traditions. With its endless family divisions and sub-divisions – its princes of Brunswick–Luneburg and Brunswick–Wolfenbuttel; of Saxe–Romburg, Saxe–Coburg, Saxe–Gotha, and Saxe–Coburg–Gotha; of Mecklenburg–Schwerin and Mecklenburg–Strelitz; of Schleswig–Holstein, Holstein–Gottorp, and Gottorp–Eutin; of Anhalt–Dessau, Anhal–Zerbst, and Zerbst–Dornburg – it was an archaic feudal anthill, bustling, and for the most part poor, highly inbred and quarrelsome, swarming in cramped conditions and on tight budgets, and with an imagination that readily soared beyond the narrow confines of the ancestral nest.[58]

Kliuchevskii was, though, capable of emotive lyricism: in particular, it was the artistry with which he evoked the Russian landscape, climate and man's relationship with the natural environment that prompted the literary critic, Iulii Aikenval'd, who had attended Kliuchevskii's courses as a student, to comment on his rare feeling for language (*redkoe chustvo rechi*): 'When you read these and other passages on Russia's natural environment, it is hard not to express deep admiration at the finesse in words and thought, or to realize that before you is not only a scholar, but a poet (...) a modern day Nestor'.[59]

Artistry of thought

Kliuchevskii's narrative gifts ensured the popularity of his *Course of Russian History* as the natural successor, if not rival, to Karamzin's original work of historical synthesis. Yet, unlike Karamzin, or Lomonosov before him, who as masters of rhetorical embellishment were read as one more literary work, Kliuchevskii's artistry was regarded as evidence of an intricate fusion of form and method: 'Language', as he claimed, and is worth reiterating, 'has retained much of the past that has been lost through time to human memory (*iazyk zapomnil mnogo stariny, sveianoi vremenem s liudskoi pamiati*)'.[60] Kliuchevskii's conviction that the past is etched in language honed his sensitivity not only to the linguistic heritage (*iazykovoe nasledie*) that he uncovered in the ancient chronicles, but also to the tonality of modern poetry and prose – Pushkin, Lermontov, Turgenev, Saltykov-Shchedrin, the plays of Ostrovskii and the lyrics of Nekrasov – that he avidly read and commented on in his mature writings.[61] In his close reading of sources, Kliuchevskii penetrated the worldview, feelings and mindset of the people he was studying with an inner artistic feeling (*chut'e*) for the peculiarities of speech, its inflections and colour. But it was his ability to refract this 'linguistic heritage' or 'poetic spirit' through the terms of his explanatory narrative and somehow co-opt it as 'the instrument of his thought' (in Presniakov's expression) that resulted in the intricate fusion of form and method just mentioned.[62] For both his contemporaries and successive generations, it was this seemingly inimitable skill that made him the exemplary 'scholar-artist' (*uchenyi-khudozhnik*).[63]

Kliuchevskii's critique of the eighteenth-century nobility in volume three of the *Course* provides a good illustration of the way in which he harnessed oral and written discourse as instruments of historical analysis. Here, as Pavel Miliukov argued in his 'in memoriam' tribute piece, Kliuchevskii spoke in the language of eighteenth-century satire; he needed (*emu ponadobilos'*) the vocabulary of Fonvizin and Novikov (two figures Kliuchevskii admired) to spell out the damning effects on the nation's moral health of the nobility's clumsy imitation of Western mores. The eighteenth century saw the creation of

> our dear cadet corpuses for the nobility, schools of engineering, educational societies for young noble or middle class ladies, academies of the arts, gymnasia. Tropical plants were cultivated in gentry greenhouses, but in the course of two hundred years not one purely national (*narodnaia*) generalist or agricultural school for the general public was opened. [...] Over the course of four to five generations the newly Europeanized Russia became a Russia of guards barracks, government chambers and gentry estates: adolescent offspring (*nedorosli*) were inducted into the first and in the second of these thanks to a little coaxing (*peregonka*) from home tutoring or an exotic boarding school, but all we got in exchange were superintendents in a uniform (*brigadir s mundirom*).[64]

In his commentary of the foregoing passage, Miliukov drew attention to Kliuchevskii's state of mind (*psikhologiia nastroeniia*) in order to grasp the significance of his scathing critique of serfdom as an institution designed to bolster the largely imported lifestyle of the nobility:

> He speaks in the voice of the 'average man' (*srednego roda luidei*), who does not shy away from a little candid vulgarity (*chestnaia podlost'*), even at the risk of offending the entire nobility. The historian replicated (*stal na pochvu*) those 'jokes in poor taste', and 'melancholy prose', which in the nation's past set the scene for the first gestures of serious social opposition, prompting the first serious danger to and reprisals by the authorities (*vlast'*). [...] Take Novikov, for example, who had also praised the former 'virtues of the Rossiian', opposing them to the same putrid tropical plants, which 'flourished in gentry greenhouses'! Both Novikov and his friends championed the first serious protest against the horrors of serfdom. Novikov, Fonvizin, Boltin were the people that Kliuchevskii loved in the eighteenth century, and about whom he wrote monographs. [...] So here we have the primary source of Kliuchevskii's negative attitude towards the culture of the eighteenth century; it was the culture of the nobility 'disfigured and ugly'. It, like 'Evgenii Onegin and his forebears' (Kliuchevskii's essay about Pushkin's famous novel in verse – FN) was a pose, a grimace, beautiful and clever [...] but pointless (*nenuzhnost'*).[65]

For Miliukov, Kliuchevskii's attitude towards the nobility, the social estate he neither pitied (*zhalel*) nor bemoaned (*zhaloval*) and the emotional affinity (*sochustvie, sostradanie*) that he expressed for the poor derived from personal experiences (*nastroenie vynesennoe iz 'byta'*) and memories that were reinforced by the great impression which the emancipation of the serfs had had on him during his student years.[66] Indeed, it was the enormous significance, both personal (Miliukov used the term 'autobiographical') and historical, which Kliuchevskii attributed to the existence and termination of peasant bondage that led Miliukov to position Kliuchevskii's narrative at the interface between autobiography (self-reckoning) and a psychological analysis of the human condition. Comments made by Kliuchevskii himself – history is 'a study of ourselves' (*izuchenie samogo sebia*), his description of Russia a historical person (*istoricheskaia lichnost'*) – arguably gave weight to Miliukov's observations regarding his seemingly unorthodox temperament as a historian.[67] Similarly, as Aikhenval'd noted:

> For Kliuchevskii, straightforward factual history was too constraining (*tesno*). He used to speak of 'the fact, expended by history (*fakt, otrabotannyi istoriei*)'. If this is so, if history drains facts, after which the latter disappear, lose their significance and meaning, then it becomes clear that history is itself provisional. For someone so drawn to permanent and unchanging values – might it be for this reason that Kliuchevskii turned to literature, even to literary criticism, where he, a major artist himself, a safekeeper of the word (*pestun slova*) enjoyed such uncontested right?[68]

Whether Kliuchevskii's celebrated talents as a 'historian-artist' made him a poor ambassador for the historical and sociological theories he otherwise advocated is a question that has troubled commentators. Both his critics and admirers recognized that Russian literature played an important part in his intellectual life, so it was in a way natural that it should inform the spirit and the letter of his work as a historian and that he should assume his audience's familiarity with the plots or protagonists that he frequently alluded to. One specific instance of this concerns his portrait of Alexander I's administrator and secretary, Mikhail Speranskii: if Kliuchevskii's account was informed by first-hand knowledge of sources, it was coloured by Andrei Bolkonskii's impressions in Tolstoi's novel, *War and Peace*.[69] Still, Kliuchevskii's artistry of thought begged the question of how far it contradicted his professed credo of 'historical sociology', which he had spelt out in the methodological introduction to his *Course*: 'History', he told his students, 'is a stepping stone towards sociology'. For the Soviet historiographer, Nikolai Rubinshtein, writing at the height of Stalinism, while there was little doubt that Kliuchevskii's 'artistry of thought' (*khudozhestvennost' myshleniia*) set him apart from both the narrative techniques typical of the Enlightenment era and the polished style of his contemporaries, Kostomarov and Bestuzhev-Riumin, it was also the Achilles heel of his work as a historian: 'The error of the artist results in a distortion of historical knowledge'; the brilliance of his historical syntheses often has 'no support in a solid scientific base, and does not withstand critical verification'.[70] The North American scholar, Edward Thaden, took a similar view suggesting that Kliuchevskii seldom defined his terminology very precisely and that he probably borrowed the terms from his peers. In Kliuchevskii's defence, however, Robert Byrnes has argued that the inconsistencies in his work were both testament to his knowledge of Russia's complicated past and in response to the massive changes affecting Russia during his last decades, which influenced his view of history.[71]

These discordances between Kliuchevskii's professed view of history and his actual handling of historical materials required extensive and imaginative defence by his admirers. For example, those who endeavoured to reconcile Kliuchevskii's artistry with reform era scholarship generally equated the latter with 'source-based enquiry'. Accordingly, they argued that rather than undermine his scholarly credentials, Kliuchevskii's literary infused historical consciousness (*soznanie*) allowed him to broaden the horizons of sociology. Nineteenth-century belles lettres, as the émigré literary critic Ilia Serman noted, taught Kliuchevskii to look beyond the economic factor and to seek explanations for change and continuity by probing human behaviour: doing so, he made the study of socio-economic history an expression of 'concrete human personality'.[72] Writing some thirty years earlier, Georgii Fedotov had expressed much the same opinion: Kliuchevskii pushed the boundaries of the sociological paradigm such that: 'social history turns into the study of social character'.[73] Even so, Fedotov conceded that the master historian was far more at home with public addresses 'where he felt free from the obligation to be scientific', echoing a point Aikhenval'd had made in his obituary tribute, namely that Kliuchevskii was too much of an artist for abstractions and too much of a historian to construct a dogmatic system. Rather, 'a living feeling for the fact' (*zhivoe chustvo fakta*), an understanding of how people lived, felt, an ability to free the fabric of reality from dry and formal abstractions and enter the past in medias res- all this allowed him to resurrect the past and not treat it as a 'laboratory preparation of sorts (*ne preparirovat' ego*).'[74] In sum, Kliuchevskii's originality of style was the entry point for grasping his originality as a historian.

Aesthetic imperatives: His master's voice and the printed word

Both Granovskii and Kliuchevskii became legendary for their public addresses. Yet in many respects, the contrast between them could hardly be more pronounced. Kliuchevskii's speech had, as contemporaries noted, a special intonation, 'which the printed version cannot destroy. Everyone who attended his lectures (…) knows that their charm resides in the shades of intonation, in the modulations of his voice (…), and this quality was retained in his books'.[75] In Granovskii's case, it was his economy of style that guaranteed his place in the pantheon of Russian nineteenth-century classics:

> In calling a writer 'chosen', we (also) have in mind certain characteristic features of his exposition, his form. And in this respect Granovskii occupies a special place in our literature. Even his most fierce detractors never questioned the elegance of his speech, which was remarkable for its clarity, simplicity and nobility of language, which was at once courageous (*muzhestvennyi*) and expressive. Among the many external traits of our author we will note only one: having begun to write at a time when foreign philosophical terminology was very fashionable in Russia (*kogda u nas byli v sil'nom khodu filosoficheskie terminy, zaimstvovannye iz chuzhogo iazyka*) – indeed, he himself had studied German philosophy – thanks both to his true sense of (*vernyi smysl*) and feeling for refinement in language (*chustvo iziashchnago v iazyke*), he managed to keep his speech free from any irrelevancy. On many occasions, he had to deal with very hard questions of science, yet, despite that, his speech never lost clarity and never tried to impress with abstruse terms. Le style, c'est l'homme, as an old wise proverb put it.[76]

In a letter addressed to Nikolai Stankevich, dated 25 September 1839, Granovskii commented on the restraint he consciously practised as a public speaker: 'I read my lectures not from a notebook, but from a detailed outline. It is not possible any other way. (…) Even when I am carried away by the narrative, I try to keep my composure; I still fear falling back into dazzling improvisation'.[77] Kudriavtsev confirmed this: 'In general, Granovskii did not like overly embellished (*slishkom sviazanogo*), complicated sentences (*izlozheniia*); he preferred a more free style – that is, "short, compact" (*szhatuiu*), occasionally "elliptic" (*otryvistuiu*), but at the same time forceful (*sil'nyu*) and expressive. And he perfected all these traits at a time in the development of literature which was characterized by a level of stylistic conformity, and which did not offer much scope for difference among writers of prose'.[78]

By contrast, it was Kliuchevskii's brilliant, trenchant wit, which captured the attention of his audience. Explanations for these differences should, I think, be primarily put down to individual temperament and only to a lesser degree to the proverbial 'sensibilities' of the age in which they lived and worked, which both men, paradoxically, resisted. As I have mentioned, already, in the late 1830s, Granovskii was beginning to speak about the need to align history with the natural sciences (physical geography) and law and to co-opt their vocabularies for historical study. In Kliuchevskii's case, if his arid humour and sobriety could be said to be typical of the 'new' realism of the 1860s or his interest in understanding what he called the 'anatomy' and 'physiology' of social and historical development symptomatic of a lexical paradigm shift brought about by the rise of new disciplines in the second half of the century, we should not neglect his capacity for lyrical evocation (his account of the Russian steppe, for example) which, as both Aikhenval'd and, more recently, Shmidt suggested, evidenced a residual 'old' style. In Shmidt's words: 'From Kliuchevskii's lectures you get the sense that he and his audience were familiar with the realist literature and its social everyday themes, but also with the terminology and Aesopic-style language found in mid-nineteenth century *publitistika* and the satire of Salytkov-Shchedrin'.[79]

Ironically, what the two men did have in common was a stammer, although, again, as one might expect from contemporary testimonies, this 'flaw' was said only to enhance the hold they had over their audiences. Granovskii's stammer and tendency to swallow his words were, Solov'ev recalled, 'but surface deficiencies (which) disappeared before the inner merits of his speech, before the inner strength and warmth, which imparted life to historical figures and events, and riveted the attention of his audience on these living, brilliantly drawn individuals and events'.[80] Kliuchevskii, the 'consummate actor', used his stutter to dramatic effect through expressive pauses, as if engaging in dialogue (*on beseduet*): 'Those who attended his lectures and conversations know that one of their charms was precisely in the melting intonations and modulations of his voice; it was impossible not to be surprised by the amount of wisdom, thought and substance charging the very phonetics of his speech'.[81] Indeed, so persuasive was Kliuchevskii's 'voice' his students felt that they were listening to a traveller recently returned from his travels to the Russian past, who was now sharing his personal impressions of what he had just seen and heard.

There are a number of circumstantial and cultural explanations as to why an emphasis on the historian's 'voice' was so pronounced in these assessments by contemporaries. Significantly, an underdeveloped print culture (specifically, a scarcity of printed textbooks in the academic field) meant that many textbooks were transcripts of lectures. Frequently compiled by students and disseminated in lithograph form (and which might or might not be authorized by the professor), these raw, unpolished, records of lecture content faithfully retained the professor's style of delivery, the cadences of his voice, his use of images, word play and anecdotes.[82] This is certainly the case with Granovskii whose published, largely posthumous, output consisted primarily of lectures, which the radical thinker, Nikolai Chernyshevskii, described as 'conversations with friends'.[83] But beyond circumstantial factors, an insistence on safeguarding the (Biblical sounding) 'living word' (*zhivoe slovo*) or the importance attached to being a custodian of the word (*pestun slova*) that we frequently come across in tributes to Granovskii and Kliuchevskii brings us, once again, back into the sphere of cultural attitudes towards scholarship.[84] For Kliuchevskii, preserving the cadences of conversational speech was a matter of principle: as commentators have noted, when preparing his *Course* for publication after 1900, he consciously retained elements of direct discourse between the speaker and his audience, periodically reminding his readers that a living voice was addressing them, actively engaged in a reconstruction of Russian history and intent on sharing it with them.[85]

Attention to the distinctive qualities of the historian's voice also goes some way to explaining why, in the Russian historiographical tradition, stylistic conventions that, elsewhere, might more typically be associated with the differentiated genres of professional academic histories, research papers, textbooks, or journalistic essays and histories written for the general public were never rigidly adhered to. It was, for example, common practice for chapters of a monograph to be serialized in a journal prior to publication in book form. To this point it is worth noting that university presses, which began to appear during Granovskii's generation, would later be matched by the rise of publishing houses sponsored by entrepreneurs and philanthropists, such as the Mamontov and Morozov families, with the intention both to establish a national intellectual patrimony and to bring it into the public arena, a trend which grew exponentially around the turn of the century as part of the ethos of mass education. In this spirit, articles on history were routinely placed in a wide cross-section of 'thick journals', predominantly 'populist' or liberal in profile (e.g. *Vestnik Evropy, Russkaia mysl', Russkoe bogatstvo, Mir bozhii, Sovremennyi mir, Obrazovanie*), again with a view to ensure broader dissemination of knowledge. While it may be feasible to see in this a potential conflict of interests arising from an ambition to advance the scholarly profile of the discipline, on the one hand, and a commitment to raise public awareness, on the other, evidence suggests otherwise. In an article on émigré historians, Sigurd Shmidt noted that the publication of solid scholarly historical articles in the broad-spectrum press (magazines and even newspapers) was a conspicuous trend among first-wave émigré historians (including Aleksandr Kieswetter and Pavel Miliukov) and that the practice was mirrored by their Soviet peers. Academicians such as Platonov, Evgenii Tarle and Militsa Nechkina all published original pieces in newspapers, 'thick' journals or in popular series, most notably 'Lives of Remarkable People'. The point that Shmidt was making here (and clearly condoning) was that 'truly gifted scholarly works are as likely to be characterized by figurative thinking as by logic. These authors paid a considerable amount of attention to literary execution'.[86] In other words, the refusal to privilege one discursive mode over another may be explained on pragmatic grounds in that a deliberate blurring of genres aided the professoriate in their role as public enlighteners to instil a sense of history, especially national history, among a wider public. But this is not quite the whole picture: to return to Kliuchevskii's work on the eighteenth-century nobility, there was, as Miliukov noted, a seamless link between his essay on Evgenii Onegin (originally a public address) and his university course in Russian history – the two worked in tandem; the former was incomplete without the other.[87] Both Granovskii and Kliuchevskii expressed disdain for 'scholarly foppishness' (*shchegol'stvo*), namely elaborate quotations 'that could either be to the point or not at all'.[88] 'Articles', in Granovskii's view, 'should not be long, and, anyway, in general, I am neither capable nor wish to write long articles. If one can convey in a few words that which fills your heart, then verbosity merely waters down quality of the feeling (*sobstvennoe chuvstvo*). This is my literary theory'.[89] As an implicit criticism of 'the dead letter of 'science' associated with 'agnostic scholarship' with its rigid classification of terms, what counted, then, was the historian's ability to integrate his person, tastes, moral outlook, his vision, in short, his cultural baggage as a 'man of letters' (the legacy of salon culture) into the specialist knowledge acquired through source-based and interpretive studies.[90] The lecture was the format most suited to the task not only of disseminating historical knowledge (both specialist and popular) but, crucially, of demonstrating the power of thought itself as the historian engaged with his public.[91]

In a series of insightful, if all too brief, essays on Russian historical culture and practice, first published in the early 1990s, that is prior to the piece just mentioned, Sigurd Shmidt addressed the topic of 'writers as professional historians and professional historians as writers'. Here he noted that 'thinking in images' (*obraznoe myshlenie*) or the 'literary composition' of real facts, no less than logical thinking, was characteristic of scholarly work: 'The scholar, like any creative person, responds to and is influenced by contemporary literature, art and other science. In short, his output depends on cultural context'.[92] From the present-day, Western post-modernist perspective, Shmidt's suggestion that the history lecture, and historical narrative as a whole, functioned as an echo (*otklik*) of the aesthetic imperatives of the age may read as a truism, but the emphasis he places on the historian's ability to 'think in images' is nonetheless pertinent in the context of nineteenth-century Russia for reconsidering accepted views concerning the fundamental distinctions between the practice of history and creative literature.[93] Ironically, among those to position themselves on this question – and to insist on these distinctions – were, quite often, creative writers themselves. Declaring an unbridgeable divide between the two modes of representing the past, creative writers were generally dismissive of the historian's ability to capture the essence of a historical event or figure through his narrative. For example, the playwright Alexander Ostrovskii (1823–86), famed for his historical dramas, and who had collaborated on Pogodin's *Mosvitianin* in the 1840s, voiced the opinion (or prejudice) that 'the learned historian merely explains history, points out causal connections, whereas the historian–artist writes like an eyewitness (*ochevidets*), transports you into the past, and transforms you into a spectator of events'.[94] Possibly one of the most trenchant dismissals of historical science came from Tolstoi in his famous epilogue to *War and Peace*. If, in the following passage, the slightly more measured tones in which he spelt out the differences in nature between literature and history read as a reasoned judgement, this did not alter his otherwise disparaging view of the profession as peddlers in useless facts:

> When describing a historical epoch the artist and the historian have two entirely different objectives. Just as the historian would be wrong if he attempted to present a historical figure in all his entirety, in all his complicated connections to all aspects of life, so an artist would not be doing his duty if he presented that figure in all of his historical significance.[95]

The point to stress here is that such observations merely reinforced negative stereotypes about institutionalized learning as pedantry – stereotypes, which, it should go without saying, most trained historians themselves strenuously rejected, and not only because of the importance they invested in their role as public enlighteners, but because, like creative writers, they, too, took a dim view of narrow 'agnostic scholarship'.

The rise of cultural historical enquiry in the late nineteenth century, and, more broadly, the anti-positivist climate after 1900, created a new context for a deliberation of this question in a more conciliatory key. Writing some forty years after Tolstoi, the young formalist critic, Boris Eikhenbaum, addressed the significance of Karamzin's *History of the Russian State* for current Russian historical culture and practice. The magnum opus was not, he wrote, 'just the foundation of historical engagement, it framed the substance of historical emotion, (...) it is a vindication – what is more, an aesthetic vindication – of the act of turning one's mental gaze towards the past'.[96] For Eikhenbaum, Karamzin had devised an original template for a literary–historical fusion, which, regardless of the introduction of empirically based methodological frameworks after 1850, proved to be quite durable. As I have argued in this chapter, it was this literary–historical fusion, which was esteemed by contemporaries as the hallmark of the true scholar. Granovskii was celebrated for his ability to negotiate the terms of science through art. As for Kliuchevskii, if he could be accused of practising double standards in his evaluations of other historians (e.g. he referenced historical '*zakonomernost*' in order to expose the flaws in Karamzin's *History*, yet upbraided his younger contemporary, Platonov, for dismissing the value of literary sources in his study of the time of troubles), he never concealed his ambivalence towards the historiographical conventions of his day.[97] It is clear from his appraisal of Kostomarov's work, cited earlier in this chapter, that he considered imaginative flair, an ability to 'disguise' learning, close archival work or the historian's 'scientific apparatus' to be the marks of excellence in historical investigation. And, it is equally clear that he was rather more innovative than Kostomarov or, indeed, Karamzin, with the interplay of narrative/authorial 'voices' and perspectives that all of them had inherited from the historical novel: the resonances of literary and popular speech patterns and inflections that the reader encounters in Kliuchevskii's *Course of Russian History* had the peculiar effect of conflating or dissolving distinctions between poetic (or psychological)/historic truth and empirical historical fact. Granted, in accordance with the accepted practices of his day, Kliuchevskii could not invent dialogues or speeches in, for example, his account of the nobility (he actually relied on poetic portrayals by Pushkin and Fonvizin or indeed, as I mentioned above, Tolstoi to do this instead), but he did shatter distinctions between 'historic' truth and excavations into historical fact, thus ensuring a place for his *Course* both within the pantheon of Russian historiography and in the history of Russian literature. In sum, just as Karamzin's outdated scientific apparatus, his patriotism and political nationalism did not diminish the importance of his History as a monument in the canon of historical writing, so too, it was the artistic qualities that ensured Kliuchevskii's place in the canon even though these were, in many respects at odds with the premises of law-based, empirical enquiry. As I discuss in the next chapter, the literary interface of historical writing is illustrated very well in portrayals of historical figures. Here, once again, historical explanation relied as much on artistic vision, psychological probing and a sense of theatricality as it did on fact-based knowledge.

4

The Historian's Literary Toolbox: Portraiture

The crafting of historical portraits constituted a major strand of Russian historical writing and remained so throughout the late imperial period. As a pedagogical tool, it allowed historians to encapsulate key episodes of the past in a memorable and compelling way and was especially effective in works of historical synthesis intended for a non-specialist readership. Foregrounding the lives of individuals was, of course, also consistent with trends in mainstream west European historiography and philosophy of history which, since the early nineteenth century, had been dominated by Hegel's theory of great men (in his Philosophy of History) as exemplars of universal traits through their function as unconscious instruments of the World Spirit.[1] As undoubtedly one of the single most powerful influences on the discipline, it generated a rich seam of enquiry into the nature of historical progress and political change. By the mid-century, however, this romantic worldview was superseded by new interpretations of historical figures in which greater attention was given to their representative function. Encapsulating the spirit of their age, these 'epochal personalities', as Lidiia Ginzburg called them, could, moreover, be drawn equally from fiction as from life. In France, the main advocates of the view that 'history was embodied in personalities and destinies' included the literary historian, Charles Augustin Saint-Beuve (1804–69), and, after him, Hippolyte Taine (1828–93). Both men studied the formation of distinctive, time-bound, personality types in light of their double, yet inextricably linked, historical and fictional origins.[2]

One does not have to search very far to discover a similar, generational paradigm shift in the work of Russian historians: the conceptual tools that Granovskii and Kliuchevskii used to frame their characterizations of pivotal figures and social types closely tracked the directions that the problem of historical personality had taken abroad. Granovskii's generation was of course familiar with Hegel's thought, and it is a topic that has been studied quite extensively.[3] By contrast, the Russian reception of Taine's work has received less attention, but there is little doubt that his views generated interest among Russian contemporaries. All of Taine's major works were translated into Russian during the 1870s and were the subject of critical review in scholarly and generalist publications. As an undergraduate in the early 1860s, Kliuchevskii was already familiar with some of the French historian's work, and in his own course on methodology in 1884 he introduced his students to the use of applied psychology in historical analysis.[4] In the spirit of Taine's judgement that 'all historical events are psychological phenomena' (which, on occasion, he cited), Kliuchevskii instructed his pupils that history was 'a popular-psychological study'. Charting the nation's past was, he claimed, the study of the 'historical personality of a people'.[5] As I argue in this chapter, this principle clearly informed his sketches of Russian tsars and leading statesmen, effectively displacing the importance he otherwise ascribed to economic, social and institutional factors as motors of historical change. The premises of aesthetic realism, moreover, allowed him not only to vindicate creative literature as a resource, but also to conflate historical fact and literary evocation.

Ivan Grevs' master's dissertation, a study of farm management in the late Roman Empire published in 1899, signalled yet another direction in historical biography. In part indebted to the example of Fustel de Coulanges, the French historian he admired most, Grevs developed what he called economic biography (or biographical method) as a tool for exploring not just the broad scheme of economic and political change but, importantly, their impact on daily life and culture, and the moral world of individuals.[6] In his words: 'Focusing on concrete case studies helps explain the complexities of historical formation; it teaches us to discern and draw links between the material and the conceptual (*ekonomicheskii/ideinyi*), between political and individual elements (*politicheskii/individual'nyi*). (…). It sharpens the historian's ability to discern – through the processes by which they emerge and develop – the impact of large-scale movements on the life of society and of the individual'.[7] Grevs' main innovation, however, was that by combining socio-economic and 'psychological-biographical' perspectives in his case studies, he was able to broaden his range of sources, notably to include impressions in verse and prose by Roman contemporaries, materials traditionally regarded as the exclusive entitlement of classical philologists.[8] Whether, then, in the form of a public address (the case of Granovskii), university lecture (Kliuchevskii) or research topic (Grevs), the ways in which these historians constructed their portraits of individuals and types offer considerable scope for exploring the interface between literary culture and historical enquiry. Granovskii's Hegelian-inspired portraits of great men, Kliuchevskii's masterfully drawn sketches of Russian tsars and Grevs' decision to include poetry as a historical source in his economic biographies all functioned as telling disclosers of the literary impulse in Russian historical scholarship.

Granovskii's typology of great men

In the spring of 1851, Granovskii delivered a series of public lectures on the lives of four major historical figures: Tamerlane (1336–1405), Alexander the Great (356–23BC), Louis IX (1214–70) and Francis Bacon (1561–1626). Each of Granovskii's chosen figures exemplified distinctive character traits – despotism; military prowess and political vision; compassion; and rationality – which, he argued, were historically pivotal for understanding the pace of socio-political and cultural changes. Great men, he believed, were chosen by providence 'to accomplish what resides in the requirements of a given epoch, in the beliefs and wishes of a given time and people. (…). Such men clothe in the living word that which lies hidden in the mind of the people, and they convert the vague aspirations and wishes of their compatriots or contemporaries into visible exploit'.⁹

Forming a leitmotif in these sketches was the concept of power, which Granovskii explored not only in relation to warfare, politics and legality, but also, and significantly for his intended audience, in terms of the power of knowledge. To begin, he contrasted the destructive consequences on state formation of Tamerlane's brutal conduct in warfare and tyrannical domestic rule with the expansion of Hellenistic territories in the wake of Alexander the Great's military campaigns. Granovskii's point here was that if military might is not combined with 'fruitful ideas', the spoils of conquest have no lasting value.¹⁰ Thus, within a century of Tamerlane's death virtually nothing remained of the oriental-style despotic 'state' (*gosudarstvo*) that he had forged through violence and bloodshed. By contrast, the legacy of Alexander, the Western (*zapadnyi*) warrior, who did not violate the traditions and customs of those he conquered, was buttressed by his decision to break down barriers and attendant privileges between Greeks and Barbarians. If Granovskii conceded that Alexander was given to acts of unwarranted vengeance, which damaged his reputation, his broad stroke characterization confirmed the canonical portrait of a legend on the battlefield and of a visionary in the arena of politics:

> Were we mentally to scan the horizon of the past, we would not find another individual whose historical activity compares in volume and influence with that of Alexander. He stands as a mediator and reconciler between the West and the East. For entire peoples he opened up routes, along which, hitherto, only a handful of brave travellers had ventured. In this respect, only Columbus could be said to match him. The Greeks were already familiar with the western parts of Asia. The northeastern regions of the Persian state and the Indian borderlands, however, were the stuff of the most nonsensical fables. Alexander turned these huge expanses to good account, uncovering for the inquiring mind of the West a new geography and nature, a whole world of distinctive religious ideas and moral values. New lands were brought into the spheres of trade and science. For its part, the East absorbed these influences, bringing to them the unprecedented wealth and plentitude of its own ideas unlocked from within the deep recesses of collective consciousness.¹¹

Even though Granovskii accepted Hegel's view that men of providence are summoned to resolve important historical tasks for the sake of progress, his portrayal of Louis IX, the subject of his third lecture, suggests, rather, a romantic yearning for a bygone age. Caught between the medieval and early modern worlds, Louis' reign contained a 'tragic beauty'. As a historical actor, the French monarch embodied 'all the beauty and virtues of a lost era': with his qualities of valour/gallantry (*doblest'*), grounded not in military conquest, rather in the Christian principles of compassion and justice, Louis was, in Granovskii's eyes, 'a knight, in the most elevated, ideal sense of this word', one of the finest representatives and valiant defenders of chivalry.

Commentators have frequently noted that historical figures like Louis the Wise elicited Granovskii's sympathies over those who, by their actions, reneged on the past 'with little care for the ruins they leave in their wake'. Nature, he argued, may have gifted the forward-looking 'great man' with a good ear and keen vision, but has denied him love and poetry. Although such men exemplified victory and progress, it was at the cost of certain moral values that Granovskii prized over the tangible gains of modernization. In a lecture given two years earlier, he had spoken of his fascination with transitional periods in history where figures such as Louis reside:

> Ever since the beginning of my studies in history these sad periods have caught my attention. It was not merely their tragic beauty that attracted me, rather the yearning to catch the fading moments of a world in decline, and to glimpse the first signs of a new order about to emerge. It occurred to me that only here is it possible for the trained ear to detect or discern (*podslushat'*) the secret growth of history, grasp it in the midst of its creative labours.[12]

Louis was a perfect case study in this regard: if his belief that the ultimate aim of war as the triumph of faith and the restoration of breached laws stemmed from chivalric principles, it was also, in Granovskii's view, an inchoate expression of a new conception of justice signalling the demise of feudal practices based on estate privilege:

> His decrees concerning judicial duels and private wars underpinned subsequent legislation. The people who helped Louis with these reforms were learned jurists, who enjoyed his special respect and trust. The reforms of which they were the authors were not, of course, envisaged by the King, who thought only about the ennoblement and consolidation of feudal institutions through greater justice and morality. He knew that the knights were bad judges and replaced them as far as possible by people who had studied law as a science. The consequences came to light after Louis' death. The jurists whom he had set on a career of practical activity constituted a whole estate inimical to the ideas and forms of the Middle Ages.[13]

True progress, then, or the purposefulness of the historical process, as Granovskii conceived it, could be traced through the gradual change over time in expressions of power, from one of brute force to the might acquired through ethically grounded intellectual endeavour. If Tamerlane had an inchoate, 'mystical respect for science' (attested by the fact that he enlisted scientists and artisans captured in battle to construct his magnificent city of Samarkand), Alexander, as Aristotle's pupil, harnessed 'the wealth of ideas developed by Greek science' to build the illustrious city named after him on the western bank of the Nile.[14] Alexandria became a hub not only of world trade but also of scholarship (*obrazovannost'*). It was host to 'a centuries-long conversation of ideas' between the West and the East. 'Without Alexander', Granovskii concluded, 'modern-day scholarship would not exist'.[15]

Francis Bacon, the subject of Granovskii's fourth historical portrait, completed this transformation towards the modern, more inclusive, knowledge-based concept of power that Alexander had initiated and to which Louis IX gave expression in the language and setting of Christian compassion and justice. Although Granovskii was openly critical of Bacon as a statesman, his duplicity, self-interest and moral cowardice in the political arena did not, he believed, impinge upon his significance as a philosopher who successfully paved the way for the development of modern (natural) science. It was Bacon's commanding grasp of the current trends across science as a whole, rather than any one particular discovery, that made him such an important historical figure whose influence was still discernible in the modern age. In Granovskii's summary: 'The hopes and demands of Bacon have been fulfilled: today, knowledge and scholarship (*obrazovannost'*) have become a necessary condition of state power and of the might of the morally conscious life of individuals'.[16]

'Four Characteristics' was warmly received. Pogodin called the lectures a 'brilliant success', his characterizations 'lively, interesting, pleasant, and clear'. According to Vetrinskii, the public deemed the subject and Granovskii's delivery to be 'too good to be scientific lectures' (*slishkom khoroshie*).[17] More persuasively than his west European counterparts, who situated great men in a tightly rational chain of causality (the name of Guizot was singled out in this connection), Granovskii had presented his heroes full of 'proud decisiveness'.[18] As his Russian commentators noted, for Granovskii, the person was not an abstract concept, rather a concrete being vested with the responsibility to ensure societal good (*blago*), and this was why he was particularly drawn to those leaders of humanity who exhibited strength of mind, courage and moral conviction.[19] As freely creative, moral beings they gave Granovskii grounds to test the faith that he and his generation shared in 'human progress'.[20] In the context of Oriental despotism associated with Nicholas I's reign, this was highly significant: for his audience, Granovskii's vigorous defence of the socially and historically meaningful role of the creative individual positioned him as a moderate Westernizer. The credentials he ascribed to 'great men' were interpreted as a 'reaction against the extreme regulation of all aspects of Russian life' that Nicholas I had imposed through his bureaucracy.[21] As such, his views suggested a common platform with those of Herzen, one of the most outspoken champions of individual rights and freedom. However, it is interesting to note that Granovskii was also careful to distance himself from his friend's more radical theory of contingency, which effectively made 'great men' an accident of history.[22] For Granovskii, by contrast, of central importance was the task of developing in his listeners an awareness of the eternal laws of historical development, a respect for the past and a striving for betterment in the future: therefore, to deny the necessity of great men in history was, to his mind, equal to claiming

> that one of the forces operating in nature had lost its significance, that one of the organs of the human body had now become unnecessary. Such a conception of history is only possible if one takes the most casual and superficial view of it. But he, for whom history is not a dead letter, he who is wont to heed its mysterious growth, sees in great men the chosen ones of Providence, those who are called to earth to accomplish what resides in the requirements of a given epoch, in the beliefs and wishes of a given people.[23]

Granovskii's portrayal of elect personalities provided him with the platform to formulate a theoretical and moral–philosophical credo, which generations of historians after him came to regard as his most significant legacy: 'History', he wrote, has two aspects: first, the free creativity of the human spirit; second, nature, the properties of which are completely distinct from the former. A new method should arise from a rigorous study of the spiritual and natural world, together with their interrelation. Only in this way will it be possible to establish solid basic principles, that is, clear knowledge of the laws which determine historical events.[24]

In his university address (*aktovaia rech'*) delivered the following year, he further refined this point: human existence, he argued, is subordinated to the same law as the natural world except that in each of these realms the law acts in different ways. Natural phenomena occur in a far more uniform and simple manner than historical phenomena (…) wherein

> the law functions as an aim or goal towards which mankind ineluctably (*neuderzhimo*) proceeds; but the law does not dictate which path to take, nor how much time is needed to reach the end goal. It is here that the person presents all her rights (*vstupaet vo vse prava svoi otdel'naia lichnost'*). Here, the individual (*litso*) acts, not as an instrument, but as an independent champion (*pobornikom*), or adversary of the historical process, taking responsibility for the events that she has triggered or prevented. This is why her character, passions, inner development are for the thinking historian an important and deeply engaging object of study. Unfortunately, historians today pay little attention to the psychological element in their science.[25]

If Granovskii's comments here anticipated the turn towards historical psychology, it is also clear that he still had to navigate a difficult course between free will and the designs of providence. As Priscilla Roosevelt notes, Granovskii did not deny the existence of historical laws, nor renege on his Hegelian pedigree, but there is, nevertheless, a sense that the emphasis he placed on the creative potential of man amounted to a 'methodological protest' against a narrowly restrictive determinism.[26] Both here in this lecture series and in other biographical sketches, his obvious enthusiasm for the personalities he portrayed was taken as a sign that he was prepared to invest these historically pivotal individuals with more free will than Hegel's 'pawns to the cunning of Reason' would allow. Ultimately, what Granovskii valued most in historical actors were the moral tools they used to assist in the historical progress of mankind. This is why he placed so much emphasis on the qualities of spiritual courage (Alexander the Great, Louis), strength of mind, 'moral beauty, and the unsullied purity of soul (*svetlaia dusha*)'.[27] For Granovskii, these qualities functioned as ethical preconditions for the personal realization of universal values.[28] The subject of his controversial doctoral dissertation (1849) about the life and thought of Abbot Suger (1081–1151), councillor to Louis VI, which was interpreted – and condemned – by his official nationalist peers as an attempt to subvert the principle of autocracy, offers perhaps one of his most eloquent vindications of the morally and socially creative role of the individual as a model for the thinking elite as Russia edged tentatively towards an era of reform:

> The peculiarity of Suger's mind and character consisted of its unusual clarity and simplicity. He is among that rare number of men who absolutely know what they

want, who are fully conscious of their goals and intentions. Blessed is he who has such clarity of understanding in himself united with that high moral conviction without which there is no durable historical achievement.[29]

In many ways, Granovskii's fascination with history's heroes was typical of what Lidiia Ginzburg described as 'post-Decembrist romanticism' with its intense interest in the inner life of the 'elect personality'.[30] If the characterizations allowed him to test his historical–philosophical viewpoint concerning the purposefulness of history, the manner in which he fleshed out these qualities in the portraits themselves was undoubtedly inspired by the novels he had read as a youth. Indeed, his credo that the goal of history is the moral, enlightened person independent of the chains of fate (*rokovye opredeleniia*) and a society that meets the demands of such a person was, in a sense, a rephrasing in historical–philosophical terms of one of the chief motifs of literary romanticism, namely the dramatic struggle for the triumph of good over evil, 'the ultimate transcendence of man over the world in which he was imprisoned by the Fall', as Hayden White summarized it.[31] The notion of honour that Granovskii and his contemporaries discovered in the novels of Sir Walter Scott, Victor Hugo or Alexander Dumas confirmed a 'belief in the inherent primacy of the realm of the ideal over "base" empirical reality'.[32] That said, it is also the case that the heroes of Granovskii's lectures, such as Abbot Suger, were not typical romantic rebels fighting a hostile environment. On the contrary, their actions reflected the spirit of their age and were conditioned by the weight of past tradition. Roosevelt reminds us that as a believer in organic development, Granovskii felt that great men, 'whatever their influence for good or evil, do not stand independently but are closely and tightly bound to their land and time'.[33] It is interesting to note that claims of this kind left later generations of Russian historians querying the extent of Granovskii's intellectual indebtedness to Hegel, Ranke and the liberal French historians of the first half of the nineteenth century. For example, Vladimir Ger'e, author of an intellectual biography of Leibniz, Kareev, and the liberal-populist critic, Vetrinskii, all cast Granovskii as a champion of the free creativity of the spirit (*lichnost'*), thereby downplaying a residual determinism in his thinking about the historical process. Others, however, disputed Granovskii's credentials as a romantic: writing on the fiftieth anniversary of Granovskii's death, the historian of ancient Greece and Rome, Robert Vipper, argued that, post 1850, Granovskii saw evidence of free will 'only in the actions of individual people; as a whole, in the general scheme of things, their actions repeat and adhere to a strict law-governed process (*zakonomernost'*)'.[34] For Vipper, Granovskii's choice of case studies suggests that, by that time, he had revised his earlier views of heroes as the prime movers of history: 'The destructive Tamerlane, the passive (…) pitiful figure of Louis XIV, the fantastical conquistador, Alexander, and Bacon – a great mind and a moral nonentity – cannot function as spiritual exemplars; rather, as witnesses of history, they exhibit in sharpest form the salient features of a given epoch'.[35]

Vipper may have grounds for making Granovskii's ideas current with the age of 'agnostic scholarship' that succeeded him, but it was arguably at the cost of ignoring the conceptual and rhetorical conventions of philosophical idealism and literary romanticism that informed his work. As Granovskii, himself, wrote, both the

Tamerlanes and the Peters (the Great), as innovators who boldly and consciously trample on the past for the sake of a new and better future, and those individuals like Louis IX who embody the highest ideals of an age about to perish 'bear responsibility only for the purity of their intentions and the earnestness of their endeavours, not for the far distant consequences of the work they have done. It is deposited in history, like a secret seed. The germination, fruition, and time of harvest are in the hands of God'.[36] Indeed, once we place Granovskii side by side with Kliuchevskii who rejected the great men theory, the contrasts between the two historians could hardly be any more pronounced. Whereas Granovskii had, in a sense, pre-selected universal moral traits as forces of historical progress, which he then 'embodied' in his chosen heroes as public figures (irrespective of whether he regarded them as prime movers, models to emulate or witnesses of their age), for Kliuchevskii, inspired by his muses of literary realism, reconstructing the lives of individuals was, rather, the key to understanding the subjective-psychological reality of a period. Unlike Granovskii's aim to uncover in each of his case studies a distinctive trait that shaped the future course of history, Kliuchevskii situated his historical figures (Peter the Great, Tsar Alexis) squarely within, rather than outside, their immediate socio-political and cultural settings in order to explore the ways in which their lives reflected or encapsulated the spirit of their age. It was as if the two historians were viewing their subjects through the opposite ends of a telescopic lens.[37]

Kliuchevskii's word portraits

'To say that the moral level of society depends on the perfection of some of its members is equal to claiming that the ambient temperature is affected by the rise in the mercury level when the thermometer is held in a warm hand'.[38] Kliuchevskii's ambivalence towards the role of leaders and prominent figures in history gave him enormous scope to ply his narrative skills. His 'word portraits', as Marshall Shatz calls them, were brilliantly crafted out of visual metaphors, similes and anecdotes in which he juxtaposed incongruous yet highly memorable detail to ironic and comic effects.[39] A single simile or troubling dichotomy captured the essence of a historical figure. Here are some examples: Peter the Great's happiest moments 'were those spent using an axe, a saw or a lathe, or wielding a correctional cudgel'; he was 'a kind man but a ruthless tsar'.[40] For Alexei, Peter's father, by contrast, 'vindictiveness and a sense of injury were as incomprehensible to him as the taste for wine is to some people, who wonder how others can drink such unpleasant stuff'.[41] Ordin-Nashchokin, one of Alexei's chief plenipotentiaries, was 'a Voltaire in an Orthodox theological jacket (…) as skilled with abstractions as a pianist playing Liszt, he advocated principles that were alien and dangerous'.[42]

Since history recorded neither miracles nor miracle workers, the arrival of authoritative, energetic figures on the historical scene was, Kliuchevskii claimed, 'for no apparent reason'.[43] He therefore tended to make use of relevant socio-political and cultural – and particularly, domestic – detail as frames for his portraits: the historical protagonist's formative years, his education, family relations, marriage all informed Kliuchevskii's psychologically probing interpretation of their (idiosyncratic) personality traits, beliefs and conduct. Typically, he identified one or two salient physical and/or behavioural traits as the main axes within which he then situated his account of a given monarch's reign.[44] He would also incorporate these personality traits as points of reference in the verdicts he almost inevitably returned on their legacy as rulers. For example, driving his account of Catherine the Great's reign was the topic of the impact of Western thought on Russian minds and institutions. This was, as Shatz notes, a central preoccupation for Kliuchevskii in his treatment of the seventeenth and eighteenth centuries, and we encounter it again in his portraits of Peter the Great and Alexis where he highlights the tragi-comical consequences arising from attempts to imitate Western mores or accommodate them to indigenous traditions. Catherine the Great's north German origins (she grew up in Stettin), however, presented Kliuchevskii with an opportunity to explore this impact through the prism of the cultural prejudices she had acquired through her upbringing and education, and which she brought with her to the Russian Court. Glossed as 'a total absence of moral principles', these prejudices gave Catherine her dominant personality traits: ambition, cold calculation and self-deception:

> A deficiency of moral consideration and independent thought deflected Catherine from the proper path of development on which her fortunate nature had placed her. She understood early in life that for every individual, knowledge of people must begin with knowledge of oneself. Catherine was one of those rather rare people who know how to look at themselves from the side, as the saying goes, objectively, as though at an interesting passerby [...]. Catherine writes of herself in her memoirs that she had a mind and character incomparably more masculine than feminine, although she retained all the agreeable qualities of a woman worthy of love. The tree of self-knowledge without sufficient moral fertilization bore unwholesome fruit – conceit.[45]

At the root of Catherine's self-deception was a 'physical handicap' that she learnt to disguise by honing an ability to charm and captivate with her mind: 'From childhood she had been told that she was ugly, and early in life this made her learn the art of pleasing, of seeking within her soul what was lacking in her outward appearance'.[46] But, as Kliuchevskii suggests, her ability to gain favour with others had the unwanted side effect of corrupting her powers of self-reckoning. This dissonance between Catherine's less than perfect beauty and her ability to charm and deceive provided Kliuchevskii with a psychological explanation for the impact of Western civilization on Russian minds: many educated Russians were drawn by the idea of the West, hoping to assimilate its refinements, its style and traditions, but first-hand experience of its reality invariably resulted in a sense of disappointment, moral confusion or tergiversation.

As a rule, the degree of admiration or contempt (or, as we saw in Catherine's case, ambivalence) that Kliuchevskii expressed for his subjects was proportionate to the degree of correspondence he detected between their physical appearance and personality traits. Most of his case studies exhibited neat psychophysiological parallels: for example, Alexei's moral and intellectual makeup – kindness, piety, yet moral sybaritism – was 'reflected to perfection in his comfortable looking, indeed, rather portly, figure, his low brow, fair skin, puffy rosy cheeks framed by a well trimmed beard, light brown hair, mild features and gentle eyes'.[47] His daughter, Sofia Alekseievna, who secured her seven-year regency (1682–9) through intrigues, crimes and bloodshed, seemed to have traded her youth and beauty for power: 'This plain and stout semi-spinster, with a thick short waist, a clumsy head and crude features, who looked forty at the age of twenty, had sacrificed her conscience to ambition and her modesty to the demands of her temperament'.[48] Without doubt, one of Kliuchevskii's finest demonstrations in this technique of correlating physical and behavioural attributes was his introduction to the personality of Peter the Great, a portrait that many consider a masterpiece:

> Intellectually, Peter the Great was one of those simpleminded people who can be read at a glance and are easily understood.
> Physically, Peter was a giant of just under seven feet, and at any gathering he towered a full head above everybody else. During the Easter service he had so much bending to do that he invariably suffered from backache. [...]. [T]races of a serious nervous disorder due either to the memories of the bloody scenes of 1682, or to his all too frequent debaucheries, or to a combination of both, ruined his health. [...]. Very soon, by the time he was twenty, he began to suffer from a nervous twitch of the head; and when he was lost in thought, or during moments of emotional stress, his round, handsome face became distorted with convulsions. This, together with a birthmark on his right cheek, and a habit of gesticulating with his arms as he walked, made everybody notice him.[49]

These visible features and mannerisms provided Kliuchevskii with the components of the tsar's psychological makeup. If Peter's simple intellect, physical dexterity and strength, his frugal tastes and coarseness made him one of the people (and decidedly out of place in royal courts across Europe), his nervous disorder, exacerbated by brutalities he witnessed first hand in the court as a boy, clouded his energy and spontaneity with an aura of cold brutality, 'as cold, but as explosive, as one of his Petrozavodsk cannons'.[50]

The image of the 'artisan-tsar' captured brilliantly the peculiar tensions between Peter's personality, his likes and dislikes, and his public role.[51] As tsar, Peter sought to establish his undisputed authority by introducing Western models of ceremonial pomp into the Russian Court; as the uncouth artisan, however, he frequently subverted these newly acquired trappings of political power by reverting to type – spontaneous, given to childish pranks, lacking in decorum and entirely unpredictable:

> Whenever he went visiting he would sit down in the first vacant seat; if he was hot he would take off his kaftan in front of everybody. When he was invited to act as Marshal of Ceremonies at a wedding he would fulfill his obligations punctiliously and then, having put his Marshal's rod of office away in a corner, would move towards the buffet, take a hot roast of meat in his hands, and start eating. It was

this habit of dispensing with knives and forks at table that had so shocked the princesses at Koppenburg. He had no manners whatsoever, and did not consider them necessary.[52]

According to Kliuchevskii, the tsar's mockery of ceremony and tradition, particularly the Church hierarchy, and even of his own personal power had a harmless, childlike quality about it ('in the same way that children imitate the words, actions and facial expressions of adults, without meaning either to criticize or to insult them'[53]). Crucially though, that Peter acted on the spur of the moment without making plans for the future was a personality trait which, for Kliuchevskii, had telling consequences for an assessment of his programme of modernization. Historically, Kliuchevskii argued, reforms are 'the product of all the previous history of a people' and are simply natural responses to long-recognized needs.[54] This view of Peter's reforms challenged broadly accepted interpretations of the tsar as the architect, ex nihilo, of Russia's modernization that had been advanced by historians and thinkers since the first half of the eighteenth century. Whether they applauded his achievements or accused him of betraying national values, Tatishchev, Lomonosov, Derzhavin, Karamzin and even Solov'ev did not disturb the underlying premise of 'modernization by design'. By contrast, Kliuchevskii's account of Peter's personality and the ways it shaped his behaviour as an autocratic ruler effectively undermined, by belittling, competing Westernizer and Slavophile images of Peter, whether as a modernizer of Russia or as a traitor to the nation's indigenous traditions. If he conceded that Peter was 'an authoritative, intelligent, energetic, and talented individual, one of those (…) who appear from time to time,' he was quick to qualify that this was 'for no apparent reason'.[55] In sum, Peter the Great's achievements were simply due to the fact that he responded to circumstances at the appropriate time, not because of foresight or genius[56]:

> Peter […] regarded everything he did as an immediate necessity rather than as a reform, and did not notice how his actions changed both people and the established system […]. Indeed, it was only during the last decade of his life, when the effects of his reforms were already fairly obvious, that he realized that he had done something new and spectacular. His better understanding of what he had done, however, did not help him understand how he might act in the future. Peter thus became a reformer by accident, as it were, and even unwillingly.[57]

Individuals as epochal personalities: Tsar Alexei and Afanasii Ordin-Nashchokin

Kliuchevskii's interest in historical personalities lay not with what made them distinctive as individuals, rather the ways in which their lives could be instructive of the complexities of a given social-economic historical context. While he accepted that their actions made them catalysts of change, the emphasis he placed on history's most visible men and women as representative, typical figures, who 'harness' all the interests and characteristics of their milieu reflected his deeper social historical preoccupations and fundamental belief that the subject of history was not man, but people.[58] We see this at work in his account of the zigzag course of pre-reform in the second half of the seventeenth century, which he placed in relation to the worldviews of Peter's father, Tsar Alexei Mikhailovich, and one of the most prominent statesmen of the age, Afanasii Ordin-Nashchokin (1605–80):

> One of the two conflicting currents [in the seventeenth century – FN] that agitated Russian society was driving it back to the old order of things, and the other was drawing it forward to dim and alien horizons. These mutually opposed tendencies gave rise to vague feelings and aspirations in the community at large, but in men who were in advance of it these moods and strivings became clear-cut ideas to be carried out in practice. The study of such representative types will help us to understand more fully the kind of life that bred them. They focused in themselves, as it were, and vividly exemplified interests and characteristics of their environment that escape notice in everyday life, where they only occasionally come to the surface as accidental individual peculiarities leading nowhere.[59]

Peter the Great's father typified the first stage of the reform process: 'Tsar Alexei Mikhailovich's attitude might be described as that of a man who firmly rested one foot on the native Orthodox ground, and lifted the other to cross the boundary – and permanently remained in this uncertain position'.[60] Not dissimilar to Granovskii's sympathetic portrayal of Louis IX, Kliuchevskii depicted Alexei as a benign, yet passive proponent of reform, which his elder statesmen Ordin-Nashchokin and Golitsyn then acted upon in a series of well-defined measures by 'taking the West as a pattern in all things and following the example of foreign lands'.[61] The tsar and Ordin-Nashchokin complemented each other as polar opposite personality types. If Alexei's gentle demeanour, piety and sybaritic indulgence were characteristic of 'old Russia', Ordin-Nashchokin's subtle, tenacious intelligence, his tendency to grumble and constantly find fault with everything were the features of the forward-looking 'new man': bold, self-confident, pragmatic and exacting in his quest for reform.[62] Both men were concerned with the welfare of the nation, but they conceived 'welfare' in diametrically opposed ways. For Alexei, welfare meant 'eternal salvation' and involved measures of diplomatic compromise in order to maintain the status quo ante. By contrast, Ordin-Nashchokin focused his attention on the nation's political and social institutions and, according to Kliuchevskii, 'managed to find something new in the old Russian way of life, to discover its still untouched and unexploited resources, and make use of them for the good of all'.[63] To this end, he and other 'new men' (Rtishchev, Golitsyn) applied Western scholarship and achievements 'not to undermine Russia's spiritual heritage, rather to defend its vital principles against deadening routine, against a harsh and narrow interpretation instilled in the masses by a bad political and ecclesiastical leadership'.[64] Arguably, then, the emphasis Kliuchevskii placed on the incompatible intentions, pledges and convictions of those most closely involved with the process of social change yielded a more nuanced account of Russia's modernization as – paradoxically – a process of cooperation, rather than one of contest, between the defender of old Russia and the advocate of change. In the case of Alexei and his statesman, sharp differences in temperament seemed to function as mutual reinforcements assuring the success of the reform process. In Kliuchevskii's words:

> They were the last and the best representatives of ancient Russia, and gave a colouring of their own to the tendencies they introduced or supported. Tsar Alexei Mikhailovich awakened a vague general taste for novelty and improvement without breaking with the native past. Good-naturedly blessing incipient reforms, he gradually accustomed timid Russian minds to them. His kindly disposition inspired belief that there was no moral harm in foreign novelties, and that we must not lose faith in our own powers.
>
> His minister, Ordin-Nashchokin, was not so good-natured or so piously devoted to native traditions as the Tsar, and his constant grumblings against everything Russian might well have reduced one to hopeless dejection and inertia. But his honest energy was irresistible, and his bright intellect converted vague strivings toward reform into such simple, clear, and convincing plans that their usefulness seemed obvious, and one wanted to believe that they were both reasonable and practical. For the first time in Russian history a coherent system of reforms was being developed from his suggestions, suppositions, and experiments. It was not a wide programme, but it was a well-delineated plan for administrative and economic innovations.[65]

Towards a study of national psychology

Robert Byrnes has suggested that Kliuchevskii may have given increased prominence to particular persons as a teaching device: certainly, his portraits mark some of the most engaging and memorable sections of the *Course*.[66] But, as Byrnes also implies, the rich gallery of portraits that he produced never really altered his views on the role of individuals in history. Rather, his decision to anchor the momentum of reform in personality types, his use of Tsar Alexis and Ordin-Nashchokin to exemplify the characteristics of old and new Russia, or Peter as a tool to expose the (comical effect of) cultural differences between Russia and the European West, was consistent with his view of history as a relentless probing for psychological explanations of the processes behind historical change. Given his deepening concern with fundamental aspects of national character, it was pretty clear that the idea of the self-sufficient individual removed from social context could be of little interest to him.[67] He therefore tended to typecast individual 'great men'. Conceived as products of the social or ethical conventions of the age in which they were brought up, Kliuchevskii's cameos of the ancient Russian prince, Muscovite boyar, or man of service throw light on the elusive and often contradictory qualities of mindset and attitudes, qualities which he integrated into his account of major political events such as military conquest or legislative reform and their effects on the population.[68] If anything, he seemed more willing to 'individualize' the common folk, 'the men and women, rich and poor who gave their goods, even their lives to their fellow men and country'. For example, in a public lecture entitled 'The Good People of Ancient Russia', which he gave as part of a fund-raising effort during the harvest failure and famine of 1892, he singled out a certain Ul'iana Ustinovna Osor'ina, the widow of a small provincial landowner, who, during the famine of 1601–4, helped the poor and needy. In Kliuchevskii's eyes, this woman's heightened sense of charity was testimony to a life lived according to morality and the dictates of the heart. But, he concluded: 'No one has ever bothered to account for how many such Ul'ianas there were in Russia nor how many tears of hunger they soothed with their good hands'.[69]

In the concluding passages of the second lecture of his course in Russian history, Kliuchevskii wrote: 'And if you are able to acquire from my presentation, however full of deficiencies, if only the most general features of the Russian people (*obraz russkogo naroda*) as a historical personality (*istoricheskaia lichnost'*), I will consider the purpose of my course achieved'.[70] As I suggested at the beginning of this chapter, Kliuchevskii's conception of history presents a number of affinities with the ideas of Hippolyte Taine. Like Taine, Kliuchevskii rejected the notion of rigid periodization, or progress, in favour of the idea of the 'flow of history'. 'History', Kliuchevskii reminds us, 'has few sharp breaks, saints, heroes, or devils. It lacks a beginning and an ending. It is organic and continuous, unspectacular and gradual, flowing like a river and sometimes spilling over the banks'.[71] It followed that, by placing men and women in the flow of history, he could not – without ruining the metaphor – present them as harbingers of a new era; rather, they encapsulated and defined the spirit of the age in which they lived. For Kliuchevskii, this made fictional protagonists no less than historical 'great men' viable candidates for deepening an understanding of national character. As I discuss in the next chapter, this was nowhere more evident than in his treatment of the eighteenth- and early-nineteenth-century Russian nobility: 'Onegin', he claimed, 'is as much historical as poetic'.[72] Fictional protagonists and plot provided him with original materials for charting the damaging socio-psychological impact of Western culture on Russian traditions and customs, namely the moral and cultural disfigurement of the nobility and the resulting chasm between it and the common folk, which Kliuchevskii so deplored.

Ivan Grevs: Economic biography

For the period, the 1890s, Grevs' study of land management in the ancient world was fairly topical: it formed part of a body of literature dedicated to socio-economic issues that had grown exponentially in the decades following the 1861 Emancipation Act. However, it was his novel anthropological approach to economic questions that drew the critical attention of peers.[73] Grevs proposed an ambitious line of historical–biographical enquiry as a tool for bridging a narrative of political and socio-economic events during the late Roman era with a cultural and intellectual history of everyday life and mentality. To his mind, researching the ways in which individual figures acquired and safeguarded their wealth during a particularly turbulent period of Roman history as it transitioned from republic to empire was instructive of certain qualitative changes within the economy which impacted both the growth of the state and the social and cultural profile of its population.[74] His choice of case studies – the prominent magnate,

Atticus Titus Pomponius, and the lyric poet, Horace (discussed in Chapter 5), was also quite unusual: both had been mainly studied by classists, Atticus for his Epicureanism, Horace for his verse. But for Grevs, integrating their worldviews into a study of their socio-economic profiles as landowners afforded a deeper understanding of what he believed to be the fundamentally organic nature of historical change. In light of this, the importance of uncovering sociological laws was not, he argued, just 'for a correct understanding of the conditions that shape society', but also 'in order to define the quality and degree of active influence on society of consciousness and of its bearer, namely, the human person'.[75]

Grevs argued that there were two types of historical–economic study: the first is based on analyses of historical–economic data contained within a single source or a clearly defined set of materials, such as the work of a single author; the second involved working with information drawn from a wide variety of 'qualitative' sources about one major land holding or a number of farms belonging to a single owner. Principal among the latter were not only personal impressions and correspondence, but also topography, architectural and painterly images, and archaeology, in other words, 'mute testimonies', which Grevs had studied as part of his research trips to Italy in the early 1890s.[76] If the first approach prioritized quantifiable juridical and economic data, the second demanded an understanding of subjective-psychological reality. In view of Grevs' underlying premise that, as he put it, 'relationship to the land was, for all classes of Romans, primordial',[77] the subjective and introspective qualities of these sources imparted a vital psychological perspective not found in runs of statistics. Moreover, it was not simply an exercise in extracting kernels of 'fact' from a mass of personal impressions in order to reconstruct the function of small and large-scale Roman estates; rather more ambitiously, Grevs' analysis of individual experiences was integral to his project of transforming the study of the economy into a man-centred historical enquiry. For Grevs, it was important not just to chart developments across the socio-economic, political and cultural arenas, but rather to analyse the ways in which these developments were processed by a given individual. Such a 'micro-historical' approach, Grevs believed, brought the historian closer to an understanding of the remote past. Methodologically, then, Grevs' incorporation of literary sources was intended as a means to counteract what he perceived as the negative effects on historical understanding of subject specialization in the humanities and social science research. To his mind, this was particularly evident in studies of the ancient world. He therefore presented the 'biographical method' and micro-historical enquiry as a way to overcome the prescriptive use of sources as practised by some of his elders and peers in the university.

Titus Pomponius Atticus (112/109 BC–35/32 BC), had, to date, mainly been studied by historians of literature and classical philologists interested in his role as a patron of the arts (for his 'Atticism', so-called) and his correspondence with the statesman and writer, Cicero.[78] But Grevs believed that his life was also highly instructive for the socio-economic historian. As he saw it, the process of aristocratization of the Roman social system, which concentrated wealth in the hands of a small number of people, yielded a number of distinctive socio-psychological types. He argued that Atticus exemplified a new category of landowning aristocracy who managed to consolidate his inherited wealth and lifestyle in a period of political upheaval and danger. Using Cornelius Nepos's biography and letters in addition to the writings of Cicero, Atticus' life-long friend with whom he corresponded, Grevs analysed the nature of his land-based wealth (*sostoianie*) paying particular attention to the ways in which he both maintained and used it to secure his position as – in sociological terms – a 'social actor'.[79] For Grevs, this remarkable expert (*znatok*), affable person (*serdets*), 'fisher of men' (*lovets dushi*) and, especially as the architect of his own, personal wellbeing (*blagopoluchiia*) had the ability equally to impress (*imponirovat'*) Roman statesmen, such as Sulla and Cicero, and the first Roman Emperor, Augustus.[80] Reared on old republican ideals, wealthy magnates like Atticus typically saw themselves as bearers of a truly national, class-based tradition, on the strength of which they claimed the inalienability of their privileges.[81] But, as Rome abandoned its republican principles for the premises of monarchical rule, retreat to the land became the only option to safeguard personal wealth and security. Once distanced from centres of political power, they focused their attention on accommodating 'the old socio-economic system of large-scale aristocratic landownership and economic prowess to the new, imperial, political system'.[82] In this connection, Grevs believed, the case of Atticus was especially instructive for the social historian: what he called Atticus' 'socio-political physiognomy', namely an 'Epicurean-inspired political judiciousness' informing the strategies he employed to maintain his position, characterized, on a micro-level, the emergence of a new type of individual (*lichnost'*). There was, Grevs claimed, a discernible shift away 'from communal expressions of republican patriotism towards a cultivation of the 'inner growth' of the individual (*lichnost'*). Predicated on the idea of autonomy and independent wellbeing, this self-determining person signified a new set of principles anchored in the life of the 'private individual' (*chastnoe litso*). Henceforth, man (*ideal cheloveka*) was conceived as the foundation stone of a new civilization.[83]

Grevs traced the origins of this idea of *lichnost'* to the power struggles and conspiracies involving prominent statesmen during the republican (Hellenistic) period. Initially expressed as a form of 'egoism' or concern for the self, it gradually filtered into the upper echelons of society where it assumed connotations of socio-political indifference and self-interest.[84] Philosophically, this paradigm shift underscored the view that the sole purpose of human activity was personal happiness and that the attainment of inner equilibrium could be achieved only by distancing oneself from the public sphere. Neither Stoics nor Epicureans, the two schools of thought harnessing this view, could, Grevs argued, be advocates for republicanism: the former rejected all possibility of reaching the goal of inner harmony in the current socio-political climate; proponents of the latter, while retaining a certain attachment to the republican model, were nevertheless guided by principles of discretion which dictated that they lead their lives out of the limelight, and away from politics. In Grevs' view, this made them better suited to the imperialist model of governance.[85] Such men, he noted, did not flaunt the wealth they had accumulated; rather, they used it as a means to encourage mutually advantageous relations among peers. The life of Atticus fitted the credentials of this 'new social type' very well: 'The philosophical teaching he embraced consisted in a form of relations among people that were mutually advantageous and justifiable from a moral perspective'.[86]

Atticus had steeped himself in Epicurean teaching, the pursuit of spiritual good over material satisfaction, while he was in voluntary exile in Athens, and, in Grevs' interpretation, it was the idea of friendship, 'a union, freely entered into, and in which the individual feels no constraints placed on him', that was to become the magnate's guiding life principle.[87] Recognizing that strong bonds and connections would help him protect his great territorial wealth and ultimately withstand the political storms, he decided to put this ethics of self-interest and individual advantage through mutually beneficial acts into practice on his return to Rome (65 BC). Using his wealth to establish connections, he soon found himself at the centre of an intricate system of 'friendly unions'.[88] Admired as a man of refined tastes and mind, knowledgeable in literature and philosophy without falling prey to pedantry, he acted as a benefactor and councillor while remaining true to Epicurean principles, namely 'to forge (*kovat'*) his own, personal happiness'.[89]

Grevs conceived the dual socio-economic and intellectual–political axes of his study as tools for attaining an 'integral cultural–historical' understanding of the nascent empire and its impact on the higher echelons of society.[90] In this connection, it is worth noting that his portrayal of Atticus as a modified revival of the old system of social relationships based on patronage differed significantly from the interpretation advanced by Fustel de Coulanges whose comprehensive studies of the ancient world had originally inspired Grevs to take up the topic. For the French historian, Atticus's retreat from the political centre stage typified the abandonment of patriotism and social responsibility for hedonism.[91] For Grevs, by contrast, Atticus' behaviour was entirely consistent with his Epicurean values, informing a new understanding of what it meant to be a good citizen. As I discuss in the next chapter, Grevs' other case study – an exercise in local history in which he endeavoured to reconstruct Horace's villa not solely with respect to textual evidence but with reference to topography, paintings and sculpture – established one further significant point of difference with the French master's famous instruction, namely to study 'texts, texts, nothing other than texts'.[92]

Biography and history

According to Nikolai Antsiferov, Grevs' former pupil and, after 1917, close colleague and collaborator,

> Grevs greatly valued the idiosyncratic (*svoeobychnoe*). Through his studies of the individual he came to understand an epoch [...], his approach to people required great care, scientific rigor and honesty so as not to distort the 'images of mankind' that he created. All this imparted to his historical characteristics a certain warmth of understanding. We should recall how the artistic truthfulness and strength of image with which he sketched Atticus, Seneca, Pliny the Younger, St Francis of Assisi, afforded a deeper understanding of the era as a whole.[93]

In some respects, Grevs developed his 'biographical method' out of necessity. The paucity of statistical and legal records relative to the period he was studying, as well as their failure to account for the ways legal measures actually filtered into the day-to-day routine existence of the population or, indeed, their impact on social wellbeing and cultural practices meant that he was more or less compelled to seek answers elsewhere. But once he applied his research agenda to a body of writing that, up until that point, had been considered the reserve of classical philologists, he recognized its enormous potential, both substantively, that is, for rethinking the historical process, and institutionally in terms of what he regarded as the negative effects of specialization within the discipline.[94] At his viva, in 1900, he listed what he believed were the advantages of his new approach:

> The broad and systematic application of the biographical method may benefit economic research into ancient Rome, significantly: 1) in the absence of statistics, it is an important support for assessing how widespread large land holdings were; 2) it affords details of the way they were managed on a day-to-day basis; 3) it affords a deeper understanding of social change and its impact on the daily life of individual; 4) it paves the way for exploring the links between the economy as a system and the political order, for understanding the relationship between the collective process in the life of a people (nation) and individual consciousness, the interaction between the material and ideal principles in history.[95]

The last two points mentioned here fed into Grevs' views concerning the historical process as a continual interaction between the individual and the socio-cultural environment, and the importance he invested in bringing the individual back onto centre stage. It was not, of course, a matter of reviving theories of great men as drivers of political change; rather, as he put it, with the help of the biographical method, 'we have the opportunity to look into the secret laboratory of ideas where reflections of the world are generated'.[96] To his mind, such 'living' concrete-historical material provided the only possible platform on which to explore general tendencies. Arguably, this was micro-history *avant la lettre*; Grevs, himself, used the terms 'microscopic' and 'miniature'.[97] As a new methodology, then, intended to bridge classical scholarship and socio-economic history, Grevs believed his case studies had broader implications as an antidote to the current trend towards specialization and the development of technical skills. While he accepted that this was part and parcel of the process of institutionalizing knowledge, he was critical of the types of historical practice that this seemed to be generating, namely an overly prescriptive use of sources, such as statistics and legal records favoured by economists (most of which, in any case, post-dated the period of transition that he was interested in) or anachronistic interpretations arising from research with strong agendas, most notably, Marxist historiography predicated on the idea of progress.[98] In a letter to his friend, Viacheslav Ivanov, which he reproduced in the conclusion to his thesis, Grevs formulated his view of the historian's task:

> Just as philologists have hardly ever tried to become economists in order to study the history of ancient economy, likewise, economists have been little disposed to acquire the philological skills necessary for understanding the life of people in the classical era. At the present time, with factual and methodological obstacles obstructing the discovery of the truth in such a difficult area in the science of

society, the obligation to be prepared for battle on several fronts has become the responsibility and the creed of historians. It is precisely the historian who has to become a 'synthetized type' of researcher and thinker so as to understand all the complexities in the process of world history as well as its core unity (*edinstvo*). He has to have the ability to discern (*urazumet'*) the diverse phenomena within all the patterns and configurations that comprise the historical process.[99]

The reference to 'synthesis' is key here: inherited from his mentor-*nastavnik*, Vasilevskii, it underpinned Grevs' bid to remedy the current trend in research culture of compartmentalizing historical knowledge, mentioned above. It was also directed at university teaching practices, which continued to privilege the history of political institutions and great men, with only the occasional excursus into the culture of a given era. As Grevs noted in his obituary tribute, Vasilevskii had developed his 'synthetic approach' as a tool for the in-depth study of more specific time spans and regions so as to highlight what he believed was the complex and fundamentally non-linear, organic character of historical change.[100] In much the same vein, Grevs contrasted what he called 'external history', that is, 'a narrative of essentially "concrete," "discrete," "momentary," "intermittent" events' (*razskazyvat' o sobytiiakh*), with 'knowledge of the formation of culture' (*poznat' slozhenie kul'tury*), which, in his view, constitutes the goal of 'inner history'. To this end, he proposed the study of 'phenomena', such as cult, forms of ownership and exchange, family life, judicial systems, poetic tastes and national temperaments: 'Only on this basis', he told his students, 'is it possible to understand the past of mankind scientifically. Only in this way may we work "*ad intelligendum*" towards knowledge and an understanding of this past (and avoid writing history "*ad narrandum*" as chroniclers, or "*ad aedificandum*" in the manner of historian–pragmatists)'.[101]

The reception of Grevs' thesis by peers suggests that he was regarded as the pioneer of a scholarly, albeit somewhat quirky, new methodology. In a review essay of the published version of the thesis, Nikolai Kareev applauded his colleague's achievements: Grevs' findings afforded valuable insights into the evolution of the Roman Empire; his methodology raised important questions about the peculiarities of the economy in the ancient world. In this connection, he added: 'Atticus is drawn brilliantly; he emerges both as a living individual and as a typical representative of an entire class of people'.[102] As the author of monographs and essays on similar questions himself, Kareev clearly welcomed Grevs' decision to ground social history in a study of the interactions between man (*lichnost'*) and his socio-cultural milieu: Grevs' treatment of the individual as the 'creator' rather than the product of a cultural milieu or as an 'illustrative example' was especially significant since it restored a level of agency that was missing in much contemporary historiography. (Kliuchevskii's view of individuals also comes to mind, here.)[103] If Kareev had some misgivings about Grevs' actual handling of lyrical material in his case study of Horace (discussed in the next chapter), he argued that his colleague's attempt to reconstruct an economic history of landownership in the Roman Empire on the basis of seemingly inappropriate (*neprigodnyi*) literary sources was truly novel and original: Grevs had demonstrated 'enormous erudition (*uchenost'*)'.[104]

'For me', Grevs wrote a few years later, 'history is the biography of mankind, and mankind is the gradual construction of a great person (*velikaia lichnost'*), a massive tree growing out of many roots which come together in a huge trunk breaking down further into a multitude of branches, expressing unity in multiplicity, the end of which we do not know and may only partially divine'.[105] The biographical method that Grevs developed in his master's dissertation would ultimately inform the two principal axes of his teaching and research throughout his entire career: the study of mentality and belief systems, and urban culture. As windows onto an age, the study of human experience required a psychological acuity, or empathy, on the part of the historian, which he, but also Kliuchevskii and Granovskii before him, recognized as an essential skillset alongside an informed critique of the written (and visual) sources available to them.[106] However, endeavours to understand past human experience and representations of the world did – as Kareev noted – incur the risk of surrendering historical accuracy (truth) to poetic licence. As I have argued, there is little doubt that Kliuchevskii's artistry in character analysis and storytelling was a condition of his intellectual authority as a public enlightener; his detailed portraits of Ivan the Terrible, Tsar Alexis, Peter the Great and others must be recognized, as Kiesewetter, yet another former pupil, put it 'as real pearls of imaginative literature'.[107] But for the Soviet historiographer, Nikolai Rubinshtein, while Kliuchevskii's portrait gallery of historical figures confirmed his literary skills, it also exposed his weaknesses as a historian.

> It is in this artistry that Kliuchevskii's celebrated strengths as a historian lie, his path of probing (*proniknovenie*) into concrete reality. It is through this living image that he sometimes succeeds in resurrecting the unity of a phenomenon (*edinstvo iavleniia*) […], touches the inner connection that binds together the disparate elements into an organic whole. But herein resides Kliuchevskii's weakness, because this synthesis has no support in a solid scientific base, it does not withstand critical verification. The error of the artist results in a distortion of historical knowledge. Take for example, his account of the *oprichnina*, which he subordinates entirely to his preconceived (*uslovno*) psychological image of Ivan IV thereby draining it of any real historical content (which Solov'ev had unearthed before him).[108]

As a richly ironical side note, it is worth recalling Kliuchevskii's rather damning assessment of Karamzin, Russia's original master of a literary infused historical account, on identical grounds.

> Karamzin's Russian princes of the eleventh and twelfth centuries (the Kievan period) think and behave in exactly the same way as the northern princes of the fourteenth and fifteenth centuries, as cyphers exemplifying one or another moral principle – duty, honour, good, evil, passion, betrayal, virtue. Karamzin had no sense of historical development and change. His view of history was informed not by historical laws (*istoricheskaia zakonomernost'*), rather by moral–psychological aesthetics […]. He did not explain or generalize; rather he depicted, moralized and

admired. He wanted to turn the history of Russia not so much into an 'ode to the Russian nation' as Lomonosov had done, but into a heroic epic celebrating Russian valour and glory.[109]

But it is also worth noting that despite his dismissal of Karamzin's ahistoricism, Kliuchevskii did not follow the example of his immediate teacher, Solov'ev, mentioned by Rubinshtein for the scientific rigour with which he reconstructed the past: for both Rubinshtein and the émigré Michael Karpovich, any concerns that Solov'ev may have had over the beauty of his narrative would have taken him a long way from his main aim to provide a detailed history of the nation. Still, as the proverbial 'historian's historian', his dedication to a balanced, detailed reconstruction of the past was not rewarded by a place in the pantheon of national historical masterpieces; simply put, his narrative lacked colour.[110]

As I discuss in the next chapter, Kliuchevskii uncovered a wealth of material in belles lettres on the basis of which he presented a highly readable, psychological–cultural account of the eighteenth-century nobility. Drawing upon a rich inventory of sources including, in addition to fiction, legal record, memoir, notes and impressions by foreign visitors, he combined real and created personages with ease to chart the moral malaise of this social estate together with the deleterious consequences of this 'moral confusion' for the outlook, tastes and behaviour of the generations that followed. For his part, Grevs incorporated literary and personal impressions into his case study of the lyric poet, Horace, as a landowner in the late Roman period. If lacking the narrative flair of his slightly older peer, Grevs' experiment nevertheless confirmed the place of creative literature as a resource in an otherwise science-led historical enquiry.

5

Literary Evidence: Realist Aesthetics and Historical Enquiry

In the 1860s, the idea that a work of realistic art could be treated as a phenomenon of actual life was commonplace: truth (*istinnost'*) or authenticity in the representation of social reality became the central aesthetic category.[1] In addition, realist fiction often had an openly didactic intention: a new breed of protagonists such as Rakhmetov, Chernyshevskii's rational egoist, the so-called new man in his influential novel, *What Is to Be Done?* (1863), and Ivan Turgenev's anti-hero, the nihilist Bazarov in *Fathers and Sons* (1862), were brought to life on the page as models (or negative portents, in the case of Bazarov) of social and cultural changes.[2] Accounts by contemporaries confirm that young radical *intelligenty* became wholly committed to the new ideologically engaged aesthetics, with some, such as the writer and social critic Dmitrii Pisarev, widely considered Bazarov's 'alter ego', even going as far as to play out their lives 'in character'.[3] As one older contemporary, the literary critic Nikolai Strakhov, noted in a fairly damning account, Pisarev had made himself the 'lyrical hero' of his articles and thus was not so much a 'theorist of *bazarovshchina*' as a peculiar clone (*inobytie*) of Bazarov himself: 'Of course, Bazarov does not look at things the way Pisarev does. Even though he denies art its real value, Pisarev does in fact acknowledge it as such, whereas Bazarov rejects it outright because he has a deeper understanding of it'. In Strakhov's eyes, Pisarev's Bazarov-style ramblings and homilies, his excessive preoccupation with his own 'Bazarov image' had taken him down a path full of contradictions, which undermined the effect he was after. In the end, it was the fictional hero, that is, the 'real Bazarov' (*nastoiashchii Bazarov*), who came across as more profound than his admirer.[4] Strakhov's words may have been intended to caution readers against Pisarev's literary–critical posturing, but the point to stress here is that his observation concerning a far-reaching confusion between fact and fiction as a feature of the post-1860s generation perfectly encapsulates the ethos of aesthetic realism: since literature was regarded as a maximally precise and direct representation of reality, it followed that it could very readily be equated with the real world.[5]

The broad assumptions of realist aesthetics as an authentic representation of reality briefly described here informed the ways Kliuchevskii and Grevs handled creative literature. Both men recognized that fiction contained evidence of everyday life and served as a valuable resource for grasping the intangible realms of human motivation, tastes and attitudes. If Grevs justified his inclusion of Horace's lyric poetry in his study of farm management during the late Roman era on the grounds of a paucity of economic and legal sources and made a case for the factual reliability of the poet's impressions, it was also his belief that the social–psychological observations they contained 'complete our understanding of this period in Roman history by accounting for the ways in which economic change impacted everyday life, social mood and not just "external facts"'.[6] As I mentioned in the previous chapter, it was Grevs' view that for all classes of Romans, relationship to the land was primordial. And Horace, a landowner himself, was no exception in this regard: as Grevs would argue in his thesis, impressions of agrarian life played a key role in the poet's imagination providing him with numerous motifs and topics. For the historian, these lyrical impressions (Grevs was referring to the Odes composed around 27 BCE) offered reliable information about the day-to-day experiences in the running of a middle-sized farm.

Kliuchevskii envied the freedom of the artist.[7] Among commentators of his work, there seems to be a consensus that his professional interests underwent a shift away from economic questions to politics and a growing interest in inner, psychological factors. If he never entirely lost his admiration for the precision of the scientist in search of natural law, and remained convinced that it was possible to reveal man's inner nature by working out the regularities of social history (one of the main points he made in the methodological introduction to his lectures), he 'yielded more than once', as Alfred Rieber writes, 'to the temptation of probing intuitively the spiritual depths of man through literary masterpieces'.[8] This is nowhere more in evidence than in his work on the Russian nobility where he brought to his arsenal of historical enquiry sources such as Russian belles lettres and unpublished archival material.[9] Alongside legal records and economic data, the novels, plays and poetry of Pushkin, Griboedov, Fonvizin and Lermontov provided him with original materials for charting social transformation in the eighteenth and early nineteenth centuries. As Chumachenko has argued, the originality of Kliuchevskii's work in this regard was that this rich inventory of sources allowed him to characterize the everyday '*byt*' (way of life) and mores of Petersburg high society, 'its colour and culture', to capture the emergence of new socio-historical types, and, specifically, the moral and intellectual disfigurement of the nobility resulting from the gulf that had grown up between it and the common folk.[10]

If, then, like Grevs, Kliuchevskii accepted the close correlation between fiction and fact, his handling of literary material was not at all limited to its value as a complement to economic and legal data nor, indeed, as evidence for a specific theme; rather, in tracing the historical template for some of the nation's most famous fictional protagonists – Pushkin's Evgenii Onegin, Griboedov's Chatskii and Fonvizin's Mitrofan – he made the literary-artist's perceptions integral to understanding the broader processes of Russian history.[11] In addition, as I have said, he took them as models for the creation of his own generational personality types – from the moral vacuity of the noble adolescent in the age of Catherine the Great, the heroic, if misguided Decembrist, to the superfluous man and the repentant nobleman – so as to reconstruct the manner in which the educated classes and the people became irrevocably separated, alienated from one another. However, as I discuss below, while Kliuchevskii's public addresses commemorating the work of Fonvizin and Pushkin undeniably confirm the importance he placed in their literary confections as a historical resource, his analyses, paradoxically, also had the effect of turning the didactic principles of realistic aesthetics upside down: rather than a 'guide to life', or a model to emulate, the gallery of grotesque figures that he created was to serve as a reminder of the disastrous consequences of emulating, in an unreflective manner, the lifestyle of others.

From Mitrofan to Onegin: The moral decline of the Russian nobility

Kliuchevskii used fiction to build on a single leading theme – the tragi-comic identity crisis of the Russian nobility resulting from the legacy of Peter the Great's modernizing reforms in the early eighteenth century. Emulating the spirit of Buslaev's wry comment about the 'high society created by Peter the Great' which he had likened to the airy void of 'German-style knickerbockers' (*Nemetskie pantalonniki*'[12]), Kliuchevskii traced the moral and cultural ruins of the nobility across three generations with reference to the domestic impact of Enlightenment thought, the Napoleonic wars and the Decembrist uprising. In an essay about Fonvizin's *Nedorosl'* (*The Minor*), for example, he took the satirical play as a starting point to speak to the moral and social complexion of the late-eighteenth nobility in the wake of Peter III's famous ukaz on the granting of freedoms and liberties to Russian nobles (18 February 1762).[13] However, whereas Fonvizin set out to poke fun at the newly emancipated landed nobility as a parasitic class leading a frivolous existence on the unpaid labours of its serfs while failing to exercise the leadership that might have otherwise justified its privileges,[14] the point, for Kliuchevskii, was to draw attention to the detrimental consequences of the new ruling for the very existence of the estate as a whole. In Ancient Rus', the title of noble *nedorosl'* designated an adolescent up to the age of fifteen. It was, as Kliuchevskii notes, an entire state institution, an entire page in the history of Russian law with detailed prescriptions concerning obligatory education in preparation for military service. Kliuchevskii reminds the reader that although Peter III's manifesto released the nobility from twenty-five years of military service, it still emphasized the need for education as a condition of its social entitlements. Obligatory military service was replaced by a moral obligation to perform civil service: as members of the privileged educated class (i.e. as owners of land and serfs), it was their moral obligation to care for the wellbeing of their serfs and to set an example. In other words, if the decree abolished obligatory service, training/education (*obuchenie*) continued to be compulsory:

> The law read: 'be good, serve, and educate your children. Failure to do so will result in expulsion from society.' The wording of the ukaz contained the 'hope' that the nobility would not evade service, but that it would engage in it zealously, and in no less degree endeavour to ensure that their offspring acquired an appropriate education. In addition, by virtue of their privileges as landowners, the nobility were morally obligated to perform a civic 'duty of care', providing their serfs with a model of good conduct worthy of emulation.[15]

As Kliuchevskii put it: 'Rights without responsibility is a juridical nonsense'.[16] But the terms and conditions of freedom outlined in the ukaz were widely misapprehended (or wilfully misread) as licence to do as one pleased, and Fonvizin's characters were testimony to this confusion. That Mrs Prostakov took it as an official sanctioning of her own lawlessness (*chto zakon opravdyvaet ee bezzakonie*) was, he argued, a naïve reading of the ukaz; yet, it was one that was entirely symptomatic of the abnormal phenomena in Russian life for which the decree had, inadvertently, become a catalyst.[17] In Kliuchevskii's reading, this nonsense informed the play's central message: Prostakova was effectively pronouncing a death sentence on the estate, which, at that time (the late eighteenth century), was not yet intending to die out. With his dominant traits of idleness, clumsy imitation of Western manners, Mrs Prostakov's son, Mitrofan (*nedorosl'*), together with the succession of generations that came after him should, Kliuchevskii argued, be seen as a casualty of the new ruling.[18] In sum, Fonvizin had not written a comedy at all, rather, a tragedy.

What Kliuchevskii esteemed as the viability of a work of fiction for the historian is evident from the strapline he gave for his essay on Fonvizin: 'Experiment in an historical explanation of an instructional play' (*Opyt istoricheskogo ob'iasneniia uchebnoi p'esy*). If, as he acknowledged, the play had lost its contemporary relevance and novelty, it had acquired interest as an artistic monument, namely as a portrayal of what he termed 'the concepts and practices implanted in a cultural soil on which we now tread, and of its fruit upon which we now feed'.[19] Interestingly, not only did Kliuchevskii consider it unnecessary to scrutinize or test the factual validity of the playwright's impressions, he even went as far as to challenge the common perception of Fonvizin's characters – Starodum, Milon, Pravdin, Sofia – as mere puppets exemplifying different moralities: 'Were their actual prototypes any more real?', he asked. Kliuchevskii's point here was that Fonvizin did not so much write a comedy, as hold up a mirror up to life, and copied what he saw: he simply took the protagonists of *Nedorosl'* directly from the maelstrom of ordinary life, ridding them of all cultural guises and set them centre stage where they exposed their messy rapport with one another and the chaos of their disorderly interests and instincts.[20] Fonvizin's caricature was thus a telling fact of life. Indeed, as the unwitting casualty of new regulations affecting the duties and privileges of the nobility, Mitrofan's upbringing had already disfigured him far more than the playwright's comedy was able to ridicule him.[21] Clever and quick witted in his own way, Mitrofan reflected upon things, not, though, with the aim of finding something out, rather with the aim of extricating himself from something. His behaviour was not funny, but repulsive. 'It is dangerous to laugh at him, for the Mitrofans will exact revenge by virtue of their proliferation as a breed (...), just like insects or microbes'.[22]

Much the same view concerning the consequences of a bad education and ugly kowtowing before the West formed the leitmotif of possibly one of Kliuchevskii's most celebrated pieces about the fictional Evgenii Onegin and his historical seventeenth- and eighteenth-century ancestors (*Evgenii Onegin i ego predki*).[23] Originally delivered as a public lecture in 1887 as part of the nation-wide commemoration of the fiftieth anniversary of Pushkin's death, 'Onegin', Kliuchevskii wrote, 'is an image that artistically reproduces a localized distortion (*mestnaia nelovkost'*) of one of the attitudes adopted by Russian society. He is not a general or predominant character-type of his time, but a typical exception. Such an image, of course, can only have historical ancestors, not genetic ones'.[24]

As Marshall Shatz argues, Kliuchevskii's genealogy of the nobility captured two elements of Russia's social and intellectual life that would have a profound impact on Russian history from Catherine's time onward: 'One was the cultural cleavage between the westernized elite and the rest of the population, a division that exacerbated social conflict and served to equate Western culture with class interest. The other was the radicalization that Western ideas might undergo when plucked from the historical context in which they had originally developed and replanted in a very different cultural soil'.[25] Both underscored a cultural identity crisis, which Pushkin captured in his account of 'Onegin' as a 'complex cultural type' (Kliuchevskii's expression), and which Kliuchevskii examined in terms of the way each successive generational reconfiguration of this type posed and dealt with one fundamental conundrum: 'Born a Russian, having recognized that a Russian is not a European, and faced with the task of becoming European'. If a noble living in the age of Catherine the Great had somehow managed this identity crisis without injury to his conscience, 'remaining happy and good', his son, exemplified by the figure of Chatskii (a reference to Griboedov's *Woe from Wit*[26]) in the age of Alexander I, would succumb to *toska* (melancholy/yearning). The Decembrists' younger brothers, Onegin and Pechorin (Pushkin's and Lermontov's protagonists, anti-heroes), who grew up in the wake of 1812, were from the outset broken men without meaning to give structure to their lives.[27] Their outer Byronic affectations were nourished by deeper, native traits – an underlying moral and intellectual disfigurement – the root cause of which Kliuchevskii located in the superficial, yet enforced, assimilation of Western values and in the severed ties with native traditions and customs that resulted from their distorted knowledge of foreign life. Their emancipation from service granted in the 1762 manifesto merely exacerbated this moral confusion, the force of which, Kliuchevskii noted, could be summarized in one single, simple rule: 'It is neither possible nor necessary to do anything'. Onegin was the embodiment of this rule.[28] In Kliuchevskii's reading, then, the root cause of Evgenii Onegin's moral and intellectual mutilation was much more than a matter of inherited personality traits; rather, it had to be sought in deeper underlying cultural–historical developments.[29] To this end, he presented a series of thumbnail sketches of Onegin's great-grandfather, an immediate contemporary of Peter the Great, his grandfather and father in the eighteenth century and, lastly, his older siblings – witnesses, sympathizers and/or victims of the Decembrist revolt of 1825.

Onegin's ancestors all belonged to the old Russian nobility. Onegin's great-grandfather lived in the second half of the seventeenth century. Typically, his upbringing consisted of a period of military training under the command of German officers to harness his spirited nature (*boikost'*) and time spent at the Spassky monastery to foster an intellectual curiosity. Here, he would receive Latin lessons from a Kievan elder: 'The religious elder introduced him to Catholic views on the holy Ghost, taught him Polish and the skill to recite doggerel'.[30] He would then be sent off to do military service (an allusion to Peter the Great's 1714 law on obligatory education for the nobility and training abroad in artillery or engineering skills with the army and navy) whereupon he began to question the value of the knowledge he had acquired from his Kievan masters, since what he now needed were practical skills to sew soldiers' leather boots (*spiridy*).[31]

After the death of Peter the Great, navigation skills gave way to other tastes: edification was superseded by entertainment, but with a tragic outcome for the noble's sense of identity. In St Petersburg, high society paid Germans generously so that they

> played the drums and stood on their head, while our navigator, finding himself in the company of his peers, felt that he was caught between two stools. Some teased and mocked him for his 'European manners'; others, themselves followers of fashion, considered that he was not sufficiently Europeanized by his experiences abroad. Our navigator eventually settled into a domestic life on his provincial estates (his wife bore him eighteen children, he went to Church, while the mathematical and navigational skills he had acquired in Holland were never put to use).[32]

Onegin's grandfather began his education in the age of Elizabeth Petrovna, completed it during the reign of Catherine II and lived out his days during the reign of Alexander I. Elizabeth Petrovna encouraged the cultivation of refined taste, the art of courtship, love and poetry. During her reign it became standard practice for a young noble to spend five to six years in the guards regiment and fifteen years as an officer, during which time he frequented the court theatre (twice a week) and high society balls. His compulsory education, 'which did not provide sufficient grounding in the sciences, prompted him to develop skills (*vyuchka*) – in the main provided by foreign tutors – in subjects not included in the official curriculum of dance and theatre'. During trips abroad (France was high on the agenda of places to visit) this generation encountered the philosophes and French enlightenment. In salons of *dames d'esprit* they discussed all manner of topics, from the immortality of the soul, prejudice, science, morality and aesthetics. Returning to Russia, they abandoned the guards for administrative service but, finding it too difficult to adapt, left for their country estates, where, out of boredom, they succumbed to the pursuit of pleasure and amusement:

> Tucked away in the depths of Tula or Penza, [Onegin's grandfather] cut a very strange figure indeed. His acquired manners, tastes, even language all drew him to faraway climes, while at home he had no organic link or attachment to his immediate surroundings. [...]. Having spent his entire life exposed to 'European customs', and reflections on the enlightenment of society, he had tried to be true to himself (*svoim*) among foreigners, only to become a foreigner among his own people. In Europe, he was regarded as a Tatar in European dress, while in the eyes of his compatriots he was taken for a Frenchman who happened to be born in Russia.[33]

Onegin's father belonged to the post-1789 generation. Albeit still educated in the 'French' tradition he was exposed to different influences, namely the anti-republican views of French nationals fleeing the reign of Terror. The influx of Marquis, cavaliers, royalists and abbots on Russian soil was a conduit for a new sensibility: questions of faith and morality replaced those of atheism and enlightenment that had been fostered by the previous generation. In addition, this generation of foreign refugee tutors encouraged their tutees to endorse politically anti-democratic views. This trend was completed in response to the rise of Napoleon as Onegin's older brothers were forced to defend their country against France, their fathers' spiritual homeland:[34]

> Their experience on the battle fields of Borodino, Leipzig, and outside the walls of Paris, taught them that the educated classes had turned their backs on their country in vein. Then, with even greater sorrow they discovered that in the Russian people themselves lay powerful resources, hidden treasures of intellect and morality, which, if left untapped, risked being squandered altogether. From this moment on they fixed their gaze on Russia.[35]

Renouncing their fathers' worldview, the sons pursued a variety of paths, setting out with nervous bravery, driven by the conviction that the existing order was evil yet could be changed: 'But they viewed their surroundings through a prism of patriotic grief, which they had substituted for the cosmopolitan indifference of their fathers'.[36] Kliuchevskii's image of a 'prism' works brilliantly here to suggest a fragmented, disjointed sense of reality, thereby thwarting attempts by members of this generation to set their aims or picture their goals clearly. How did members of this generation propose to rectify social injustice? Kliuchevskii identified several courses of action:

> Some simply hoped that they could upturn the existing order with a single blow.[37] Others stood to one side, and looked around them, nurturing hope and illusions. Even before 1812 they had begun to notice that the reform movement launched by the government was grinding to a halt for which neither Speranskii nor Arakcheev could be held accountable.[38] They realized that what was blocking change was Russian reality itself (what Speranskii called a 'coarse thickness' [*grubaia tolshcha*]) that neither their preparation nor that of their fathers could help them rectify. This discovery destroyed a worldview nurtured by successive generations who had grown used to taking their example from the West. In despair, some then enlisted as active accomplices of Nicholas I's harsh regime, others bade farewell to the civilized world (retreating into spiritual solitude), others, still, began to study the civilized world in the minutest detail.[39]

The effects of this patriotic grief on their younger brothers who did not take part in the Napoleonic wars (i.e. Onegin), nor were implicated in the movement culminating in the Decembrist uprising, were, however, quite different. Schooled in the capital where they acquired the tools necessary for entry into polite society (though not skills that would be of any intellectual or practical service), once they reached the age of maturity they witnessed the grief and despair of their older siblings, which they then imitated:

> To this secondhand acquisition of disappointed hopes (*razocharovanie*), they added ideas about their inutility bequeathed by their freethinking fathers,

throwing a dose of ennui into the mix as well. These young men came to despise high society yet they were incapable of managing without it. They felt shame for doing nothing, but had no work ethic. They were the chattels of an intellectual and moral inheritance handed down from their fathers and grandfathers encrusted with a layer of bitter or angry feelings on which their older brothers had fed.[40]

It was this mixture of Byronic 'disenchantment' (*razocharovanie*) and home spun moral depravity, the ethos of which, as I mentioned above, Kliuchevskii rendered as '*nichego cdelat' nel'zia i ne nuzhno delat'* ('it is neither possible nor necessary to do anything'), that anticipated by some twenty years the entry into the literary canon of the superfluous man, one of the defining personality types crafted by novelists and literary critics, such as Turgenev, Goncharov, Lermontov and Belinskii, as an unfortunate intellectual and moral by-product of Nicholas I's reign.

'Onegin', Kliuchevskii claimed, 'is as much historical as poetic'.[41] As fictional creations, the names of Mitrofan, Chatskii, Onegin and, later, Pechorin entered the national lexicon where they acquired historical and cultural meaning and thus legitimacy for use by the historian. Already in the early nineteenth century, 'Mitrofan' had become a common noun, a short-hand term for a stupid ignoramus and spoiled brat, or 'adolescent', as Pushkin noted of his own age – referring to it as a period of the most recent Mitrofans.[42] Kliuchevskii co-opted this device of typecasting to make a number of didactic points about the intergenerational decline of the nobility. We see this at work in the following example: the enlightenment, he argued in an essay on the life and career of the writer and philanthropist, Nikolai Novikov (1744–1818), produced from within the nobility a handful of (historical) individuals sensitive to political issues which they were bold enough to articulate (Kliuchevskii named Fonvizin, Novikov, Radishchev as constituting an 'intelligenstia stratum'). But their immediate successors to the Decembrist movement included Onegin and Pechorin, that is, representative, fictionalized figures that embodied the main characteristics of Byronic revolt and despair.[43] Kliuchevskii integrated literary material into historical analysis in other ways, too: as I mentioned earlier, he used Andrei Bolkonskii's impressions, Tolstoi's fictional hero in *War and Peace*, to bring 'colour' to his portrayal of Mikhail Speranskii.[44] And, as Raisa Kireeva suggests, in his analysis of Pushkin's tale he seemed to bridge the gap between fact and fiction by using 'Tatiana's method' (the heroine of Pushkin's tale) to provide a historical contextualization for Pushkin's fictional protagonists and anti-heroes. Like Tatiana in Chapter 7 of the novel, who endeavours to learn more about Onegin through the books he had read, Kliuchevskii '*probiraetsia ukradkoi*' (enters stealthily) into the studies of the people of the time, scours their bookshelves and inspects marginal notes and question marks they made.[45] In this way, Kliuchevskii fleshed out Pushkin's depictions of the eighteenth-century nobility; inversely, by elucidating the concrete-historical circumstances of their lives, he integrated Pushkinian images into the living tissue of historical reality.

Was Kliuchevskii's creation of a rogues' gallery of fairly grotesque portraits of the Russian nobility little more than a playful, albeit 'scholarly', joke? Perhaps. But there is every reason to suggest that, like most jokes, it had a deeper underlying seriousness.

In presenting the genealogy of a literary protagonist through the prism of national historical developments, it was Kliuchevskii's intention to demonstrate that Onegin was not a chance mistake to be explained in terms of genetics, rather the consequence of cultural–historical developments stretching back some two hundred years.[46] But, in addition to their function as catalysts of historical understanding, Mitrofan and Onegin also resonated with Kliuchevskii's audience for their contemporary significance: the moral dysfunction these characters exemplified made them especially relevant as diagnostic tools to explain the mounting social tensions associated with the reforms and counter-reforms, which Kliuchevskii witnessed as an acute yet pessimistic observer of his own age.[47] Lastly, one should not overlook Kliuchevskii's distinctive populist, anti-aristocratic temperament and innate affinity with the underlying ethos of literary realism and criticism. His disdain for aristocratic dandyism was, of course, a feature of realist criticism: for the revolutionary literary critics such as Pisarev or Nikolai Shelgunov, conventions of polite behaviour that had formerly been accepted by the previous generation of the 1840s now deserved to be treated as little more than a manifestation of the lies and the hypocrisy of the age in which they lived. There is every reason to believe that Kliuchevskii sympathized with this view: certainly, it was registered as such by his pupils.[48]

Horace's world: Poetry as an empirical source (Ivan Grevs)

'Literary monuments, even works of poetry, often contain valuable if not always sufficiently exploited information for understanding social processes or economic phenomena (…). If these are not enough for us to draw definitive conclusions they do, nevertheless, allow us to make some important generalizations'.[49] In many respects, Grevs' handling of literary material was quite different from Kliuchevskii's. Whereas Kliuchevskii readily embraced creative imagination as a refractor of the intangible realm of tastes, attitudes and human prejudice, for his younger contemporary, it was a matter of extracting 'factual' information from the subjective, impressionistic colours of the lyrics. His approach was measured, more circumspect: the historian had to: 'rid these impressions of the admixture arising from the poetic treatment of a given topic, correct one-sided explanations, moderate its extremes and even disregard the forms of expression and interpretation so as to assess its unique essence'.[50] Possibly taking his cue from a saying popularly attributed to Horace, namely that the purpose of poetry is 'to teach and delight',[51] Grevs contended that 'Horace was neither a fantasist nor utopian in outlook, but a "genre artist" (*zhanrovyi khudozhnik*)', that is, a dependable recorder of his immediate world:

> He takes motifs from everyday life, which disturb him, prompting him to philosophize, motifs that move, uplift, anger, amuse or sadden him. Thanks to their content, his verses offer a lively and concrete reflection of contemporary life; they are replete with thoughts about it, or allusions to it. Out of this living material he builds allegorical figures exemplifying particular moral codes. From it he creates his various stylistic effects, metaphors and similes; it is the canvas

on which he pens his outlines and sketches; it offers him a palette of colours with which to give his lyrics depth and shade.⁵²

How exactly did Grevs work with Horace's poetry? First, he used the poet's impressions to establish the topography of the Sabine estate, the layout of the villa and surrounding land used for livestock and crops, his aim being, as he put it, to describe the location, as far as possible, in the poet's own words, 'walking alongside him as a reliable guide'.⁵³ By comparing the topography of the estate gleaned from Horace's lyrical evocations with other contemporary pictorial images, Grevs hoped to gauge roughly the size of his territory. Second, on the basis of the poet's descriptions of life in the villa, his account of the crops, vineyard, livestock, meadows and surrounding woods, Grevs broadened the scope of his enquiry to sketch out the everyday running of small- and medium-sized land holdings as a system of land management.⁵⁴ Grevs' case study of the poet's farmstead therefore involved rigorous filtering of artistic embellishment in order to attain informative empirical data about the structure of the typical or average-sized Roman estate at the moment of the establishment of the empire, that is, when the question of land management had taken the form of a serious social crisis.⁵⁵

Grevs spoke of being able to 'extract a kernel of truth' from the poet's imaginative designs, and he did this by formulating a set of questions which he used when working with any given source in order to determine its authenticity, as well as the purpose for which it was produced.⁵⁶ Such information, he contended, may take

> the form of 'vignettes' written with a philosophical-cum-moral purpose in mind; sometimes a detail or trait might be couched in a lyrical or satirical rendering of current historical events (*proisshestvie*), or linked to the experience of one or another person, if not the author himself. Lastly, images could be derived from the sphere of agriculture, and likewise characterize land management in the form of poetic embellishment (*v vidakh ukrasheniia poeticheskogo*).⁵⁷

The *Satires* (published in 35 BC), for example, reflected Horace's adhesion to the attempts of Octavian (the future Augustus) to deal with the contemporary challenges of restoring traditional morality, defend small landowners from large estates (*latifundia*), combat debt and usury, and encourage *novi homines* (the 'new men') to take their place next to the traditional republican aristocracy. In addition, the poems often exalted the new man as the creator of his own fortune, free of any association with noble lineage. As specialists in the field have noted, Horace developed his vision with principles taken from Hellenistic philosophy: *metriotes* (the just mean) and autarky (the wise man's self-sufficiency). The ideal of the just mean allowed Horace, who, like Atticus, discussed in the previous chapter, was philosophically an Epicurean, to reconcile traditional morality with hedonism. In other words, the basis for his aspiration for a quiet life, far from political passions and unrestrained ambition, was self-sufficiency.

Grevs' view, then, was that a source is not some kind of self-contained component (*istochnik ne sam po sebe*), rather, as he counselled his seminar students, material for familiarizing ourselves further with 'already established questions' (*material dlia oznakomleniia s uzhe izvestnymi voprosami*).[58] In other words, it was an open-ended endeavour involving extensive cross-referencing with other types of source. It followed that if Horace's otherwise realistic representations of an everyday scene (e.g. life in the household) were charged with social or moral significance, such resonances might be evaluated with reference to other contemporary texts. Specifically, in addition to a variety of written records pertaining to small- and medium-scale farm management in central Italy where Horace's Sabine estate was located, Grevs used topographical and recently uncovered archaeological evidence to crosscheck the poet's impressionistic depictions of the layout of his villa and surrounding meadows and woodland. To complement his fieldwork, he researched architecture and paintings, frescos, mosaics and sculptures housed in museums, as well as other archaeological sites relative to the period so as to gain an as comprehensive understanding as possible of Horace's day-to-day life. However, given that the prime focus – and originality – of his research was a body of work celebrated for its subjective (autobiographical), lyrical, but also satirical qualities, it was essential to establish the poet's credentials as a dispassionate observer of his age. Accounting for the poet's upbringing and activities as a landowner (his economic biography), his experiences in public service, his friendships, together with the political events, which shaped, tested and confirmed, his personality was therefore key. In this regard, a point of major concern for Grevs was to demonstrate a fundamental consistency in the poet's outlook on life irrespective of the turmoil of war and regime change and their effects on his personal circumstances.

Born into a relatively modest family (his father had a small holding on the southern border of central Italy which was confiscated during the civil wars), Horace's career as a scribe and minor official in the treasury in the period following an amnesty in 39 BC for supporters of Brutus (Horace had fought for the republican cause) meant he did not experience a radical 'rise and fall' in personal – material – circumstances. Albeit an erstwhile supporter of Brutus, Horace gradually reconciled himself to the new imperial order under Augustus (27 BC–AD 14), and little by little came to embrace Caesarism as a form of governance even though this entailed the erosion of political freedom and the erstwhile engagement of male citizens in state affairs – possibly one of the most celebrated hallmarks of the Roman republic. Once Augustus was awarded the title of *princeps*, or first citizen, the idea of citizenship and the 'right to vote' became mostly irrelevant. (In this connection, Grevs spoke of the subordinate citizen (*grazhdanin-poddannyi*), henceforth subject to private law.) The gift of the Sabine estate, which Horace received from his patron Maecenas in the mid-30s BC, as well as his rise to prominence as the foremost lyric poet in the age of Augustus meant that he became a beneficiary of the new regime. But he was, by temperament, Grevs insisted, never given to excesses; rather he retained a wry impartiality as an observer of contemporary mores. Thus, as he endeavoured to set out the foundations for a new 'monarchical' ideal (here, Grevs references Mommsen), he did not deny himself the right to observe and describe exactly what he saw. He retained an interest in life and always demonstrated a presence of mind to grasp the essence, significance and effect of the factors he observed, and to draw from them serious social and ethical lessons.[59]

Grevs, of course, recognized that Horace's intentions were often satirical and that they contained moral judgements, meaning that the poet would distort reality. But these distortions, he argued, were minimal.[60] For Grevs, the poet's levelheadedness (wise, just, measured, sober are the epithets Grevs frequently used to describe him) qualified him as a reliable witness – 'one of the most socially aware, interested and knowledgeable':

> He is calm, independent and thus capable of providing a more or less impartial opinion; he is also so honest that he will always be agitated by evil, since he possesses the perspicacity necessary to notice it. These qualities which illuminate the personality and worldview of Horace reduce to a minimum the drawbacks of using his poetry as a historical source.[61]

Moreover, Grevs argued, it was important to note that Horace was not an exception in this regard; on the contrary, all Roman poetical literature was of value to the historian. Thus, besides the odes, satires and epistles of Horace, 'whose lyrics are especially interesting', the heroic and historical poems of Virgil and Lucan, the morality tales of Petronius (which Grevs presented in a case study to the Historical Society a few years later), the elegies of Tibullus or Ovid, and Martial's epigrams all contained themes drawn from everyday life and presented a concrete, nuanced picture of it.

The reception of Grevs' thesis was mixed. On the one hand, his area of interest – property and management of the agrarian sphere – was highly topical; on the other, his inclusion of literary material as an empirical source seemed to test the ambitions of his peers for the development of history as a scholarly discipline. For one, Grevs' friend and sometime epistolary interlocutor, the symbolist poet and classical scholar, Viacheslav Ivanov, could not see the analytical potential of Horace verse, even though he had translated some of Horace's lyrics at his friend's request for inclusion in the thesis. At his viva, Grevs was challenged by F. F. Sokolov, professor of World History and a specialist in epigraphy: 'There are many fascinating pages in the thesis, but they are hardly significant. The author is rather like Walter Scott – a fine storyteller, but not a scientific historian'.[62] What Sokolov meant by this was Grevs' tendency to fuse his analyses with personal impressions of, for example, the archaeological site he had visited while conducting his research and the emotionally laden, introspective descriptions, which he sourced in Horace's lyric poetry. When Sokolov took this further to ask, possibly for rhetorical effect, whether anyone would ever attempt to reconstruct the history of the Russian peasantry on the basis of *Evgenii Onegin*, Grevs' reply – 'in my opinion, Pushkin, Turgenev, Saltykov-Shchedrin are important sources for understanding the *krepostnoe* countryside'[63] – suggests two irreconcilable views of 'science' and the 'discipline'. I will return to this point presently.

Representing the public at his viva, Kareev was, seemingly, the most receptive to Grevs' novel approach. As I mentioned in Chapter 4, he applauded Grevs' decision to foreground the person in social history, no doubt because it was germane to his own work in the field. Yet, like F. F. Zelinskii, specialist of Ancient Greece, who took issue with Grevs' description of Horace's estate, Kareev contended that Grevs did not so much create a typical portrait of a Roman estate, as an 'ideal' one.[64] These reservations aside, Kareev endorsed the principle of including works of literature in economic–historical research. This aspect of Grevs' study was, he said, 'truly novel and original'.[65] Four years later, however, Kareev was among those who took issue with precisely such methodological innovations.

In 1904, Grevs completed a further case study of household management in the late Roman era, this time basing his account on the 'Cena Trimalchionis' (Dinner with Trimalchio) in Petronius' *Satyrikon*: 'The artistic form of Petronius' work', Grevs wrote, 'requires that the historian handles his evidence with caution (*kriticheskaia ostorozhnost'*); but the realism of his depictions, the purely descriptive intentions of the author (*byto-opisatel'naia zadacha avtora*) prompt the reader to accept the veracity of the picture he creates. It confirms, in a vibrant, colourful and non-pedantic way other documentation and/or materials'.[66] Titled 'Closed Household Economy in the High Imperial Roman Period' ('Zamknutoe domovoe khoziaistvo v epokhu rastsveta imperii'), Grevs used Karl Bucher's (somewhat contested) concept of *oikos* to argue that despite the size of Trimalchio's estate it not only functioned as a closed, self-sufficient or autarkic household economy, that is, bringing in little from the outside (*malo pokupat'*), but also prepared to 'sell a lot' (*mnogo prodavat'*) to the outside world, thereby demonstrating a certain economic prowess. The thrust of Grevs' paper was to argue (after Bucher) that the running of Trimalchio's household provided a socio-economic paradigm that was characteristic of the late Roman period: all phases of production, from raw materials to finished goods, were united under the control of the master, in the *familia*, that is, the *oikos*: although technical specialization in crafts did exist, there was no exchange of goods in the various stages of manufacturing and completion.

Grevs presented his study for debate at a meeting of the University Historical Society where he faced considerable criticism from peers – including Kareev – who, this time, was hostile to Grevs' use of literary material, thereby reneging on his earlier more favourable tribute. Zelinskii and A. A. Kaufman challenged Grevs' interpretation of household economy. Kaufman, for example, positioned his critique in line with the 'modernizers', the German scholars, Eduard Meyer and Karl Beloch, in that he regarded the economy in ancient world as 'thoroughly modern': Trimalchio was a banker, a trader who produced a lot for the market, and, like Atticus, his household was run on principles that scarcely differed from modern-day capitalism.[67] Both men in Kaufman's view were 'contemporary large-scale capitalists' (*sovremennye Grosskapitalisten*).[68] Kareev's criticism targeted Grevs' biographical method on the grounds that his case studies were no more than illustrations; he even expressed doubts about the value of working with a literary artefact (*pridumannyi poetom obraz*). In his reply, Grevs vigorously defended his view of Trimalchio's economic self-sufficiency, pointing out that modern-day capitalist ventures were unthinkable without supporting integrative economic structures.[69] His closing remarks, however, were directed at Kareev: while he welcomed the bulk of the criticisms, Grevs could not but lament (*posetovat'*) the baselessness of his colleague's fault finding with the biographical method. In response to Kareev's accusations of a fantastical subjectivism, lack of discerning analysis and muddling of scientific research with artistic representations, he insisted that he remained faithful to the demands of science.

Towards a multi-faceted approach to culture and mentalities

How well founded were such criticisms of Grevs in regard to respecting 'scientific' norms? As I mentioned in the previous chapter, Grevs' work with lyric poems and personal correspondence was intended to rectify what he saw as the detrimental effects of the increasing compartmentalization of knowledge. In particular, his quarrel lay with the (in his eyes) artificially created chasm between specialists in intellectual and moral culture (classical philologists) and specialists in material culture (economists). As he repeatedly argued, the material world of agriculture, of production and management, was one of the central features of life in ancient Rome, all of which had an impact on the poet; these things fed his imagination about man's relation to the land, providing him with numerous motifs and plots. In short, the work he produced was, itself, a record of society.[70]

In the introduction to his thesis, Grevs announced a shift away from the history of events (historical dramas) to a growing interest in inner state of society, its culture:

> Thanks to this paradigm shift, let us hope that 'cultural history' will henceforth be studied and structured as an integral picture (*kartina*) – an account of human development – and, by the same token, that the not entirely justified (undesirable) opposition between the history of social and intellectual (*dukhovnyi*) development will disappear. Then, with greater interest, the historian's attention will be given to the uncovering of global trends in the intellectual, moral and religious planes of human experience. In so doing, science will impart human understanding with fresh discoveries and ideas.[71]

In this connection, Grevs made explicit reference to Leopold von Ranke's call for a universal history ('depictions of the lived experience of all peoples and all times in their connectedness (...) [should] form a unified whole' – in Grevs' rendering), although he was careful to reset the 'moral pitch' of Ranke's original remark to a scientific register: 'And if it is impossible to be all-encompassing, the well-trained historian should nonetheless always keep in mind a universalistic historical point of view'.[72] For Grevs, then, his project was intended as a means to test his ambitions for the historical discipline: for a history to be truly comprehensive, he believed, one had to engage with all aspects of human activity – the socio-political, economic and material as well as the religious and moral, scientific and artistic.[73]

Were we to translate Grevs' ambition into modern-day parlance, we could well liken his 'genetic' study of the inner wholeness of history as a fusion of micro- and macro-history – Grevs did, in fact, speak of micro-historical analysis, as I have mentioned.[74] To recall, also, the initial impulse for this position came from the example of his first mentor, Vasileveskii. Like Vasilevskii, Grevs was critical of the still-dominant trend in university instruction of privileging political institutions, the lives of great men and narratives that presented the historical process as linear or 'law given' (*zakonomernost'*). In its stead, Grevs co-opted Vasilevskii's arguments in favour of an organic, non-linear unfolding of growth and decline (or an 'unfurling' and atrophy), an approach which required differentiating between 'external' and 'inner' history.[75] The former, external history, as he explained in a lecture course delivered in the academic year 1902–3, consisted of 'a narrative of events' (*razskazyvat' o sobytiiakh*) that are concrete, discrete, momentary and intermittent, and reliant on an arbitrary periodization; in contrast, the latter dealt with organic, dynamic phenomena, such as the role of worship, family and friendship ties, or forms of ownership and exchange and so on, which were analysed within shorter, specific time frames. Grevs' aim, therefore, was to draw attention to the complexities and slow rate of historical movement by privileging the study of problems rather than reconstructive explanatory narratives.

During the mid-nineties, Grevs cofounded a small study group with his peer group of friends, Lappo-Danilevskii, S. F. Oldenburg, A. E. Presniakov, M. A. Polievktov, I. I. Lapshin and A. A. Kaufman. At their regular meetings, held in the flat of Lappo-Danilevskii, they worked on theory and methodology of social science paying particular attention to contemporary developments abroad.[76] And, indeed, from a cursory overview of contemporary methodological developments in Continental Europe, we may discern a number of interesting parallels between Grevs' understanding of the remit of the socio-economic historian, his ambitions for the discipline and the current European-wide debate on the nature and aims of history. In France and Germany, as Donald Kelley notes, broadening the range of sources for history had in part been prompted by the introduction of prehistory (*Vorgeschichte*) across Europe in which the study of monuments, memorials and material objects 'offered historians access to a deeper past than that afforded by written records'.[77] But historians of the medieval and modern era were also beginning to draw not only on history and philology but also on archaeology and anthropology (understood as a systematic extension of ethnology in which field research was essential to its method) as part of the turn to the 'multi-faceted' study of 'culture'. Kelley describes cultural history as 'unreservedly interdisciplinary, proposing to include not only all aspects of human behaviour beyond politics and war but also to subsume the political and military aspects in a wider social field'.[78] Moreover, as part of the turn to culture, he writes that 'the literary moment' revived the quarrel concerning the credentials of the historical discipline as a science, that is, whether it should adopt the terms of modern natural science as its basis for exploring cause and effect, or whether its natural home was that of the creative muse.[79] As I discuss in Chapter 8, this quarrel also brought back onto the agenda questions pertaining to the relation of (general) history to the newly emerging field of literary history.

In the German-speaking world, the credo of the Renaissance scholar, Jacob Burckhardt (1818–97) – 'history finds in poetry not only one of its most important, but also one of its purest and finest sources' – anticipated a partial 'literary turn' within the positivist paradigm. To my knowledge, Grevs never mentioned Burckhardt; yet, the coincidences between them are hard to miss. Burckhardt's best-known studies, *Die Kultur der Renaissance in Italien* (1860) and *Geschichte der Renaissance in Italien* (1867), used the visual arts as a source for historiography alongside other factors such as poetry, music, natural science, social etiquette, morality and religion. (Much like Grevs, he was criticized by contemporary readers for his limited use of official documents and over-reliance on literary sources.) Burckhardt, who held the chair of History and Art History at Basle University, also authored a guide to Italian art treasures. Based on materials gathered during a research trip to Italy in 1855, his published *Cicerone* contained sections on architecture, sculpture and painting, that is, 'artefacts' which, some fifty years later, Grevs would, likewise, prioritize in his own research agenda as a medievalist and 'excursion historian'.[80] Grevs' aim to combine material factors with the realm of ideas, moreover, suggests a number of potentially rewarding, if coincidental, parallels with the famous '*Methodenstreit*', which raged in late-nineteenth-century Germany. Associated with the work of Karl Lamprecht (1856–1915), this 'new history' was, again, in Kelley's summary: 'Actually a continuation of the old tradition of cultural history, which he pursued along two lines: that of material culture, to which he contributed in his massive study of medieval German economic and social history, and a second, Burckhardtian sort of art history, emphasizing "spiritual" factors'.[81] Turning away from politics and the state to the study of everyday customs and usages, of lowlife (*Kleinleben*) in its most minute details – rather than the spiritual and moral character of the people – Lamprecht, Kelley writes, conceived his approach as part of modern scientific history: 'He cited advances in linguistics, archeology, art history, and especially recent psychology, which he believed should be the foundation of scientific history'.[82] Grevs', himself, though, always spoke of his indebtedness to the French school of historiography, and his formal training as a historian in the late 1880s and early 1890s clearly attests his familiarity with French models, from his reading of Guizot, Michelet, Thierry and Fustel de Coulanges to the lectures of Gabriel Monod, A. Loucher, Ch. Langlois, Ch. Bémont and P. Violet, which he attended at the Collège de France, the Sorbonne and the Ecole des Hautes Etudes in the early 1890s.[83] As I have mentioned, Grevs' main point of reference for his thesis was Fustel de Coulanges (1830–89).[84] However, if anything, his differences with the French master, both in terms of approach and interpretation, made him a renegade pupil.[85] Recognized as the foremost authority in the history of ancient Greek and Roman social and legal institutions, including, notably, private property, Fustel de Coulanges was notoriously dismissive of 'conclusions drawn from poetic sources, and anything not immediately inferable from the documents, especially laws and charters'.[86] Likewise, the next generation of French scholars, including the medievalist and palaeographer, Charles-Victor Langlois (1863–1929) and Charles Seignobos (1854–1942), specialist in the history of the Third Republic, eschewed the 'literary' approach to history, although they did 'emphasize the value of poetic sources for social and political history' as part of their positivist/scientific credo.[87] The notable exception in France was Hippolyte Taine, whom Grevs met just prior to the former's death while he was studying in Paris. Acknowledged as a key, if controversial, figure for understanding the relationship between literature and history,[88] Taine developed a scientific–historical theory of literature in which he argued that literature was largely the product of the author's environment and that an analysis of that environment could yield a perfect understanding of a work of literature.[89] Grevs' own approach to literary sources was in much the same vein, except that he seems not to have employed the hallmark terms of Taine's theory – *race, milieu, moment* – nor, indeed, seems to have mentioned him in this connection: for explicit reference to and use of these terms we must consider the work of Grevs' colleague, Kareev, who dedicated a series of lectures to the question of the relationship between history and literature.[90] In this connection, one last potential (but, again, unacknowledged) source of inspiration that should be flagged up here, and to which I will return in Chapter 8 below, was the work of Grevs' older Russian contemporary at St Petersburg University, the historian of literature, Aleksandr Veselovskii. Best known for his theory of historical poetics, Veselovskii treated literature as a social phenomenon and, on that basis, offered a definition of literary scholarship as a social science.

If, then, the accent Grevs placed on the literary world as an object of 'scientific' historical enquiry met with criticism from some of his peers, the reality was that his more inclusive approach to historical sources was in fact both characteristic of recent developments within the positivist paradigm abroad and (as I discuss in Chapter 8) consistent with the lasting methodological overlaps between historical and philological enquiry, at home. As Donald Kelley notes, most agreed that historical enquiry should be scientific but there was little agreement as to what science actually entailed. What however seems to be the case was that the growing interest in culture involved a multi-disciplinary approach and that the questions this posed with respect to the status of the historical discipline (as a science or an art) was a feature of European-wide historiographical developments. Moreover, both in Western Europe, and in Russia, these questions informed ambitious projects to establish the theoretical underpinnings of the human sciences as a whole.

Kliuchevskii and Grevs provide two distinct uses of the literary document. As we have seen, Kliuchevskii used literary representation as a tool of historical enquiry, often blurring distinctions between fact and fiction, to characterize, through a series of socio-historical types of his own invention, the '*byt*' (daily life, mores) of modern Russia. Drawn from life – and fiction – these composite personages evidenced the problematic impact of Western culture on pre-Petrine Russian traditions and customs. For his part, Grevs incorporated artistic impressions as a source to explore socio-economic reality in ancient Rome and (later on) medieval Continental Europe. However, as I mentioned at the beginning of this chapter, Grevs' interest in the way socio-economic change was experienced by people meant that his recognition – indeed justification – of a 'social-psychological' perspective in economic history arguably bridged the distance between his own empirically led inquiry and Kliuchevskii's unquestioning acceptance of the poetic imagination as an intrinsically valuable resource for the historian interested in understanding 'collective psyche'.[91] Granted, their respective reasons for incorporating the world of literary imagination in historical explanation were quite different: in Kliuchevskii's case it may ultimately be due to his temperament (he was too much an artist to be constrained by historical facts); as for Grevs, the initial driver for his turn to literary monuments might best be understood in the spirit of 'necessity as the mother of invention', that is, the absence of economic records relative to the period he was working on. But, whether used as a source or resource, for both men the literary artist's perceptions of the minutiae of reality played a role no less important than the use of economic records for a reconstruction of the large-scale events in history. For Kliuchevskii, this made fictional protagonists no less than historical 'great men' viable candidates for his deepening interest in national character. Onegin, recall, was 'as much historical as poetic' in his view: works of fiction taught him to look beyond the economic factor and to seek explanations for change and continuity by probing human behaviour. In doing so, he made the study of socio-economic history 'an expression of concrete human personality'.[92] Grevs' achievement was what Sveshnikov calls the 'anthropologization of economic research' where the accent is placed not on the objective, impersonal character of historical processes, rather on the economic management of real people in light of the attitudes and worldviews they expressed through their activities. Working with Horace's poetry, even the grotesque (Petronius' *Satyricon*) he managed to offer glimpses of daily life in the ancient world. Moreover, as I have argued, it was an approach that in some degree resonated with (if not inspired by) developments in west European positivist historiography. In sum, if there is little doubt that Kliuchevskii's use of literary imagination as a tool of historical enquiry was more adventurous than that of his younger contemporary, they each, in their own way, helped reset the terms of the historical study of society and the economy. In Grevs' case, his study of the lyric poet Horace as a small landowner contained the hallmarks of an approach to the past that would later define his career: intellectual biography, the use of literature as an empirical source, visual perception of the past (topography), microhistory and the study of mentality – in short, cultural history understood as the 'total picture of human development (…) in which distinctions between the histories of social and spiritual development disappear'.[93]

As I discuss in the next chapter, Grevs' reconfiguration of the socio-economic problematic into a study of 'man' and 'culture' provided him with the principal axes for his research seminars on medieval Italy and France that he led after the turn of the century and during the final years of Tsarist rule. With his seminar students he analysed medieval spiritual culture through the prism of biography (from St Augustine and Boethius to Francis of Assisi and Dante). His early experiments in economic biography (in conjunction with fieldtrips) also served as a building block for his work on urban culture which became his specialist field at St Petersburg University and the Bestushevskie Higher Courses for Women, and for which he is perhaps best known. By the end of the first decade of the twentieth century, however, as Russia entered its turbulent years of war and revolution, field trips abroad effectively became impossible. It is really at this point, then, that Grevs honed the biographical method to explore the (emotional) life and work of his favourite writers – Ivan Turgenev, Romain Rolland and, of course, Dante – in the context of the mentality, belief systems and events of their age.

6

Place: Excursion History and the Question of Literary Sites

One of Grevs' favourite pedagogical watchwords for the study of history was 'visuality'/tangibility and 'authenticity' (*nagliadnost'*/*podlinnost'*).[1] While the latter term related to careful philological analysis of sources, it also implied – as the former term did more explicitly – fieldwork. Early on in his career, Grevs had learnt that a powerful way to render the past meaningful was to experience first hand its material traces: 'The adage proclaimed by all the great historians', he wrote, citing the names of nineteenth-century masters, Niebuhr, Savigny, Ranke, Mommsen, Renan and Fustel de Coulanges, 'is that to become a historian you need to distance yourself from the present and immerse yourself in the past. If this is so', he continued,

> then what better way to experience the aura of a period than through direct contact with its physical traces that history has left behind? The Roman ruins, the palaces and churches of Florence or Venice, the monuments of Babylon and Athens, Paris, Strasburg and Bruges, Jerusalem (…), Moscow and Kiev – they all place us, as it were, in medias res. They awaken within us a desire to participate in the construction of culture, and to capture the sounds of human existence buried deep in ancient texts.[2]

For Grevs, such tangible remnants of the past were as equally important as the written sources housed in archives and libraries, and he frequently counselled his students to 'go from books to monuments, from the study of history to the real stage of history; then, from the free unbounded air of history, back to the library and the archive'.[3] In his seminars, which he ran between 1902 and the First World War, he combined analyses of the lives and writings of pivotal figures in the spiritual culture of late Antiquity and the Middle Ages with work on the history of towns in northern Italy and France. Here, the emphasis was placed on the distinctive hallmarks of a location, the 'face' (*litso*) of a town, as he often referred to it. Guided by this fundamental conception of the urban world as a 'living organic entity', he introduced his students to architecture, artefacts, paintings, even the layout of streets as cultural products and refractors of daily life in the community.

The dual accent that Grevs placed on individual 'voices' (his biographical method) and 'silent witnesses' of the past (architecture, monuments) came together in 'excursion history', a multi-faceted – topographical, architectural, aesthetic and philological – approach to locations, understood as 'cultural–historical complexes' and the people (principally creative and spiritual thinkers) who inhabited them. 'Excursions', Grevs wrote, 'should become a permanent and integral component in the study and teaching of history, both in technical schools and gymnasia. In the university, it is indispensable as a form of historical seminar'.[4] As I discuss in this chapter, excursion history or 'excursionism', 'monument(al) history' or '*gradovedenie*', as it was called interchangeably, also functioned as a portal to the literary dimension of historical enquiry, both in Grevs' own writings dating from the pre-war years and in the early 1920s, but especially in the work of one of his closest pupils, Nikolai Antsiferov, who would play a pivotal role in advancing literary excursionism as part of a Narkompros-funded (Commissariat of Enlightenment) project to transform secondary and higher education in the wake of the October Revolution.[5] Antsiferov's studies of city monuments and districts (his work privileged St Petersburg) through the prism of the emotive responses that they generated in the lives and work of creative writers not only brought a new dimension to the study of urban culture and collective psychology, but also afforded some valuable insights into the nature of the creative process itself.

From classroom to fieldwork: Spiritual culture and cityscapes

Grevs' university seminars covered a wide range of topics, but there was always an accent on 'historical biography'. Among the figures studied were the early Christians, Lactantius (advisor to Constantine the Great and tutor to his son), the Roman senator and bishop of Nola, Saint Paulinus, Julian of Eclanum and St Augustine.[6] Several cycles of seminars were dedicated to St Francis of Assisi and early Franciscanism (a theme which his pupil, Lev Karsavin, later took up in his master's dissertation[7]), and Dante. As a rule, the format of these seminars observed the long-established practices of close philological analysis. Attention to the material form of a document, modalities of production and classification was typically framed by a broader thematic enquiry conceived as prerequisite for building a portrait of a given historical figure. For example, the topic 'St Augustine and Pelagianism' involved close reading of the *Confessions* in conjunction with other works by St Augustine and his contemporaries. Driving the analysis was an attempt to understand both how St Augustine saw himself and how he was understood by his successors. For Grevs, Augustine's *Confessions* uncovered (*raskryvalo*) the worldview of a man who, as witness to a period of transition, highlighted the tensions between ancient philosophy, paganism and Christianity. Then, to complement these textual-based analyses of religious and political thought, Grevs dedicated a number of seminars and lecture courses to the study of urban culture in medieval France and Italy. Florence figured prominently in his seminar agenda along with Assisi, Venice, Padua and Rome, while his lecture series carried titles such as: 'Municipal Culture in Italy, from the tenth to thirteenth century (society, institutions, spiritual life)', 'The Genesis (*zarozhdenie*) of Social and Spiritual Culture in the early

Middle Ages', 'The Development of Spiritual Culture in the late Roman empire and early Middle Ages', 'A History of the Development of Municipal Culture in Italy from the break-up of the Roman world to the so-called Age of Renaissance', 'A History of Culture in the late Middle Ages (Rome, Venice, Florence)', 'The Genesis of Medieval Spiritual Culture', 'The Development of Social Order and Spiritual Culture in France in the period of Feudal and Estate monarchy' and 'Intellectual and Religious Movements of the high Middle Ages (in Romanic countries)'.

A core concern for Grevs as a teacher was to equip his students with the necessary analytical and conceptual tools they would need to be able to engage with not just the leading ideas of a given author and their various inflections within a single body of work, but also their resonances and/or reconfigurations in different historical contexts.[8] In this connection, analysis of an author's lexicon and the mapping out of the various contexts affecting the meaning of a word, paying particular attention to the inflections of the authorial voice was key. For example, in his seminar on 'the political ideas of Dante and his contemporaries' (1910), each student had to take up a chapter of Dante's treatise *de Monarchia*. The basic concepts in a given chapter – pace, justizia, carita, etc. –were rigorously commented and compared to other works by Dante. Antsiferov described the procedure in his memoirs: 'Working on the chapter on peace, for example, we had to comment on the meaning Dante ascribed to the concept in different contexts, the various ways he employed the term. It was in this manner that we gradually compiled a lexicon of the fundamental concepts that defined the great Florentine's world view'.[9]

Pedagogically, the dictionary project was an excellent tool for promoting independent research using tried and trusted methods of semantics, and, as I suggested in Chapter 2, it was quite likely inspired by the rather better known Pushkin dictionary that Grevs' colleague in the department of literature, Semen Vengerov, had been compiling since 1908 with the help of his students. In addition, the ideas of Vengerov's predecessor, the literary theorist and founder of literary comparative studies, Aleksandr Veselovskii, whose courses Grevs had attended as a student, may have helped define the 'conceptual landscape' of his seminars on the medieval world. I will return to this topic in Chapter 8, but it is worth mentioning here that Veselovskii's expertise in medieval Italian literature – including the writings of Dante (for Veselovskii, Dante was a watershed moment in the history of literature as his creative output posed the issue of individually aware creativity) – meant that both the substance of his research and the methodological comparative approach he developed were directly relevant to Grevs' own cultural historical enquiry and the spirit in which he conducted it: for Grevs, as a self-styled 'humanist-realist', professor-enlightener and classical Russian liberal, the approach of his older contemporary seemed best to answer his own endeavours to rethink the terms and aims of historical enquiry in a 'positivist key'.

Grevs' ambivalence towards some of the more extreme expressions of the so-called Silver Age in the early 1900s has been commented on by a number of scholars and is very well summarized in Nina Perlina's observation that he (and Antsiferov) 'were not just contemporaries of the symbolists, but saw themselves as scholar–humanists germinating on the cultural soil of Russian symbolism'.[10] By this, Perlina meant that if Grevs' interest in spiritual culture, religious sentiment, eternal values and the importance he placed in man over the 'impersonal blind forces of history' (one of the leading tenets of the French positivist school formulated by Auguste Comte) tracked the shift in the wider cultural, philosophical and aesthetic sensibilities associated with Russian symbolism and neo-idealism, he never abandoned a methodological faith in positivism, that is, in the convincing nature of pragmatic data and historical facts in which he had been formally trained.[11] His indebtedness to positivism is readily attested by the presence of a vocabulary derived from a natural and social-scientific lexicon. As we shall see, this is especially evident in the terminology Grevs' favoured as he set out to devise an excursionist methodology: the emphasis he placed on the physiology, anatomy and psychology of a city, and a tendency to anthropomorphize, even spiritualize the features of townscapes was, in fact, symptomatic of developments in historical and literary critical discourse, which, since the latter part of the nineteenth century, had been exposed to the expansion of the natural sciences into the sphere of humanities studies. If anything, then, Grevs' repeated references to 'the soul of the city', 'the face (*lik*) of the city', 'the restoration of its image as a living (*real'naia*) collective person' and genius loci (*mestnyi dukh*) which he sourced in Western studies about collective psychology are traceable to a lexicon and conceptual apparatus dating from the 1860s and popularized by figures such as Hippolyte Taine (his view of historical events as psychological phenomena) and Ernest Renan's 'spiritual principle' in his concept of the nation (1882).[12] Likewise, the intention of border crossing between disciplines and areas of studies such as geography, ethnology, history and literature was to equip scholars with 'scientific/ empirical' (positivist) pathways towards a study of the intangible psychological resonances of place for human existence, not to overhaul the empirical inductive rationale of positivism itself.

'An important teacher for me', Grevs recorded in his notebooks towards the end of his life, 'was travel. For that I am grateful'.[13] Grevs' decision to combine close reading of sources pertaining to the life and works of certain key individuals with the study of medieval and early renaissance (urban) culture as a basis for pedagogical excursions abroad introduced a dimension to the history syllabus which, for its time, was quite novel in higher education.[14] Pedagogical excursions had, though, already been tested with some measure of success in secondary school curricula as part of the pedagogical reform in the 1890s and early 1900s.[15] The goal of this reform was to provide the basis for a more rounded education by harnessing the best of classical instruction (book learning) and combining this with 'real life' subjects such as modern languages and natural science, that is, staples of the more 'technical' Realschule which had been introduced into Russia during the reign of Nicholas I after the German model. As Emily Johnson argues in her study of *kraevedenie* (regional studies – which were to become so prominent during the Soviet era), Grevs' personal involvement with the excursion movement can be traced to the methodological innovations he had encountered first hand in 'the heady idealism of the Tenishev School' in St Petersburg where he taught following his suspension from the university.[16] Founded in 1898, the Tenishev School was, Johnson writes, an optimal laboratory to develop and trial a new, more progressive yet 'humanized' approach to education in which the needs of the 'whole child' would be met. Key to their methodological innovations was the idea of *nagliadnost'* (visuality): 'Pupils had to be taught to learn through observation and independent work, to collect and correctly interpret information received from both the surrounding environment and from reference books'.[17] The advantages of incorporating excursions into the syllabus were obvious: 'Even more than laboratory experiments and classwork with visual aids, they resembled immersion in the world at large'.[18] At the Tenishev School, excursions were initially used in geography and natural sciences classes. Their introduction into the history curriculum in the academic year 1900-1 was enthusiastically endorsed by Grevs as his comments published in the school's *pamiatnaia knizhka* (commemorative pamphlet) for the same year make resoundingly clear. He wrote: 'Excursions are the best available means of bringing students closer to the object of their study – to natural things and phenomena, to monuments, the environment, and the facts of human life; they intimately acquaint pupils with the authentic sources of those pieces of knowledge that have been communicated to them by the words of the teacher and reinforced in textbooks'.[19] In another early piece, published in 1903, and, again, probably intended for a more junior audience, he opened with a quotation from Pushkin (Adriatic waves!) as a device to impress upon the reader the benefits of 'immersive learning' through travel. Not to embrace risk and adventure, he cautioned, could have detrimental consequences for one's intellectual and spiritual growth. Just look at the narrow existence of the aged Prince Shcherbatskii or Iv. Iv. Aianov, both of whom eschewed risk and adventure for the security of home comforts and the familiar. The point to stress here is that, for his readers, Grevs' allusions to these fictional characters from Tolstoi's *Anna Karenina* and Goncharov's *Obryv* (*The Precipice*) required no explanation, since as literary types they were well established in the canon. Grevs could, therefore, confidently refer to them in a rhetorical manner in order to drive home a didactic point about the advantages of excursionism for the historian and a student audience.[20]

There is little doubt that Grevs' ambition to incorporate carefully structured trips into the university humanities curriculum was nurtured by his experience at the Tenishev School. But it was also entirely consistent with the 'local method' (as Antsiferov later called it) that he had experimented with in his master's dissertation about the layout and daily life on Horace's villa, and a natural corollary of his 'biographical method', which he developed through his seminars on the medieval world.[21] 'Grevs always looked for individual traits, "the face of an age," "the face of culture," or "the face of a town" (*litso*)', Antsiferov recalled in his memoirs.[22] For Grevs, the city was the quintessence of cultural processes. As an object of research in its own right, then, it demanded an 'integral', 'organic' approach in which material, written and oral sources would function as mutually reinforcing components, and the core point that he reiterated time and again was the need to acknowledge the value of material sources in terms of their parity, as mutually reinforcing components, with written and oral sources. Embodied in monuments, architectural styles, paintings and urban topography, these visible and tangible traces of the past, Grevs argued, afford a direct encounter with the past, a sense of immediacy, which illustrations in books could not recreate. The 'immediacy of the past', a visual/tactile encounter with it, was, in his view, the defining characteristic of excursion history.

In 1907, Grevs took a group of sixteen University and Bestuzhevskie graduate students to Italy on what would be the first of only two field trips abroad to complement the study of documents with 'monumental history'. They visited Venice, Padua, Ravenna, Florence, Perugia, Assisi and Rome. Grevs' principal goal was to give his students the tools with which to immerse themselves in the medieval world, to grasp the unarticulated connections between place, experience and intellectual or religious reflection. With their grounding in cultural history, the history of the everyday and art history, his students, Grevs hoped, would, upon arrival at the location, perceive traces of the past in contemporary structures and thus understand cities as living organisms rather than an assemblage of individual buildings and institutions. By way of introducing excursion history, classwork with sources was designed to promote an awareness among his students of man and place: for example, the Florentine chronicles of Dino Compagni, Giovanni Villani, Dante and religious poetry were studied for the insights they afforded into the social and intellectual (*dukhovnyi*) cultures of the medieval and renaissance eras, but also as records of everyday life.[23] In addition, Grevs spent considerable time preparing his students for the detailed itinerary of the trips themselves. Using a method of his own devising, he would show his students how to work with histories, maps, guidebooks and, importantly, illustrations, where the aim was to impart a real understanding of the locality's finest works of art and their significance in a global context. Strictly speaking, this latter aspect of the programme fell within the domain of art history, and, so, for his second excursion in 1912 with students from his Dante and St Francis of Assisi seminars (they visited Tuscany, Umbria, Venice and Rome), he turned to specialists in the art history department to assist him.[24] He also instructed his graduate students, Karsavin and Ottokar, (both men were teaching at the Higher Courses for Women) to focus on Italy in preparation for the trip: Karsavin ran a course on Francis of Assisi and the Franciscans; Ottokar charted 'a year in a medieval town', an in-depth study of Florence in the thirteenth and fourteenth centuries using chronicles, laws, statutes and myths as his main sources.[25] For his part, Grevs offered a special course on daily life in the Middle Ages through the prism of topography and the rise in the number of monuments. With its focus on the three major cultural sites of Venice, Rome and Florence, the intention was to complement not only his seminar on Dante and his epoch, but also his survey course on the history of the Italian Middle ages.[26]

As part of his efforts to integrate excursions for students of history at university level, Grevs wrote a number of articles (pedagogical and local historical – *kraevedcheskii*) outlining the notion of excursions as a method of knowledge of culture.[27] In terms of developing a strictly methodological template for excursion history, however, his endeavours may best be described as 'experiential', a tentative trial and error approach that was heavily reliant on descriptive accounts of places he had already visited. For example, in his first proper methodological statement on excursionism, published in 1910, he used the experience of the 1907 trip – and the lessons learnt – 'as a blueprint for future excursions'. The upshot was that most of what he actually had to say about 'methodology' consisted in a detailed description of their itinerary, basic organization and time management. Still, in the process, he did identify a number of defining features, which as Emily Johnson puts it at least in embryonic form (...) later became standard for pedagogical excursions in the humanities and social sciences: an interest in literary sites, the use of maps to trace the 'biography' of cities, attempts to recreate the atmosphere of history by combining visits to actual sites with stirring narrative, a concern with group dynamics, and a conviction that weather and time of day needed to be factored in when considering how to present a site for the greatest emotional effect.[28]

An unpublished follow-up piece in 1912 (again, most likely drafted as a report on the field trip itself) further refined the 'method': The idea behind 'monumental tours on foot', Grevs wrote, 'was to reflect on the characteristic features (*cherty litsa*) of the sites visited. These afford an initial understanding of the soul of the town as reflected on its face. It is as if vital currents emanate from the living tissue of the town'.[29] Specifically, this required the study of the topography, cultural type, and the physiognomy (*lik*) and soul of a town, which Grevs classified as a cultural historical approach and history of the everyday, together with an art historical analysis of the artwork associated with a given locality.[30] As I discuss below, the introduction of an anthropomorphic vocabulary (references to the 'soul' (*dusha*) of the city, its 'face' (*lik*), the city as a 'living organism'), and a more clearly articulated multi-disciplinary framework, which we see the beginnings of here, would figure more prominently in Grevs' publications dating from the post-revolutionary period when the programme was officially endorsed by the new regime's first Commissar of Enlightenment, Anatolii Lunacharskii, and granted an institutional base with government funding.

Because of what can only be described as a fortuitous coincidence of aims between the old professoriate and the Bolshevik programme of educational innovation, Grevs was able to integrate his 'biographical method' into a more comprehensive multi-disciplinary study of urban sites. It is, perhaps, then, an irony of history that for all his attempts to gain recognition for his new methodology, Grevs' original experiments in excursionism never entered the mainstream of humanities scholarship in the late Tsarist era; rather, it would enjoy, albeit briefly, the support of the Bolshevik government during the heady years of revolution. For the Imperial Ministry of Education its 'learning for life' ethos and cross-disciplinary optic were too radical a departure from the classical canon taught in gymnasia, and possibly too time consuming in terms of management and funding to be fully integrated into university curricula; for the Bolshevik regime, by contrast, it seemed to answer a requirement to revolutionize education. It is perhaps, also, a cruel irony to note that despite Grevs' personal fate as a *byvshii* (has-been) in the new regime, the practice of combining classroom study with pedagogical tours of literary and historical monuments became so popular in Soviet Russia.

After October: The Excursion Institute (1921–4)

Much has been written about the educational strategies of the Bolsheviks in the immediate aftermath of the revolution. The general consensus is that the new leadership recognized the importance of the 'cultural front' as integral to the task of constructing a radically new society on Marxist–Leninist principles. Equally though, as many commentators have noted, until roughly the mid-1920s, the party was in fact relatively open to experiments in curricula and prepared to co-opt the expertise of non-Marxist scholars and academics. In this connection, the role of Anatolii Lunacharskii, first commissar of Narkompros (1917–29), was key. As Sheila Fitzpatrick argues, his relatively non-partisan approach to education built on two premises for an enlightened government: recognition of the autonomy of the sciences and the arts to pursue their respective goals, and support for their endeavours through generous subsidies in the belief that the advances made would ultimately benefit the state. It was Lunacharskii's view that respect for scholarship was a mark of enlightenment, and so he made it a point of principle to protect prominent traditional institutions, such as the Academy of Sciences, from challenges to their legitimacy by party hardliners.[31] Thanks, then, to this relatively clement cultural climate, the early 1920s witnessed a number of educational experiments, which, if short lived, demonstrate the creative means by which established scholars were able to apply their expertise acquired during the final decades of tsarist rule to the task of building new educational programmes in the spirit of revolution. Excursionism was one of these. Set up during the winter of 1920, the aim of the Petrograd Excursion Institute was to advance a multi-disciplinary approach to urban environments as reflected in textual documents and as shaped by monuments. Comprising three departments – Natural History, Economic–Technical, and Humanities – the institute developed a programme of research and pedagogical seminars. Recruited to run the Department of Natural History were Professors Fedchenko, Rimskii-Korsakov and Raikov; the Economic-Technical Department was led by Professors Dmitriev and Zelentsov. Grevs was appointed director of the Humanities Section, tasked to devise a series of cultural excursions within Petrograd and other, nearby regional towns and cities.[32] In the classroom, the principal aim was to develop a typology of urban spaces and, by the same token, perfect a method for 'reading cities' as a historical document in order to gauge their impact on collective psychology and the fate of the individual, past, present and future.[33] To assist him in this project, Grevs enlisted the support of Faddei Zelinskii (specialist of the ancient world) and his former student, Olga Dobiash-Rozhdestvenskaia. The sector also worked in close contact with the Moscow group of excursionists where Antsiferov played an active role as a leading spokesman for the approach and as a mediator between the two affiliates.

Shortly after the opening of the Excursion Institute, Grevs published a series of articles for the in-house journal, *Ekskursionnoe delo*, in which he endeavoured to provide some kind of theoretical ballast for the study of urban sites as cultural-historical complexes.[34] Here he defined the city as a complex of groups, families, a synthesis of the life of people and their communities:

> Cities are both laboratories and reception points, cultural repositories and the supreme indices of civilization. In them, cultural processes are condensed, their results saturated; they are the largest form in which the elements of civilization are combined, the confluence and balanced intersection of its various constituents and trends. A city is simultaneously a centre of cultural attraction and of radiating

energy; it is the clearest and most visible measure of the level of culture. The history of the city is a wonderful guide to determining [a culture's] course and fate.[35]

The rationale for making the town an object of historical study was not, Grevs argued, merely (as was often the case) 'to familiarize ourselves with its outer physiognomy (…). What is needed is its biography, to uncover its peculiarity as a collective personality (…) to establish its "geniia." We have to comprehend the processes by and out of which its soul (*dusha*) arose, the chain of influences and changes in circumstances towards that which, in the end, a city's past has brought it'.[36] Since the biography of a collective being (*kolletektivnoe sushchestvo/kollektivnaia lichnost'/zhizn' litsa*) comprises many facets, it followed that the study of a city or a district, street and even a parish should involve its economy, daily life (*byt*), as well as its social, political, intellectual, artistic and religious profile: 'Only the aggregate of these processes, studied separately with reference to official documents, memoirs, poetry and belles lettres, will yield a picture of culture and its development in a given setting'.[37] Specifically, as Grevs conceived it, this multi-pronged approach could be broken down into the study of the city's geography and its relation to the natural surroundings, demography and the history of the role of leading figures in shaping the city, namely founders, rulers, architects and reformers, together with an analysis of monuments and buildings as sites of major political events.[38] Equally central to the biographical method was the study of daily life, art and culture. Grevs placed a major accent on the aesthetics of a city and its function as a catalyst of cultural production, in terms of both the visual arts and, more broadly, material culture in the form of everyday objects such as clocks or crockery which he regarded as refractors of patterns of everyday life and collective beliefs. For Grevs, then, excursion studies presented a revolutionary new educational programme in which theory, pedagogy and fieldwork each played an indispensable role. In his conception, the tools of physical geography and human geography provided a methodological baseline of sorts for a cultural historical study of man's material and spiritual worlds. As natural pre-determinants of culture, physical geography, he believed, was crucial for understanding the environmental setting, out of and within which customs and forms of social behaviour develop: human geography or anthropogeography (*anthropo-geografiia*), a term Grevs borrowed from the nineteenth-century German scholar, Friedrich Ratzel, articulated the idea of 'human rootedness' of man and the place he shapes, over time, through labour. Unlike factors of local geography, which describe the soil, flora and fauna, anthro-geography is the history of *byt* in which the entirety of a local culture comes to expression. Its ultimate object is man defined topographically and historically (*chelovek mestnyi*).[39]

Literary excursionism: Urban myths and literary topography – Nikolai Antsiferov's Petersburg

If the overall goal of excursionism was to capture the image of the city based on an analysis of its monuments, and from that characterize the city as something individual with its own peculiar history and way of life (namely its physical landscape and the historical conception of it), a major concern for both Grevs and Antsiferov was to understand the power of a locality on the psyche of its inhabitants.[40] This is where literary excursions as a sub-category of cultural historical excursions came in. The inclusion of creative literature as a vital resource for understanding man's sense of connectedness to place was, of course, something Grevs had already recognized in his pre-revolutionary writings, but he did not really address the question how best to study the literary resonances of place in any meaningful way at that time. In his programmatic statement of 1921, he spoke only very briefly of a 'literary/aesthetic approach' which he defined as 'reflection of the city at various points of its "life" in accounts by creative artists, a study of its nature as interpreted by the greatest poets'.[41] And he recognized its potential as a branch of excursionist research for the insights it afforded into the lives of writers and poets themselves through their connections with the life of the city: 'In this way', he wrote, 'we have a picture not only of the Petersburg of Pushkin, Gogol, Turgenev and Dostoevskii, but also of these writers *in* Petersburg'.[42] At the time of writing, however, it was, bar a few exceptions, a line of enquiry that was still largely unexploited. Of these, Grevs singled out (in a footnote) the, as yet, unpublished monograph by his colleague and former pupil, Antsiferov, *The Spirit of Petersburg* (*Dusha Peterburga*), a study based on literary material which aimed to capture the psyche (*psikhicheskii lik*) of the nation's former capital.[43] As I discuss in the next chapter, Grevs himself would, following the closure of the institute, harness the literary dimension of excursionism in a monograph about the novelist Turgenev's tours to Italy in the 1840s and 1850s. But in terms of devising a methodology of literary excursionism, it was Antsiferov who assumed the task and became known as the foremost authority on literary Petersburg and literary *kraevedenie*.[44] A leading figure in the activities of the Petrograd Excursion Institute, which he cofounded, Antsiferov helped ensure that the literary component in cultural historical excursions would have a methodological base. To his mind, works of creative literature brought to view the impact of the urban environment on human psychology: the strongest expression of the image of city, the spirit of city, he believed, is captured in literature.[45]

In 1919, as Petrograd became the stage of Civil War, Antsiferov began work on a series of related monographs about his adoptive city. The first of these, *Dusha Peterburga*, published in 1922, was an exploratory study of genius loci. As a setting within which various cultures coalesced – whether organically, or by design – Petersburg, he argued, fostered a distinctive mythopoeic culture, its monuments, nature, climate, topography and history correlating many complex layers of unconscious and symbolic meaning in collective experience.[46] Poets and novelists, from Lomonosov to Maiakovskii, harnessed these raw, unmediated responses to the cityscape and its watery surroundings in their fictional characters, plot and lyrical evocations, thereby giving rise, over time, to one of the nation's most enduring myths: the 'tragic essence of the city with its universal soul'.[47]

Two further studies about literary St Petersburg – *Peterburg Dostoevskogo* (1923) and *Byl' i mif Peterburga* (*Petersburg – Reality and Myth*) (1924) – were intended for use as primers and contained practical guidance for three main categories of excursion: geographical/topographical, historical and literary. For the first two of these, where the aim was to reconstruct the city's origins and subsequent expansion, Antsiferov devised detailed itineraries, drawing on popular tales and literary citations primarily for their contrasts with standard factual sources such as maps, street plans and other official municipal documents. For the third, literary component, he returned to his hypothesis concerning the self-contained links between popular image, myth and literary representation. In *Byl' i mif Peterburga*, for example, he examined Pushkin's narrative poem, *Mednyi vsadnik* (*The Bronze Horseman*), in light of popular attitudes to Peter the Great. His point here was that in composing his tale, Pushkin was in fact giving epic form to a myth (a creative, ordering force confronts watery chaos in a cataclysmic struggle) that had deep roots in popular historical imagination. This 'myth of the miracle-working builder' (Peter the Great), as Antsiferov called it, also figured in his study of Dostoevskii's Petersburg published a year earlier. Using the Mokrushi region of the city as a backdrop, here he explored the novelist's complex attitude to the capital, showing how he reworked, in darker, more sombre tones, the archetype lying at the heart of Pushkin's poem.[48]

Antsiferov's early experiments with creative literature as cultural constructs took the pedagogical excursion into territory that, at the beginning of the 1920s, was still relatively unexplored.[49] Beyond a visual perception of the past, he recognized the need for a trained 'inner eye', which he later likened to the 'intuitive method of cognition of the artist', to grasp the city's 'spirit' (or '*psikhicheskii lik goroda*', in Grevs' words).[50] His attention to works of poetry and fiction as expressions of St Petersburg's 'tragic essence' showed that while they might not be empirically viable records of the city's architectural or topographical history, as witnesses to deeper layers of collective psychology they afforded the historian valuable insights into 'the power of place as a source of knowledge' about man and his sense of connectedness to the world that surrounds him. In sum, for Antsiferov, Petersburg harnessed or was the embodiment (*vyrazitel'*) of cultures (in the plural), which it had absorbed at various levels – individual and collective, unconscious and symbolic – and the correlations between them. It followed, he argued, that by studying texts not only at the level of meaning (in terms of signification), but in terms of their shared links with the deeper, unconscious 'collective psychology' which generated individual and collective mythopoetic creativities, it would become possible to understand why they merged into a single syncretic artistic image: tragedy.[51] As a side note, one cannot help but note a poignant contemporary resonance in this last remark. Given the period in which he was writing, Antsiferov's bid to 'connect with the past' reads as an oblique reminder of the importance of safeguarding a cultural heritage threatened by economic demise, the effects of war, if not the Bolshevik policy of renaming streets, demolishing statues and monuments as a means to consign the pre-revolutionary world to oblivion.[52] As we know, by 1920 Petrograd had been reduced to a 'provincial town', its population effectively halved (through death and migration). Factories and shops had been shut down, and private residences left to ruin. Eyewitnesses spoke of grass beginning to push through the tramline tracks on Nevskii Prospect. If the introduction of the New Economic Policy in 1922 promised a partial recovery of the city's infrastructures and allowed for some degree of architectural preservation (a cause taken up by numerous intellectuals – including Antsiferov, himself, as an appointed member of the Old Petersburg Society), this was not, of course, with a view to revering a bygone age.

Again, as contemporaries noted, the bells of the Isaac cathedral, the city's largest place of worship, which had not chimed since the Bolshevik seizure of power, remained silent: Pushkin's Petersburg, Nekrasov's 'cradle of revolution', had become a graveyard.[53] Perhaps, then, it was this poignant sense of a lost world, which gave the excursion method – particularly literary excursionism – its distinctive pathos as an enquiry into the realm of what was ultimately invisible, intangible, namely the 'soul' of the city, or as Antsiferov later called it the aetiology of place as myth (*etiologicheskaia legenda mestnosti*).[54] By mapping the past through fiction, Antsiferov's work arguably helped safeguard not just memory/historical knowledge of Petersburg's pre-revolutionary topography, but, importantly, the experiences and worldviews of successive generations of the city's inhabitants.

As one of the driving forces behind the creation of the Institute's Humanities Sector, Antsiferov was instrumental in ensuring a methodological base for literary excursions as part of its programme. In a mission statement published in 1923, 'Concerning the Methods and Types of Historical and Cultural Excursions', he built on Grevs' template by breaking down the multi-disciplinary approach to the study of towns into five main axes. The social anthropological axis involved the study of the material and spiritual culture of people's past and present; physical geography was an important tool for gauging the natural conditions in which culture develops; the focus of art history included architecture, art and sculpture. Antsiferov then sub-divided the cultural–historical approach into two interdependent categories: the cultural–historical, properly speaking, and the literary. The cultural–historical perspective involved the study of 'tangible' objects, such as monuments, streets or houses in relation to household management (daily life) and material reality. Excursions falling into this sub-category would engage a variety of approaches – from the topographical, technical, economic to the aesthetic.[55] Finally, the literary component was flagged as an innovative dimension of excursion/urban history. Antsiferov acknowledged that the method was not yet fixed, but he believed that it had great potential both for the study of the biographies of writers and for the historical monuments referenced in their writings (e.g. Pushkin and Dostoevskii in Petersburg, Herzen and Tolstoi in Moscow).[56]

Literary excursions, then, albeit vaguely defined, had the rather more ambitious aim of prompting a reflection on the creative writer's ability to channel historical reality into symbolic images. Students were prompted to study representations of popular settings in Russian literature, such as Tsarskoe Selo, Gatchina or the backstreets of St Petersburg, paying special attention to the emotive resonances of certain place-related words, such as *zemlia* (earth) or *kamni* (stones), in a given author's lexicon. To illustrate this, Antsiferov took the personality of Paul I as drawn by Dmitrii Merezhkovskii in his play, *Pavel Pervyi* (1908). In this instance, an excursion to Gatchina Palace, the Tsar's beloved imperial residence, he suggested, would prompt a reflection on the literary image and its creator (the figure of Paul and Merezhkovskii as a poet and playwright).[57] More broadly, though, he hoped that the study of place through the prism of emotional attachments would encourage pupils to think about 'the psychology of creativity', a phenomenon which, to date, had received little attention among historians.[58] As Antsiferov readily acknowledged, the approach was especially challenging, but he believed that in addition to sharpening the students' awareness of their environment, integrating the literary component into historical–cultural fieldwork opened up a wealth of untapped material for the excursion movement as a whole:

> We shall be looking for an understanding of the city's surroundings, of boring ordinariness, and, in light of this new approach, this boring ordinariness, this tedium will appear new; it will speak to us through the stones of bridges, through the forms and groupings of houses, street names, through all the things that we have got used to looking at with unseeing eyes. Then a new, interesting book will open its pages, which we will learn to read [...]. The ordinary will be filled with the fascinating content of the past, which brings us closer to an understanding of those lives [of writers – FN] that were so filled with creative endeavour.[59]

This last comment might well read as an allusion to ideas of aesthetic distancing (*ostranenie, vnenakhodimost'*) that were gaining currency in contemporary literary theory. Certainly, Antsiferov was familiar with the formalist and dialogic methods of Skhlovskii and Bakhtin, and, as some have argued, his approach to the past through the prism of literature presents some intriguing points of comparison with the concept of chronotope which became one of the hallmarks of Bakhtin's theory of meaning in language and literature.[60] But I would suggest that Antsiferov's appeal to the reader to 'look again' at St Petersburg and to explore a writer's sense of attachment to his surroundings remained fundamentally consistent with the principles of historical enquiry that he had first encountered as a student in Grevs' seminars on the medieval world. In particular, it was, as he later recalled, the experience of his field trip to northern Italy (1912) as part of Grevs' Dante seminar which taught him that 'the past is contained in the present' and that, in order to 'connect' with the past (*priobshchit'sia k proshlomu*), one had to 'do an inverted reconstruction of lost monuments so as to discern the "pulse" or spirit that once "animated" them'.[61] Above all, he was, at his own admission, indebted to Grevs' view that artistic creations are one of the most reliable (*vernyi*) historical documents preserving the atmosphere of a given locality in different ages.[62]

'I chose Grevs as my teacher'

Antsiferov's advocacy of excursion studies consisted in highlighting its versatility as a resource for cultural studies and local history. In his words: 'Grevs' "local method" allows both the historian and philologist in equal measure to engage (*priobshchit'sia*) with the aetiology of the myth/aura of a place, with the complex social and natural processes that affect it and change it over time. For the historian, the local method yields an understanding of the realia of a locality, for the philologist it affords insight into 'place' as an embodied idea, and into the emotional individuality of a creative writer'.[63] Specifically, Antsiferov conceived his popular and scholarly studies of national literary sites, in particular those associated with the writings of Puskhin and Dostoevskii, as an adaptation of, and faithful tribute to, Grevs' experiments with the methodology that he had originally devised for his study of Horace's villa in the province of Rome.[64]

Certainly, as Emily Johnson notes, Grevs' influence is felt in the way Antsiferov organized his Petersburg tours, which he detailed in his 1924 monograph: structured as a series of four excursions, 'the first three routes covered topics that corresponded to the initial and most extensively described section of the program Grevs outlined in "the monumental city," namely, his characterization of the circumstances of Petersburg's origins, its nucleus and early settlement'.[65] (In this connection, Grevs had introduced a comparative dimension by referencing the more typical patterns of development of ancient Russian towns.) Likewise, the focus of Antsiferov's excursions gradually shifted from geography and prehistory to street plans documenting the colony's growth from a central point.[66] Yet, even though Antsiferov inherited Grevs' excursionist glossary of physiological and psychological terms and, throughout his career, took a broadly 'essentialist' approach (as opposed to a functionalist or formalist one) to the study of urban culture, there was a note of tension between his call for a 'visual understanding of history' and the repercussions arising from a question he had posed in the opening pages of his first monograph about St Petersburg: 'How', he asked, 'is one to learn to understand the language of the city?' (*kak zhe nauchit'sia ponimat' iazyk goroda?*).[67] On this one occasion, Antsiferov seemed to be suggesting that the city might be considered as a single, composite text with its own peculiar semantics and language. Indeed, as Dmitrii Likhachev argued, while the literary citations in Antsiferov's studies generally functioned according to scholarly convention as supporting evidence, in some instances they seemed to assume a 'self-sufficient semantic entity' in their own right. For example, the extensive range of literary citations making up the second part of *Dusha Peterburga* had no traditional explanatory function; rather, they appeared to coalesce into a new 'supra-text' or 'Petersburg text' as Antsiferov's own personal evocation of the city's beautiful, yet tragic essence (*lik*).[68] As a contemporary of Russia's Silver Age culture, Antsiferov was, like Grevs, certainly receptive to its syncretism and semantic thinking. Not only did his work on the founding myth of St Petersburg build on motifs present in Russian symbolist poetry and prose, the unusually lyrical, evocative quality of his own 'scientific' prose was, itself, testament to the cultural sensibilities associated with Russian symbolism. Still, it remains that the main point of difference between Antsiferov, the historian, and his literary contemporaries was that rather than perpetuate the myth of St Petersburg's 'tragic essence' (*Dusha Peterburga* excepted) his goal was to uncover its sources and to reconstruct the process by which historical reality became mythologized.

The immediate reception by contemporaries of the excursion project was mixed, and we may easily appreciate why this was so: it reads as a peculiar hybrid of ideas that were at once outmoded and ahead of their time. If Grevs and Antsiferov were direct contemporaries of the avant-garde, their positivist inheritance, and what one might call an 'ethos of nostalgia' running through their work, placed them among an older generation of scholars, thereby obscuring the otherwise experimental nature of the ideas they were testing. But it is equally the case that while Antsiferov's approach to literature received mixed reviews by contemporaries as a return to the old era of symbolism, his latent grasp of the semantics of cityscapes anticipated – whether by accident or design – the semiotic approach to urban culture (*gradovedenie*) and myth that was developed in non-conformist literary theory during the Brezhnev era.[69] A number of scholars affirm this, citing some rewarding parallels between the model that Antsiferov devised in the early 1920s and collaborative articles by Iurii Lotman and Boris Uspenskii on the symbolism of Petersburg and the semiotics of the city.[70] Like Antsiferov, Lotman and Uspenskii argued that, well before Pushkin, Gogol and Dostoevskii 'turned the Petersburg myth into a fact of national culture, the real history of Petersburg was permeated with mythological elements', evidenced, they claimed, by the customs, beliefs, rumours and urban folklore patterning the lives of ordinary people.[71] There are other correspondences, too, between the two generations of scholars. Some may be considered incidental, such as the excursionist idea of the city as a 'cultural historical complex' and the semioticians' concept of the city as a deeply 'historical organism', which they defended against the 'technical', functionalist accent current in much twentieth-century scholarship.[72] Other similarities are more consequential in that they feed into broader questions concerning the nature of historical understanding: the spatial–temporal characteristic of the city, which both excursionists and semioticians addressed, is a case in point. According to Lotman, architecture, municipal ceremonies, even the city plan, street names and the thousands of other relics of past ages 'act like coded programmes (*kodovye programmy*), continually regenerating texts (*teksty*) from the historical past. The city is a mechanism that constantly engenders its past, which is given the possibility to align itself (*sopolagat'sia*) with the present as if synchronically'.[73] If, then, the semiotic theory of 'reading' the city as a 'complex semiotic mechanism' transposed to a new discursive context the visual and anthropomorphic metaphors (*lik, obraz*) of excursionism, this did not fundamentally disturb their shared premises concerning the significance of the city as a site in which past and present (or the synchronic and diachronic perspectives, in semiotic terminology) converge.

Closure of the institute

In June 1924, the institute was merged with the Institute of Scientific Pedagogy and the Pedagogical Museum and thus vanished as an organized entity. The reasons for its premature closure were ostensibly financial: the Commissariat of Enlightenment faced budgetary cuts as funding was redirected to Moscow, the new capital. But there is little doubt that the decision to support *kraevedenie* by establishing the central Bureau of Regional Studies (Moscow) as its administrative hub was both a strategic and political one.[74] With its focus on the history and culture of more remote regions across the Soviet Union, *kraevedenie* was arguably better suited as a scientific adjunct to *korenizatsiia*, the Soviet policy of assimilation through indigenization, than its urban-centred excursionist counterpart. On paper, there were, of course, some obvious similarities between regional and urban studies: both were multi-disciplinary in approach and advocated the pedagogical principles of 'learning by doing'. Moreover, as one of several calques, along with *rodinovedenie* and *stranovedenie*, for the German *Heimatkunde*, the coinage *kraevedenie* had entered the language around the turn of the century, that is, at roughly the same time as excursionism, and, again, like excursionism, was originally used to bolster the campaign for educational reform.[75] However, as Emily Johnson argues, with the exception of specialist literature, the term, as such, never really gained currency in either pedagogical or public discourse until after the revolution. During the Civil War, it was used as a qualifier (*kraevedicheskoe dvizhenie*) for measures to coordinate the efforts of local volunteers to protect valuable documents and artefacts that were at risk of being destroyed. It was only in 1921 when delegates at the first conference of Scientific Societies for the Study of Local Regions chose *kraevedenie* rather than its more familiar synonym, *rodinovedenie*, to designate a comprehensive approach to the study of local resources, heritage and folklore that its position as a comparable, yet potentially, rival discipline was acknowledged among excursionist contemporaries. Symbolically, by endorsing this relatively obscure term the regionalists had the advantage of a tabula rasa: unlike the excursionists who explicitly drew on their pre-revolutionary origins to remodel the discipline in line with Narkompros expectations, the regionalists were able to announce a clean break with the past and thus launch *kraevedenie* as a revolutionary new science.

It is interesting to note that among excursionists, Grevs was one of the very few to incorporate the terms '*krai*' and '*kraevedicheskii*' into his excursionist lexicon, and as early as 1922, when the regionalists received their first institutional base under the auspices of the Academy of Sciences, he had begun arguing – against considerable opposition – for closer collaboration between the two disciplines.[76] Two years later, as the future of the institute was under discussion, he made a spirited, if somewhat misguided, attempt to negotiate an institutional partnership by proposing to accommodate *kraevedenie* as a new 'social studies' (*obshchestvovedenie*) axis of excursionist enquiry.[77] A draft essay found among his papers, dated 1924 – so presumably around the time the fate of the institute was under discussion – summarized the main lines of research pursued by the Humanities Section of the Institute. In many respects, the piece merely reiterated comments from his unpublished 1912 essay, but it also included references to Antsiferov's mission statement of 1923. Thus, as before, methodological issues remained high on the agenda, issues that, in Grevs' view, were especially challenging because they were inextricably linked to some of the most fundamental questions in the science of education. With this in mind, he advised a two-pronged, analytical-deductive and empirical approach combining pedagogical ideas and pedagogical praxis ('in the laboratory of day-to-day work'). In tandem these would, he believed, help forge a substantially new discipline – the theory, methodology, psychology, didactics and technique of excursion studies (now coined as *ekskursievedenie*).[78] Another major task involved the classification of excursions. Here, again, Grevs more or less repeated the guidelines Antsiferov had set out. He identified five main areas that were best suited to the dual theoretical and practical (fieldwork) approach he envisaged for the discipline: geography and ethnography (focusing on the material and spiritual culture of populations, past and present); physical geography, which he argued was crucial for understanding the natural/environmental conditions in which culture(s) develop; cultural history, which he broke down into two subsets, namely: the study of painting, sculpture, architecture and the decorative arts; and a rather clumsily labelled 'aesthetic, artistic-historical, culture of the everyday (*kul'turno-bytovyi*)'. Next came creative literature – a new type of excursion, which had emerged simultaneously, though independently of each other, in Moscow and Leningrad. If methodologically, this category of excursions was the least developed, based on work conducted thus far (on Puskhin's and Dostoevskii's Petersburg, Tolstoi's and Herzen's Moscow), it promised, Grevs argued, to be an extremely valuable tool in the study of the lives of artists and in assessing their relation to the urban settings and monuments depicted in their writings. The final category of excursions – contemporary regional studies (*kraevedicheskii*) – was possibly the most significant in that it represented a last ditch attempt to save the excursionism project. What Grevs had in mind here, moreover, had little to do with a multi-disciplinary study of borderland regions: the first set of case studies he envisaged were thematically organized excursions within the Leningrad district: Petersburg – the imperial capital; military Petersburg, merchant Petersburg, and in an attempt to accommodate current social and political change he proposed the themed excursion – Proletarian Petersburg, Old Petersburg and New Leningrad. Alluding to, but not naming, the October Revolution ('the old is disappearing and the new is taking shape in peoples' lives'), Grevs argued that it was becoming all the more necessary to 'fix the bygone age through study, take note of the rise of new forms and trends, and elucidate the social, material and spiritual impact of these transformations (*peremena*) on populations across the regions'.[79] But by that time, Grevs' hopes to bridge cultural historical and sociological enquiry on the basis of interdepartmental collaboration were, of course, no longer practicable: the underlying rationale of his proposal belonged to a tradition in scholarship, which, ultimately, could not be readily co-opted to the task of consolidating the new Soviet space. If Grevs' 'scientific-empirical' pedigree might have assured him a place, however tenuous, in an emerging intellectual climate increasingly dominated by a Leninist–Stalinist reading of Karl Marx, the 'man-centred' nature of his enquiry, his attachment to questions of mentality, emotions and collective psychology, and his view of the historical process as something fundamentally complex, slow moving, and non-linear would rapidly find him branded as persona non grata. Neither the experimental scope of excursionism, then, nor its underlying premises of uncovering the spiritual resonances of a locality answered the increasingly prescriptive demands of Bolshevik ideology.

From a political–ideological perspective, explanations for the rapid demise of excursionism as a recognized discipline are self-evident: its 'science for science's sake' ethos was obviously out of kilter with the increasingly prescriptive expectations of the Bolshevik leadership in its drive to consolidate the regime. As I mentioned above, with the exception of Grevs, excursionists failed to recognize the challenge posed by *kraevedy* whose remit – at least during the 1920s – was clearly better suited to the leadership task of maintaining its border regions. And even as he endeavoured to bridge the two subject areas, Grevs could never abandon his view that the ultimate object of excursionist study was the person, man defined topographically and historically (*chelovek mestnyi*). As I have suggested, it was a view that remained consistent with the methodology he developed as a medievalist. In Soviet literature, however, both Grevs and Antsiferov were typically thought of as *kraevedy*, rather than medievalists, especially when, for a brief period during the latter part of the 1920s, regional studies (*kraevedenie*) became such a major discipline.[80] Its fortunes, though, changed dramatically in the early 1930s, once Stalin launched his massive industrialization and collectivization project: from that point on, the study of localities was driven by an interest in the potential of sites for industrial development, rather than by a disinterested enquiry into localities as 'cultural-historical complexes.'

Following the demise of the Excursion Institute, both Grevs and Antsiferov were employed by the Petrograd (Leningrad) Department of the Central Regional Study Bureau, where, for the next few years, they were able to pursue their work in urban studies.[81] Grevs visited towns in the Volga region – Rostov, Iarovslavl, Kostroma, Nizhnii Novgorod and Vladimir – and published a number of articles on historical (cultural) geography intended for schools. In these pieces, he remained wedded to the idea that geography and history needed to be studied together as kin disciplines in the family of sciences: 'Without geography', he wrote, 'our knowledge of the earth, its countries, and regions lacks analysis and is ideographic (*sinteticheskoe-obraznoe*); without history, the evolution of life is lost'.[82] In other words, to study urban sites, an understanding of the natural preconditions (*prirodnye predposylki*) facilitating their emergence was indispensable. As for Antsiferov, the provisional nature of literary excursionist methodology (if not the difficulties in defining one at all) remained a constant theme in his writings in this immediate post-institute period. In 1926, he published a further piece with guidelines for types of literary excursions. Titled *The Theory and Practice of Literary Excursions*, he again outlined various ways of incorporating literature into excursion work. More narrowly defined, the focus of literary excursions should, he argued, be based exclusively on material relative to a given author's biography; within the context of local studies, however, the inclusion of literary references was for illustrative or didactic purposes only and did not constitute a 'literary excursion' as such.[83] For example, an excursion to a large city street might conclude with a citation from a poem by Maiakovskii in order to draw attention to some of the key features of urban life – the movement of the crowd; fragments of conversations and phrases; the bells on trains, car horns and the hum of wheels; the cries of newspaper boys, 'as short and garish as posters'.[84] Or an excursion to a museum might serve as useful background information for deepening the pupils' understanding of classic texts. Ultimately, though, he recognized that these variants were, by far, the most difficult to conduct and, 'in view of their peculiarities', might well 'never be broadly practiced'.[85] 'Of course', as he put it, 'the "Three Pine Trees" (Tri sosny – a short story by Turgenev), the inn of "the unknown Woman" (neznakomka), and "the statue in Tsarskoe selo" (Tsarskosel'skaia statuia) exist "outside of space," that is, outside of any connection with concrete places (...), they exist in the special world of art. Their value does not depend at all on whether or not there is a sweet girl with a pitcher in the Catherine Park, whether there exist three old pine trees on the road to Trigorsk or whether, on the outskirts of the northern capital there really is an inn frequented by a pensive poet which is reflected in one of his best creations'.[86] What really mattered was an ability to capture the imagination of the students as they visited key landmarks in the nation's history and, in the process, impress upon them what he believed to be the 'sovereign significance of the artistic work'.

Antsiferov was arrested in 1929 and sentenced the following year in connection with the Academic affair (1929–31). In late 1931, he was sent to the BelBaltLag, a hard labour camp set up to construct the White Sea–Baltic Canal. After his release in 1934, he settled in Moscow, and for the remainder of his professional life he worked in a number of pedagogical institutions, managing to resume his research in literary urbanism, although, with the exception of his master's *kandidatskaia* thesis, which he defended in June 1944 at the Institute of World Literature (IMLI), most of what he published dating from this period consisted of popular studies about literary Moscow.[87] The thesis, itself, a study of Dostoevskii's Petersburg and questions of urbanism in the Russian literary canon (*Problems of Urbanism in Russian Creative Literature: Constructing the Image of a City – Dostoevskii's Petersburg – Based on an Analysis of Literary Traditions* [1944]), marked an obvious return to one of his main preoccupations during the 1920s.[88] Even from the most cursory overview, one can discern a seamless continuity with his earlier work: the principal task of urban history, he claimed, was to capture, through the inflections of a literary or philosophical document, the '*litso goroda*' and to explore the power of place as a peculiar historical individuality on the psyche of its inhabitants. For Antsiferov, understanding the physical and non-material qualities of 'place' was key for understanding the historical process more broadly. On another level, though, one may perhaps appreciate how, at the time of writing, his analysis of the highly personal resonances of the words '*zemlia*' or '*kamni*' (earth/stones) in Dostoevskii's lexicon reverberated with questions relating to cultural legacy that were both deeply emotional and value laden. For example, in the preface, we note his tribute to the city that, just five months earlier, had been released from the horrors of the blockade: 'As far back as 1919, I began working on images of Petersburg as refracted in the nation's literary classics. At that time, Petrograd was torn by the civil war; the Blockade has sucked the lifeblood out of our great country (…). In my book, *The Soul of Petersburg*, I tried to convey (…) a sense of the tragic essence of this city with it universal soul (…). Now, more than twenty years on, undertaking a new study on a similar theme, I hope that, although it deals with Leningrad's past, it has some bearing on the events that have assailed this great city, as tragic destiny raises this city–hero through a path of suffering to the heights of world glory'.[89] And, as we glean from his memoirs, in Antsiferov's own life, war and the blockade had reduced places linked with personal and family memory – Detskoe Selo, Pavlovsk, Gatchina, Tsarskaia Slavianka, located on the outskirts of Petersburg – to ash and rubble. Even more poignantly, though, the sense of uprootedness, of being forcibly detached from 'stone and the earth' through collectivization, war and resettlement was, we know, an experience shared by millions.

Local history and the medieval world: Festschrift for Grevs, 1925

In a questionnaire conducted for the Excursion Institute, Grevs listed his field of expertise as scientific–historical research in ancient and medieval history, and in the social history of the renaissance with an emphasis on questions of spiritual culture.[90] As I have suggested, the 'man-centred' nature of his approach encompassing spiritual and daily life, which became the hallmark of his seminars during the final decade of imperial rule, was certainly innovative for its time. Indeed, some Western and

Russian scholars regard Grevs' early prescriptions for historical study as an incidental precursor of the French *Annales*.[91] Certainly, the career paths of Grevs and Marc Bloch as medievalists were remarkably similar: trained in socio-economic history but quickly turning to the study of culture and historical geography, both men rejected the conventions of political historical narrative of national events with its inbuilt assumptions of progress, and its 'obsession with origins' for a multi-disciplinary study of human experience, beliefs and values and the way these were articulated in local contexts. We should not, though, overlook the notable differences between the Russian and French historiographies, namely the *Annales'* emphasis on enduring structures versus the diachronic accent in excursionism or 'generic man' versus 'vernacular' man. Perhaps, then, it may be more accurate to speak of complementary endeavours to grapple with historical explanations predicated on the well-established 'view from above' that we typically associate with political and diplomatic history, and which still prevailed in university instruction.

'Every age', Antisferov recorded in his memoirs about Grevs, 'has its aroma, its own particular "sound," a sort of "couleur temporelle" just as we would speak of a "couleur locale." But only a historian-artist is capable of rendering this aura, this colour. Not a historian-aesthete, an admirer of heroic acts and strong personalities, or of the most striking, eye-catching aspects of culture; rather, someone who attains the depths of all movements (...). It is precisely the historian-artist who captures these sounds of time within his own being, imparting to them the luminosity of a moral light, and conveys these to others'.[92] Without a doubt, Grevs' contribution to excursion history constituted his most enduring legacy: he trained several generations of students, both at the university and the Bestuzhevskie courses, in methods of investigating the culture of select topographical regions; and, as I have just mentioned, his own work in the field established his reputation in the Soviet era as one of the founders of *kraevedenie*, a label which eventually superseded the clumsy, ill-sounding pre-revolutionary term of excursionism. Even if Grevs only managed to lead two excursions to Italy with his university and Bestuzhevskie students, the local history methodology which he made integral to his seminar programme was rewarded by a sense of total immersion ('*effekt pogruzheniia*') into the spiritual (*dukhovnaia*) culture of the medieval world, that, hitherto, the curriculum had not managed to provide.[93] Two Festshrifts dedicated to the 'master' (1911 and 1925 celebrating twenty-five and forty years of teaching) attest the dual excursionist and biographical approach used by former students in their tribute essays to him.[94] The second collection of essays, for example, contained a research paper by Matvei Gukovskii on 'jousting' (*turnir*) in Italy – a study of the rules of the game as a distant precursor of modern-day sport such as lawn tennis and fencing, and of its function as a great public attraction albeit frowned upon by the Church.[95] Anna Khomentovskaia wrote about the Tuscan city of Lucca, an important centre of cloth making and trade during the age of the merchant dynasty of Guinigi. A further topic was life and commerce on the Petit Pont in Paris during the twelfth and thirteenth centuries: using a range of sources – archaeological, topographical, architectural, chronicles and poetry – the author, Maria Tikhanova-Klimenko, took the bridge as a framework or microcosm to study urban life, trade, customs, taverns and hostels in the French capital. Specifically, she considered the successive reconstructions of the bridge and its layout, the ways in which it was populated by tradesmen, hostels, taverns, Jews and foreigners (English, German, Danish); provincials from Burgundy, Gascony, Normandy; and by butchers from Brittany. Antsiferov contributed a piece about the residual features of agrarian life in a French town on the outskirts of Paris at the turn of the thirteenth century. By studying the agricultural resonances of place names, and the day-to-day rhythms and customs typically associated with rural life, which the new urban settlers continued to practise, he traced the peculiar cohabitation of urban and agrarian life within the perimeters of the city.[96] A certain A. Stepanovich explored the evolving symbolic significance of the cockerel on the gothic church spire – from that of sunrise/resurrection in the ancient world and New Testament, to vigil, guide, warning or comforter in the Church Fathers and popular belief.[97] One last example worth mentioning is Elena Skrzhinskaia's account of a medieval thermal bath (*kurort*), which she based on a didactic poem, de Balneis Puteolanis, by Peter of Eboli, an early thirteenth-century poet to the court of Fredrick II Hohenstaufen: her analysis of the poem provided the context for a discussion of the rise of medicine and healing in the High Middle Ages.[98]

In their various ways, these studies of place, things and practices each answered Grevs' early instruction to visualize the past and experience first hand its material traces. They also attest a peculiar hybrid of historical and philological (textual–literary) analysis. I will return to this topic in Chapter 8 where I consider the rise of literary history and its overlap with general history during the course of the nineteenth century. As to why this remained an enduring practice in the early Soviet period, one has, I think, to consider the historians' status as persona non grata in the new regime which more or less coerced them into making a career switch (the case of Antsiferov, as we have seen[99]). But equally, the skills they acquired as historian-medievalists meant they were able to cross over into literary criticism and culture with relative ease; at the root of their literary-critical work lay the same methodological principles and approaches they had worked with under Grevs' tutelage.

7

The Historian's Literary Compass: Modern Poets and Novelists

For any student of Russian society and culture, to say that the reading public vested the nation's modern literary masterpieces with the power to raise historical consciousness is a truism. However, the repercussions of this for the epistemic authority of trained historians could be quite damaging in the sense that the intellectual capital afforded to creative writers made them potential rivals competing with the university discipline for ownership of the past. Indeed, among novelists and poets, themselves, it was not uncommon to encounter dismissive opinions of historical scholarship. Tolstoi and Dostoevskii, for example, both perpetuated a prejudice against institutionalized forms of knowledge production: 'One can express incomparably more about our history through fidelity to historic truth than through fidelity merely to history', Dostoevskii wrote in his *Diary of a Writer*; and, in Tolstoi's opinion: 'The new history is like a deaf man replying to questions which nobody puts to him'.[1] Whether substantiated or not, Tolstoi's cruel parody of textbook histories in his epilogue to *War and Peace* as a compromised, misguidedly naïve, or simply 'boring' science was a commanding one and goes some way to explaining why members of the academic community felt compelled to address, if not challenge, the historical insights of literary masters.[2] Kareev, for example, took a fairly dim view of Tolstoi's philosophy of history, but he nevertheless regarded the novelist's viewpoint seriously enough to engage with it in some detail. No one, however, questioned Pushkin's genius as a historian-poet. As the consummate 'divinatory of historical truth', he had, as Kliuchevskii argued, earned his place in Russian historiography.[3]

Historians used a variety of platforms – public address, essay, monograph, personal notes and jottings – to offer a predominantly social and cultural historical critique of the nation's modern literary canon: the life of the artist, his worldview, and the intellectual and socio-political environment in which he wrote poetry and prose all provided valuable insights into the peculiar correlations between individual and historical experience. Yet, if, as a rule, historians tended to contextualize or generalize the personal experiences shaping the artist's historical sensitivities, in some instances their engagement with works of fiction took an unexpected departure from established practices of enquiry. Reflections on human emotions and values, topics that we more commonly associate with the remit of literary criticism (or psychology), informed a body of commentary, which, although small, is nonetheless instructive of certain patterns within Russian historical culture. It is, of course, true that this literary–historical confluence was often due to force of circumstance affecting the career path of a historian. The prohibitive Jewish quota, for example, compelled Mikhail Gershenzon (1869–1925), a highly talented student of ancient history, to adapt his skillset to the study of literature, and, as I mentioned in the previous chapter, regime change in 1917 also necessitated career switches. But, this is not to say that the questions and hypotheses driving these small studies of the human condition were necessarily ancillary to historians' main field of expertise: on the contrary, as the writings of Kliuchevskii and Grevs demonstrate, they could occupy a central place in their reflections on the purpose and object of history itself.

This chapter examines a body of work by historians on the nation's modern literary pantheon – Pushkin, Tolstoi, Lermontov and Turgenev. I begin with an overview of commemorative speeches and essays about creative writers in which historians singled out specific motifs/conceptual issues for their intellectual historical resonances: the artist as the voice of historical consciousness (Pushkin); the artist as a historian and philosopher of history (Pushkin and Tolstoi); the life of the artist as a historical source (Turgenev). The underlying question here is whether these essays and lectures were merely a sideline to the historian's preoccupations as a scholar or whether they might legitimately be considered integral to his endeavours to deepen historical understanding. In the second part of this chapter, I turn to their handling of questions relating to 'the human condition' and the manner in which this fed into broader definitions of the historian's task. Finally, I consider the literature–history node through the prism of (enforced) changes in career paths in the late nineteenth century. The case of Mikhail Gershenzon, a casualty of the Jewish quota, which prevented him from pursuing a career as a professor of history, is especially interesting as, independently of Grevs, his work on the national literary canon focused on (imagined) places and the inner world of creative individuals.

The lives of artists

From the Voice of Historical Consciousness to Historian and Philosopher of History

The practice of commemorating the life and work of the nation's most celebrated literary masters offered a wide platform for historians to perform as public intellectuals. Written or delivered to mark a special anniversary, the format of these addresses generally combined the established conventions of encomium with arguments highlighting not just the value of creative literature as a key factor in enhancing historical understanding, but also the conscious life of the artist as integral to this process. Numerous tributes to Pushkin, in particular, stressed his importance in this regard. 'Three things', Kareev wrote, alluding to Taine's tri-part theory of literature (race, milieu, moment), 'determine the physiognomy of every poet and his literary activity: the personality (*lichnost'*) of the poet; place of birth or origins (spiritual and natural environment); the inheritance of his native land. (…) His poetry is not just a reflection of the poet himself – it reflects, rather, the history, epoch, and historical moment in which the poet lived'.[4] For Kareev, Pushkin was both a Russian and a European poet in the sense that his poetry articulated points of connection between individual and historical experience that were equally nation bound and universal in their ramifications. 'Modern poetry', he wrote, 'was the first voice of self-awareness in the field of art, the first artistic profession of noble, humane, liberal ideas of the century'.[5] Comparing Pushkin's cultural significance to the political vision of Peter the Great whose 'window on to the West' launched Russia as an important player in European politics, Pushkin, he argued, helped position Russian poetry in the mainstream of contemporary European culture: similar to Lord Byron, Pushkin was fully aware of the power of his poetry as the voice of public opinion.[6]

'The life of the poet', Kliuchevskii recorded in his diary, 'is only the first part of his biography: the posthumous history of his poetry constitutes a second and more significant part'.[7] Pushkin remained an inexhaustible source and inspiration for Kliuchevskii throughout his career. In the various essays and lectures he wrote on the poet's life and work, he aimed to uncover the national indigenous roots of his poetic genius, explain his place in the nation's history, and assess the extent of his influence. Like Kareev, Kliuchevskii drew attention to Pushkin's poetry as 'a national echo of universal endeavour'. And, again, like Kareev, Kliuchevskii took note of the way Pushkin himself conceived 'nationality', less in terms of the specificities of language or in the choice of subject matter as in respect of the particular form of thoughts and sentiments that were (putatively) an intrinsic part of a 'nation's moral and physical physiognomy'[8]: 'The source of Pushkin's genius (*istochnik genii*) as a poet is to be found', Kliuchevskii wrote, 'in the depths of popular Russian thought and feeling, in our songs and proverbs (…); it (*istochnik*) is rooted in the entire course of the history of our people'.[9] In other words, as an echo of the voice of the Russian people, Pushkin's poetic voice became in its own right a catalyst of national self-consciousness.[10]

'Pushkin was a historian where he did not think he was one'.[11] If historians were sensitive to the ways that creative artists articulated a sense of history or reflected on the meaning of history through the mediums of poetry, drama and the novel, they were also interested in the way creative writers actually processed historical material, that is, how they worked with archival sources, and the degree to which they relied on – or indeed refuted (as Tolstoi did) – established historical interpretations. Pushkin's ventures into history have been widely commented upon.[12] His first topic, Boris Godunov, a play in verse (written 1825), for example, drew heavily on Karamzin's *History*.[13] But during the last decade of his life he undertook intensive historical study of his own based on consultation of documents in the national archives. In addition to a two-volume history of the Pugachev Rebellion (*Istoriia Pugacheva*, 1834[14]), at the time of his death in 1837, he was working on a History of Peter the Great. At first sight, then, Kliuchevskii's observation, cited here, is puzzling. What exactly did he mean by it?

Reflecting on the relation between history and creative literature in Pushkin's work, Kliuchevskii presented a somewhat paradoxical argument: more than works that clearly announced historical themes in their titles, such as *Poltava* (1829) or *Boris Godunov* (1825), it was his romantic tale, *The Captain's Daughter* (1836), that offered a deeper and more accurate rendering of the epoch (in this instance, the late eighteenth century).[15] Modelled after Walter Scott, Pushkin's novel combined historical documents and fictitious letters. It brought together in various chance meetings two historical antagonists – Catherine II and Pugachev – with Mironova, the captain's daughter and the fictional first-person narrator, Grinev. Through his eyes, the reader is given not only a portrait of Mironova (and the romantic love story), but also an account of life and domestic customs in a small border garrison town as a local setting within which the impact (and human cost) of one of the most significant events in Catherine's reign – the Pugachev rebellion – was experienced.

Although, as Kliuchevskii remarked in his 1880 speech, *The Captain's Daughter* had grown out of Pushkin's extensive historical research into the Pugachev rebellion, in his view, the earlier, non-fictionalized account functioned as little more than dry commentary to the novel.[16] It was, by contrast, the prose novel that captured far more powerfully Pushkin's strengths as a historian-artist, which Kliuchevskii identified as an ability to craft his protagonists from a blend of fact and fiction. Specifically, what he meant by this were not just the staged encounters and juxtaposition of the two historical antagonists with the fictional protagonist and narrator, but also the way in which the latter – Captain Mironov and especially the first-person narrator, Grinev – belonged to a gallery of eighteenth-century cultural types, namely 'those Russians who grew up in the knowledge that they were not European, but compelled to become European', as Kliuchevskii put it with such acuity.[17] Here, in this novel, Pushkin captured this brilliantly in his portrayals of the adolescents (*nedorosli*), Captain Mironov and Lieutenant Grinev, as the typical average low-ranking nobility (they were more or less contemporary with Fonvizin's Mitrofan) who fought alongside the generals Suvorov and Rumiantsev celebrated for their valour on the battlefield. But that he did so in other novels, too (Kliuchevskii mentioned Ibrahim in Pushkin's unfinished tale about Peter the Great's Negro/Moor, *Arap Petra Velikogo*, written in 1827–8, and published shortly after the poet's death in 1837, and *Dubrovskii*, published in 1841), made him indispensable for the historian. In sum, Pushkin truly was the master of 'artistic-historical' (*khudozhestvenno-istoricheskie*) portraits.[18]

As I argued in Chapter 5, Kliuchevskii's articles on literature and the literati were closely related to his understanding of the historical process, and regardless of whether he was narrating the life of a tsar or characterizing the typical noble, he worked imaginatively with a variety of sources, from historical documents, legislation, chronicle, to folk legend and some of the classics of modern and contemporary fiction.[19] Thus, his appreciation of Pushkin's historical sensitivity and of his work as a 'historical document (…), a poetic chronicle of his age through the personages he portrays',[20] is hardly surprising since it was entirely consistent with the emphasis that he, himself, placed on portraiture as a means to harness the historical process – the flow of history – in socio-psychological terms. In other words, like Pushkin, Kliuchevskii made the historical past present by means of literary art. For the poet and, arguably, for the historian as well, it was the impact of large-scale events on the lives of people who experienced them that mattered rather more than the power of individual tsars and/or governments who orchestrated them. And indeed, even in their characterizations of the latter both men tended to enclose their subjects within domestic settings so as to scrutinize with greater ease the psychological factors governing their actions.[21] Pushkin's portrayal of Catherine the Great is a case in point: it is intimate, familial, and unlike the ceremonial, triumphalist poses referencing classical models with which we tend to associate her, Pushkin foregrounds her traits as a woman and mother, a 'lady of about forty', seated on a bench in the park, 'with red cheeks' in a 'white morning dress.' Suffice it to recall Kliuchevskii's characterization of Peter the Great (discussed in Chapter 4), whom we first encounter genuflecting at an Easter liturgy, and not at some grand court ceremony. Indeed, it is tempting to read Kliuchevskii's study of *Evgenii Onegin* and his real-life historical precursors, written seven years after his Pushkin Speech, as a tribute, through imitation, to Pushkin's ability to create a collection of artistic-historical portraits, all of which embody one and the same cultural type and its complex variations across generations: Troekurov and Prince Vereiskii (in *Dubrovskii*), the Mitrofans 'of all sorts' were the predecessors of Onegin.[22]

In his article, 'Poetic Genre and the Sense of History in Pushkin', Jurij Striedter shows how changes in a poet's sense of history may be documented in his preference for certain poetical genres and, conversely, how the specific structures of given genres accommodate certain aspects of history and the sense of history, yet hinder others. As Striedter argues, it was the novel that afforded Pushkin (and later Tolstoi) the greatest scope to explore not just the impact of great historical currents and events on personal and family destinies, but, importantly, the role of chance in human experience. This last point also had implications for understanding the historical process itself. As I discuss below, the idea of chance gave creative artists licence to question 'the laws of history', free will and causality.

'For history', Lev Tolstoi wrote, 'the admission that the free wills of men are forces capable of influencing historical events, that is, not subject to laws, is the same as would be to astronomy the admission of free will in the movements of heavenly bodies.'[23] Like Pushkin in the *Captain's Daughter* (and equally, *The Bronze Horseman*), Tolstoi's depiction of the historical process in *War and Peace* correlated personal and historical experience, his sympathies as a writer lying firmly with the people, 'those small differentials', as Tolstoi called them, who were often overlooked in historical accounts. Tolstoi famously reserved his sharpest criticism for historians who tended to venerate the historical singularity of so-called great men, such as Napoleon, at the expense of the ordinary, inglorious Russian or French foot soldier. In this connection, he named Thomas Carlyle (his *On Heroes, Hero-Worship and the Heroic in History* [1841]), Edward Gibbon and Henry Thomas Buckle, and, of course, was, as Isaiah Berlin noted, familiar with Hegel's description of Napoleon as 'the world-spirit on horseback'. 'Life', Tolstoi wrote, 'consists of innumerable events, but history chooses only an insignificant, arbitrarily patterned part of these events with which to document a special theory as the primary cause of social or political change'. In his view, it followed that in historical scholarship, ascriptions of 'free will' to great men were misguided and delusional: Napoleon and 'great men' like him (such as Louis XIV), who thought of themselves as supremely free, vested with the power to command the movement of thousands of people from west to east to die and slay in battle, were, in fact, mere 'servants of history', as much caught up in that 'swarm-like' existence as the meanest hussar. In other words, great events, like the Napoleonic invasion, happen not because one man dictates the movement of history, but because hundreds of thousands of motives and accidents and reactions occur at once. The 'real' history of human beings, then, resided not in social, political and economic phenomena (which Tolstoi categorized as mere outer accidents), but in ordinary, day-to-day life and in the 'inner' (private) events affecting the lives of human beings, which he captured so brilliantly in the sentiments and experiences of the fictional protagonists he created. As the most real and immediate experiences, 'they and only they are what life in the last analysis, is made of'.[24] As Tolstoi understood matters, then, his overriding task was to uncover a single explanatory doctrine or law for all these multiple and seemingly disconnected events that make up reality, even as he was fully aware of the difficulties confronting him – on the one hand, a call for laws and a tone that implies their existence; on the other, a complete lack of any kind of coherent statement of these laws: 'The driving force (or motor) of history, as the cause of movement, comprises the sum total of people's arbitrary will (*proizvol*), while the final (*poslednaia*) cause/force in a given moment is such because in the given circumstances any other combination is unthinkable'.[25]

Tolstoi formulated his understanding of history in the second section of the epilogue to *War and Peace*, thereby creating scope for a critique of contemporary historiography (questions of causality, laws) and for a highly personal reflection on the irrational, on good and evil, free will and determination as competing forces of history in a manner not confined or conditioned by the conventions of the novel.[26] But how far he succeeded in countering established 'scholarly' explanations given in terms of 'chance', 'genius' or 'cause', which he considered as little more than 'thin disguises for ignorance', became a topic of debate among contemporary historians. In his notes for the epilogue, he wrote:

> I understand the entire difference between my stated view of history and that of all historians. The difference is such that it is clear: either I had the misfortune to go out of my mind and to couple an insane discussion of history to a work that was having great success, or else all that is called historical science, that is written, taught, and published so seriously is empty and idle chatter. (…) Either I am crazy or I have discovered a new truth. I believe I have discovered a new truth.[27]

The majority of Tolstoi's first readers thought the former, however: the great novelist's view of history (and trenchant dismissal of historical science) perplexed many as maladroit and as a form of posturing. Ivan Turgenev called it 'farcical', literary specialists regarded it as 'trivial and superficial (…), the denial of the decisive influence of individual personalities on events (…) nothing but "charlatanism"'.[28] Among university-based historians, too, the issues Tolstoi raised became a point of contention, but not because of his tirade against the political historians who, Tolstoi claimed, by writing history as a series of public events 'are talking shallow nonsense', rather because of what they saw as the inherent contradictions in Tolstoi's own theory and (for some) his misplaced targeting of a Hegelian-inspired approach foregrounding the role of Great Men as the driving forces of history, or the role of 'ideas' as primary causes: by the closing decades of the nineteenth century such ideas (in Russia) were, if still residual in some historical studies, for certain, no longer mainstream.

Among historians, Nikolai Kareev was one of very few to take Tolstoi's doctrine seriously enough to offer a reasoned refutation of it, both from the standpoint of social history and by exposing its inherent contradictions. For example, with respect to the main points of Tolstoi's theory of causality, just cited, Kareev took the novelist to task for terminological sloppiness:

> Tolstoi calls this 'force' a law (*zakon*), ignoring his own advice to 'smash up (*drobit'*) causes, since they are all subsumed under a single 'law'. Tolstoi himself does not clarify what he means by cause, or indeed, the term 'law'. If the sum total of people's arbitrary wills frames the process of history, the question arises whether the constituent parts of this total are equal. If not, how then are they configured in terms of the influence they exert over the course of events? Tolstoi's answer is highly unsatisfactory: he denies the role of the individual in history, reducing it to zero before the masses, or the '*rosva*' of force. Second, if will is not free then what is it subordinated to? Again, since Tolstoi denies the role of the individual he cannot offer a convincing answer.[29]

Kareev did, though, acknowledge the value of Tolstoi's critique of Hegelian-inspired historiography in the name of realism: he agreed with much of Tolstoi's protest against theories premised on the notions of 'power' or 'ideas' as the driving forces of history, and welcomed the importance that the novelist invested in reconstructing concrete, empirical facts. Tolstoi was also right in calling for the integration of the infinitesimals of history. But, if Kareev had no quarrel here, and while he welcomed Tolstoi's categorical rejection of 'objective teleology'[30] (namely, the goal of history is freedom, enlightenment and civilization, which, we saw, Granovskii advocated), it was the novelist's indifference towards social questions and the manner in which he prioritized purely moral questions relating to the individual that ultimately explained his failure to produce any kind of persuasive counter-theory. For Kareev, then, the historian–sociologist and left-wing intellectual, Tolstoi's inability to overcome his own, personal subjectivism prevented him from understanding the true nature of history. In Kareev's words:

> As an opponent of the idealization of historical reality, namely a total rationality of the general path of history, Tolstoi takes a radical stand against objective teleology, and is categorical in his belief that 'the end goal of history is unknown to us' […]. But he goes too far: if his refusal to idealize life's phenomena in general does not prevent him from forging ideals of a personal ethic, then he ought to have made these the basis of social ideals as well; if he allows himself to pronounce judgment on life from the point of view of an ethical ideal, then he ought to apply this to an evaluation of […] the social ideal, understood in the widest sense of the term. However, not only does he not do this, he exhibits an astonishing indifference towards social questions insofar as the latter have their own independent content irrespective of purely moral questions. […]. For him, the changing forms of life, which leave their mark on the person and man's fate, simply do not exist. From here it is one small step to a belittling of history, reducing it to a purely mechanical sequence of facts, which have no inner substance. Such is Tolstoi's philosophy of history.[31]

Tolstoi's blind spot regarding the impact of society on man's world formed the leading thread of Kareev's critique. Repeatedly, he reminds the reader that the action of history on man does not consist uniquely of the direct influence of events on the inner life of the person and that the life of the individual is conditioned by certain social forms which change with the historical process: 'The plenitude, freedom and well being of the individual are entirely shaped by the overall structure of social life, and the task of outlining the impact of history on man from this perspective falls to the sociologist'.[32] This perspective also framed Kareev's response to Tolstoi's views on free will and determinism in terms of their implications for historical understanding. If Tolstoi was right to say that the impersonal 'forces' and 'purposes' assumed by an older generation of historians (and which, apparently, still had some purchase within the profession) were dangerously misleading myths, these could not, Kareev believed, be dismissed altogether: 'Tolstoi's philosophy of history in *War and Peace*', he wrote, 'comes down to a denial of the role of individual initiative in history. History, for Tolstoi, is a mass movement (...); great men function as "labels of events" (*iarlyky sobytii*), and have no independent significance'.[33] For Kareev, by contrast, it is men, doubtless, who make social forms, but these forms, that is, the ways in which men live, affect, in turn, those born into them. In other words, while individual wills may not be all-powerful, neither are they totally impotent, and some are more effective than others: Napoleon may not be a demigod, but neither is he a mere epiphenomenon of a process which would have occurred in the same way without him. Unlike Tolstoi, to whom the intimate inner life of individuals alone seemed real, in Kareev's understanding, individuals have social purposes, and, thanks to a strong will, some may be capable of transforming the lives of communities (as empirically based historical evidence has demonstrated countless times). From this perspective, Tolstoi's notion of inexorable laws which work themselves out whatever men may think or wish seemed to be an as oppressive myth as the theory of inexorable 'forces' which he eschewed. For Kareev, then, just as the achievement of *War and Peace* resided in the author's realism, the omission from his philosophy of history of 'social forms, social questions, and social ideals' meant that his 'realism' became one sided, not far removed from naturalism.[34] This, combined with his acknowledged fatalism, was, as Berlin observed, more than likely to provoke a negative reaction in many readers and critics to Tolstoi's historiosophical disquisitions.

According to Isaiah Berlin, Kareev's objections were entirely reasonable but did not engage with the deeper source of Tolstoi's obsession with history which, as Berlin notes, was rooted in 'something more personal, a bitter conflict between his actual experience and his belief, between his vision of life, and his theory of what it, and he himself, ought to be, if the vision was to be bearable at all'.[35] This conflict was famously captured in the classical motifs of 'hedgehog' and 'fox', which Berlin used as the title of his essay. Tolstoi was by nature a fox but believed in being a hedgehog, that is, in Wachtel's summary of Berlin's argument: 'Tolstoi was capable as no other writer before or since of noticing and capturing the multiplicity that surrounded him, but at the same time he had an irresistible desire to reduce that multiplicity to a single, overarching system'.[36] Was Berlin entirely justified in his remarks about Kareev, though? In the introduction to his essay about *War and Peace*, Kareev noted: 'History and the novel are two forms within which one and the same is contained (…) namely the depiction of the person and the movement of history in a reciprocal relationship'.[37] Certainly, Kareev argued that Tolstoi had failed in his designs at a theoretical level to provide a unifying law of history, but he also acknowledged that the clarity and passion with which he spoke as an artist was the most powerful way to restore into the continuum of history all the infinitely small human actions and events that had been egregiously overlooked in the arbitrarily segmented accounts of professional historical discourse. As a writer and as the creator of a gallery of individuals that he depicted in all their unique differences, Tolstoi had, indeed, succeeded in integrating the infinitesimals of history: using artistic-psychological means he had managed to penetrate the very depths of the interrelationship between individual experience and broad-scale historical events.[38] If, then, in his appraisal of Tolstoi's philosophy of history, Kareev appeared to be drawing a clear line of demarcation between the historian and the novelist, it was not to dismiss the value of creative literature in historical understanding, quite the contrary. To appreciate this, we need to place Kareev's commentary of Tolstoi within the context of a broader project that he was working on at that time, namely to integrate creative literature into a comprehensive theory of the humanities. I will return to this in the next chapter.

The life of the artist as a historical source: Grevs on Turgenev

'Turgenev', Grevs wrote in an unpublished draft essay,

> is one of my all-time favourite Russian writers (…). I love him, I am in awe of him; I delight in his words, images and thoughts. I revere him like a good teacher of truth (*pravda*) and beauty. I feel his wide-ranging influence as countless threads spiritually binding me with him. The principal secret of this link resides, I think, in the signification of one single word: humanity, *humanitas*.[39]

Recently published notes and excerpts from Grevs' diaries (dated 1925) relate with quite disarming frankness his sense of intellectual and spiritual affinity with the novelist and are worth quoting at length as evidence of the importance he invested in literature as a guide to life. More specifically, they shed light on the theme of love and friendship, which Grevs addressed in his home seminar during the war, and which he would write about (and publish) during the first decade of Bolshevik rule:

> Throughout my gymnasium years I read and reread the main works, each time finding new artistic enjoyment, social and moral exhortation […]. I was particularly drawn to the social message of his writing, which tied him to Russian life, yet for which he became the victim of heavy blows […], those repeated instances of incomprehension by the intelligentsia crowd or radical youth, as well as their reactionary fathers. It is precisely for this reason that I called him 'master' (*uchitel'*). […]. I can say that throughout my life (apart from a brief lapse during my student years), the works of Turgenev have never left me. With friends in the

brotherhood[40] I was always defending him against those who were in thrall to Lev Tolstoi, and later, Dostoevskii. During my research trips to Paris (1890-2) he was a great comfort to me. At that time, I was thinking of writing about him as an interpreter of social movements in Russia; but to this day I have not carried out this plan. As a teacher, I tried to instill students with a love for Turgenev: I gave talks and readings at literary evenings at the Petrovskaia and Tagantsev gymnasiums. And I was saddened when I saw that the youth did not like him. This happened on my second excursion to Italy when A. I. Anisuimov started criticizing him as a boring writer.[41]

In a letter dated 12 October 1921, addressed to one of his former students, E. Ia. Rudinskaia, then residing in Kiev, Grevs wrote:

What really set last winter apart was that I was able to give public lectures on a number of topics which, though hardly my specialism, are dear to me. I lectured on historical idealism, on great figures in the history of religion in antiquity and the Middle Ages, on Dante, Romain Rolland, on images of Italy in the writings of Turgenev. It was interesting to see that through these lectures for a wide public I found my audience, which kept coming back, and with whom a special (*dukhovnyi*) connection was established.[42]

Beginning in 1918, to mark the centenary of Turgenev's birth, Grevs embarked on a series of studies focusing on the intellectual and emotional life of the artist.[43] Two monographs were published in quick succession following the closure of the Excursion Institute – *Turgenev and Italy: A Cultural-Historical Study* (*Turgenev i Italiia: Kul'turno-istoricheskii etiud*) (1925), followed by *A History of One Love* (*Istoriia odnoi liubvy: I. S. Turgenev i Polina Viardo*) (1926), in which he charted Turgenev's life-long emotional involvement with the opera singer, Pauline Viardot. A further project dealing with what Grevs called Turgenev's 'religious drama' (1927) was, to my knowledge, never printed, but, again, as with the themes of Italy and love, the choice of topic was significant for the insights it affords into Grevs' own spiritual and emotional world. As he put it in a diary entry: 'I dream of writing a study of Turgenev's religious drama. It is a major question. Turgenev was a religious spirit, and even though he broke with it, he was not able to assume his doubts fully. Turgenev has always been close to me, first as a teacher then as a friend. We are very different people, but are bound by common cultural–genetic and individual traits. I am more fortunate than he, having overcome pessimism and lack of faith, but admire him all the more for this, and feel for him'.[44]

Grevs' work on the lives and works of modern and contemporary literary artists dates from the outbreak of war. As we shall see, he used the same analytical tools that he had worked with as a historian: his study of images of (ancient) Italy in Turgenev's poetry, fiction, correspondence and diaries, for example, brought together cultural history and intellectual biography. Combining these two strands, his aim was not only to reconstruct Turgenev's Italy, that is, the Italy he depicted and commented on, but also to highlight the significance that Italy had in Turgenev's life. Grevs' study was not, he stressed, a literary critical one (*na chisto literaturnoe znachenie moia rabotka ne pretenduet*'[45]); rather, by using Turgenev as a 'cultural source', he wanted to gain a deeper understanding of the writer's spiritual world (*dukh*) and through it confirm some of the distinctive ideas and styles/tastes (*vkus*) of Russian educated society, namely its long-standing attraction to Italy, the origins of which Grevs traced to the reign of Ivan III in the fifteenth century.[46] For Grevs, Turgenev's sentient and spiritual universe, his tastes, style, reflections on life, his position as a critical admirer of Europe, of Russia and his love for the classical world made him an ideal, yet insufficiently exploited, historical source: 'As such, he is especially valuable to the cultural historian who has the ability to look for truth through beauty' (*'iskat' istinu cherez krasotu'*).[47]

'My task is to collect material and provide commentary.'[48] Turgenev visited Italy twice: in 1840 and again during the winter of 1857–8 (this second trip was cut short by illness). On his first visit he spent a large part of his time in the company of Nikolai Stankevich with whom he visited ancient Roman ruins, studied Latin and read Roman classics. From Rome he went to Naples, before travelling north, stopping in Genoa, Milan and Lake Maggiore. His return to Rome nearly two decades later confirmed his first impressions of the city, where, again, he engrossed himself in classical literature and the work of historians – ancient and contemporary[49] – as part of an extensive programme of visits to art galleries and monuments. Grevs suggested two ways of organizing his monograph. One way would be to group Turgenev's Italian material (poems, prose, notes and correspondence) thematically: this would provide a composite picture of his world of Italian culture through the prism of its constituent parts, namely its nature, people, ruins and monuments (e.g. the Villa Borghese, Doria Pamphilj Palace and the Villa Farnesina situated on the bank of the Tiber), as well as daily life in the town and countryside. Alternatively (Grevs' preferred option), one could take individual poems and short stories as separate 'living entities' (*zhivye tsely*) noting how his allusions to nature, people and places were configured and combined within each individual piece: 'In this manner we acquire a glimpse of how Turgenev actually studied Italy, and may derive from the sum total of his sketches and lyrics a more general picture (Grevs used the term "synthesis") of what Italy meant to him.'[50]

Grevs tested out this approach on an early poem, Parasha (1843), and the tale 'Tri vstrechi' (composed in 1851, and published in 1855). For Grevs, 'the setting of Parasha in the blistering heat of a southern land, most likely (*naverno*) recalled his experience of Naples'. The 'Three Meetings' included allusions to the Mediterranean, its nature, sun blinding days, dusty streets, orange groves, pavilions, shutters, music, guitars, song and love, which Grevs cross-referenced with contemporary correspondence.[51] Why, in Grevs view, did this second approach work better than the former? Simply because Turgenev did not offer a reliable topography of the places he evoked in his stories; rather, his accounts subordinated visual detail to emotional responses, to the beauty he saw around him and which he experienced both in an immediate, existential way, and in cultural terms, mediated, as it were, through his encounter with artworks and literature.[52] In sum, he captured a 'mood'.[53] Accordingly, Turgenev's Rome was one of Antiquity and the Renaissance (Raphael). In his account of Florence, likewise, he offered no identifiable concrete image of the city[54]; instead, he conveyed its renaissance qualities, thanks in part to his study of Dante. (In this connection, Grevs highlighted instances in Turgenev's prose poem *Lazurnoe tsartsvo*, 1878, of Dantean inflections and motifs inspired by lyrics that the Italian master had composed as a young man in the 'dolce stil nuovo'[55]). Turgenev's Venice, which featured in his novel, *On the Eve*, 1859, was static – a cultural *lik*, eternal, monumental and very different, Grevs noted, from Herzen's dynamic portrait which captured the stormy current of the life of the sea and its people.[56]

It was also Grevs' view that Turgenev's affective responses to Rome were bound up in a culturally grounded belief system, namely his liberalism. Politically, Turgenev sympathized with the Risorgimento activists and Garibaldi. Although, unlike his friend, the revolutionary Mikhail Bakunin, he was not a utopian thinker, the ideas of the freedom of the nation and the freedom of the person constituted the bedrock of his own social ideal. As Grevs writes: 'His soul protested against the *gnet* (knout), which at the time deprived Italy of its freedom, and with bitter sympathy he recalled the words of the Italian poet, Mazzini, in which he had spoken of the cruel, unjust enslavement of the nation to foreign despots'.[57] It was, above all, Turgenev's view of Italy as the embodiment of *humana civilitas*, which, for Grevs, confirmed a set of socio-political values grounded in individual freedom. Given the period in which Grevs was writing – the first decade of the Soviet era – the poignant resonances of his remarks are hard to miss: 'And in the depths of the collective personality of the Italian nation (or *genius populi*) there is always that free human individuality without which culture for Turgenev is meaningless'.[58] In sum, for both the novelist and his commentator, the appeal of Italy resided in its eternal (*vechnie*) elements, that is, in its vibrant individual nature. Both men recognized and celebrated a gifted people, its rich history, a revitalized present, its heroic and simply 'human' individuals and groups, their daily lives, their sense of nationhood (*national'nyi byt*) and the fruits of their creativity – works of art as 'emanations of their particular beauty'.[59]

The inspiration that Turgenev drew from his impressions of Italy stood in sharp contrast with the absence in his novels of his native city – Petersburg. In an appendix to his monograph, Grevs included a brief account of Turgenev's negative attitude towards and depiction of the Russian capital. Drawing on Antsiferov's *Dusha Peterburga* (1922), he charted the different phases of literary evaluations of the city, from exaltation in the eighteenth century (Grevs mentions Derzhavin's 'Severnaia Pal'mira' (Northern Palmira) and Pushkin's more nuanced appreciation) to apathy and indifference in the second half of the nineteenth century (Turgenev's age) followed by a revival of exuberance as expressed by Alexander Benois in his World of Art movement on the eve of the city's two-hundredth anniversary in 1903.[60] Within this range of evaluations, Turgenev's account of the city as a mosaic of fragments, thereby failing to impart a sense of the city as a whole, sat alongside the literary realism of the poet, Nikolai Nekrasov, the writer and literary critic, Ivan Panaev, and Dmitrii Grigorovich, all rather better known for their writings about the rural community and peasant way of life. Again, for Grevs, this is where Turgenev's value for the historian of Russia lay: as he reminds us, in the topographical and monumental domain, Turgenev's favourite objects of observation and depiction were the peasant countryside and the gentry estate (*usad'ba*). He was especially interested in the 'human soul of the simple folk', the inhabitants of the village hut (*izba*). And even if he wrote more about the 'Russian intelligentsia, 'those men and women in the countryside and towns who bore the heavy cross of their historical destiny', for the cultural historian interested in Russia's transitional period between serfdom and emancipation, 'there is in Turgenev a wealth of unexploited material for restoring the epoch'. By contrast, the monumental physiognomy of St Petersburg and the integral form it had once taken during the eighteenth and early nineteenth centuries had to a great extent been ruined by Nicholas I and Alexander II: their reigns marked two periods of high society, '*rastsvet svetskogo bleska*' and showy militarism that was utterly tasteless. Petersburg had lost her lustre, and her new attire (namely the ugly and senseless painting of buildings) completely screened out her beauty. As Grevs notes, this explains why the dominant colour in Turgenev's verbal palette about the northern capital was grey.[61]

Although the monograph was warmly received by peers and pupils who recognized its fit with his long-standing interest in '*kraevedicheskaia rabota*', excursion history and historical biography, it was largely dismissed by Formalist critics as the work of an amateur literary historian who had over-indulged in sentimental pathos.[62] For sure, Grevs recognized that his approach to literature had become unfashionable, and he was aware of the critical reception of his study by contemporary avant-garde theorists. But, against the Formalists' disregard for approaches focusing on anything other than the nature of literary/poetic language, he argued that the content is not separate from the form. Rather, the inner world of the writer, his ideas, his 'worldview' engender the form, which organically merges with the content; the theme/subject must not be detached from the style, whether it be poetry, music or the fine arts.[63] Grevs therefore defended his approach as cultural–historical, rather than literary critical in the sense that he was using Turgenev's impressions of the ancient Roman (and Greek) world through its monuments as a source for knowledge about human culture (which elsewhere he termed 'our self-knowledge').[64] To his mind, Turgenev embodied Russian and European culture, and while he needed to be studied in terms of the character, process, forms and fruit of his creativity (i.e. the literary point of view), it was primarily as a source – the historical point of view – which 'helps us understand the cultural environment in which he grew up, the world which surrounded him with its traces of a bygone age, (…), and which made him an interpreter of the past'.[65] His study of Turgenev's emotive responses to Italy could, moreover, be situated within a broader history of Russian ties with Italy encompassing material evidence, such as Russian architecture dating from the thirteenth century, diplomacy and trade, as well as expressions of emotional attachment which travellers recorded in their diaries and memoirs. In this connection, he mentioned Buslaev ('Rome is the homeland of my moral existence' ('*Rim – rodina moego nravstvennogo sushchestvovaniia*'[66])), Pogodin and his own erstwhile friend and interlocutor, Viacheslav Ivanov, whose lyrical impressions of Italy (again, especially Rome) were particularly pronounced. Finally, Grevs' study functioned as an autobiographical mirror of his own personal and professional trajectories: the themes covered in the book spoke to a 'spiritual affinity' which Grevs believed he had found with the author and the itinerary covered by the novelist allowed the historian to revisit in his mind's eye the research trips that he, himself, had conducted as a student and as a teacher.

The human condition: Love, friendship and melancholy

Grevs' companion study about Turgenev's years-long infatuation for the Spanish-born mezzo soprano Pauline Viardot (a 'biography of his heart', as he called it[67]) was, likewise, poorly received by the new generation of literary critics: it was considered to be out of pace with the experimentalist tendencies of the avant-garde, on the one hand, and lacking in socio-political relevance by proponents of proletarian literature on the other. But its subject matter is pivotal for understanding Grevs' development as a historian. 'The historian', he wrote, 'addresses eternal truths that are common to mankind, and celebrated in poetry and philosophy. Among these is love'.[68] Based on Turgenev's letters – which Grevs described as a remarkable 'human document', worthy of study by the philologist, historian, psychologist and philosopher'[69] – the topic of the book answered the mature Grevs' understanding of the task of history, namely to address eternal truths common to all mankind:

> The inner life of a genius and generally a remarkable personality will forever remain an important 'universal' (*obshchechelovecheskaia*) theme in any social stratum, or culture. It touches anyone in whom *humanitas* is awakened irrespective of class origins or ideology. [...]. We need to remind ourselves that in any historical endeavour we should proceed from an understanding of the individual peculiarities of the cultural life of the society that we are studying. And for our 1840s intelligentsia, love and friendship constituted a solid, original emotional element and creative motif in the life of the mind (*dukh*); their spiritual journeys both shaped and reflected the cultural foundations of the era. Turgenev was without question a child of this epoch.[70]

According to Antsiferov, Grevs was especially drawn to the topic of love and friendship,[71] and it is not difficult to appreciate that the importance he ascribed to the latter, in particular, mirrored (in an idealized way) his own experience as a founding member of the fraternity with the Oldenburg brothers in the 1880s, as well as his efforts to forge a sense of community with his students in the settings of the seminar and excursion trips which he organized after 1900. Friendship (which, as Antsiferov noted, Grevs believed had greater value than love) was true and durable when the friends complement each other while remaining wholly distinctive as individuals. For this reason, friendships between men and women were especially significant as relational ties needed (ideally) to be balanced by, if not facilitate, a sense of individual agency and moral worth. These principles informed both Grevs' personal sense of vocation as a teacher and life mentor, as well as the choices he had made with respect to his research into late antiquity and medieval Europe. As we saw in his study of Horace and Atticus dating from the 1890s, for example, the notion of friendship and sense of community functioned as a leit-motif and analytic tool with which to explore the formulation of worldviews in response to the challenges of regime change which both men experienced as Rome transitioned from Republic to Empire. Both Horace and Atticus, recall, professed an Epicureanism, meaning that they invested great importance in friendship, but also individual self-sufficiency as the basis for leading a quiet life, away from the arena of political intrigue.

> To support one another in difficult times, in my circle of closest pupils we studied the history of ideas about peace and the theory of friendship. And, in this context, I managed to connect them (*srodnit'*) with Rolland; and Rolland, in turn, helped us strengthen our own spiritual union.[72]

The onset of war in 1914 and the revolution that followed in its wake more or less forced Grevs to abandon fieldwork abroad, and it is really from this point that he turned his attention to more intensive study of friendship/affective ties both in the lives of historical figures and in literary representations. In the summer of 1915, he set up a series of home seminars to discuss Epicurus, Cicero, Gregory Nazianzen and Basil the Great; St Augustine, St Francis of Assisi and Jacoba (Jacqueline) of Settesoli, Dante and Beatrice, Michelangelo and Vittoria Colonna, friendships among the Jena romantics, Byron and Shelley, Herzen and Ogarev, Marx and Engels. This, then, was the origin of his study of Turgenev and Viardot, as well as his translation project and commentary of the novel or roman fleuve, *Jean-Christophe*, by Romain Rolland, mentioned in the quotation above, where he explored the eponymous hero's friendships with Olivier and Grace.

Grevs had come across Romain Rolland's roman fleuve, *Jean Christophe*, in late 1914.[73] What attracted him to the tale was its uplifting message: it charts the life of the hero in his struggle to overcome ugliness in the world and shows how a person may become morally strengthened through adversity, whereas others might succumb and thus be decimated by it. The central character, Jean-Christophe Krafft, is a German musician of Belgian extraction (apparently modelled on Beethoven) who endures great hardships and spiritual challenges. Conscious of his talents as a musician, he is also duty bound to care for those around him and thus has to take on menial work in order to provide for them. However, it is his acute sense of social injustice that inevitably brings him into direct conflict with the authorities (on several occasions) forcing him to flee. Finally, after a period of self-imposed exile in a remote corner of Switzerland, Jean Christophe returns 'in triumph' to Paris. As critics of this largely (and no doubt deservedly) forgotten novel have commented, Rolland was an admirer of Tolstoi, and as Tolstoi had done in *War and Peace*, he chose to interrupt his narrative with long disquisitions on subjects ranging from music, feminism, militarism, national character and social changes in the Third Republic. But, as Antsiferov recalled in his memoirs, it was the novel's central message – life is a tragedy, hurrah! – which struck a chord with Grevs: 'This embracing of life in all its tragic essence struck a chord with the padre, even as his own "hurrah" did not resound with the same note of defiance'.[74]

How exactly did Grevs work with the novel? In addition to identifying the fairly evident literary realist parallels between Rolland's and Tolstoi's creative genius, Grevs explored the novel's (arguably equally obvious) symbolism, attested to in the name choices for the main characters, and which he traced back to motifs in old French epic poetry: Kraft embodied life force; his friend, the fragile and delicate, Olivier (tree of life) is the symbol of peace. Jean Christophe's uncle, Gottfried, is God's peace, while other characters including Grace; Emmanuel; Oliver's son, George (victor); and Grace's daughter, Aurora (dawn) all carried names that translated into easily recognizable character traits of strength, physical and moral courage, youth, wisdom, and so on. Where, however, Grevs' analysis of the novel was possibly more original was the way in which he brought to bear his skillset as a historian-medievalist and his conception of history. In an unpublished draft introduction to a paper about the life and work of Rolland, he used Dante as a foil to draw out the universal significance of the novel as a tale about the human condition and as a defence of humanist principles. Titled *Lichnost' i delo Romena Rollana: opyt istolkovaniia dushi'* ('The man and his craft: an attempt at interpreting the inner world (soul) of Romain Rolland'), Grevs spoke of an affinity of minds between the Florentine master and Rolland's talent.[75] Like Dante, Rolland's muse 'is serious, pure, majestic, and assiduous; she is summoned to resolve the problems of being/existence through poetry'. In Grevs' view, Rolland shared with Dante the same elevated conception of the world and a faith in the supreme law. And in a somewhat telegraphic style, Grevs jotted down a number of non-sequential explanations for his rationale in tracing Rolland's spiritual lineage to Dante's genius:

> There is no need to compare the strength given to each of them, … the invincibility of creative work … irrespective of differences, one should not be afraid of comparing two figures so many centuries apart, … it is important to point out the deeply rooted affinity between Dante and Rolland, the way in which Rolland's thought signals a return to the image of Dante. Dante's genius shines on Rolland summoning within him a symphonic echo. It would not be an empty paradox to see in *Jean Christophe* traits of the *Divine Comedy* for the modern–day world. Engaging with the man and oeuvre of Rolland is a deeply significant task whatever his flaws as a writer or human being might be. There is a moral obligation (which the heart experiences joyfully) to connect him with our own Russian idealists.[76]

Grevs was fully aware that current critical appraisal of Rolland tended to be fairly dismissive of his talent as a novelist. But for him, what mattered most, especially at the time of writing as Europe plunged into war, was, as I mentioned, the tale's underlying vision of human triumph through adversity: 'On reading *Christophe*, the soul is fortified by a curative source, by a strength that is vital for overcoming the crisis that has crippled all being, our lifeblood (*sushchestvo*)'.[77] Regardless of whether or not Rolland could be classed as a first-rate writer, Grevs saw in him a seed of genius ('a fertile seed of genius that is authentic and gifted by nature', as he put it):

> In the figure of the author there is something supremely old, but also something that is forever new. In his literary intuitions (to which he always gives expression with principled modesty) we witness the emergence of a powerful (*krupnyi*) son of his age, a son of mankind – a powerful yet subtle interpreter of the destinies of people. Hidden within the restrained pose of an ordinary citizen, one discerns the presence of a cultural leader.[78]

It was in connection with these ideas about Rolland and his novel that Grevs included his comment, cited above, about the importance for his circle of pupils of studying, as he put it, 'the history of ideas of peace and the theory of friendship'. Ultimately, then, the value for Grevs of Rolland was likely more existential than it was purely intellectual. Overall, what we see in his discussion of *Jean Christophe* is a fundamental consistency with the analytical tools he used as a historian: close textual analysis, an interest in intellectual biography and a conception of history that combined a Rankean sense of the specificity of a given age with a quest to uncover in the culture and belief systems of the medieval world 'eternal values' that are relevant to all eras of historical development.[79] It was precisely this understanding of history that gave Grevs a platform on which to bring Dante and Rolland together as spiritual interlocutors across time.

From historian to literary critic?

It is worth restating that, from the beginning of his career, Grevs had always insisted on the scientific and synthetic characteristics of the history of culture which embraces not only the development of material culture, but above all of the mind, viz., conceptions of the world, of justice, religion, all of which are, in part, captured in artistic expression. If, then, his work on the literary world has to be seen as a consequence of changes in the political climate, it was, as I have argued, also consistent with the approach he developed in his master's dissertation and an integral part of the interdisciplinary approach that he worked on with his seminar students, after 1900. In many respects, the same held true for Kliuchevskii: his interest in both fictional characters and historical figures was driven primarily by a concern to enhance our understanding of past Russian society. The literary critic, Iulii Aikhenval'd, made this point in his obituary comment. However, in his view, if Kliuchevskii's historicization of Pushkin's significance was highly valuable, it, diminished what he called the author's 'eternal qualities' or the eternal aspect of his genius. As a result, Pushkin's verse now read as a form of 'social or moral archeology'.[80] What, by contrast, redeemed Kliuchevskii, in Aikhenval'd's eyes, were his opening autobiographical comments in his essay about *Evgenii Onegin* where he recalled his discovery of Pushkin as a youth, and the pledge he made with his friends never to treat a woman so devoted in love as Tatiana was for Onegin with such cold indifference.[81] For his generation growing up in the 1850s, Kliuchevskii wrote: Onegin 'was the event of our youth, it traced our common biography, those turning points in our lives marked by the completion of our school years or our first love'. The novel provided lessons in life. Kliuchevskii and his school friends thus initially read it as a means to navigate their way through their own trials and tribulations as adolescents: 'Reading Onegin, we began (…) to articulate our emotions, make sense of inchoate drives and ambitions (…). We understood that the novel was set in a different period. But we felt that it wasn't just a tale, that its heroes exist somewhere and at some time in Rus', even in a period close to our own'.[82] As Aikhenval'd noted, it was this different discursive register – a highly personal elegiac reflection about self-identity – which was the distinctive feature in a later essay Kliuchevskii wrote on the theme of melancholy in the poetry of Lermontov. This unsigned piece, published in the journal *Russkaia mysl'* in 1891 as a contribution to commemorate the fiftieth anniversary of the poet's death, differed from his other excursuses into creative literature because here he highlighted personal emotions and endeavoured to probe the self-contained inner world of the author's individuality.[83] As Alfred Rieber notes, it was precisely this engagement with a highly personal expression of melancholy that paradoxically was more universal in its ramifications than his treatment of Onegin, which Rieber rightly describes as the aesthetic expression of a historical fact.[84] 'Lermontov', Kliuchevskii wrote,

> did not cultivate his poetry from a poetic seed, hidden in the depths of his spirit; rather, like a sculptor, he carved it out of the formless mass of his impressions and feelings, throwing out anything unnecessary. Do not go looking for a poetic light of the kind that a poet- philosopher throws on the world and its creation in order to comprehend his relation to the parts that compose it [...]. Lermontov's poetry is not a quest for the meaning of life; rather, in life's twists and turns (*iavleniia*) he sought his own reflection which helped him understand himself in the way that we might look in a mirror to capture an expression on our face. Lermontov considered his image in the various phenomena of nature, he listened to himself in the hurly-burly of life, turned over one poetic motif after another in order to divine which of them was truly his native poetic range. Having chosen the sounds germane to him, he merged them into a single poetic cadence that echoed his poetic spirit. This cadence, this Lermontovian poetic gamut – is melancholy (*grust'*), which captures the nature of individual existence; it is not an expression of the meaning of life more generally. It is the mood of a singular spirit. Lermontov tells of personal grief, not of world sorrow. If, from a lexicological perspective the words are synonymous, from a psychological one they are antitheses. Underlying world sorrow is disaffection, a loss of an ability to believe in an ideal, but not a denial of the ideal as such. Once this faith has gone it is no longer a matter of *razocharovanie* (disillusionment), but *otrezvlenie* (sobering up), which by definition cannot be the source of sorrow, rather a celebration of common sense.[85]

Kliuchevskii's definition of *grust'*, then, is a state of being that derives its energy from the experience of loss and suffering. It is not just a question of coming to terms with one's loss, but of drawing nourishment from the state of suffering, which in turn provides comfort and joy. (The intended allusion here is Christian grief as a form of joy.) Reflecting on what might have triggered this mood in Lermontov, Kliuchevskii suggested that its origins were closely linked to the moral history of Russian society: 'Lermontov's poetry will forever be a curious psychological phenomenon and will never lose its artistic beauty, but it is also significant as a historical symptom'.[86] What did he mean by this? In Kliuchevskii's reading, the poet's leading message was that we should not look for happiness (*schast'e*) as an antidote to 'sadness/melancholy' (*grust'*); rather, we should learn to manage without it. With its connotations of naivety, and as a by-product of material gain and social advancement (the damaging effects of which Kliuchevskii presented in his essays on Nedorosl' and especially Onegin), happiness was anathema to Lermontov, Kliuchevskii argued. Yet, if he disavowed it, he was, at the same time, clearly a victim of it having been brought up in the same kind of society as his fictional peers and subjected to the same process of artificial Europeanization with its vain allure of social refinement: like them, Lermontov was doomed to a socially destructive role. In Rieber's words, 'The intensity of their isolation, drove them to speculate upon the future of Russia, and their reflections were suffused not with despair and even less with high hopes, but with melancholy'.[87]

Kliuchevskii's assessment of Lermontov differed from those of contemporaries such as the philosopher, Vladimir Solov'ev, and the symbolist poet, Dmitrii Merezhkovskii, who foregrounded Lermontov's demonism, the Obermensch traits of his personality and his pride. For Kliuchevskii, the question of a Byronic accent in Lermontov's poetry with its dominant mood of disaffection (*razocharovanie*) and the demonic personage that was generally regarded as his alter-ego (in poems such as Portrait, Moi demon and the various guises he assumed in his short stories – from vengeful lover, savage Cossack mountain dweller or bored son of a *barin* [gentry landowner]) were the result of his early eclectic reading, but were not intrinsic to his poetic nature; rather, they were tools allowing him to probe deeper into his talent.[88] Kliuchevskii detected a paradox here: the more the poet deliberately paved a way towards death, mentally storing a mass of gloomy thoughts, the more bright notes would erupt into his song.[89] In Aikhenval'd's opinion, that Kliuchevskii treated these demonic traits as a tragic mask, an attempt to conceal a deep inner and genuine melancholy (*grust'*), rewarded him with the means to express sympathy not so much for Lermontov's protagonist, Pechorin (in *Hero of Our Time*), as for the author himself.[90] His poetry mirrored the poet's personal state of mind, and it was a disposition with which Kliuchevskii empathized. Behind the sarcasm and the challenge he presented to high society, there was another quality, namely a tenderness towards the fatherland, the land, nature, the people, towards his fellow comrades who simply and selflessly live and die carrying out their duty.[91] In effect, Kliuchevskii was reading Lermontov 'against the grain' as he claimed that the poet tried to hide these feelings from 'high society' and that in his lyrics these motifs of tenderness and melancholy, which are virtually indiscernible, require a trained ear. Perhaps, as Rieber notes, Kliuchevskii's attention to the poet's 'native sentiments' was an outgrowth of his own, early love for Russian folk songs, and that, albeit indirectly, it registered the historian's formative indebtedness to his 'master', Buslaev. Citing a letter from his student years, dated 27 October 1862, to a friend in Penza, where he extolled the 'Igor Tale' – 'in every song the Russian bemoans his fate' – Rieber suggests that Kliuchevskii later came to see 'the same expressive line' in the entire history of Russian poetry.[92] By the same token, it is tempting to suggest that this motif underpinned all of his historical critical writings about the Russian literary world as well.

In their obituary tributes, Bogoslovskii, Miliukov, Platonov and Aikenval'd all noted the sharp correspondences between the topic of Kliuchevskii's essay and his own dark mood, the elegiac strains in his writings and a tone of 'poetic resignation' that few typically associated with the historian.[93] Miliukov referred to a 'historical pessimism', seeing the piece as a reflection of Kliuchevskii's own pessimistic state of mind during a period – the early 1890s – dominated by renewed censorship, the rescinding of Alexander II's administrative reforms and worsening hardships for the peasantry. The essay showcased his ability to work with the tools of literary criticism, but as a psychologically probing account of the poet it was equally telling (as Platonov suspected) of the way in which

Kliuchevskii's mocking irony (which he used to great effect as a rhetorical device in his *Course of Russian History*) was no longer able to shield him from his own, very personal sense of despair: his empathy for Lermontov allowed him to indulge in his own emotional elegy for the Russian people. Endeavouring, then, to uncover the source of these complex, fundamentally contradictory states of mind, and to retrace their dynamics and development, Kliuchevskii explored the poet's creativity as a '*sootechestvennik-odnodumets*' (a like-minded thinker and compatriot).⁹⁴ Granted, Kliuchevskii did assume the stance of the historian, stepping back to consider Lermontov as an emblem in the moral history of Russia. But even here, it was about probing the unchanging essence of that history rather than charting developments or change over time. Kliuchevskii identified this 'essence' as a peculiar Russian temperament: caught between a spineless fatalism of the East, and the energetic self-confidence of the West (where melancholy gives way to fatalism), melancholy in Russia took on the peculiar hues of the national religious experience and became 'a historical fact'. Lermontov's later, more mature poetry came close to capturing this national religious mood. Expressing resignation (i.e. liberated from earlier Byronic traits of *razocharovanie*) his grief transformed into an artistic rendering of the common prayer that best captured the Russian religious mindset: *da budet volia tvoia*' (thy will be done).⁹⁵ His lyrics, Kliuchevskii concluded, 'resonate with Russian song, which is neither happy nor sorrowful (*pechal'nye*), but melancholic (*grustnye*). Look at any Russian landscape in life or as depicted on canvas. Is it happy or sorrowful? Neither. It is melancholic'.⁹⁶

In a colloquium dedicated to problems of creative literature and history, Richard Wortman drew the following distinction between the two modes of thinking: 'the writer's inventory derives from individual experience, whether the narrator's or the hero's, and is elaborated to reveal the meaning of that experience. The historical account places the individual experience within the context of the collective experience of the time'.⁹⁷ Kliuchevskii, like Grevs, was interested in the life of the artist and the ways in which poetry and prose were a record of that life and of society more broadly – in this instance, a record of the emotional (psychological) climate of Russia during the oppressive rule of Nicholas I. Yet, more than any other essay about the literary world that he wrote, in this one, Kliuchevskii (who, recall, published this piece without signature) demonstrates literary-critical rather than historical skills: it is testament to his training and the importance he placed on language. In support of this, suffice it to mention his critique of Platonov's study of seventeenth-century Russian tales as a historical source (*Drevnerusskie skazaniia i povesti o smutnom vremeni XVIIv kak istoricheskii istochnik*, [1888]) in which he rejected the inclusion of literary 'visions' (*videnie*), personal records or polemics as a viable source on the grounds that they do not yield any factual material for the historian, and because they required rigorous critical verification. Kliuchevskii's acerbic response throws light on his understanding of historical facts: 'There is not one historical source, which does not require critical verification. Besides, what does factual material for the historian entail? Historical facts are not simply events: the ideas, viewpoints, feelings, impressions by people in a given period are also facts, they are very important and equally require critical study'.⁹⁸ The point was well made.

History as literature: The modernist interpretation of historical personalities as literary heroes: Mikhail Gershenzon

As I mentioned at the beginning of this chapter, late tsarist political culture prevented many talented historians of Jewish origin from pursuing a career in their elected field of interest. The case of Mikhail Gershenzon (1869–1925) is just one example of how trained historians managed to re-channel their skillset to produce quite innovative analyses of the nation's literary and intellectual–historical canon. Perhaps best known to students of Russian political thought as the figure who initiated a reflection on the meaning of the 1905 revolution,[99] Gershenzon's views about history, literature and biography – as well as politics – may be traced to his work as a historian-classicist and, in particular, to his interest in the inner spiritual world of ancient thinkers as creators of history.[100]

Gershenzon matriculated 'by a fluke' as part of the extremely limited quota of places for Jews in the Historical–Philological Faculty of Moscow University in 1889.[101] In his second year, he attended Kliuchevskii's lectures, but his interest in ancient history and political theory drew him closer to Pavel Vinogradov, whose lectures and seminars on the ancient and medieval worlds, and, especially the example he set in terms of source criticism, that is, to resist blindly adhering to any rigid positivist and sociological methodology or preconceptions, made him the ideal intellectual patron. For his part, Vinogradov recognized Gershenzon's talent, encouraging his work on various research topics, for example, a study of 'Aristotle and Ephorus' (1894), which won a gold medal, and 'Aristotle's *Athenian Constitution* and Plutarch's *Lives*' (1895). Vinogradov also procured fellowships and translation work for him, as well as review articles to write for some of the leading 'thick journals', such as *Russkaia mysl'* and entries for the encyclopaedic dictionary, *Granat*. The relationship lasted until Vinogradov's departure for England in 1901.

It was Vinogradov's suggestion that Gershenzon apply for training towards a professorship, but Gershenzon's refusal to convert to the Russian Orthodox faith (a decision which Vinogradov respected) meant that he was effectively obliged to forgo a career in academia.[102] Perhaps, though, in terms of 'intellectual temperament', he would have been ill suited to the task. As Brian Horowitz notes in the opening pages of his comprehensive study of Gershenzon's Pushkin scholarship: 'Early in his career as a historian, Gershenzon developed his own, idiosyncratic method. Instead of involving himself in the explication of what is usually considered history – the significant events and salient political movements of a period – he concerned himself with the illumination of forgotten individuals, and focused his attention on their private relationships'.[103] Gershenzon, himself, spelt out his position in his programmatic introduction to *A History of Young Russia* (*Istoriia molodoi Rossii*, 1908) about the generation of the 1830s and 1840s, as follows:

> The essence of a movement is always embodied in a few individuals, combining in themselves the sharp, innate receptivity to the main idea of a time with an inescapable force of the spirit. Such an individual does not always stand at the head, and does not always visibly influence it – that does not matter. What does

matter is that, only in him, in the single, receptive, and gifted individual, does the core of the movement yield its full blossom: only in him is the purpose of the main historical task revealed.[104]

For Gershenzon, such a hero is the intellectual or artist. These individuals, with all their complicated and contradictory baggage as personalities, bring to view the distilled spiritual essence of an age, which the historian can grasp and retrieve, provided he is sensitive to psychology. To understand history, the historian must, in Horowitz's words, 'penetrate the hero's psyche, dig deeper into the subconscious and emotional strata of the self; only in this way can he discover the salient features of an epoch'. It was not a matter of studying every individual, rather a representative few because Gershenzon believed that they, better than anyone else, embodied the ideals, motivations and subconscious inclinations of an entire culture.

In the foreword to his first monograph, *A History of Young Russia*, just cited, Gershenzon bemoaned the current state of intellectual history: 'It is hard to find any other type of literature that ranks lower in our country than the history of the intellectual (*dukhovnyi*) life in our society'. This was because, to date, historians had studied society as some sort of abstraction, blind to the fact that 'society does not seek, or think, or suffer – only individual people suffer and reflect'.[105] For this reason, Gershenzon chose to concentrate on the worldviews, inner life experiences, dramas and friendships of a number of key figures and contemporaries – in this instance, the military hero in the war against Napoleon and later convicted Decembrist conspirator, Mikhail Orlov, the exiled Catholic monk and priest, Vladimir Pecherin, Nikolai Stankevich, Timofei Granovskii, Ivan Galakhov and N. P. Ogarev (the last two were friends of Herzen) using a body of correspondence and private diaries as his principal sources.[106] It was his view that letters best retain the actual emotional and intellectual, or religious–philosophical core of a person, the way they lived, and that, in them, it is possible to hear the live voices of the past. Gershenzon did not, however, use these as evidence in the usual way, that is, to reconstruct, for example, the factual details of Pushkin's exile, Chaadaev's experiences in Europe or Turgenev's career as a writer in Russia and abroad; rather, he used them as tools to analyse mental patterns and themes pervasive in their work that, in turn, mirrored the intellectual and spiritual climate in which they lived.[107] 'The [book]', Gershenzon wrote, 'does not consist of a series of portraits, but rather an entire picture of the epoch marked by the successive change of personal experiences. This is why I have called it a *history*'.[108]

Where did Gershenzon's ideas come from? As I mentioned above, the example that Vinogradov set for working with sources confirmed his disdain for overly prescriptive methodologies. More specifically, Vera Proskurina, author of a study of Gershenzon's life and career, has argued that a critical attitude towards positivistic history is discernible in some of his earliest publications dating from the 1890s: 'not only for its treatment of facts (i.e. tied to universal categories which, by definition, were extraneous to the period under discussion), but also for its mode of explanation, which, for Gershenzon, lacked colour (*koloritnost'*) and tonality'.[109] By contrast, Gershenzon tried to intuit the underlying, implicit, yet deeper meaning of the text. As Horowitz notes, very early on, when he was working on ancient Greek thought and history,

Gershenzon (…) trespassed beyond the limits of verifiable textual analysis. Extrapolating and recreating the thoughts of his subjects through creative empathy, he was able to 'enliven' or to present these ancient Greek intellectuals as if they were 'living and speaking'. Even as a student, then, Gershenzon did not consider the written word a record of abstract ideas, but treated it as a symbol of potentially animated feelings which the reader can awaken.[110]

If Vinogradov's example facilitated Gershenzon's early break with current positivist and sociological conventions, intellectually, as Vera Proskurina argues, his view of history as dependent on the conscious lives of individual people whose experience of the world may be said to reflect, if not transform, reality was heavily indebted to Thomas Carlyle. Gershenzon first read *On Heroes and Hero Worship and the Heroic in History* (1841) as a student in the early 1890s, and, as Proskurina suggests, it was this discovery of a romantic historiosophy, according to which history was governed not by 'interests', but by the Spirit and the Word as articulated by leaders of humanity – prophets, priests, poets and literati (Mohammed, Shakespeare, Dante, Rousseau, John Knox, among them) – that sparked his historical imagination.[111] In fact, Proskurina contends that Thomas Carlyle was a major influence for Gershenzon's generation more broadly, but I suspect that the Scotsman's ideas divided opinion: if there was agreement on the importance of reflecting upon the lives of individuals as agents of history (a trait we have seen in the preceding chapters of this book), many resisted the dangerous implications of charismatic leadership.[112] For one, Antsiferov recalled how as a student (some twenty years after Gershenzon) he was interested in '*lichnost*', but, he stressed, 'not as a factor making history, nor, he insisted, as a hero who shapes historical destiny (as Carlyle had argued, and to whom Antsiferov explicitly referred), rather as a symptom of the age, as a fragment of a given epoch, aiding comprehension of the whole.'[113] In Gershenzon's case, by contrast, Carlyle's theory seemed to answer an existential angst that he was grappling with as a student. What most impressed him was the way in which Carlyle's 'heroes' resolved their own spiritual concerns to become what he called 'holistic' or integrated personalities, that is, cultural leaders vested with a transformative inner creative energy, vitality and courage. Most critics agree, then, that Gershenzon's views on Russian nineteenth-century history that he became known for were quite unconventional: Horowitz summarizes this well when he writes that Gershenzon's 'historical scholarship' provided a 'literary portrait' of early-nineteenth-century Russia in the form of interpretive essays about the personal life of some of the nation's leading, representative intellectuals. The point to stress, however, is that the terms of this scholarship were entirely consistent with his work as a historian-classicist and his early studies of certain personalities, such as Aristotle and the historian, Ephorus of Cyme, as architects of history, and remained largely unchanged throughout his career.

Stylistically, Gershenzon's monographs were highly distinctive for their narrative artistry in a modernist key.[114] What became known as the 'Gershenzon method' was a peculiar coupling of two narrative voices – that of his own views as the 'author' with that of his subject, his 'hero'. The effect, in some instances, as critics noted, was to transform historical topics (e.g. his discussion of Herzen and the Slavophile thinker,

Ivan Kireevskii, in *Images of the Past* [*Obrazy proshlogo*]) into something approaching the novelesque.[115] *Griboedovskaia Moskva* (1914), in particular, was received by critics as a kind of tale (*povest'*), or as a 'sketch for a historical novel'.[116] Basing his study on the correspondence of the Rimskii-Korsakov family, his aim was to reconstruct the *byt* (daily life, family and domesticity) of Moscow in Griboedov's time (1810s–20s). The idiosyncrasies of each individual were intended to represent a quality of Moscow's aristocracy: Maria Ivanovna's home in 1816–23 'was in all respects a typical home of Griboedov's Moscow. It was precisely during those years, in that circle and in the family of the Rimskii-Korsakovs that Griboedov observed Moscow society'.[117] The central figure, the aforementioned Maria Ivanovna Rimskaia-Korsakova, is the devoted mother who worries anxiously about her children. Her son, Grigorii, cares little about promotions, giving most of his thought to his personal comfort and pleasure, and her daughters think only about making a 'brilliant' marriage. Generally, within the family, an inordinate amount of attention is given to the consumption of rich food and evening balls. Gershenzon wrote:

> The book offered here is an experiment in illustrating historically *Woe from Wit* (*Gore ot uma*), an attempt to present in the clearest way possible that corner of authentic reality that Griboedov depicted and creatively transformed in his remarkable comedy. [...] (The historian) does not make things up, he only relates: from his heroes' diaries and correspondence he carefully depicts their moods in the course of the real events of their life. In his narrative, excerpts from their letters accomplish the same goal as a conversation in a novel: [they] lead the reader directly into the feelings of real people, and give the reader the possibility to hear their voice and manner of speech.[118]

As Horowitz notes, Gershenzon maintained that the historian had an advantage over the novelist because he had access to the actual letters, the writings of his heroes; there is none of the artificiality of fiction: 'And one has to say: an excerpt from an old letter can be so psychologically sharp and so full of the spirit of the time that a conversation between invented people in the best historical novel cannot compare. What is particularly valuable here is the actual reality of feelings and speech'.[119] In this regard, again as Horowitz rightly observes, Gershenzon assumed a Tolstoian defence of history as a conglomeration of all the individual experiences occurring at any given moment: each individual will is as significant as any other. And, importantly, Horowitz argues, despite their superficiality, Gershenzon attributed to these people a spiritual holism, which he sourced in their upbringing and way of life and which, he believed, was missing from his own 'fragmented' age on the brink of war. In Gershenzon's words:

> Do not throw stones at Maria Ivanovna. Was she guilty because she did not know? I strongly fear that a historian in a future generation will condemn us in the same way that we condemn Maria Ivanovna, because, after all, our lives also contain too little creative work and in turn must seem unavoidably empty and superficial from the viewpoint of higher consciousness. I do not want to say that our age is as

equally bad as that one: no, it is immeasurably better, closer to truth, weightier; but the same poison runs in our blood, and the poison can be felt in us, just as in those people with their emptiness and frivolity. Only then it found other forms – balls and picnics, the whole pretentious juvenile debauchery of their life – while with us it is the nasty complexity and fruitless subtlety of feelings and ideas.[120]

If, then, Gershenzon's idealization of the early-nineteenth-century aristocratic family was a literary construct, it was nevertheless consistent with his view of history, dictated by a concern to engage with the inner world of holistic or integral personalities. As Thomas G. Winner suggests, his approach must be seen within the context of the anti-positivistic movement that dominated the Russian intellectual scene of the early twentieth century.[121] In literary studies this meant opposition to the historical–cultural school, associated with the names of Professors Veselovskii, Tikhonravov and the *publitsist,* Alexander Pypin, author of a multi-volume history of Russian literature, but whose method Gershenzon characterized as a form of glorified journalism. As I discuss in the next chapter, the Tainean approach of this school (as reviewed by Kareev in his own project to elaborate a comprehensive theory of the humanities) viewed literature as a social phenomenon and literary scholarship as social exegesis. Against this, Gershenzon stressed the need to differentiate between a study of the evolution of literary forms and the cultural–intellectual outlook of a given period: literature had to be released from its function as material for the study of social thought, and the study of literature should, he believed, concern the realm of artistic form.[122] This did not mean that Gershenzon advocated, or indeed occupied, himself with the Formalist view of the autonomy of literary form that was currently being developed by a young generation of literary scholars. Rather, Winner argues, his reasons for discarding the cumbersome historical apparatus of his predecessors were dictated by an overriding concern to capture the spirit of a creative personality, and to deduce from works of art an integral personal philosophy.

At one level, Gershenzon's innovation in literary-historical studies by breaking with all existing positivistic conventions requires a reconsideration of my leading premise in this book concerning what I have claimed to be the close ties between creative literature, historical enquiry and literary critical studies in the late imperial era. But I would argue that Gershenzon's insistence that the study of literature be liberated from the extra-literary concerns of historians and sociologists does not fundamentally disturb my hypothesis once we remind ourselves of the origins – in historical research – of Gershenzon's own literary scholarship or, indeed, of his repeated reminders that he intended his studies to be read as history: Gershenzon's views about the reconstruction of a given author's inner spiritual biography as a tool to understand the meaning of their work as artists were intrinsically linked to his formation as a historian. His views may strike us as idiosyncratic (as they did his immediate peers), but they still attest to a fertile interplay, during the late tsarist era, between historical and literary imagination in the production of monographs and essays about the nation's past. Indeed, as Horowitz notes, although Gershenzon was critical of the Russian 'literary-historical' positivists, he did acknowledge their influence 'for their employment of literary works as source material for nonliterary study'.[123] As I discuss in the next chapter, it was, of course, this historical–cultural and/or sociological approach to creative literature which dominated the field of *slovesnost'* throughout the nineteenth century: in their various configurations, these extra-literary readings of poetry, folklore and creative prose by literary historians were all paralleled in mainstream or generalist historical enquiry.

8

Historical and Literary Historical Scholarship: A Hybrid Science?

Across Europe during the first half of the nineteenth century, conventional wisdom had it that folklore is deeply, even uniquely, expressive of the community in which it was produced and thus could be of great value to the historian. Among the major sources of inspiration for this view were, of course, Johann Gottfried Herder (his name is often associated with the term Volksgeist[1]) and the mythological and linguistic theories of Jacob Grimm. In France, Augustin Thierry and Jules Michelet both championed this way of thinking about the past. For Michelet, the oral tradition captured in song and legends provided a profound sense of historical reality because it retained 'the warmth of people's voices and the presence of their bodies'. And Thierry, in his three-volume study, *Histoire de la conquête de l'Angleterre par les Normands* (1825), was, as Donald Kelley notes, equally clear that literary remains rendered most truthfully the spirit of the tribes that lived in Britain at that time: 'The ancient Britons lived and breathed poetry', Thierry wrote. 'The expression may seem extravagant, but not so in reality: for, in their political maxims, preserved to our own times, they placed the poet–musician beside the agriculturalist and the artist, as one of the three pillars of social existence. The poet had but one theme: the destiny of his country, its misfortunes and its hopes'.[2]

Around 1850, as the romantic ethos gradually gave way to empirical evidence-based enquiry, the importance ascribed to 'feelings', 'spirit' or the senses was, as I have argued, eclipsed by endeavours to establish the credentials of historical study as an exact (empirical) science. In practice, this required the strict exclusion of the spoken language (oral tradition) as a viable historical source. Historical explanation and style of presentation also needed to be revised. Addressing this matter, one of the chief architects of the 'scientific method', Gabriel Monod, called for the removal of what he termed 'vague generalities or oratory': instead, 'every statement would be accompanied by proofs, by references to sources and quotations'.[3] It remained, however, that if the demands of 'science', understood as commonsense empiricism, were now deemed premium, the question of whether imaginative literature could be of any evidential value did not go away; rather, it was brought back on to the agenda in response to developments in literary historical scholarship as a branch of positivist-scientific study and to questions pertaining to the types of relationship between the two disciplines:

should the history of literature be considered a separate branch with its own distinctive methodology and practices, or should it be subsumed under historical scholarship? Debates concerning the place of imaginative literature in historical research, moreover, fed into broader questions about the scientific/scholarly credentials of the discipline, and possibly the most vexed question of all that historians posed in tandem with reflections on the relationship between literary history/history of literature and 'generalist' history was an age-old conundrum: is history itself a science or an art? In France, a catalyst for the revival of these questions was the highly influential, yet controversial thought of Hippolyte Taine. A committed positivist, empiricist, he encapsulated the cult of physical and chemical science that characterized his age.[4] And yet, at the same time, he called for the reinstatement of the imagination in historical research 'L'histoire', he wrote in his introductory remarks to what ranks as possibly his best-known study, *Histoire de la littérature anglaise* (1863–9) 's'est transformée depuis cent ans en Allemagne, depuis soixante ans en France, et cela par l'étude des littératures'.[5]

Taine set out to apply the 'scientific method' to the study of the humanities. Every piece of writing, he argued, was causally defined by three 'external' factors: *race* (the inherited dispositions of national character), *milieu* (the pressures of the natural environment) and *historical moment*. But he also insisted on the importance of studying 'facts of the highest kind', that is, 'internal' modes of feeling and thought, which he believed were best harnessed in creative literature: 'on a découvert qu'une oeuvre n'est pas un simple jeu d'imagination, le caprice isolé d'une tête chaude, mais une copie des moeurs environnantes et le signe d'un état d'esprit. On en a conclu qu'on pouvait, d'après les monuments littéraires, retrouver la façon dont les hommes avaient senti et pensé il y a plusieurs siècles'.[6] For Taine, this idea that, with the help of the poem, novel or confession, one may resurrect mental and sentient world outlooks of people living in the distant past, indeed, the way they conceived the world around them, was a factor of prime importance.[7] One statement in particular, which Russian contemporaries cited quite frequently in their appraisals of his theory, captured both the essence of the French historian's position and the significance that they, his Russian audience, attached to it: 'I would give fifty volumes of charters, a hundred volumes of diplomatic records for the memoirs of Cellini, the epistle of St Paul, (…) or Aristophanes' comedies (…). The more feelings are tangibly expressed, the more literary it becomes. And the more literary its qualities, the greater its suitability as a document for psychological history (…)'. 'This is why', Taine added, 'that among documents which account for feelings (the sentient reality) of past generations, creative literature occupies such an important place. It follows that to write a moral history, to comprehend the psychological laws governing events, this should be done in the main through the study of literature'.[8]

The terms for writing about the past that Taine announced were received by his immediate peers in France as a troubling advocacy of two opposing standpoints about the nature of history.[9] But if his approach triggered controversy, it also necessitated renewed efforts to rethink the terms of the discipline, and, by the same token, address the relationship between the history of literature and history in light of the 'scientific turn' in contemporary human and social sciences. As I discuss in this chapter, in Russia, such debates prompted endeavours to devise a comprehensive theory of history in which creative literature was conceived as an integral component with its own clearly delineated method and field of application. However, it was, above all, Taine's contention concerning the transformative impact of the study of literature on historical enquiry itself which, if it distanced him from his French peers, Monod, and Fustel de Coulanges, clearly resonated with Russian contemporaries: 'History', Taine argued, 'is, in essence, the task of psychology'.[10]

The importance ascribed to literature – especially poetry and folklore – as a historical artefact, and, inversely, debates over whether literature had any place at all in historical enquiry, was undeniably a European-wide phenomenon and not a distinctive feature of Russian historical culture and practice. What, however, was arguably more peculiar to the Russian case is that the advent of positivism in the second half of the century did not produce a clear split between literature and history and thus the need to 'retrieve' or recover a lost tradition (the literary 'moment') thereafter. Rather, the discovery, in the 1830s and 1840s, of folklore and popular songs as invaluable indices of the spirit of a bygone age and of the nation's truly distinctive cultural heritage became the hallmarks of, to borrow Lidiia Lotman's term, an indigenous 'hybrid' philological–historical science, which, as I argue below, proved to be rather more enduring than the vicissitudes in historiographical developments experienced abroad.[11] Initially associated with the romantic nationalistic aspirations of the Slavophiles and advocates of official nationality, the importance of this discovery for creative artists and intellectuals, especially those who espoused cultural particularism, needs little explanation. For university-based scholars active in the pre-reform era, the study of oral traditions opened up the field of enquiry, providing them with valuable tools to, for example, reconstruct domestic life (*byt*) and family relations in the pre-Petrine age, to comprehend the spiritual realities of people and the ways in which they interpreted the world around them. In other words, besides its obvious political and ideological resonances, which fuelled Slavophile and nationalist discourses, the romantic conception of Volksgeist harnessed an ethnologically based conception of culture that prioritized the study of the material and spiritual universe of distinctive 'peoples' (*narod*/Volk) and communities. 'Poetry', Kostomarov wrote, 'is a human attribute (*poeziia est' prinadlezhnost' cheloveka*) without which we cannot breathe'.[12]

While Russian humanities scholars continued to track developments abroad, both responding to and, without doubt, contributing to the emergence of a new positivist historical consciousness at home, for reasons I discussed in the Introduction to this book, the boundaries between historical and literary scholarship during the second half of the nineteenth century continued to be quite fluid: Fedor Buslaev (Moscow) and Alexander Afanas'ev (1826–71), active in the pre- and early reform eras, as well as their successors Nikolai Tikhonravov (Moscow), Aleksandr Veselovskii (1838–1906) in St Petersburg and Alexander Pypin (1833–1904), who dominated the field at the end of the century, were all as much historians as specialists in folklore and the literary process.[13] 'Tell me how a nation lived', Veselovskii famously declared, 'and I will tell you how it wrote'.[14] Figures such as Veselovskii exercised considerable influence on their peers and pupils in the Department of History, and it would arguably not be beyond the bounds of credibility to suggest that, as a branch of positivist-scientific enquiry, the work of literary scholars aided the growing trend among historians to move away from histories of the state to focus instead on aspects of society, the economy and culture.[15] For both historians and philologists/literary scholars 'folklore, art, history, contemporary literature and the most ancient layers of culture presented an integral object of knowledge', and it was this common ground of intellectual enquiry and shared 'scientific' vocabulary that strengthened the ties between, and the popularity of, cultural history and literary studies in the closing decades of tsarist rule.[16] As historians and philologists began to tackle a wider range of sources – written, oral and material – their findings helped broaden the sphere of knowledge not only about Russia's cultural legacy, but also to place its distinctive characteristics in a comparative perspective at regional and national levels.[17] In response, then, to the new directive coming out of France for a scientific method based on irrefutable empirical 'fact', together with its call (Taine excepted) to disregard legends, oral traditions, or any 'expressions of human passions' as viable sources for the study of the past, Russian historians and philologists reconfigured the terms of their enquiry so as to manage the current expectations of greater scientific rigor. Specifically, as I discuss below, they began to theorize distinctions between 'history of literature', 'literary history' and 'cultural history' while continuing to build upon aspects of an indigenous historical–philological practice. In sum, if they abandoned the pathos of the romantics and their quest to uncover 'the soul of the people' (Kostomarov is, however, a noted exception in this regard), they incorporated 'the literary monument' (poetry/song/folklore) as an authentic record into wide-ranging ethnographic, historical, semantic studies to learn more about the way the common folk lived their lives on a day-to-day basis. In light of these developments, then, it seems reasonable to suggest that, after 1850, Russia's scholarly relations with Western Europe evolved from one of relative dependence (attested by instances of conscious borrowings, if not the circulation of ideas across borders) to one where similarities between Russian and west European historiographical developments may, I believe, be best described as coincidental points of convergence.

The rise of Russian literary scholarship, particularly in terms of the history of literature as a sub-discipline, has been analysed by others.[18] What concern me here are its various interconnections with 'mainstream' historical scholarship as the latter transitioned from the age of romanticism and philosophical idealism to that of realism and positivism. With this in mind, I shall begin with an account of the way verbal art functioned as a resource for historians with a nationalist or cultural particularist agenda (the case of Kostomarov) before turning to the way it was used to support theories of cultural production in a comparative perspective by historians of literature. Fedor Buslaev, as the first professor of World Literature (named in 1863), is a pivotal yet transitional figure in this regard; but it was his pupil, Aleksandr Veselovskii, who, brought up in the tradition of positivistic thinking, advanced a theory of the history of literature (historical poetics) which resonated with historian-peers in the faculty as they endeavoured, for their part, to reflect upon the relationship between history and literature. Here, I will take as my case study a series of lectures delivered by the historian-sociologist, Nikolai Kareev. An immediate contemporary, Kareev's arguments both responded to those of Veselovskii and Taine and, more ambitiously, informed an attempt to classify the humanities disciplines as a whole.

Romantic era commonplaces

'Every sound of a song', Gogol wrote in a letter to the folklorist, Izmail Srevnevskii, 'communicates more to me about the past and in a livelier way than those short spineless chronicles'.[19] Among historians of Gogol's generation, Nikolai Kostomarov arguably did more than anyone to ensure that the boundaries between history and literature remained porous. His doctoral dissertation [defended in 1843; published in 1845] in which he treated folk poetry as the most authentic, insightful, truthful 'factual' (and psychological) record of the national past is a perfect illustration of what Lotman calls 'the fusion of historical and philological interests'.[20] Kostomarov opened his study, *On the Historical Significance of Russian Popular Poetry* (*O Istoricheskom znachenii russkoi narodnoi poezii*), with a cogent explanation of the relevance of his topic and of his approach in the current intellectual and political climate. Beyond an enduring love and respect that most nations typically express for their folkloric tradition (he mentioned Sir Walter Scott and Goethe), the study of popular culture (*narodnost'*) could, he argued, be more specifically linked to: the decline of literary classicism in its struggle with romanticism; recent government interest in the people (an allusion to Nicholas I's policy of 'official nationality'); and, more importantly, developments within historical scientific enquiry, namely an engagement with sources in light of the contexts in which they were produced. In Kostomarov's words: 'We need sources in which the people express themselves unconsciously. Literature (especially poetry) is precisely that source. In sum, all literature is the authentic expression of society'.[21]

Like, Gogol, Kostomarov was critical of certain practices in contemporary historical enquiry, in particular, an over reliance on chronicles recorded by monks and a tendency to embellish the 'facts' '*na svoi manyer*' (in one's own way): 'For all his talent, Karamzin', Kostomarov wrote, 'committed the error of looking at past events from a present day perspective, judging them in respect of present day tastes and expectations (*prilichnoi svoemu vremeni*)'.[22] By contrast, if analysed correctly, *narodnaia poeziia* (songs and tales) offered a glimpse of the ways in which the people not only saw their own lives, historically and societally, but also afforded a deeper understanding of their beliefs, attitudes and spirituality. In this connection, Kostomarov identified four ways in which folk songs might enhance historical enquiry. First, as records of events, folk songs contained valuable evidence for political ('external') history. Second, as expressions of *narodnyi byt* they afforded insights into 'inner history', namely social structures, domestic life, mores and local customs. However, while such glimpses of the day-to-day life of the people were highly revelatory, Kostomarov was conscious that the evidence they yielded tended to be patchy and fragmented, lacking in clarity, and thus required corroboration through the critique of other sources. Third, as an object of philological enquiry, the study of folklore was, Kostomarov believed, of great – though still regrettably – neglected value for the historian: while, at the time of writing, the 1840s, such findings had gained purchase among specialists in the history of language, they had not, as yet, been sufficiently exploited as supporting evidence in historical studies of the nation/people. Lastly, as a 'monument' (*pamiatnik*) attesting to the way the people viewed their own lives and their surroundings, folk songs encapsulated traits of the national character. For Kostomarov, this could potentially yield the most valuable insights of all for the historian endeavouring to capture popular perceptions of higher being and nature, and of the political world, past and present 'as conveyed orally by the people themselves'.[23] As a source, then, 'songs express feelings in their raw state, the authentic movement of the soul, notions that are not contrived. In song, people are who they are. The song is truth'.[24] Moreover, the absence of 'authorship' or ownership imparted a quality of 'universality' (*vseobshchnost'*): 'No one can say when or who wrote a given song; it was moulded out of a whole population; it is as if anyone who performs it makes it his/her own composition; in no other instance does a people assume such unity (*edinoe litso*) as it does through these notes; or, it follows, give such expression to its soul'.[25]

In developing his thesis concerning the differences between Great and Little Russian (Ukrainian) folkloric traditions, Kostomarov was able to draw upon a body of work compiled by contemporary ethnographers and philologists.[26] But, according to Iurii Pinchuk, author of a monograph-length study of Kostomarov's life and work, it was his first-hand acquaintance with some of these scholars (Pinchuk mentions G. F. Kvitkoi, I. I. Sreznevskii, A. L. Metlinskii and A. O. Korsunov) and the conversations he enjoyed with them that goes some way to explaining the origins of his interest in the life and history of the people through the prism of folklore and ethnology. Of equal note was Kostomarov's acknowledged indebtedness to contemporary creative writers. As an admirer of the satirist playwright, Kvitka-Osnovianenko and Gogol (*Vechera na khutore bliz Dikan'ki/Evenings on a Farm near Dikanka*; *Taras Bul'ba*), but also as an accomplished poet and novelist in his own right, he produced, in parallel with his historical studies, a series of literary compositions in the style of 'Ukrainian romanticism' into which he infused elements of factual detail to create a blend of legendary tale and historical narrative.[27]

Kostomarov's engagement with the distinctiveness of his own native 'Malorusskaia' cultural heritage was a fairly typical expression of the cultural sensibilities, which dominated his age. As one of the components of official nationality and a key motif in Slavophile discourse, the idea of *narodnost'* informing his various studies of Russian, Cossack and South Russian folksong inevitably played into these wider, more ideologically charged questions about collective identity. Indeed, as I argued in Chapter 1, scholars active in the pre-reform era were more or less expected to position themselves as advocates or dissenters on these questions. Some, such as Kostomarov's contemporaries at the University of Moscow, Pogodin and Shevyrev, championed Russian *samobytnost'* (uniqueness) through source-based studies of folklore and the early chronicles.[28] Shevyrev, for example, discerned 'historical' traces of the worldview (*mysl'* and *filosofiia*) of the people 'in our bylina', the distinctiveness of which, he argued, should form the basis of current Slavophile thought. Granovskii, we know, strenuously tried to distance himself from the Slavophile-nationalist sentiments overshadowing historical–philological scholarship, and this was without doubt one of the factors prompting him to call for an institutional alliance between history and the natural sciences in his famous speech of 1852 (mentioned in Chapter 2 of this book), which so confounded his contemporaries because it seemed to be a violation of his innately poetic temperament. As his successor, Kudriavtsev noted: 'Poetic monuments of different periods and peoples were his favourite objects of study. Recognizing their direct link with life itself, he frequently turned from his historical studies to them in order to '*doprashivat'sya u nikh*' (source in them) things left unsaid by history'.[29] If, then, in temperament and upbringing – all scholars were reared on the literary classics – Granovskii was a romantic through and through, it was, by contrast, in his role as a 'thinking historian' set on making history 'scientific' and wary of the claims made by his official nationalist opponents that he repeatedly reminded his audience of the need to differentiate between poetic and historical truth: 'The task of the thinking historian', he wrote in his tribute to Niebuhr, 'is to point out the boundary separating pure history from the poetic for the purpose of evaluating the latter. Aside from the fact that poetry is a pure and direct reflection of the enduring qualities of a people, it also contains within it indications of the reality of events, and frequently uncovers their inner connections'.[30] It was this marginally more qualified acceptance of poetry as a resource in historical enquiry (along with standard philological practice) that we see at work in the, admittedly few, instances where he analysed 'literary monuments'. A case in point was a lecture he delivered on the Icelandic Eddas where his approach conformed to the philological practice first introduced by Schlözer (and adopted by Niebuhr) in order to reconstruct the tale. In his view, while one should not demand chronological accuracy from Scandinavian sagas, they do not contain deliberate misrepresentations of events: as 'history and poetry, in which the folk believe, these tales and legends have their own independent value and significance'.[31]

Throughout his career, Kostomarov remained loyal to his commitment to write about the common man, and, increasingly, in later life concentrated on the specificities of his own Ukrainian cultural origins.[32] As such, his contribution to literary historical scholarship remained firmly anchored in the age of romanticism dominated by attempts to harness the spirit of a people through historical ethnographic study and analysis of language. By contrast, the work of Fedor Buslaev (1818–97), Kostomarov's immediate contemporary, tracked the transition from romanticism to what one might call a more 'secular' positivism. Between the two scholars there were, of course, many similarities: like Kostomarov, Buslaev believed that 'language is the treasure trove of beliefs and traditions imprinted in the collective memory of a people'[33]; epic folk poetry housed all the distinctive features of that people (*narodnyi byt*).[34] Since poetry was meant to be the form by which the nation's language was injected with 'life', and hence served as an indispensable interface between linguistic form and the popular spirit, Busleav, again, like Kostomarov, used the term 'poetic' primarily to legitimate the expansion of scholarly discourse into the study of popular myths and beliefs.[35] But Buslaev also challenged the nation-centred (*samobytnyi*) approach of Kostomarov and the Slavophiles by insisting on a broader comparative perspective in his linguistic and ethnographically based analyses of the folklore, myths and belief systems of ancient Rus'.[36] In doing so, he laid the groundwork for the advancement of a scientific, document-based conception of the genealogy and development of cultures in a historical comparative perspective, the scope of which resonated both with literary scholars and with historians interested in questions of national identity and social institutions.

Developments in historical literary scholarship: From Buslaev to Veselovskii

In the early 1860s, Fedor Buslaev was officially authorized to offer a course in comparative literature as part of government measures to restructure the curriculum. Memoir accounts by those who attended his lectures, however, suggest that he had, in fact, been incorporating a comparative perspective into his courses on the history of national literature well before the era of reform: already, in the late 1840s, he was giving voice to the idea that the origins of epic poetry were as ancient as the birth of language itself and that the similarity between beliefs and traditions may be explained by the blood ties of the Indo-European peoples. For Buslaev, this meant that the mythological legends and traditions of the Slavs should be studied in connection with the legends of other medieval tribes, especially the Germanic.[37] Initially inspired by the comparative–philological theories of Jacob Grimm, Buslaev's interests soon broadened beyond linguistic history into a more inclusive study of literature and folklore, which he approached using an ethnographical and art historical methodology in addition to the tools of philological analysis. As one of his former pupils confirmed, Buslaev had become interested in the study of Russian iconography following his trips to Italy: he recognized that such visual, highly stylized representations imparted a deeper understanding of ancient spiritual and aesthetic values, religious and moral norms, and that studying these was equally pertinent for literary and historical scholarship.[38] This multi-pronged approach, which he developed, allowed him to extend the linguistic field of enquiry beyond Church Slavonic (and points of comparison within a matrix of common linguistic roots) to uncover a rich tradition of 'lay' folk legend, myths and poetry in ancient texts. He therefore began placing emphasis on the phenomenon of interplay and cross-fertilization, of conscious borrowings and adaptations among peoples of their oral and written traditions that were largely brought about, he posited, as a natural consequence of direct and indirect contact among peoples, for example, through trade or in the theatre of war and military conquest.[39] At the heart of Buslaev's research, then, was the rather more ambitious task to elucidate, with the aid of a comparative lens, Russian medieval culture and world outlook as a whole.

According to S. Iu. Zimina, in an analysis otherwise concerned with literary-historical scholarship in the early twentieth century, one of Buslaev's major achievements was that, by virtue of making extensive use of 'semiotic methods and approaches to the problem of the unconscious', he was able to open up new avenues of enquiry.[40] Post-modernist parlance aside, Zimina's underlying point is, I think, a valid one: what Buslaev uncovered in religious texts announcing a Christian worldview – particularly those such as iconography and hagiography in which stereotyping and pictorial tropes were especially prevalent, while references to concrete events rare – was a deeply embedded culture predicated on popular beliefs and folk legends. In other words, thanks to his analysis of language, myths and folkloric themes, Buslaev made collective psychology and belief systems of old Rus' visible objects of enquiry.[41] Anecdotally, the innovative character of Buslaev's research may be corroborated by the reaction it elicited from his peers: suffice it to mention the national conservative Mikhail Katkov's negative reaction to Buslaev's Masters thesis, *O vliianii khristianstva na slavianskii iazyk*, which he defended in 1848. Accusing him of *'dvoeverie'* (a confession of two faiths), Katkov asked: 'Who, precisely, is the master (*khoziain*) of this book – the philologist or the historian'? In his reply, Buslaev simply stated: 'I am the master'.[42]

By the latter part of the century, Buslaev's findings and the path of enquiry he adopted would become as relevant to social history as they were already 'native' to the study of literary production. I have already discussed the deep impression he made on the young Kliuchevskii: as a student in the early 1860s, Kliuchevskii read and was inspired by Buslaev's recently published *Istoricheskie ocherki russkoi narodnoi slovesnosti* (1861), his major monograph in which he explored the correlation of history and philology, and the significance of folklore for historical research.[43] What Kliuchevskii took from Buslaev's scholarship was an appreciation of simple folk language as a repository of worldviews, 'a complex network of primary (unprocessed) worldly impressions (…), a set of basic popular representations of god, the world, and of man as deposited by these impressions'.[44] And, as I have mentioned, Kliuchevskii repeatedly reminded his own students that the Russian language (*rodnaia rech'*) was an extremely valuable and original historical–philological source, an imperishable monument of the past, and that it was precisely in language that a bygone age is ensured its immortality: 'The first and main work of popular literature (*proizvedenie narodnoi slovesnosti*) is the word itself, the language of a people. A word is not an accidental combination of sounds, a mere tool for communicating thoughts, but the creative moment of a people's spirit, the fruit of his poetic creativity. It is an artistic image in which a people's self-observation and observation of the surrounding world is imprinted'.[45] Similarly, for Vsevolod Miller, it was Buslaev's ability to situate the 'literary interests of the period' in relation to the entire gamut of artistic expression that was the key to unlocking 'the spiritual life of the Russian people in its various guises'.[46] Buslaev's range of expertise, then, not only positioned him as the 'master' of a hybrid historical–philological science as he, himself, had professed to be in his defence against Katkov's criticism; more importantly, it earned him the accolade of 'scholar artist' (*uchenyi khudozhnik*), the qualities of which were flagged up time and again by contemporaries as crucial to the task of consolidating a tradition of learning in Russia.[47]

'In the broad sense', Veselovskii wrote, 'the history of literature is the history of social thought in so far as it has come to expression in philosophical, religious and poetic trends, and is fixed by the word (*zakreplena slovom*)'. And, he went on: 'If, as I believe, we should pay particular attention to poetry, then within this narrower field, the comparative method presents a completely new task: to follow how new content of life (*soderzhanie zhizni*) (…]) filters into (*pronikaet*) old images'.[48] There is little doubt that Buslaev's cultural historical and comparative approach to the study of ancient Rus' prefigured some of the hallmarks of 'historical poetics', which his pupil, Aleksandr Veselovskii, one of the most prominent intellectuals in the closing decades of the nineteenth century, developed over the course of his career as professor of World Literature at St Petersburg University.[49] Defined as 'a comprehensive theory of the gradual evolution of literature through a large-scale inductive–comparative study of poetic forms', in recent years it has become the subject of some interest among literary scholars.[50] It is important to note, however, that, during his lifetime, Veselovskii never actually presented, in published form, a theory of historical poetics in its entirety, although it was central to his teaching and its main premises were developed in some detail: the task fell to his students who pieced together the theory from various fragments, lecture notes, conspectuses and articles after his death.[51] Among contemporaries, Veselovskii was equally, if not better, known (and highly regarded) for his encyclopaedic knowledge of the history of Russian and European literature and culture. Like Buslaev, he lectured and published on the Italian Renaissance (studies on Dante) medieval literature and folklore, Russian romanticism, comparative German and French literatures,[52] often drawing on political thought, social practices and referencing architectural forms.[53] It remains, though, that, throughout his career, as specialists have argued, one of his key concerns was to vest the study of literature with distinct contours so as to construct a 'science of literature' and establish its place as an autonomous branch of positivist enquiry within general historical and cultural historical scholarships.

Beginning in the 1860s, while studying in Berlin under the tutelage of the philologist, Professor Heymann Steinthal, Veselovskii produced a series of reports for the Russian Ministry of Education about the state of literary studies in his host country.[54] What is clear from his comments is that the problem of defining literary history and the challenge of instituting world literary history were just as actual in Berlin as they appeared to have been partially resolved at home, thanks to the recent creation of the Chair of World Literature in Moscow (held by Buslaev). But just how did Veselovskii define literary history/history of literature? It was, as we see from the quotation below, a very broad, all-inclusive definition:

> For our part, we explain matters as follows. There is a rubric by the name of literary history: its boundaries are unclear, expanding from time to time to adopt elements that have become specialized fields. It was necessary to draw boundaries – to define how far the history of literature was allowed to go and where foreign proprietorship began. The alien territories are political history, the history of philosophy, of religion, of the hard sciences. As a result, what remains as the share portioned to literary history is only so-called belles lettres; [literary history] becomes an aesthetic discipline: the history of refined works of verbal art, or historical aesthetics. This is what one calls the legitimization and the effort to make sense (*osmyslenie*) of that which exists. Without a doubt, the history of literature can and should exist in this sense, replacing the stale theories of the beautiful and the lofty with which we have thus far been compelled to occupy ourselves. And in the hands of Steinthal it would so remain. […]. Instead of leaving a cautionary loophole for ourselves, we would do better to acknowledge that the boundaries of literary history must sometimes be defined much more widely than as an exclusive selection of belles lettres. While we seek to make sense of the existing rubric, it is possible, I believe, to offer a new, alternative rubric. We have offered [such an alternative]: the history of cultural formation (*obrazovanie*) and of social thought insofar as it is expressed in poetry, science, and life. The hard sciences will be

included, of course, only with their results; in any case, they have generally begun to influence culture only in recent times.[55]

In 1870, Veselovskii devoted his inaugural lecture as professor of World Literature at St Petersburg University to the subject, elaborating on themes mentioned in these earlier reports. The purpose of the lecture was to establish the discipline's institutional status.[56] First, he differentiated between philology (with its focus on texts, language, etc.) and literary history understood as more ambitious project to analyse, for example, the place of sagas (he mentioned the Icelandic Eddas and Beowulf) within the tradition, or their resonances in later works. Such a comparative perspective, he argued, required the application of the inductive method so as to account for recurring phenomena relative to the material, intellectual and cultural environment, conventions and legacies or tastes of a given age. All of these feed the poet's creativity: 'In order to determine the degree of individual imagination or initiative (*pochin*) we must first establish the mechanisms/processes which underpin his creativity by breaking these down into a history of poetic language, style, literary topics, through to questions about the historical succession (*posledovatel'nost'*) of poetic genres, such as its law-like regularity (*zakonnost'*) and links to socio-historical development'.[57] Veselovskii's underlying premise here was that as a reflection of life, poetry functions like objective data which may be compared, placed in causal relations, or recur:

> Literary scholarship has to start with the most elementary observations of literary-historical facts. After comparing a great number of them, one may reach relatively firm partial conclusions. These may then be gradually combined into more and more general conclusions until one eventually reaches the definitive, integral view of the subject, the only true scholarly one in so far as it would be overarching yet systematically rooted in empirical detail.[58]

In practice, Veselovskii noted, the method was already being used in the study of mythology, folk poetry, *stranstvuiushchie skazaniia* (wandering tales about the Bogatyri, the Russian equivalent to tales of the knights-errant in west European medieval literature) as well as in geography and juridical customs: 'The success of linguists in this approach encourages us to expect if not identical but equally exact results from the study of historical and literary phenomena'.[59]

What fell within the remit of literary history for Veselovskii? If it were to be limited to the written word (*pis'mennost'*), one would have to exclude folklore; understood as *slovesnost'* (letters), then the subject would cover 'history of science, poetry, theological questions, economic systems and philosophical constructs'.[60] Just as he had done in his 1860s' reports, then, Veselovskii vigorously dismissed out of hand the idea that literature is just about the beautiful aesthetics or form (*iziashchnyi*); in his view, this was the legacy of Kant's notion of a universal–subjective understanding of aesthetic experience that was still common across Western Europe.

As Igor Shaitanov and Ivan Gorskii both note, Veselovskii's definition of the subject remained constant for most of his career, except that, by the 1890s, the decade in which he formulated his 'historical poetics', he had narrowed his focus to place more emphasis on artistic expressions of public thought – especially poetry – that is, 'thought' experienced in images and embodied in forms. Literary history, then, in Veselovskii's mature definition was the 'history of social thought as experienced (*perezhivanie*) in poetic imagery (…). History of thought is a broader notion, literature a partial manifestation of this'.[61] The implications of this narrowing were highly significant and on a first reading have all the hallmarks of a volte-face. But, according to Andy Byford, Veselovskii's explicit concern here was to construct a new platform for truly autonomous literary studies while remaining committed to a vision of literature as a social phenomenon and thus to a definition of literary scholarship as social science.[62] What Veselovskii meant by this was that as a natural–historical process, the history of literature was governed by the same laws as those found in the social sciences. To quote from Maslov's translation:

> Growing on the soil of general culture and nourished by its juices, poetic works gradually form a separate stratum or literary sphere. In this milieu, creative works are born, thanks to it they develop in a way specific to it, and in decomposing are swallowed up by it. Across a long history, they appear in various connections, develop or cease, their components interchange with others as one genre gives way to another (from the epic poem into tales or *lubok*, from tales into the novel and so on).[63]

In sum, historical poetics brought together the study of the historicity of artistic forms and theoretical reflection on cultural continuity and change. Maintaining the ties between philosophy, philology and history, it sought to construct a theory of verbal art that would be true both to the specificity of its medium and to the realities of its existence in the social world.[64]

How far Veselovskii succeeded in carving out territory for literary studies has been discussed by scholars and specialists in the field and goes beyond the scope of this book. Of importance here for the question of an interconnection between literary historical and historical scholarship, however, is that Veselovskii's theoretical/methodological lexicon with its key terms – empirical, inductive method, cause and effect, *zakonnost'*, evolutionary, naturalist – derived from contemporary positivism and Darwinism and expressed a hostility towards romanticism. It was, of course, an attitude shared by many contemporary sociologists and historian peers.[65] The upshot was that, despite his efforts, Veselovskii's insistence on a fact-based, empirical inductive analysis of *slovesnost'* inevitably provided fertile ground for exchange with historians with a positivist agenda. After all, Veselovskii himself claimed there was a correlation between 'the evolution of poetic consciousness and its forms' and the more general historical development of 'social and individual consciousness'.[66] As we shall see, this was precisely one of leading premises of Kareev's account of 'literary evolution' which he developed in a series of lectures and *publitsistika* during the 1880s: 'History depicts (*predstavliaet*) the process of evolution (*izobrazhenie evoliutsii*), of development in one or another domain in the life of society (…)'; the subject of history of literature concerns 'the evolution of the artistic production of life in connection with the evolution of individual and social ideals, as well as of the forms and directions of creativity'.[67]

Kareev's project for a general theory of the human sciences

Beginning in the early 1880s, Kareev devoted a series of articles and lectures to literary scholarship as part of an ambitious project to devise a general theory of historical knowledge.[68] In the first of these, published in 1883, he set out to define the history of literature as a discipline, but as we shall see, in addition to forging close links between socio-political and literary history, he used the occasion to offer some broader considerations about the public function of scholarship. Doing so, he traded in much the same prejudices regarding Western (aka German) scholarship that we saw earlier with Granovskii and Kliuchevskii.

'In general', Kareev wrote, 'the historian deals with events/phenomena of life (*ialveniia*), the historian of literature, in the main, with artifacts (*pamiatniki*) that are produced by life. If the distinction appears obvious, in practice historians and literary historians have blurred the line of division'.[69] As Karrev saw matters, part of the problem was how to determine what is creative literature. Is it just belles lettres? Or is it broad enough to include everything other than maps and documents such as statistics, charts etc., which fall into the province of diplomatic, political history? Although in this particular text he made no mention of Veselovskii, there is little doubt that Kareev recognized and admired his peer's erudition: his concern to factor in the material, intellectual and cultural environment informing poetic creativity all resonated with the type of enquiry that Veselovskii was currently conducting. Like Veselovskii, Kareev argued that the object of literary history (as *slovesnost'*) had to include oral traditions[70]: 'For both the literary historian and "generic" historian these *pamiatniki slovestnosti* are representations of the past in terms of its spiritual, as opposed to social, life'.[71] Possibly, anticipating Veselovskii's later statements on historical poetics, though equally drawing on a commonplace of romantic era historiography, Kareev stressed that the primary object of literary history is poetry: 'It captures the soul of a people, its pulse, expresses its religion, philosophy, morality, politics, its understanding of life'.[72] To his mind, poetry harnessed 'forms' (the prerogative of the arts) with 'ideas' (the prerogative of the sciences) in the most synthetic way and thus speaks to the whole human being: 'In popular poetry, or folklore (*narodnaia poeziia*) we find a synthesis of the religious, philosophical, scientific, moral, political, juridical, and historical conceptions present in primitive society. Thereafter, everything became increasingly differentiated, everything received its own dedicated literature, and the more specialized everything became, the less it reflected life'.[73]

> If science reproduces reality in dry, analytic descriptions, dissecting it with an anatomical knife, if science endeavours to grasp reality having resolved to compartmentalize it into a system of abstract concepts, if in the verdict on life which it returns it addresses man's reason alone [...], then, in works of art, which reproduce reality yet retain its essence in its entirety and vitality, and speak to man as a whole sentient and thinking being [...], that verdict acquires a particular force: it becomes more readily understood, more widely accessible, its effects on man far more powerful. [...]. Should the source of life, beating inside poetry, really be sullied by the dirt of archeological excavation?[74]

The view that poetry as a source yields knowledge of the distinctive sentient characteristics (emotional life) of a people was, of course, fairly commonplace and played into the canonical narrative about the literary-centredness of Russian culture.[75] But the point of Kareev's repeated reminders of this here had possibly more to do with the importance that he (like many of his peers) invested in the task of extending the reach of scholarship into the public sphere. Time and again in this piece, Kareev stressed the value of learning with the proviso that it be widely accessible and of general interest (*obshcheinteresnoi, udobnoponiatnoi, obshchdostupnoi*[76]), in sum, that it refract life and speak to all of human experience. The same rationale explains why he admitted other discourses such as literary criticism, *publitsistika*, philosophical and some academic writing into his pantheon of creative living literature. At their best: 'All of them express and determine the views and attitudes of society; in their works they reflect the life of society or shed light on it, inserting into this understanding a personal, subjective element, which should not be present in specialist literature'.[77] Thus, at its finest, scholarly discourse becomes 'art' a 'reflection of life'. History, for example, 'may be raised to the level (*podymat'sia*) to art, and serve as a means (*orudie*) in bringing ideas to life'.[78] If, though, historiography, he added, should be the subject (*predmet*) of a specialist discipline, 'art history, history of philosophy, subjects which are often treated in *publitsistika*, closely intersect with the domain of the historian of literature'.[79] The task, then, was to raise public awareness of the value of scholarship: provided it retained a connection to 'life' (distinct from arid abstract learning), it could serve as a tool of individual empowerment.[80]

If literature may be the object of history, the history of literature 'is by its very nature capable of being art itself'.[81] What Kareev meant by this was that, whereas in other branches of history, such as economic or diplomatic history, a source is used as evidence of a fact that cannot itself be resurrected before the reader in all its past reality, for the historian of literature the source (a work of art) is precisely that very fact about which he is speaking. For this reason, history of literature was, in his view, the discipline most capable of managing a perfect union between science and art:

> History of literature should represent literature in precisely the same way as literature depicts life, i.e. without separating the idea from the individual fact connected to it (…). The highest ideal of a history that is of general interest, that is universally understood and accessible to all, is to resurrect the dead man and make him speak, – and (indeed) the life of these individuals (that is, writers) was fullest, and they spoke most clearly, precisely in their literature.[82]

Kareev's misgivings about ivory tower scholarship (academic specialization with no regard for the bigger picture) were, as I mentioned, shared with Kliuchevskii and Grevs (and Granovskii before them) as part of an endeavour to gain public acceptance for true scholarship and thus secure the influence of the professoriate as 'legislators of knowledge' (to borrow Zygmunt Bauman's term) in a climate of government oversight. Almost without exception, though, such endeavours involved trading in stereotypes about German science as arid and remote from any public interest, *Vorstudien dazu*, as Kareev termed it. History of literature, he wrote, should not be limited to specialist studies of literary works as 'finished products' (*an und für sich*); rather, it has to be a history of creativity, an understanding of its tasks and aims that come to expression in ideas and ideals. Conceived as a creative process, literary works involve writers and readers, their critics and followers; they come into existence and play a role in a specific 'milieu' (*sreda*): 'It is time for all sciences concerned with the fruits/products of human activity to adopt a psychological point of view (*stat' na psikhologicheskuiu tochku zreniia*)'.[83] This last comment was a clear indication of Kareev's enthusiasm for the work of Taine, whose *Histoire de la littérature anglaise* he described as the finest example (*obrashchik*) of the French conception of science – so very different, as he reiterated, from German scholarship, which he disparagingly dismissed for its obsession with compilations, classification and for its focus on the laws of creativity and technique.[84]

I shall return to Kareev's engagement with Taine's ideas below. What is important to stress here is that the proximity he established between history of literature and other branches of historical enquiry which 'describe and narrate, elucidate and pass judgment, recreate (*vostanavlivaet v pamiati*) the general and the particular, the individual and the collective' was central to his broader ambition of formulating an integral theory of humanities scholarship.[85] Of note, also, is that, in this connection, he defined all history, and especially the history of literature, as a 'phenomenological' rather than a 'nomological' science. In Kareev's words: 'Phenomenological sciences are capable of acquiring artistic forms and history more so than any other science since it reproduces that same human life that art itself recreates. Only a thin line separates a good historical novel from an artistically written history: in the former it is *Dichtung* that prevails, in the latter it is *Wahrheit*'.[86]

In 1884, Kareev began lecturing at the University of Warsaw on the topic of 'literary evolution in the West'. Serialized in ten parts in *Filologicheskie zapiski* (January 1885–May 1886) and published as a separate monograph in 1886, the study was intended as one facet of a general theory of historical 'evolution' (Kareev's term), that is, a general theory of the historical process.[87] The book contained a number of leading premises that clearly spoke to a critical engagement with Veselovskii, whom he designated as the pioneer, in Russia, of the study of the history of literature as a science. Kareev's intention, then, was to 'put forward the view of a generalist historian who must familiarize himself with the historical research of colleagues whose object of enquiry are works of literature'.[88]

How did Kareev conceive literary evolution and the remit of the historian of literature in relation to that of the generalist historian? His leading premise was that literary developments must be placed in a broader social and intellectual context: even as it develops, carves out its own distinctive sphere of activity and charts its own evolutionary course, literature nevertheless retains its ties with other spheres of life and so cannot be studied independently of the history of society in general.[89] In terms of its intrinsic qualities, literary evolution should be considered in relation to the weakening of traditions, on the one hand, and the growth of individual creativity, on the other. Literary traditions, Kareev argued, might be altered through cross-national encounters or – particularly in the modern era – through the recovery of past traditions (he cited the influence of the classical world on European literature of the Renaissance era, and medieval poetry on 'neo-romanticism' (sic) of the nineteenth century).[90] But, by far and away the most important phenomenon was, in his view, the emergence of individual creativity. On this point, Kareev took issue with some of the claims that Veselovskii had made in his mission statement of 1870. As Kareev interpreted matters, Veselovskii's view that 'the content of current literature is cast (*otlivaetsia*) only in fixed (*ustoichivo*) traditional forms meant that he could not account for the potential for individual creativity and originality'.[91] In response, Kareev inverted the terms of the relationship between tradition and creativity to suggest that in contemporary literature (e.g. Gogol, Zola) what we find are old ideas presented in new forms: 'Herein lies scope for individual creativity. The Iliad, for example, is the product of the collective creativity of many generations in which the *pevets* (singer/ performer) worked in a single tradition and shared spirit.' By contrast, the *Divine Comedy* is first and foremost the expression of individual genius, the work of an original, independent being who plays freely with his cultural heritage: 'History brings the individual person (*lichnost'*) into being, and creativity provides her with new material.'[92] For Kareev, then, individualized literary creativity was commensurate with historical progress and the development of society. [93]

'Like any evolution, literary evolution is an interplay between creativity and tradition, of activity and milieu (*sreda*). We come across this everywhere in history, and it is none other than the interplay between pragmatism and culture'.[94] Kareev did not define what he meant by pragmatism, but I take it to infer a view of the historical process as one of contingency, expediency, accident, or the unforeseen, which may or may not be dependent on, or related to, human agency; 'culture' suggests the realm in which man (more consciously) shapes his world. When used as a qualifier, the term pragmatic–cultural research may be taken to mean non-doctrinal, albeit equally concerned with the ascription of meaning, as just described.[95] At least this is suggested in the following quotation, which is worth quoting in full as it brings us back to Kareev's main argument concerning the relationship between general history and the history of literature:

> The first task of any historian is to study facts [...] to uncover the cause and effect for every action (*deianie*), the underlying context and cultural circumstances [...]. For this we need to compile sources, analyse them, compare, differentiate and categorize [...]. Every specialist domain – for example, politics, religion, the economy or literature [...] and every era [...] has its own specific methodology determined by the quantity and type of source, or the task involved [...], all of which, however, is merely a preliminary, preparatory elaboration (*razrabotka*) of historical material for further surveys and source criticism, or for more specialist pragmatic and cultural research. In this connection, the materials a historian of law works with differ from those of a historian of literature; their methodologies differ, too. [...]. But, irrespective of all these specialisms [...], the overriding aim of history itself is [...] always and everywhere the same, namely to characterize/represent (*predstavit'*) the pragmatic–cultural evolution in a given domain. Whether it be a series of legislative acts and changes in the law, religious movements and change in dogma, economic activities and change in economic relations, or artistic achievements and the changes these

may undergo in terms of content and form [...], all these specialisms exist in an organic interrelation (*nakhodiatsia v organicheskom vzaimodeistvii*) and, in their movement (*dvizhenie*) they each influence the pathways (movement) (*dvizhenie*) of the others. Changes in the economic sphere are reflected in the political, legal, technical, customs and mores; political transformations leave their mark on law, the economy, religion, philosophy, as well as on literature; religious movements affect the life of the state as well as philosophy, art, literature, law, and so on.[96]

Within this totalizing view of the historian's task, Kareev then spelt out the task of the history of literature, which, again, is best quoted at length:

The history of literature must be the cultural–pragmatic characterization (*izobrazenie*) of literary development (evolution) both within the more general evolution of society and in connection with other partial evolutions, which may have a direct bearing on literary developments. If a historian of literature understands his task in the narrow sense, he merely provides a preliminary elaboration of historical–literary materials; if he takes it in the broader sense, then he enters the realm of the history of intellectual and social development [...]. If, in the first instance, he is working solely *for* the historian of literature (for example, studying the relationship between Shakespearean heroes and protagonists of Italian novellas), in the second, he is providing the generalist with more than he has the right to expect. Both have a role to play, though the latter is not history of literature in the strict sense [...]. One cannot call a historical–literary study one in which the general characteristics of the spirit of a given age are depicted, albeit relying exclusively on literary works; rather, it would be more accurate to call this 'literary history'.[97]

Kareev's attempts to differentiate between the task of the historian of literature and the more diffuse practice of the literary historian, which could be co-opted by historians, might strike the modern-day reader as laboured, but his argument is nonetheless a valid and commonsensical one: if typically used interchangeably, Kareev believed that these designations were in fact governed by two ways of thinking about the relationship between literature and life. The task of the historian of literature is to depict the social role of the 'writing class', its production and activities, or the relationship between creativity and tradition together with the reasons and conditions affecting their evolution. For the historian of literature,

life explains the literary work: life is not explained by literature. He focuses on his material (*pamiatnik*) in and of itself, not as a tool for highlighting the 'spiritual physiognomy' of an individual, his epoch or of the nation: this falls within the remit of literary history, that is, a documentary history based on archives, memoirs, for example. It is not a history of literature as such: you can have a literary history of political life (based on a critical and interpretative study of morality or religion, although a literary history of the economy or trade is unlikely.[98]

In making this distinction Kareev referred to Taine's *Histoire de la littérature anglaise* as a model of literary history, simply because he prioritized works of literature as evidence. For Taine, as quoted and summarized by Kareev, the value of a work of creative art is as a tool for probing the psychology of man (as an individual, and generically). If properly analysed, it is a rich document affording insights into the human soul and the 'psychology of the age, sometimes the psychology of a race'.[99] In short, studying the poem, novel or the confession could afford a far deeper understanding of the past than a 'pile of historians with their histories' – a point of principle that Kareev thoroughly endorsed: 'For the general historian, the literary expression of thought and mindset (*nastroenie*) is important only insofar as literature is socially relevant (*imeet znachenie obshchestvennogo faktora*), that is, affords the most influential and sharply defined expression of ideas and ideals'.[100]

Kareev's sociological analysis of the remit of the history of literature and literary history confirmed the difficulties of carving out a distinct disciplinary space for the former and the manner in which the latter – as practised by both historians and literary scholars – had encroached on the former.[101] His contemporary, Aleksandr Pypin, likewise struggled to establish the specificity of literary scholarship in relation to other disciplines in the humanities. In an article entitled 'Questions of Literary History', published in 1893, he adopted a critical historical approach to address the same problem of determining the scholarly (scientific) identity of literary–historical studies in the post-reform era.[102] Charting developments in the field since the late eighteenth century – from a mechanical compilation of titles to the comprehensive 'philological' understanding of the subject (scare quotes in the original Russian) which it became at the end of the nineteenth century – he observed that

> today, literary history is all inclusive (…). It is no longer confined to purely artistic/ aesthetic considerations (as exemplified by Belinskii); rather, it engages with the concurrent phenomena of popular and social thought and sentiment, it considers literary material as material for analyzing the psychology of the people and society; finally, it studies literary phenomena in a comparative perspective, in terms of cross-border (*mezhdunarodnoe*) exchange.[103]

Pypin argued that the shift in accent from a narrow interest in aesthetic criteria, typical of early-nineteenth-century approaches to cultural historical enquiry, could, in part, be explained by the fusion of the historical and philological sciences, which, by the mid-century, had become almost indistinguishable from one another in the sense that a comprehensive study of language and literature in their historical context was practised by both historians and scholars of *slovesnost'*. Thus, whereas, for Schlözer or Tatishchev, old Russian literary texts presented a rich source of factual historical data, by the 1830s and 1840s, a period dominated by questions of 'national psychology' (*narodnaia psikhologiia*) and anthropology, they became valued as windows onto an, as yet, largely unexplored cultural and spiritual world.[104] Literary texts thus became objects of historical enquiry in their own right: once again Taine's view that 'the history of literature should become the psychology of the nation' seemed incontrovertible.[105] Moreover, Pypin argued, irrespective of the competing interpretations they produced, studies by Slavophile thinkers and their rivals, Konstantin Kavelin and Sergei Solov'ev, all facilitated a change in the perception of these pre-Petrine documents from 'curiosities' or objects of 'archeological interest' to vital components of reflections not just on the nation's spiritual heritage, but also, thanks to the publication of compilations of songs and folk poetry, of ethnographical studies of everyday life (*byt*) in the commune.[106] In other words, with the onset of populism in the 1860s, the notion of *narod/narodnost'* had transformed from its original romantic connotations of cultural specificity into an engagement with 'the people's side of history' (*narodnaia storona*) and the implications of this in charting the development of the state.[107] 'More than ever, historical *pytlivost'* (inquisitiveness) is addressing those periods and phenomena of history where the active role of the nation/people came to expression'.[108]

There were numerous institutional and cultural factors (education, upbringing, censorship, attitudinal ones) contributing to the methodological parallels, convergences and overlapping contents between literary and historical scholarship that lasted well into the reform and counter-reform eras as Pypin and Kareev confirm. It goes without saying that the research questions that scholars took up in their lecture courses and publications in the closing decades of the century registered changes that were occurring in the current intellectual and political climate. Since the early years of Alexander II's reign, the most significant catalyst for a paradigm shift in humanities scholarship had, of course, been the Emancipation Act of 1861: historians began increasingly to direct their attention away from the state to the study of social and economic institutions (serfdom, village life and the rise of the factory), and, for their part, literary scholars had begun to invest the concept of *narodnost'* (the cradle of romantic study) with a more specifically socio-political colouring. In Pypin's view, this explained the blurred boundaries between literary history and history within the broader matrix of 'positivist' enquiry. This is also why historians working in a positivist-empirical and comparative key, such as Kliuchevskii or Miliukov, whose expertise lay primarily in socio-economic and political history, employed current philological approaches to research features of popular culture, such as day-to-day customs and religious ritual. Common to both disciplines was an inductive, empirical methodology, shared assumptions concerning the social role of literature, but also a residual romanticism, which, if disavowed, was nevertheless still discernible in their work. Kliuchevskii's handling of cultural institutions in his course of Russian history, as I have stated, owed much to the historical–philological methodological paradigm of his formative years (the 1860s) – notably, the influence of Buslaev – in the sense that he stressed the importance of a mutually reinforcing 'philological' and 'factual' critique of sources: the first (lower – *nizshii*) involved establishing the authenticity of the source, an accurate reading of it and the study of its language. The latter, higher (*vysshii*) factual critique, engaged with the substance of the author's thoughts which imparted a sense of, or an attitude towards, everyday phenomena – from events to thoughts and feelings.[109] Taking this a step further, Kliuchevskii contended that a historical critique may be either a critique of texts, which communicate historical facts, or a critique of facts produced by the texts. 'A vita (relating the life of a saint)', he wrote, is not a historical source (*istoricheskii istochnik*) but a "literary memorial" (*literaturnyi pamiatnik*). A vita should first and foremost be analysed as a reflection of religious ideas and norms of the times in which it was written, rather than as a source for discovering material reality. The purpose of hagiography is to provide examples of righteous behaviour, and its characters and events are thus idealized at the expense of certainty and exactness of their representation. The ideals represented by the vita, in turn, reflect the culture of the given epoch.[110]

Regardless, then, of attempts by historians and literary scholars to address questions of definition, and, notwithstanding the quite different definitions they offered, historical–philological research in the nineteenth century presented, as Lotman argued a non-differentiated (*neraschlenennyi*), non-specialized genus (*vid*): historians and literary scholars (or literary history in Kareev's terminology) occupied a common ground of historical ethnographic, philological and literary critical research.

Was this unique to Russia? This is a difficult question to answer without falling into the trap of unhelpful generalizations, or overlooking the proverbial 'exceptions to the rule' in Western Europe: as I have discussed, Hippolyte Taine, for one, was a noted, and seemingly influential, example of a 'counter-current' in France, and we may appreciate why he enjoyed a strong following in Russia. What, I think, we can confidently say about the Russian case is that the frequency with which historians of the modern era co-opted the tools of philology (medieval history was another matter, as Kareev moaned about[111]) gives us grounds to suggest that it was a hallmark of Russian historical practice and that the reasons for this, as I have repeatedly argued, are to be located in institutional developments and government oversight, as well as in formative cultural and attitudinal factors, such as upbringing, peer relations and the rather more elusive 'sensibility of the epoch'. It is also important to keep in mind the many parallels between Russian and west European historiography and literary historical scholarship. In his study about west European history of literature, Rens Bod identified a single methodological principle unifying all the various philosophies and conceptual tools informing humanities scholarship throughout the nineteenth century: 'Whether in a Darwinian, naturalistic sense as championed by Taine in his theory of race, milieu and moment, or by way of the Herderian Zeitgeist and Volksgeist, governing literary–historical enquiry was the view that a work can be explained causally, either in light of the spirit of the age, or the life of the author'.[112] Conceived as cultural artefacts, songs, drama, narratives and lyrical poetry were studied in the contexts of their production and in light of the responses they elicited. As we have seen in this chapter, in Russia, this 'causal-explanatory principle' was shared equally by literary specialists and mainstream historians, and, as Bod notes, this was the main point of difference with formalism that developed around the time of the First World War and revolution.[113] But, even though Bod's broad observations serve as a useful reminder of the dangers of insisting unduly on Russian cultural specificity, one cannot ignore some noted exceptions, this time in the Russian camp: suffice it to mention Grevs' concern to 'problematize the past'. If the difference is almost too subtle to be discernible, it is nonetheless worth reiterating that rather than ask how past events might be explained, he was asking what can we learn from them? Finally, we must mention Kliuchevskii, who strongly cautioned against engaging with explanations of cause and effect. For him, what was important was not the unravelling of a sequence of events; rather, the remit of the historian was to examine the qualities that man and society exhibit under given conditions, even though their provenance may be inexplicable or completely accidental:

> If a historian wants to speak in his own language corresponding to the nature of the subject studied, he may not speak of causes and effects, categories taken from the field of logical thinking. Reducing historical phenomena to causes and effects, we impart to historical life a type of well defined, reasonable, planned process, forgetting that in it reside two forces which are alien to these logical definitions, namely, society and the natural world.[114]

Epilogue: The Forgotten Legacy

In his study of Russian history, Dmitrii Bagalei, a relatively little known but highly prolific historian of Russia and Ukraine, cited Hippolyte's Taine's famous remark about the ideal historian: 'In the historian there is the critic who verifies the facts, the scholar who gathers them, the philosopher who elucidates them, but all of these should be concealed behind the artist who narrates'. And he went on to comment – 'Unfortunately, very few historians have possessed this gift, and figures such as Gibbon, Macaulay, Thierry, Taine, Kostomarov are the exception rather than the rule'.[1] The handful of Western authors in Dmitrii Bagalei's list of model historians is a timely reminder that the literary impulse in historical writing was certainly not unique to Russia; nor is it a claim I have made in this book. Moreover, nowadays, in the climate of post-Modernism, there have been numerous concessions to the presence of fictional elements in historical writing: that 'fiction' somehow informs 'history' is a commonplace (albeit not an uncontested one).[2] I have, though, argued that, in Russia, the ties between history, as a university-taught discipline, and literature remained constant throughout the period under study and that among the principal reasons for this was a shared belief, across the generations, in the need to empower the population through knowledge. As a pedagogical tool, the use of rhetorical devices and a degree of poetic licence in the creation of historical portraits, for example, facilitated this task of broadening public education. But, as I have tried to demonstrate, the literary world also informed approaches to and an understanding of history itself. The various historians presented in this book turned to creative literature for a whole range of reasons: for Karamzin and the romantics, poetry and novels performed a civilizing role[3]; for historians of Kliuchevskii's generation and after, who were educated in the combined disciplines of history and literary history, imaginative literature, alongside legal records and the study of material traces, acquired meaning as sources that could be important for historiography. And finally, if the change of political regime after 1917 compelled historians to, as it were, renegotiate the terms of scholarship to meet the demands of Bolshevik ideology, the basic requirement for mass instruction remained unchanged: as a means to bring history to the common reader fictionalized accounts continued to be the perfect adjunct.[4] Thus, rather than an irrevocable split between history and literature in the mid-nineteenth century, the latter was co-opted to enhance historical understanding in an extended range of usages – from verbal art, supporting evidence, to source, and resource in the study of man's attachment to his local environment.

As I mentioned in the Introduction to this book, broad linear surveys of developments in historiography generally point to a break between literature and history following the entry of the latter into the university and that the rise of 'scientific history' in the second half of the nineteenth century completed this process. And yet, there were so many exceptions to this, both in the European West and in Russia. Part of the difficulty in identifying the point at which literature and history parted ways has to do with the fact that, as Donald Kelley notes, if 'scientific discourse' became the standard by which histories were judged, what science actually meant for historians remained open to interpretation: was it simply a call for accuracy? Was it related to the establishment of large-scale 'laws' of development analogous to those in natural science?[5] Likewise, a companion question, 'what is history?', yielded so many responses: if the French positivists of Fustel de Coulanges' generation insisted on a complete, let us say, 'quantifiable' objectivity in historical enquiry, later generations of scholars revised the relation between history and the social sciences in favour of what one might call a 'qualitative' appreciation of subjective factors and motivations. Karl Lamprecht (1856–1915), for example, whose name became associated with the famous '*Methodenstreit*' in the 1890s described history as 'primarily a socio-psychological science'; Wilhelm Dilthey (1833–1911) renewed focus on history as '*Geisteswissenschaft*' and argued that, whereas the task of social sciences was to explain from the outside (*erklären*), the task of history was to understand from within (*verstehen*).

In Russia, reflections on the defining features of the discipline mirrored such controversies abroad. From Granovskii to Grevs, Russian historians addressed – openly and/or implicitly – the perennial questions relative to their practice as teachers and researchers: is history a 'science' or an 'art'? What are the best 'authorities' (sources), and how are they to be employed critically? Which disciplines may be drawn on for assistance in historical enquiry? Yet, as I have suggested, such clear parallels with west European developments in historiography were offset by a number of different accents in the answers supplied: in other words, while between Russia and the West we may track instances of acknowledged influence, evidence of the flow of knowledge eastwards from France and Germany, equally, the coincidences in methodology that we encounter have no clear explanation. Take, for example, the striking similarities between Lamprecht's study of medieval German economic and social history and Grevs' work on medieval Italy: for both men, cultural history involved multiple strands of historical enquiry – in addition to philological analysis of textual evidence (in their work, poetry/popular lyrical evocations functioned as a bridge between material and spiritual culture), they used the methodologies of anthropology and archaeology, even art history to explore the visible, more tangible traces of the past. However, whereas Lamprecht conceived his approach as a departure from Ranke, Grevs, we saw, situated the findings of his master's dissertation in line with a Rankean type of enquiry.[6] One other example worth mentioning to illustrate this point of coincidental parallels (although, in this instance, Grevs' writings function as an incidental precursor) is the work of the Dutch scholar, Johan Huizinga (1872–1945), best known for his study of medieval Burgundy (1919), and Erasmus (1924) and, for what Kelley rightly describes as his 'meta-anthropological masterpiece', *Homo Ludens* (1938).[7] Again, what the two historians had in common was an intention to expand the discipline beyond its political, military and economic components, and to make culture, customs and the emotional or attitudinal aspects of human behaviour an integral part of historical enquiry. Grevs found a template for this in the teachings of his own *nastavnik*, Vasilevskii; according to Kelley, Huizinga's interest in representation, social psychology, symbolism, rhetoric, ceremony and popular entertainments, and his disregard for 'the artificial narratives demanded by chronology' owed a lot to the example of the mid-nineteenth-century historian of art and culture, Jacob Burckhardt, whom Grevs never seemed to have mentioned.[8]

Writing in the early 1990s, Siguard Shmidt contended that

> the history of historical thought, and even more so, the history of historical knowledge is not reducible to historical conceptions. It is, rather, about the history and methods of historical research, the teaching of history, and the dissemination of various representations of history in *publitsistika*, belles lettres, fine arts, and the ways they are perceived. By the same token (*tem samym*) belles lettres and fine arts acquire meaning as sources that are important for historiography.[9]

One of the reasons prompting me to embark on this study was the fact that this last feature of historical enquiry – the literary artistic –mentioned by Shmidt was lost from view in both Soviet and Western appraisals of the late imperial historiographical traditions. Unsurprisingly, the sequence of Soviet historiographies largely sidelined this feature altogether as the profession took on the task of canonizing a science-based, law-governed, Marxist–Leninist narrative, a pattern, which, by and large, framed west European and North American analyses, regardless of whether these were intended to reproduce or refute the version authorized behind the Iron Curtain. On both sides, this resulted in a blind spot with regard to late imperial historiography. Granted, a number of publications dating from the 1990s, and after, have since rectified this trend, with a few, such as Thomas Sanders, focusing specifically on the writing of history in a multi-ethnic empire.[10] Still, these are few and far between: patterns of historiography in nineteenth-century Russia and the ways in which its traditions may have been integrated into Soviet-era historical writing continue to be a relatively neglected area of research. Rather, scholars have elected to address the question of the recovery of culture and the role of human agency in post-Soviet historical writing with reference to the political collapse of the Soviet Union, and from this vantage point have identified a number of resources for these newly developing trends in the era of perestroika. As we know, this was a period in which creative artists, literary scholars and historians began competing for purchase over the past as part of the broader and difficult process of overcoming what has often been described as mass historical amnesia. Paradoxically, the numerous roundtable discussions and articles published in journals with large print runs during the final years of Soviet rule often spoke to a polarization of views and methods between establishment historians and literary scholars; equally though, the discussions helped foster an alliance between the latter and erstwhile non-conformist historians who came to prominence as public intellectuals. The period also witnessed the emergence of the 'everyman historian' whose personal memories helped catalyse the development of historical awareness.

A number of west European and North American observers have located the origins of the post-Soviet 'cultural turn' in non-conformist thought, which emerged in the 1960s and 1970s, especially the prestigious Moscow–Tartu school of semiotics headed by Iurii Lotman and Boris Uspenskii.[11] Yet, even a cursory glance at establishment historiography during the Khrushchev and Brezhnev eras testifies an awareness among historian-apparatchiks of the role of creative literature in historical enquiry. Suffice it to quote a 'directive' issued by a Central Committee member, Boris Ponomarev, in a speech delivered to the All-Union Conference of Historians held in December 1962, at the height of Khrushchev's 'Thaw':

> Although the persons assembled here are primarily representatives of historical scholarship, I do not believe that anyone will challenge the fact that the notions held by many of the Soviet people of the epoch of Peter I or the Civil War, for example, were shaped not only by their school texts and specialized studies but also by the novels of Aleksei Tolstoi and Mikhail Sholokhov, and by certain other works of Soviet writers. It may be stated boldly that historical novels on the Soviet era and on our Party's history, written on a high level of literary competence, may become a deep source of the people's love for and understanding of their own history.[12]

Ponomarev's official endorsement of creative literature as a historical source and 'style guide' sanctioned debates during the 1960s and 1970s among establishment historians concerning the uses and limits of fiction in historical enquiry; it also saw the publication of a slew of anthologies and school textbooks designed to introduce pupils to the national past through the prism of literary representations.[13] A number of historians also wrote introductory essays to classic works of fiction. Of course, as one might expect, the inclusion of creative literature as a tool to assist instruction in history was authorized by reference to Karl Marx, but the takeaway message is that the literary interface of historical enquiry was always and everywhere discernible. During the 1920s and 1930s, despite the call for a rigorously science-based (Marxist–Leninist) approach to the past, the requirement for mass instruction resulted in the production of historical textbooks, which, stylistically, were indebted to classical literary genres (hagiography, panegyric, epic), albeit reconfigured in the idiom of contemporary socialist realism. The writings of Mikhail Pokrovskii, erstwhile pupil of Kliuchevskii and a leading figure during the first decade of Soviet rule, is one such example, while commissioned (single-authored) history textbooks intended for secondary schools all privileged use of colourful metaphor, adjectives and adverbs in portrayals of designated heroes and villains. And if, by contrast, the sequence of collective *Histories* of the USSR published in the post-war period charted the process by which the subject of history acquired its distinctive narrative and explanatory tools in the form of a depersonalized langue de bois and excessive quotations from the works of Marx, Engels, Lenin, the upshot was that, by the 1970s, establishment historical production had lost its credibility: for the school pupil, it was indigestible, a problem which the authorities endeavoured to rectify by the inclusion of the aforementioned literary/ historical anthologies; for the discerning reader, the 'untruths' contained in authorized accounts of the past led him or her to engage with the 'voice' of historian-amateurs and their role as conduits for uncovering highly personal truths about the recent Soviet past. Sourced in memory and/or family archives, their works of historical fiction (Anatolii Rybakov's famous *Children of the Arbat*) and (semi)-autobiography (Lidiia Ginzburg's *Blockade Diary*, Aleksandr Solzhenitsyn's *Gulag Archipelago*, Roy Medvedev's *Let History Judge*) received belated public acclaim during the Gorbachev era. As bitter truth-telling ventures, they contributed, along with historical journalism by revisionist historians and sociologists, to the collapse of the discipline.

Notes

Introduction

1. 'Rech', proiznesennaia v torzhestvennom sobranii Moskovskogo universiteta 6 iiunia 1880g v den' otkrytiia pamiatnika Pushkinu', in V. A. Aleksandrov (ed. & intro), *Kliuchevskii. V.O. Istoricheskie portrety. Deiateli istoricheskoi mysli* (Moscow, 1991), p. 399.
2. L. Gossman, *Between History and Literature* (Cambridge, MA, 1990), p. 255.
3. Ibid., pp. 169, 192–3.
4. D. Kelley, *Fortunes of History: Historical Inquiry from Herder to Huizinga* (New Haven, 2003), p. 200.
5. On late-nineteenth-century developments in Russian historiography, see, for example, T. Sanders (ed.), *Historiography of Imperial Russia. The Profession and Writing of History in a Multinational State* (Armonk, NY, 1999); A. Mazour, *An Outline of Modern Russian Historiography* (Berkeley, 1939); G. Vernadsky, *Russian Historiography: A History* (Belmont, MA, 1978); V. S. Ikonnikov, *Opyt Russkoi istoriografii* (Kiev, 1891–1908); V. M. Khvostov, *Teoriia istoricheskogo protsessa*, 2nd edn (Moscow, 1914); V. P. Buzeskul, *Vseobshchaia istoriia i ee predstaviteli v Rossii v XIX i nachale XX veka*, in two volumes (Leningrad, 1929–31); N. L. Rubinshtein, *Russkaia istoriografiia* (Moscow, 1941); S. N. Pogodin, *Russkaia shkola istorikov: N.I. Kareev, I.V. Luchitskii, M.M. Kovalevskii* (St Petersburg, 1997). See also note 20, below.
6. The so-called 'literary-centredness' of Russian intellectual culture is generally associated with the intelligentsia, the nation's critically-thinking elite whose emergence in the early nineteenth century coincided with a tightening of censorship measures by the government in order to suppress any potentially dissenting voices. The function of literature is summarized well by Boris Gasparov: 'Literature was regarded, and even regarded itself, as containing the solution to moral problems and the answer to cardinal philosophical questions. It was a political program for the transformation of society, a codex of individual behavior, a way of understanding the national past, and a source of prophesy about the future'. Boris Gasparov in A. D. Nakhimovsky and A. Stone Nakhimovsky (eds), *The Semiotics of Russian Cultural History. Essays by Iurii M. Lotman, Lidiia Ia. Ginzburg, Boris A. Uspenskii* (Ithaca and London, 1985), Introduction, p. 13.
7. For definitions of philology, see, for example, Rens Bod, who charts its development from the reconstruction and authentication of ancient and medieval texts to its broader connotations in the nineteenth century as 'the complete study of language and literature in their historical context', that is, a hermeneutical study of source materials as practised by professors in both the History and Literature departments: R. Bod, *A New History of the Humanities. The Search for Principles and Patterns from Antiquity to the Present* (Oxford, 2013), p. 279.

8   On the wide-ranging meaning of the term *slovesnost*', see A. Byford, *Literary Scholarship in Late Imperial Russia: Rituals of Academic Institutionalisation* (London, 2007). It is 'the widest possible reference to poetic verbal artefacts that could incorporate the notion of poetic language or discourse in general, and was often used specifically as a way of legitimately including folklore in the realm of "literature," as in the phrase *narodnaia slovesnost*'. Byford, Literary Scholarship, p. 32.

9   The Russian term *nauka* may be translated into English as 'science' or 'scholarship'. By and large, in this book, I have opted for the latter. This is because, in Russian, *nauka* is often used in relation to research in the humanities and, in this respect, comes closest to the German concept of *Wissenschaft* denoting a research culture, broadly understood, that is, as a complex process involving the establishment of networks and institution-building as necessary adjuncts to the pursuit of knowledge rather than any particular field of study. However, the caveat applies to late-nineteenth-century debates about the status of history as a 'science' or an 'art'. In this context, 'science' referenced the rise of the so-called scientific method associated with French positivism. In part taking its cue from developments in the natural sciences, French historians, such as Fustel de Coulanges and Gabriel Monod, produced a more narrowly defined view of the remit of historical enquiry, namely, work with more rigorously quantifiable data. As I argue in this book, if contemporary Russian historians mastered the new lexicon of 'scientific history', as a rule they tended to resist this more restrictive view of the discipline. See, below, Chapter 8. I am grateful to the anonymous reviewer of my draft manuscript for flagging up this issue for further clarification.

10 See 'Universitet', *Entsiklopedicheskii slovar*' [Brokgauz-Efron] (St Petersburg, 1890–1907), t. XXXIV, pp. 751–803; S. G. Smirnov (ed.), *Pamiati Fedora Ivanovicha Buslaeva* (Moscow, 1898), p. 50.

11 Byford lists distinctive trends and phases in nineteenth-century literary scholarship as classified by Soviet scholars: 'the mythological', represented by Fedor Buslaev (1840s–60s); the 'cultural-historical' and 'comparative-historical' methods pioneered by Aleksandr Veselovskii, and which dominated the reform and counter-reform eras. *Literary Scholarship*, pp. 26–31.

12 Historical studies highlighting the distinctiveness of Russian national traits include, among others, those by Nikolai Polevoi (his *Istoriia russkogo naroda* [Moscow, 1829]) and Ivan Sakharov, who produced several multi-volume compilations (with commentary) of Russian songs and tales during the 1830s and 1840s. Works dating from the reform era include those of the Ukrainian historians, Nikolai Kostomarov (1817–85) and Ivan Zabelin (1820–1908). I discuss this in Chapter 8. See L. M. Lotman, 'Russkaia istoriko-filologicheskaia nauka i khudozhestvennaia literatura vtoroi poloviny XIX veka (vzaimodeistvie i razvitie)', *Russkaia Literatura*, Vol. 1 (1996), pp. 19–44.

13 This generation of literary scholars shifted the accent away from problems of the genesis of art and its interrelation with myth to issues of praxis (*bytovanie*), namely, the development and change of artistic forms, which were studied from a comparative, cross-border perspective. As Byford writes, scholars tracked 'the migration of topics, literary motifs, processes of their assimilation, adaptation and creative reworking' (Byford, *Literary Scholarship*, p. 30). In addition to collating and publishing source materials, a practice begun in the pre-reform era, scholars published 'theoretical' papers on questions of popular culture (*narodoznanie*) in 'thick journals': *Sovremennik, Otechestvennye zapiski, Russkii vestnik*, and *Vestnik Evropy*. See also Lotman, 'Russkaia istoriko-filologicheskaia nauka', p. 21.

14　Byford, *Literary Scholarship*, p. 4. See also Lotman, 'Russkaia istoriko-filologicheskaia nauka', p. 19; S. M. Kashtanov, 'Istochnikovedenie', in *Ocherki istorii istoricheskoi nauki v SSSR*, t. II (Moscow, 1960), pp. 585–6.

15　Wladimir Bérélowitch, for example, suggests that although the state-sponsored *Zhurnal Ministerstva narodnogo prosveshcheniia* was intended as a channel for promoting its policies, the editorial board played an important role 'as a meeting place and legislator' in the professionalization of history. W. Bérélowitch, 'History in Russia Comes of Age. Institution–Building, Cosmopolitanism, and Theoretical Debates among Historians in Late Imperial Russia', *Kritika: Explorations in Russian and Eurasian History*, Vol. 9, No. 1 (Winter 2008), p. 120.

16　B. S. Kaganovich, *I.M. Grevs i Peterburgskoe kraevedenie: sbornik statei k 150 letii* (St Petersburg, 2010); A. V. Sveshnikov, *Peterburgskaia shkola medievistov nachala XX veka. Popytka antropologicheskogo analiza nauchnogo soobshchestva* (Omsk, 2010); Danièle Beaune-Gray, 'Vers une histoire des mentalités', in Marc Weinstein (ed.), *La Geste russe. Comment les Russes ecrivent-ils l'histoire au XXe siecle?* (Aix-en-Provence, 2002), pp. 329–43. Also by Baume-Gray, *I.M. Grevs. Un historien russe à travers les révolutions (1860-1941)* (Paris, 2017).

17　Both Grevs and the French originators of the *Annales*, Marc Bloch and Lucien Febvre, developed their approach from within the framework of socio-economic history. But whereas the French *annalistes* took geography or the milieu as their starting point to think about the past, the Russians focused on art, architecture and fictional representation in order to explore religious mentality and sentiment.

18　In the early Soviet era, Grevs himself wrote a number of essays and monographs on the writers he most admired: Turgenev and Roman Rolland, author of the ten-volume roman fleuve, *Jean-Christophe* (1903–12). See below Chapters 6 and 7.

19　See, for example, J. C. McClelland, *Autocrats and Academics: Education, Culture, and Society in Tsarist Russia* (Chicago & London, 1979); S. D. Kassow, *Students, Professors, and the State in Tsarist Russia (Studies on the History of Society and Culture)* (Berkeley, CA, 1989); H. D. Balzer (ed.), *Russia's Missing Middle Class: The Professions in Russian History* (Armonk, NY & London, 1996).

20　V. S. Ikonnikov, *Opyt russkoi istoriografii*, 2 vols (Kiev, 1891–1908); N. I. Kareev, 'Vseobshchaia istoriia v universitete', *Istoricheskoe obozrenie*, 3 (1891) pp. 1–22; P. Miliukov, 'Iuridicheskaia shkola v russkoi istoriografii (Solov'ev, Kavelin, Chicherin, Sergeevich), *Russkaia mysl'* (December 1886), pp. 80–92; also by P. Miliukov, *Glavnye techeniia russkoi istoricheskoi mysli*, 3rd edn (St Petersburg, 1913); V. P. Buzeskul, *Vseobshchaia istoriia i ee predstaviteli v Rossii*; N. L. Rubinshtein, *Russkaia istoriografiia*, 2nd edn (St Petersburg, 2008). As a rule, Soviet scholars treated developments in modern historical writing as a succession of paradigms, beginning with historicism, through to positivism, neo-idealism and Marxism–Leninism (see, for example, Rubinshtein). Among émigré historiographical surveys, see P. N. Miliukov, Ch. Seignobos, L. Eisenmann et al., *Histoire de Russie*, 3 vols (Paris, 1932–3) and G. Vernadsky, *Russian Historiography*. Works published since Gorbachev's perestroika and the collapse of the Soviet Union include: V. I. Chesnokov, *Pravitel'stvennaia politika i istoricheskaia nauka Rossii 60-kh–70-kh godov XIX v. : issledovatel'skie ocherki* (Voronezh, 1989); G. P. Miagkov, *Nauchnoe soobshchestvo v istoricheskoi nauke: opyt 'Russkoi istoricheskoi shkoly'* (Kazan, 2000); E. A. Rostovtsev, *A.S. Lappo-Danilevskii i peterburgskaia istoricheskaia shkola* (Riazan, 2004); A. N. Shakhanov, *Russkaia istoricheskaia nauka vtoroi poloviny XIX-nachala XX veka: Moskovskii i Peterburgskii universitety* (Moscow, 2003); V. S. Brachev and A. Iu. Dvornichenko, *Kafedra russkoi istorii Sankt-Peterburgskogo universiteta (1834–2004)* (St Petersburg, 2004).

21 See, for example, Mikhail Osipovich Koialovich, *Istoriia russkogo samosoznaniia po istoricheskim pamiatnikam i nauchnym sochineniiam* (St Petersburg, 1884). Written from an ultra-conservative, Slavophile point of view, Koialovich's book was re-edited three times in quick succession. Less tendentiously, Buzeskul contended that the 1860s–1930s corresponded to the birth and consolidation of a 'Russian School of historiography'. Miliukov positioned historians and historical trends in respect of the original Slavophile/Westernizer controversy in the 1830s and 1840s, and its subsequent revivals in the latter part of the century. This practice of labelling was, as Hayden White notes, common throughout Europe in the nineteenth century and 'could carry either "national" designations (the Prussian school, the Kleindeutsche school, the French school, the English school, and so on), or labels of a more particularly political sort, labels indicative of the political or ideological coloration of the historians (Conservative, Liberal, Radical, Socialist, and so on)'. Hayden White, *Metahistory: The Historical Imagination in Nineteenth-Century Europe* (Baltimore, 1973), p. 269.

22 S. N. Valk, 'Istoricheskaia nauka v Leningradskom universitete za 125 let', in Valk (ed.), *Izbrannye trudy po istoriografii i istochnikovedeniiu* (St Petersburg, 2000), pp. 7–106; V. M. Paneiakh, *Tvorchestvo i sud'ba istorika: Boris Aleksandrovich Romanov* (Moscow, 2000), pp. 401–2.

23 Grevs was reinstated in 1902 and Kareev in 1906. During his three-year ban, Grevs taught at the Higher Women Courses (*Bestuzhevskie*), private gymnasia and contributed articles to the Brokgaus–Efron 'Encyclopedic Dictionary'.

24 Bérélowitch, 'History in Russia Comes of Age', pp. 116, 117–18 where he writes: 'One cannot help being struck that the "two schools" thesis generally ignores ancient historians and historians of medieval and early modern Europe. In Moscow, Vinogradov was at once a vigorous "theorist" of social history and an explorer of archives, since he was the first Russian to send his students to the British archives. In St Petersburg, the same applies to Kareev and Grevs, and later Rostovtsev and others'. On the difficulty of establishing a workable definition of 'schools', see also for example, Sveshnikov, *Peterburgskaia shkola medievistov*, pp. 3–40. Reassessing the meaning of 'schools' and scholarly communities has also informed some recent research led by Lorina Repina, a specialist in historical theory. See L. P. Repina, *Istoricheskaia nauka i obrazovanie v Rossii i na Zapade: sud'by istorikov i nauchnykh shkol* (Moscow, 2012).

25 Byford, *Literary Scholarship*, p. 5. In his correspondence, the St Petersburg-based historian of Russia, Sergei Platonov, repeatedly expressed his admiration for Kliuchevskii's work, even though he was fully aware of his difficult personality ('*lichnaia shchekotlivost*', as he put it in a letter to Ia. L. Barskii dated 27 January 1885). Indeed, Platonov based his own teaching on the Moscow professor's lectures. See his letters dating from the 1880s recording his efforts to acquire copies of the transcripts of Kliuchevskii's *Course in Russian History*, in V.C. Bukhert (ed.), *Akademik S.F. Platonov. Perepiska s istorikami. Tom pervyi. Pis'ma S. F. Platonova 1883–1930* (Moscow, 2003), p. 15.

26 G. M. Hamburg, 'A. S. Lappo-Danilevskii and the Writing of History in Late Imperial Russia', in E. A. Rostovtsev, *A. S. Lappo-Danilevskii i peterburgskaia istoricheskaia shkola*, Introduction, pp. 10–11.

27 Studying the professional lives and outlook of historians has been the focus of a group of scholars at the University of Omsk under the direction of V. P. Korzun and A. V. Sveshnikov, which, since 2005, has edited an annual historiographical anthology, *Mir istorika* (*The World of the Historian*). Other publications in a

similar vein include: A. N. Dmitriev (ed.), *Istoricheskaia kul'tura imperskoi Rossii: formirovanie predstavlenii o proshlom* (Moscow, 2012); L. P. Marinovich and L. T. Mil'skaia (eds), *Portrety istorikov: vremia i sud'by* in two volumes (Moscow-Jerusalem, 2000); L. P. Repina (ed.), *Soobshchestvo istorikov vysshei shkoly Rossii: nauchnaia praktika i obrazovatel'naia missiia* (Moscow, 2009); N. N. Alevras, N. V. Grishina and Iu. V. Krasnova (eds), *Istoriia i istoriki v prostranstve national'noi i mirovoi kul'tury XVIII – XIX vekov* (Cheliabinsk, 2011). Also worth noting is the excellent study by Vera Kaplan, *Historians and Historical Societies in the Public Life of Imperial Russia* (Bloomington, 2017). I am grateful to the anonymous reviewer of my draft manuscript for suggesting that I flag up these publications.

28 The concept of 'scholarly selfhood' or 'scholarly persona' has, in recent years, been taken up in the history of science and theory of history. See, for example, H. Paul, 'What Is a Scholarly Persona? Ten Theses on Virtues, Skills, and Desires', *History and Theory*, Vol. 53 (October 2014), pp. 348–71. Paul offers the following definition: '[S]cholarly personae affect historians not merely in their professional role identities – in the roles they play "at work," as distinguished from "at home" – but mold them more fundamentally by cultivating certain dispositions (attitudes, character traits, abilities) that can never be detached from their possessor. Dispositions, (…) are deeply ingrained in the self. (…). Intentionally or not, scholarly personae make their impact felt, to a greater or lesser extent, in other roles and capacities that the scholar fulfills in life' (p. 355).

29 Richard Wortman's comment concerning the intersection between personal lives with political or institutional issues is very much to the point here: 'I have found', he writes, 'that childhood experiences, marital relations, friendship, all figure in the relationship to power and the social world, and thus demand attention'. R. Wortman, 'Biography and the Russian Intelligentsia', in Samuel H. Baron and Carl Pletsch (eds), *Introspection in Biography. The Biographer's Quest for Self-Awareness* (New Jersey & London, 1985), p. 158.

30 Cited in W. Mills Todd III (ed.), *Literature and Society in Imperial Russia, 1800–1914* (Stanford, 1978), p. 82.

31 See Harley D. Balzer, Introduction in Balzer, *Russia's Missing Middle Class*, p. 4. Byford tackles the question of professional identity by examining discourses of self-representation among literary scholars: Byford, *Literary Scholarship*, pp. 36–7. As I discuss in Chapter 2, historians used similar discursive tools (aphorisms, dedicatory verses, obituaries, jubilees) to enhance both the profile of their discipline and its leading figures.

32 Generalist journals which covered historical topics include: *Russkaia mysl', Vestnik Evropy, Russkoe bogatstvo, Otechestvennye zapiski*.

33 Like the intelligentsia, certain historians experienced degrees of victimization (by the state and/or their peers within the faculty) on the grounds that their pledge to serve the people through enlightenment was regarded as an expression of opposition to the tsarist government. See Balzer, *Russia's Missing Middle Class*, pp. 9–10. See also McClelland, *Autocrats and Academics*.

34 The *vospitatel'* could be a family member or surrogate. See Balzer, *Russia's Missing Middle Class*. See also R. Wortman, 'Biography and the Russian Intelligentsia', p. 157f; S. D. Kassow, *Students, Professors, and the State in Tsarist Russia*. Referring to Granovskii's contemporary, Fedor Buslaev, Byford makes the useful distinction between 'true' scholarship and 'pure' scholarship: 'true' scholarship had a moral dimension and was conceived as the love of truth, goodness and beauty (Byford, *Literary Scholarship*, p. 97). See, below, Chapter 2.

35 Aleksandr Stankevich was the brother of the more famous Nikolai Stankevich and author of the first, comprehensive biography of Granovskii (1869). Quoted from 'Biograficheskii ocherk', in *T. N. Granovskii i ego perepiska*, 2 vols (Moscow, 1897) Vol. I, p. 289.
36 F. Schleiermacher, *Gelegentliche Gedanken über Universitaten im deutschen Sinn. Nebst einem Anhang uber eine neu zu errichtende* (Berlin, 1808), 33, note 36, cited in Christophe Charles in W. Ruegg (ed.), *A History of the University in Europe. Volume III: Universities in the Nineteenth and Early Twentieth Centuries* (Cambridge, 2004), p. 48
37 S. V. Eshevskii, *Petr Nikolaveich Kudriavtsev kak prepodavatel'* (Moscow, 1858), pp. 4-5.
38 See, for example, Grevs' obituary of Vasilevskii where he writes of '*sila mysli*': '*Vasilii Grigorevich Vasilevskii kak uchitel' nauki. Nabrosok vospominaniia i materialy dlia kharakeristiki. (Posviashchaetsia ego bybshim slushateliam i slyushatel'nitsam i studentam-filologam Peterburgskogo Universiteta)* (St Petersburg, 1899), p. 43. See also his comment in the foreword to his dissertation on farm management in the late Roman Empire: 'Knowledge is power (*znanie – sila*): it generates and casts a spiritual light; enlightenment is the most powerful instrument of progress. Its organ is scholarship, and fortunate is the country where mature people value this and the young engage with it. If only in our country those who dedicate their lives to scholarship could find support from the various classes and social groups'. I. M. Grevs, *Ocherki iz istorii Rimskogo zemlevladeniia (preimushchestvenno vo vremena imperii)*, Vol. 1 (St Petersburg, 1899), p. xxiii. Again, in his memoirs, he hinted at the need for true scholarship by virtue of its absence from the teaching profession. Most professors, he recalled, exhibited a fairly dismissive attitude towards the students, to which students responded by characterizing them as 'priests of lifeless erudition' *(zhretsi bezzhiznennoi eruditsii)*. See O. B. Vakhromeeva (ed.), *Chelovek s otkrytym serdtsem. Avtobiograficheskoe i epistolyarnoe nasledie Ivana Mikhailovicha Grevsa (1860-1941)* (St Petersburg, 2004), p. 156.
39 Well into the Soviet era, members of the academic profession claimed allegiance to a mentor, not infrequently tracing their pedigree as scholars back to a nineteenth-century 'master' through a succession of master–pupil linkages. (In this respect, Kliuchevskii, for example, had a particularly long line of successors, with Melitsa Nechkina (1901-1985) as one of the last, dating from the late Soviet era.)
40 Tolstoi was responsible for the college reform of 1871, which promoted the study of Latin, Greek and Ancient Literature. Appointed Minister of the Interior in 1882, he co-authored the 'temporary regulations' heralding the era of counter-reform, which, more or less, remained in place until the collapse of tsarism in 1917.
41 On Granovskii as 'the Pushkin of history', see P. N. Kudriavtsev, 'O sovremennykh zadachakh istorii', in *Sochineniia*, 3 vols (Moscow, 1887), Vol. 1, pp. 33-69; Ch. Vetrinskii, *T. N. Granovskii i ego vremia. Istoricheskii ocherk* (Moscow, 1897). On comparisons between Kliuchevskii and Tolstoi, see, for example, A. A. Kizevetter, 'V. O. Kliuchevskii kak prepodavatel'', in *V. O. Kliuchevskii: Kharakteristiki i vospominaniia* (Moscow, 1912), pp. 164-76. According to Alfred J. Rieber, Kliuchevskii was remarkably similar in temperament to Tolstoi: '[L]ike his great contemporary Leo Tolstoy, Kliuchevskii had a corrosively skeptical intellect which in its relentless pursuit of truth gave him no peace. Like Tolstoy, too, Kliuchevskii was a destroyer of systems, an enemy of abstract reasoning whose temper both matched and expressed the spirit of the times (...). He freed history from its subservience to

philosophy and cleared the way for multidisciplinary study of the past'. A. Rieber, Introduction to the English translation by Natalie Duddington of *A Course in Russian History: The Seventeenth Century*, pp. xxiii, xix–xx.

42 Iurii V. Nikulichev, 'Neprochitannaia literatura: vek deviatnadtsatyi', *Otechestvennaia istoriia*, Vol. 1 (2002), pp. 49–60; D. Ungurianu, 'Fact and Fiction in the Romantic Historical Novel', *Russian Review*, Vol. 57, No. 3 (July 1998), pp. 380–93; S. O. Shmidt, 'Pamiatniki khudozhestvennoi literatury kak istochnik istoricheskikh znanii', *Otechestvennaia istoriia*, Vol. 1 (2002), pp. 40–9.

43 D. Ungurianu, 'Fact and Fiction', p. 389.

44 V. Belinskii, *Polnoe sobranie sochinenii*, Vol. 1 (Moscow, 1953), p. 134, cited in ibid., p. 387.

45 A. Wachtel, *An Obsession with History: Russian Writers Confront the Past* (Stanford, CA, 1994), p. 7.

46 Ibid., p. 17. For example, Nikolai Karamzin's 'Natalia, the Boyar's Daughter' (1792) and 'Martha the Posadnik' (1803) illustrated themes that he addressed in his *History of the Russian State* (1816–29); Pushkin wrote both a fictionalized account and a narrative history of the Pugachev uprising (*The Captain's Daughter* and *A History of Pugachev*); Gogol shadowed his historical novel, *Taras Bul'ba*, with a history of Ukraine. In *War and Peace*, Tolstoi incorporated a disquisition on the meaning of history. For a discussion of the critique by contemporary historians, see Chapter 7.

47 Wachtel does not include the historical novel, as such, in his definition. As a recognized genre, 'the standard conventions of the historical novel […] consciously tries to level the difference between fictional and historical narration by fictionalizing everything. In scenes like these, so standard in Walter Scott, the historical figure acts unconstrainedly because the situation in which he is placed has no historical significance. The historical personage becomes, momentarily at least, unbound, for his actions fall out of the teleological path that the backward-looking historian sees. Indeed, in most historical novels these are the only kind of passages in which world-historical individuals appear'. Ibid., p. 114.

48 Ibid., pp. 221–2.

49 The 'flow of history' metaphor is Kliuchevskii's. See Chapter 4. See also R. F. Byrnes, 'Kliuchevskii's View of the Flow of Russian History', in T. Sanders (ed.), *Historiography of Imperial Russia. The Profession and Writing of History in a Multinational State* (Armonk, NY, 1999), pp. 239–61.

50 I use the term 'mentality' in the way it was understood by the French *Annales* historians, and which Aaron Gurevich's definition, cited here, renders quite faithfully: 'Research into mentality is not concerned with philosophical, religious or political convictions or doctrines as such, rather the "soil" (*pochva*) out of which they grow (*proirastaiut*)'. This cultural soil provides the setting within which traditions and social practices take shape and spontaneously change over time, 'usually outside the control of their day to day conscious lives'. A. Ia Gurevich, *Istoricheskii sintez i shkola 'Annalov'* (Moscow, 1993), pp. 10–11.

51 See, below, Chapter 6.

52 Donald Kelley has also touched on this theme in *Fortunes of History* and in his *Frontiers of History. Historical Inquiry in the Twentieth Century* (New Haven & London, 2006).

53 White, *Metahistory*, p. 427.

54 Ibid., pp. 136–7. 'To be sure', White continues, 'it was clear that the historian should try to be "scientific" in his investigation of the documents and in his efforts to

determine "what actually happened" in the past, and that he ought to represent the past "artistically" to his readers [...]. As an art form, historical writing might be "lively" and stimulating, even "entertaining," so long as the artist–historian did not presume to utilize anything other than techniques and devices of traditional storytelling'.

55 Ibid., p. 427. For this reason, White famously dropped the more conventional categories of Romanticism, Idealism and Positivism designating different 'schools' of historical writing, as well as those of 'specific ideological movements, such as Liberalism, Radicalism, and Conservatism that also served as historiographical identity tags of sorts'. Instead, his focus on the 'linguistic protocol' of a given historian's explanatory/interpretative strategies' allowed him, as he put it, 'to specify, on different levels of engagement – epistemological, aesthetic, ethical, and linguistic – precisely wherein a given historian's "liberalism" or "Romanticism" or "Idealism" consists and to what degree it actually determined the structure of the works he wrote'.

56 Ibid., p. 268.

57 P. Roosevelt, *Apostle of Russian Liberalism: Timofei Granovsky* (Newtonville, MA, 1986), p. xii

58 As Pavel Miliukov put it: Granovskii 'always loved "the poetry" in history regardless of the philosophical meaning of history'. See P. Miliukov, 'Universitetskii kurs Granovskogo' [1845–6] in *Iz Istorii russkoi intelligentsii. Sbornik statei i etiudov*, 2nd edn (St Petersburg, 1903), p. 262.

59 Kliuchevskii, cited in Byrnes, V. O. *Kliuchevskii, Historian of Russia* (Bloomington, 1995), p. 240. In an unpublished review of Bestuzhev-Riumin's *Russkaia istoriia* [1872], Kliuchevskii was highly critical of his older, Petersburg contemporary for his lack of 'literary art' (*literaturnoe iskusstvo*). See Kliuchevskii, *Neopublikovannye proizvedeniia* (Moscow, 1983), p. 153. He also criticized Bestuzhev's successor, Sergei Platonov, for dismissing the relevance of literature (i.e. the chronicles) as a source. See, below, Chapter 7.

60 See E. G. Chumachenko, *V. O. Kliuchevskii – Istochnikoved* (Moscow, 1970), p. 8.

61 Granovskii's comments on the subject echoed those of Thomas Babington Macaulay: 'In fiction, the principles are given to find the facts: in history, the facts are given to find the principles; and the writer who does not explain the phenomena as well as state them performs only one half of his office. Facts are the mere dross of history. It is from the abstract truth, which interpenetrates them, and lies latent among them like gold in the ore, that the mass derives its whole value. [...] The perfect historian is he in whose work the character and spirit of an age is exhibited in miniature. [...] By judicious selection, rejection, and arrangement, he gives truth to those attractions that have been usurped by fiction. In his narrative a due subordination is observed: some transactions are prominent; others retire. But the scale on which he represents them is increased or diminished, not according to the dignity of the persons concerned in them, but according to the degree in which they elucidate the condition of society and the nature of man'. T. B. Macaulay, 'History', *Edinburgh Review* 1828. Cited in Gossman, *Between History and Literature*, p. 356, note 156.

62 See, for example, Grevs' views on the topic which he addressed in correspondence with his friend, the Symbolist poet and classical scholar, Viacheslav Ivanov: 'Just as philologists hardly ever tried to become economists in order to study the history of ancient economy, likewise, economists have been little disposed to acquire the philological skills necessary for understanding the life of people in the classical

era. At the present time, the obligation to be prepared for a battle on several fronts […] has become the responsibility and conscience of historians'. Letter dated 4/16 October 1894, in G. M. Bongard-Levina, N. V. Kotreleva and E. V. Liapustinoi, *Istoriia i poeziia: perepiska I.M. Grevsa i Viach. Ivanova* (Moscow, 2006), p. 83.

63 Wachtel, *An Obsession with History*, p. 1.
64 In addition to some of the principal studies listed above (notes 5 & 20), see A. Mazour, *Modern Russian Historiography* (Westport, CT, 1975); E. Thaden, *The Rise of Historicism in Russia* (New York, 1999); K. J. Mjor, *Reformulating Russia: The Cultural and Intellectual Historiography of Russian First-Wave Émigré Writers* (Leiden, 2011) and the *Journal of Modern Russian History and Historiography* (Leiden, 2008–present).
65 For example, Nathan Reingold, ' The Peculiarities of the Americans, or, Are There National Styles in the Sciences?', *Science in Context*, Vol. 4 (1991), pp. 347–66; Jonathan Harwood, *Styles of Scientific Thought: The German Genetics Community, 1900–1933* (Chicago, 1993).
66 See, for example, Laura Engelstein, 'Culture, Culture Everywhere: Interpretations of Modern Russia, across the Revolutionary Divide', *Kritika*, Vol. 2 (Spring 2001), pp. 363–93, and the review essay by Stephen Lovell, also in *Kritika*, Vol. 1 (Winter 2009), pp. 205–15. On the rise of revisionist paradigms in the 1960s and 1970s, see Roger Markwick, 'Cultural History under Khrushchev and Brezhnev: From Social Psychology to Mentalities', *Russian Review*, Vol. 65 (April 2006), pp. 283–301. Also by Markwick, *Rewriting History in the Soviet Era: The Politics of Revisionist Historiography* (Basingstoke & New York, 2001).
67 On the topic of personhood (*lichnost'*) as a prevalent theme in Russian nineteenth-century intellectual culture, see, for example, G. Hamburg and R. Poole (eds), *A History of Russian Philosophy 1830–1930: Faith, Reason, and the Defence of Human Dignity* (Cambridge, 2010); A. Haardt and N. Plotnikov (eds), *Diskurse der Personalitat. Die Begriffsgeschichte der 'Person' aus deutscher und russicher Perspektive* (Paderborn, 2008).
68 Wachtel, *An Obsession with History*, pp. 47–8.
69 A. Veselovskii, 'Envisioning World Literature in 1863: From Reports on a Mission Abroad', in B. Maslov (ed.), *PMLA* (Publications of the Modern Language Association of America), Vol. 128, No. 2 (2013), p. 444.

Chapter 1

1 According to Harley Balzer, this Continental pattern contrasted with British and North American practices, which saw the emergence of 'independent professional groups seeking to invoke state authority to enforce their control over training and membership'. Harley D. Balzer, Introduction, in Balzer, *Russia's Missing Middle Class*, p. 6. It is also worth noting that developments in France and Germany more or less coincided with those in Russia and considerably predated those in Britain where the first chair in history was established as late as 1866. As Hayden White notes, 'Chairs of History were founded at the University of Berlin in 1810 and at the Sorbonne in 1812. Societies for the editing and publication of historical documents were established soon after: the society for the Monumenta Germaniae Historica in 1819, the Ecole des Chartes in 1821. Government subsidies of these societies – inspired by the nationalist

sympathies of the time – were forthcoming in due course, in the 1830s. After mid-century, the great national journals of historical studies were set up: the *Historische Zeitschrift* in 1859, the *Revue historique* in 1876, the *Rivista storica italiana* in 1884, and the *English Historical Review* in 1886). (…). In this disciplinization of the field of history, England lagged behind the continental nations. Oxford established the Regius Professorship of History, first held by Stubbs, only in 1866; Cambridge followed thereafter, in 1869. But English undergraduates could not specialize in historical studies as a distinct field until 1875'. White, *Metahistory*, p. 136. See also Susan Gross Solomon, 'Circulation of Knowledge and the Russian locale', *Kritika*, Vol. 9, No. 1 (Winter 2008), p. 25; *A History of the University in Europe*.

2 See J. Flynn, *The University Reform of Tsar Alexander I, 1802–1835* (Washington, DC, 1988). The study of ancient/medieval Russia was facilitated by the creation of Archaeological Commissions and the Russian Historical Library, which published their transactions. The Moscow Society of Russian History and Antiquities (1804), the Russian Archaeological Society (1846), the Russian Historical Society of Petersburg (1866) were set up to gather and process materials and documents of Russian history.

3 A great deal has been written on this topic. See, for example, C. Whittaker, *The Origins of Modern Russian Education: An Intellectual Biography of Count Sergei Uvarov, 1786–1855* (Dekalb, Ill., 1984); P. Miliukov, 'Universitety v Rossii', in Brokgauz-Efron (ed.), *Entsiklopedicheskii slovar'*, Vol. xxxiv (a) (Leipzig–St Petersburg, 1902), pp. 788–803; B. Glinskii, 'Universitetskie ustavy, 1755–1884', *Istoricheskii vestnik*, vols 1, 2 (1900), pp. 324–51, 718–42; W. Brickman and J. T. Zepper (eds), *Russian and Soviet Education, 1731–1989: A Multilingual Annotated Bibliography* (New York, 1992).

4 As one example of this sentiment, see the introduction to the second volume of Pogodin's lectures on Russian history: 'Having demonstrated the reliability of the Nestor Chronicle (Vol. 1), I now turn to the study of the earliest period of Russian history, for which the chronicle serves as the main source. The first question to concern us is "how did the Russian state originate? (…)." What were the foundations of a state that was to surpass all other states in the world, past and present, by its might; that could still quite easily grow in strength, that is, self-sufficient in material needs, and requires no foreign aid to sustain her, that occupies the first place in the political arena of Europe, and that disposes of its own fate, the fate of the entire world, of all mankind?' M. P. Pogodin, *Issledovaniia, zamechaniia i leksii Mikhaila Pogodina o Russkoi istorii*, Vol. 2. (Moscow, 1846), p. 1 [My translation – FN]. On the so-called Norman period of Russian history, see N. Riasanovsky, 'The Norman Theory of the Origin of the Russian State', *The Russian Review*, Vol. 7, No. 1 (Autumn 1947), pp. 96–110.

5 There exists a vast literature on the 'Russia and the West' debate. For a solid introduction to the question, see, for example, V. Tolz, *Russia*, published in the series 'Inventing the Nation' (London, 2001) and R. Bova (ed.), *Russia and Western Civilization: Cultural and Historical Encounters* (Armonk, NY, 2003). For a detailed historical–philosophical analysis, see A. Walicki, *The Slavophile Controversy* (Oxford, 1975).

6 T. Granovskii, pubic lectures (1843–4) as discussed by Thaden, *The Rise of Historicism in Russia*, pp. 110–11.

7 See Roosevelt, *Apostle of Russian Liberalism*, p. 61. Setbacks to this process, evidenced by certain 'immoral laws and institutions', such as the Spanish Inquisition

or the English Star Chamber were not, Granovskii believed, irreversible and, thus, ultimately, did not obstruct the path towards a higher stage of human development.

8   Ibid., p. 81. See also Thaden, *The Rise of Historicism in Russia*, pp. 101–14. While this holds in particular for historians of western Europe, it was also a feature of the so-called 'statist school of Russian historiography' that developed in the mid-nineteenth century, associated with the names of Boris Chicherin, Konstantin Kavelin and Sergei Solov'ev. Likewise, the next generation of positivist historians, headed by Kliuchevskii and Miliukov, tended to situate Russian history in the broader world context, the effect of which (especially in Miliukov's case) was to downplay claims to her uniqueness, if not differences from patterns of development in the West.

9   T. Granovskii, *Sochineniia T.N. Granovskogo*, Vol. 2 (Moscow, 1900), p. 211, cited in Ch. Vetrinskii (pseudonym for Vasilii E. Cheshikhin), *T. N. Granovskii i ego vremiia: istoricheskii ocherk* (Moscow, 1897), p. 105.

10 For example, the professor of world history, Mikhail Kachanovskii, who taught at Moscow University in the 1820s, also lectured in fine arts, archaeology, Russian history, 'statistics' and *'slavianskoe narechiia'*. See Thaden, *The Rise of Historicism in Russia*; also by Thaden: 'Historicism, N. A. Polevoi, and Rewriting Russian History', *East European Quarterly*, Vol. XXXVIII, No. 3 (September 2004), pp. 299–329. Russian contemporaries themselves attested the gradual emergence of subject specialization during the first three decades of the nineteenth century. See A. S. Arkhangel'skii, '*F.I Buslaev v svoikh 'Vospominaniia' i uchenykh trudakh* (Kazan, 1899), p. 8 and F. I. Buslaev, 'M. P. Pogodin kak professor', Pamphlet (Moscow, 1876).

11 A. Kiesewetter, 'Klyuchevsky and His Course of Russian History', *The Slavonic Review*, Vol. 1. No. 3 (March 1923), pp. 506–7.

12 P. Vinogradov, 'Issledovaniia po sotsial'noi istorii Anglii', in *Zhurnal Ministerstva narodnogo prosveshcheniia* (1886–7). Quotations are taken from the English version, which appeared under the title *Villainage in England* (Oxford, 1892). For 'mutual guarantees', Vinogradov used the expression *krugovaia poruka*, a term which, in the rural Russia of his day, connoted the practice of an unpopular system of taxation. Other original English language publications by Vinogradov include: *The Growth of the Manor* (London, 1905, 2nd edn, 1909), translated into Russian as *Srednevekoe pomest'e Anglii* (SPb., 1911); *English Society in the XI Century* (Oxford, 1908); and his celebrated *Outlines of Historical Jurisprudence*, 3 vols (Oxford & London, 1920–4). See also his 'Folkland', *English Historical Review* (January 1891), pp. 1–17.

13 P. Vinogradoff, *Villainage in England*, 'Conclusion', p. 2.

14 Ibid.

15 Ibid., 'Preface', p. 1.

16 Vinogradov, paraphrased in Buzeskul, *Vseobshchaia istoriia i ee predstaviteli v Rossii*, p. 177.

17 As Vinogradov put it: 'Historians are in quest of laws of development and of generalizations that shall unravel the complexity of human culture, just as physical and biological generalizations have put into order our knowledge of the phenomena of nature'. *Villainage in England*, 'Preface', p. 2. On developments in methodology, see, for example, A. Vucinich, *Social Thought in Tsarist Russia. The Quest for a General Science of Society, 1861–1917* (Chicago & London, 1976), p. 233. See also J. Hecker, *Russian Sociology. A Contribution to the History of Sociological Thought* [1915] (rpt: New York, 1969).

18 Outside commentators were also aware of the parallels existing between the European past and the Russian present, and drew attention to this in their reviews of works by

their Russian peers. The jurist and historian, Frederic William Maitland, for example, who reviewed Vinogradov's work on the English manor, noted that the author's first-hand experience of 'Russian agrarian communism', as he put it, 'allowed him to see in English medieval documents things that remained obscure for a nation that had long since lost sight of the reality of rural communal life'. Cited by V. P. Buzeskul from N. Fisher's biography, *Paul Vinogradoff. A Memoir* (Oxford, 1927), p. 21. See Buzeskul, *Vseobshchaia istoriia i ee predstaviteli v Rossii*, Vol. 1 (1929), p. 177 note 2.

19 Harley D. Balzer identifies the following as constituents of the institutionalization of knowledge: 'Members of a profession share a knowledge base acquired through formal training; they adhere to standards of conduct reinforced by a socializing process emphasizing service; and the professions are self-governing, asserting that the professionals themselves are the most competent gatekeepers and arbiters of appropriate behavior. Training, socialization, and regulation are carried out through institutional structures including universities, specialized journals, and professional organizations. Scientific societies, study circles, and various informal groups also play a role in developing and maintaining professional identity'. Balzer, 'Introduction', in Balzer, *Russia's Missing Middle Class*, p. 4. See also A. Briggs, 'History and the Social Sciences', in Ruegg (ed.), *Universities in the Nineteenth and Early Twentieth Centuries*, pp. 459–91.

20 See, for example, Thomas Sanders, 'The Third Opponent: Dissertation Defences and the Public Profile of Academic History in Late Imperial Russia', in Sanders (ed.), *Historiography of Imperial Russia. The Profession and Writing of History in a Multinational State* (New York, 1999), pp. 69–97.

21 Using history as a means to galvanize political/social change was of course a feature of historical writing in western Europe, but in this instance, the initiative often originated from within the academic community itself, and debate was conducted more openly in the press. See, for example, Jacques Barzun, 'Romantic Historiography as a Political Force in France', *Journal of the History of Ideas*, Vol. 2, No. 3 (June 1941), pp. 318–29.

22 See Harley D. Balzer, in Balzer (ed.), *Russia's Missing Middle Class*, 'Introduction'.

23 For Humboldt and Schleiermacher, the 'ideal' university was a setting in which to 'stimulate the idea of science in the minds of the students'. Schleiermacher, *Gelegentliche Gedanken uber Universitaten im deutschen Sinn*, pp. 32–3, cited in Ruegg, *Universities in the Nineteenth and Early Twentieth Centuries*, p. 5. In practice, though, across Europe, universities became increasingly subjected to state bureaucracy, which managed affairs as part of national education policy. See Barzun, 'Romantic Historiography as a Political Force in France'. However, according to Hayden White, during the second half of the nineteenth century, 'The profession became progressively academicized. The professoriate formed a clerisy for the promotion and cultivation of a socially responsible historiography; it trained and licensed apprentices, maintained standards of excellence, ran the organs of intra-professional communication, and in general enjoyed a privileged place in the humanistic and socio-scientific sectors of the universities'. White, *Metahistory*, p. 136.

24 As Christophe Charle notes: 'On the one hand, the state, in line with its tradition of enlightened despotism, saw the universities as bearers of modernization and westernization. On the other hand, reactionary forces which regularly gained the upper hand after periodic outbursts of endemic revolutionary agitation were quick to curb the universities as breeding grounds for subversive ideas and conspiracies against the social order'. C. Charle in Ruegg, *Universities in the Nineteenth and Early*

Twentieth Centuries, p. 66. For contemporary accounts of censorship and prohibition (notably of religiously sensitive topics such as the Uniate Church, and the prophet Mohammed), see also V. Vorob'ev, 'K istorii nashikh universitetskikh ustavov', *Russkaia mysl'*, Vol. 12 (1905), pp. 1–11; D. I. Bagalei, *Russkaia istoriia*, Vol. 1 (Moscow, 1914), p. 9.

25 Harley Balzer, who offers a comparative perspective on the history of the professoriate, suggests that government control over Russian educational institutions differed from other Continental European countries in degree, rather than in nature: 'While different in each national context and each profession, the professional programs inevitably involved a tension between establishing some degree of autonomy and status, protection, and control over credentialing that the state provided'. See Balzer, *Russia's Missing Middle Class*, p. 6. See also Ruegg, *Universities in the Nineteenth and Early Twentieth Centuries*, who points out that in other European countries the university became a training ground for the professions, such as medicine and law from around the mid-nineteenth century on.

26 For an account of the background to Voltaire's *History of the Russian Empire under Peter the Great* [1760–3] commissioned by Elizabeth Petrovna, see C. Wilberger, *Voltaire's Russia: Window on the East* (Oxford, 1976). Prince Shcherbatov was appointed official historiographer during the reign of Catherine the Great; Nikolai Karamzin was named historiographer to Alexander I in 1801. The practice of appointing state historiographers originated in France in the mid-eighteenth century.

27 St Petersburg University was closed twice during the academic year 1861–2 following student unrest, and, again, on multiple occasions during the late 1890s and early 1900s as a prelude to the revolution of 1905. See, for example, P. Miliukov, 'Universitety v Rossii'.

28 Cited in V. I. Ger'e, *Timofei Nikolaevich Granovskii* (Moscow, 1914), p. 11.

29 See Vetrinskii, *T. N. Granovskii i ego vremiia*, p. 265; A. Stankevich, 'Timofei Nicholaevich Granovskii. Biograficheskii ocherk', in *T.N. Granovskii i ego perepiska*, Vol. 1, 3rd edn (Moscow, 1897), p. 222.

30 T. Granovskii, *Zapiska i programma uchebnika vseobshchei istorii* [1850], *Sochineniia*, Vol. 2 (Moscow, 1892), pp. 439–40 [my translation – FN]. Robert Vipper mentions that Granovskii was prohibited from lecturing on the history of revolution. See R. Vipper, 'Obshchestvenno-istoricheskie vzgliady Granovskogo', *Mir bozhii*, Vol. 1 (1905), p. 180. See also L. P. Repina (ed.), *Timofei Nikolaevich Granovskii: ideia vseobshchei istorii* (Moscow, 2006). On this point it is also worth bearing in mind the fate of 'politically oppositional' professors in western Europe in the same period. As Hayden White notes: 'As a matter of fact, in both France and Germany, the academic fortunes of left wing historians and philosophers of history waxed and waned with the fortunes of Radicalism itself. This meant that they mostly waned. In 1818, both Victor Cousin and Guizot were fired from the Sorbonne for teaching 'ideas' rather than 'facts'. Feuerbach and D. F. Strauss were denied careers in the German academy for their 'radical' ideas. In 1850, freedom of instruction was rescinded in the French universities in the interests of protecting 'society' from the threat of 'atheism and socialism'. Michelet and Quinet and the Polish poet Mickiewicz were fired, 'dangerous books' were proscribed, and historians were specifically prohibited from departing from the chronological order in the presentation of their materials. And this time Cousin and Thiers, themselves formerly victims of political discrimination, supported the repressive actions'. White, *Metahistory*, p. 138.

31 Vladimir Ivanovich Ger'e (1837–1919), for example, studied French political history, exploring issues of republicanism, the historical role of the monarchy in France and democracy (*narodovlastia*). Some of his findings were published in government-sponsored publications such as the *Sbornik gosudartsvennykh znanii* (*Collections of State Expertise*) in the 1870s. Ger'e's early analysis of the French Revolution as proof of civic progress and state unification mirrored quite closely the general thrust of Tocqueville's views on democracy. But his encounter with the work of Hippolyte Taine, whose contested theses in *Les origines de la France contemporaine* he introduced to the Russian public soon after its publication in 1876, prompted him, in later work written after 1905, to reassess the gains of the revolution in light of the 'Jacobinism' that followed, and which Taine had condemned as a betrayal of the interests of the French people: V. I. Ger'e, 'Republika ili monarkhiia ustanovitsia vo Frantsii' in *Sbornik gosudartsvennykh znanii*, Vol. III (St Petersburg, 1873). Ger'e was also the author of an 'intellectual biography' of Leibniz, published in the 1860s.
32 They include: *Trudy i letopisi. Chteniia v obshchestve istorii i drevnostei rossiiskikh* (1846–1918), *Russkii arkhiv* (1863–1917), *Russkaia starina* (1870–1918), *Istoricheskii vestnik* (1880–1917) and *Istoricheskoe obozrenie* (1890–1916).
33 See, above, note 17.
34 Vinogradov's main Russian language publications on this topic include: 'Feodalizm v Italii' (Feudalism in Italy); 'Issledovaniia po sotsial'noi istorii Anglii' (Research into the social history of England); Kareev's master's thesis dealt with the peasant question in France: *Krest'iane i krest'ianskii vopros vo Frantsii v poslednei chetverti XVIII v* (Moscow, 1879). Grevs, *Ocherki iz istorii Rimskogo zemlevladeniia* is discussed in Chapters 4 and 5. Articles and transcripts of public lectures using historical topics as vehicles for addressing the social, cultural and political impact of current reform policies were placed in generalist journals, such as *Russkaia mysl'*, *Vestnik Evropy*, *Russkoe bogatstvo* and *Otechestvennye zapiski*.
35 Closer ties with the West were forged through a number of concrete measures. For example, Maxim Kovalevskii founded the Ecole supérieure russe des sciences sociales (1901) in Paris, which became 'a place of cross-fertilization among the social sciences, among Russian and Western academics, and among Russian specialists on Russia and other countries'. Bérélowitch, 'History in Russia Comes of Age', p. 133. Of the Russian scholars involved with this institution, Bérélowitch mentions Kareev, Vinogradov, Luchitskii, Miliukov, Chuprov and Gambarovets; their French counterparts included Seignobos, Leroy-Beaulieu, Sorel, Worms, Tarde and Mauss. Translated works included: V. I. Ger'e, *L'abbé de Mably, moraliste et politique. Etude sur la doctrine morale du jacobinisme puritain et sur le dévéloppement de l'esprit républicain au XVIII siècle* (Paris, 1886). A French translation of Kareev's *Krest'iane i krest'ianskii vopros vo Frantsii v poslednei chetverti XVIII v* appeared in 1899 (Paris). For Vinogradov's English-language publications, see note 12 above.
36 From 1882 to 1889, Tolstoi was minister of the interior and head of the Gendarmarie where he played an instrumental role in implementing the counter-reforms.
37 S. Kassow, 'Professionalism among University Professors', in H. D. Balzer (ed.), *Russia's Missing Middle Class*, p. 199. See also A. A. Kizevetter, *Na rubezhe dvukh stoletii. Vospominaniia 1881–1914* (Moscow, 1997), pp. 46–73.
38 Philosophy was relabelled 'logic, psychology, history of philosophy'. Out of a total of eighteen hours a week of compulsory classes, fourteen were given to classical languages, ancient history, ancient literature, ancient philosophy and classical art. The remaining four hours were divided between history and philology. See N. I. Kareev,

Prozhitoe i perezhitoe [1923] (Leningrad, 1990), p. 17. By contrast, the 1863 Charter had made provision for a wider and more diversified syllabus to cover the following subjects: philosophy; classical philology; comparative theories of Indo-European languages and Sanskrit; Russian language and literature; Slavic philology, geography and ethnology; world history, Russian history, history of west European literatures, Church history, theory and history of the arts. In addition, instruction was offered in political economy; ancient Greek language; modern languages (French, German, English, Italian, Spanish) and Oriental languages. The 1884 Charter incited a petition to the Ministry of Education to reconsider its decision. Among the signatories were Ger'e, Vinogradov (Moscow), Luchitskii and Fortunatov (Kiev), F. I. Uspenskii (Novorossiiskii, Odessa) and Kareev (St Petersburg).

39 Kassow, 'Professionalism among University Professors', p. 201.
40 V. Kliuchevskii, cited in *Aforizmy. Istoricheskie portrety i etuidy. Dnevniki* (Moscow, 1993), p. 386. Katkov, a former liberal, became one of its staunchest opponents in the wake of the 1863 Polish uprising. He was also highly critical of models of public instruction, which prioritized the study of natural science and technical skills.
41 Kassow, 'Professionalism among University Professors', p. 203
42 Ibid., p. 204.
43 Ibid., p. 212.
44 Ibid.
45 Grevs, 'Zabytaia nauka i unizhennoe zvanie', *Nashi dni*, 28 December 1904, pp. 2–3.
46 A. Byford, *Literary Scholarship*, p. 20
47 A. Byford, 'Initiation to Scholarship: The University Seminar in Late Imperial Russia', *The Russian Review*, Vol. 64 (April 2005), pp. 321–2.
48 See I. Grevs, *Vasilii Grigorevich Vasilevskii kak uchitel' nauki*, p. 32.
49 Ibid. Bérélowitch notes that 'Kareev took great interest in the theory of knowledge in history, which formed the subject of his thesis and several subsequent presentations and publications at the Historical Society, and tried in particular to define the specific place of history and sociology within the "social sciences". Bérélowitch, 'History in Russia Comes of Age', p. 128. As Kareev conceived it, the aim of the Society was to unify the discipline on the basis of 'certain methodological premises' (ibid., p. 130). In his memoirs, Kareev singled out the following French historians as major interlocutors in this regard: Alphonse Aulard (historian of the French Revolution); Gabriel Monod (editor in chief of the *Revue historique*); Charles-Victor Langlois and Charles Seignobos (both principal figures of the so-called 'école méthodique').
50 On Kliuchevskii, see Kiesewetter, *Na rubezhe dvukh stoletii*, p. 59. According to Maxim Kovalevskii: 'Vinogradov had a gift for gathering dedicated students around him and forming a school that was united by shared scholarly interests. At the time, P. G. Vinogradov's hospitable home, in the small house of Father Slavtsov on Mertvyi Pereulok, was the centre of an animated association of Moscow historians. At these gatherings we listened to papers by Miliukov, Fortunatov, Vipper, A. Guchkov, Korelin, Ivanov, Shamonin, Beliaev, Kudriavtsev, Petrushevskii, Gusakov, Brune, Manuilov, and many others'. See M. M. Kovalevskii, 'Otryvki iz vospominanii', in V. B. El'iashevich et al. (eds), *Moskovskii universitet, 1755–1930: iubileinyi sbornik* (Paris, 1930), pp. 275–93. See also P. N. Miliukov, 'Moi universitetskie gody', in ibid., pp. 262–74. Both cited in Melissa Stockdale, 'The Idea of Development in Miliukov's Historical Thought', in T. Sanders (ed.), *Historiography of Imperial Russia*, pp. 262–85.

51 According to Stockdale, if Miliukov was inspired by Kliuchevskii to specialize in national history, his approach had already been shaped prior to joining the Moscow faculty in 1879, thanks to the existence of this peer group of young professors that 'coalesced in the 1870s'. Rejecting idealism and 'metaphysics' for empiricism, the group's 'multidisciplinary and comparative approach to the history of culture, law, and beliefs, and search for "regularities" or laws (*zakonomernost'*) in history and social life all left their imprint on Miliukov's mature sociological views'. See M. Stockdale, ibid., p. 263.

52 Barbara Walker, *Maximilian Voloshin and the Russian Literary Circle. Culture and Survival in Revolutionary Times* (Bloomington, IN, 2005), p. 10.

53 See A. Byford, 'Initiation to Scholarship', pp. 306, 314. See also A. N. Shakhanov, 'Neformal'nye soobshchestva uchenykh Peterburga vtoroi poloviny XIX–nachala XX', in *Russkaia istoricheskaia nauka vtoroi poloviny XIX – nachala XX veka* (Moscow, 2003), pp. 352–71.

54 Like Grevs and Kareev, Vengerov was dismissed from his teaching post on political grounds in the run-up to 1905 revolution. He then taught at the Bestuzhevskie Higher Women's Courses where Grevs and Kareev also worked. Reinstated in 1906, he set up his Pushkin seminar two years later to coincide with his editorial work on the complete works of Pushkin. Byford, ibid., pp. 316–17. Vengerov's students included the future originators of Russian formalism – Iurii Tynianov, Boris Eikhenbaum and M. L. Lozinskii. See also M. Gamsa, 'Two Million Filing Cards: The Empirical-Biographical Method of Semon Vengerov', in *History of Humanities*, Vol. 1, No. 1 (Chicago, 2016), pp. 129–53.

55 See N. Antsiferov, *Iz dum o bylom* (Moscow, 1992), p. 500 (editorial note). Antsiferov would use this method himself years later in his 1940s study of Dostoevskii, a case in point being his analysis of the cultural resonances of the terms '*zemlia*' and '*kamni*' in the novelist's lexicon. As a student, Nikolai Antsiferov was on friendly terms with Tynianov and Eikhenbaum and maintained ties with them after the October Revolution.

56 Grevs later published a (contested and disproved) piece on this, linking *de Monarchia* with *Divine comedy*: 'Kogda byl napisan traktat Dante "O monarkhii"' in *Nikolaiu Ivanovichu Kareevu. Ucheniki i tovarishchi po nauchnoi rabote* (St Petersburg, 1914), pp. 354–85; 'Iz "Studii Danteschi": Pervaia glava traktata Dante "De monarchia" (Opyt sinteticheskogo traktovaniia', *Iz dalekogo i blizkogo proshlogo* [a collective volume compiled by Kareev's students] (Petrograd–Moscow, 1923).

57 Antsiferov, *Iz dum o bylom*, p. 171. Antsiferov recalled one of Grevs' early attempts, in 1909, to hold evening discussion classes with students on topics which were related to, but not part of, the curriculum. Held in one of the university lecture halls, the format failed. During the war, however, Grevs set up an informal literary–historical study group at his home that was much more successful. At the university, he harnessed the seminar format as a basis for scientific excursions (historical field trips) with university and Bestuzhevskie students. See Chapter 6.

58 The library was closed down in 1887, two years before the circle/fraternity itself was disbanded, as part of the government response to an assassination attempt on Tsar Alexander III. See Vakhromeeva, *Chelovek s otkrytym serdtsem*, p.156.

59 Kaplan, *Historians and Historical Societies in the Public Life of Imperial Russia*, pp. 159–60.

60 C. Charle in Ruegg, *Universities in the Nineteenth and Early Twentieth Centuries*, pp. 35–6.

61 There is evidence of this in memoir accounts of pre-reform university instruction. For example, the historian of literature, Fedor Buslaev, whose courses Kliuchevskii attended as a student, incorporated a world historical perspective in his lectures on the history of Russian literature at a time – 1861 – when a dedicated course on the subject did not yet exist. The future professor of literature, Aleksandr Kirpichnikov, also noted how Buslaev rapidly moved from analysis of byliny songs to the Scandinavian Eddas, Beowulf, and old German tales. In his second year course, Buslaev discussed chansons de geste and the Cid: 'It was not a transition from one section to the next (…) but a completely natural, organic fusion of homogenous materials, the scientific study of which was only possible if undertaken as a whole'. A.I. Kirpichnikov: 'Buslaev, kak osnovatel' istorii vseobshchei literatury', in V. Miller et al., *Pamiati Fedora Ivanovicha Buslaeva* (Moscow, 1898), p. 58. Similarly, Kirpichnikov noted, Buslaev's colleague, Nikolai Tikhonravov, read and commented French neo-classical (pseudo-classical) literature in a course ostensibly dedicated to modern Russian literature. Courses in world literature were eventually set up as part of the University Charter of 1863: two of Buslaev's former pupils, Alexander Veselovskii and Nikolai Storozhenko, were appointed chairs in St Petersburg and Moscow.

62 Although Granovskii found fault with the university for being so remote from life, he also disliked salon culture. To his mind, the salon acted like a purveyor of fashionable historical and philosophical quotations, ready made for light conversation. For this reason, he turned down an invitation to give a course in history for 'ladies'. See his letter to Frolov, 4/i/1840 in A. Stankevich (ed.), *T. N. Granovskii i ego perepiska*, Vol. 2, pp. 415–16.

63 A. Pypin, *Kharakeristiki literaturnykh mnenii* (St Petersburg, 1890), p. 517. Cited by Vetrinskii in *T. N. Granovskii i ego vremiia*, p. v.

64 Kassow, 'Professionalism among University Professors', pp. 197, 214–15.

65 This is discussed in more detail in Chapter 2.

Chapter 2

1 See H. Paul, 'Sources of the Self: Scholarly Personae as Repertoires of Scholarly Selfhood', *Low Countries Historical Review*, Vols 131–4 (2016), pp. 135–4.

2 Images of Granovskii, for example, were fixed in poetry and prose to celebrate his memory. In his 'Medvezh'iaia oxota', N. A. Nekrasov captured the historian's radiant purity: 'pered riadami mnogikh pokolenii/proshel tvoi svetlii obraz; chistykh vpechatlenii/i dobrikh znanii mnogo seia ty/drug istiny, dobra i krasoty'. See V. A. Sokolov (ed.), *Izbrannye sochineniia T. N. Granovskogo* (Moscow, 1905), a volume of selected publications to commemorate the fiftieth anniversary of Granovskii's death. However, in his novel, *The Devils*, Dostoevskii, who reputedly modelled the character, Stepan Trofimovich Verkhovenskii, a pure and idealistic Westernizer, on Granovskii, was gently mocking what, by then, had become the received view.

3 See A. A. Formozov, *Klassiki russkoi literatury i istoricheskaia nauka* (Moscow, 1995), p. 148.

4 For example: 'His noble, pensive appearance was pleasing, his sad eyes with knit brows and his sorrowful–benevolent smile; at that time he had long hair and a blue Berlin topcoat of a special cut, with velvet lapels and cloth buckles. His features, dress, dark hair – all this gave such elegance and grace to his person, on the borderline between vanishing youth and richly–developed maturity, that even for

a man not attracted to him, it was impossible to remain indifferent to him. I have always respected beauty and considered it a talent, a strength'. A. Herzen, *My Past and Thoughts*, cited in P. Roosevelt, *Apostle of Russian Liberalism*, p. 45. 'Peacefully, majestically, his arms folded on top of the lectern, the professor spoke of the fate of the historical world.' N. Dmitriev, 'Studencheskie vospominaniia o Moskovskom universitete', *Otechestvennye zapiski*, Vol. 119, Part 4 (August 1858), pp. 81–95.

5   Ger'e, *Timofei Nikolaevich Granovskii*, p. 74.
6   A. A. Kiesewetter, cited in Vernadsky, *Russian Historiography*, p. 89.
7   Granovskii's output consisted of lectures on early modern Europe, two series of public lectures (which attracted all of educated society), the first in 1843-4, and a second series, a comparative history of France and England, in the winter of 1845-6. A further series of public lectures, given in 1852, was a study of historical personalities (see Chapter 4). His two dissertations were *causes célèbres* prompting the first student demonstrations in support of him. In his Master's thesis (1845), a study of the legendary Slavic settlement of *Volin, Iamburg and Vineta* 'cherished as a Slavic Atlantis which had vanished beneath the waves', Granovskii exploded the myth of a *Rus'* golden age; for his doctoral thesis (1849) on Abbot Suger of St Denis, friend and councillor to Louis the Fat, he was severely reprimanded for disturbing, by implication, one of the pillars of Russian autocracy, namely, the divine right of kings. Among his unrealized plans was a series of articles entitled 'Historical Letters' on the topic of history as a discipline, and research on the town (*gorod*). See Priscilla Roosevelt, *Apostle of Russian Liberalism: Timofei Granovsky* (Newtonville, MA, 1986). Some of the manuscripts were lost, a factor that, in a sense, adds to the myth of a scholarly tradition that Granovskii spearheaded. As such, then, his written legacy consists of transcripts of speeches and lecture courses based on student notes. See Miliukov, 'Universitetskii kurs Granovskogo', in *Iz istorii russkoi intelligentsii. Sbornik statei i etiudov*, 2nd edn (St Petersburg, 1903), pp. 212–65, where he discusses Granovskii's lecture course given during the academic year 1845-6 on the medieval West.
8   Kliuchevskii, 'Pamiati T. N. Granovskogo', *Russkie vedomosti*, No. 263 (8 October 1905). Smirnov (ed.), *V. O. Kliuchevskii. Literaturnye portrety* (Moscow, 1991), p. 200.
9   Kliuchevskii's remark, '*istoriia – kolovorot uzhazov*', was cited by Iulii Aikhenval'd', 'Kliuchevskii. Myslitel' i khudozhnik', in *V. O. Kliuchevskii. Kharakteristiki i vospominaniia* (Moscow, 1912), p. 119; 'padre sereno' appeared in the foreword to a volume of essays written by Grevs' students marking his twenty-fifth anniversary as a teacher. *1884–1909. K dvadtsatipiatiletiiu ucheno-pedagogicheskoi deiatel'nosti Ivana Mikhailovicha Greva. Sbornik statei ego uchenikov* (St Petersburg, 1911), p. v. In his memoirs, Antsiferov also used this term to describe his mentor. See N. Antsiferov, *Iz dum o bylom*.
10 Chernyshevskii, in a review of Boris Chicherin's 'Oblastnye uchrezhdeniia v Rossii v xviii veke', *Russkii vestnik*, 1 (1856), pp. 568–84. Quoted from *Polnoe sobranie sochinenii*, Vol. 3 (Moscow, 1947), pp. 222–3.
11 P. N. Kudriavtsev, 'Izvestie o literaturnykh trudakh Granovskogo' [15 iv 1856] cited in V. A. Sokolov (ed.), *Izbrannye sochineniia T. N. Granovskogo*, p. viii. Other reminiscences in the Sokolov volume include those of Ivan Turgenev, 'Dva slova o Granovskom', in pp. xii–xv and a further piece by Kudriavtsev: 'Vospominanie o Timofee Nikolaeviche Granovskom' pp. xvi–xxvi.
12 Kudriavtsev: 'Vospominanie o Timofee Nikolaeviche Granovskom', p. xx; N. Chernyshevskii, 'Zametki o zhurnalakh', *Sovremennik*, Vol. 2 (1856), pp. 219–22, cited in *N. G. Chernyshevskii. Polnoe sobranie Sochineniia*, Vol. 3 (Moscow, 1947),

p. 631. See also Byford, who notes with reference to Buslaev: 'A "professor" was not just a (university-based) "scholar." Crucial to professorial identity was the professor's relationship with his students. The professor–student relationship was, in turn, essential to the ideological definition of *nauka* itself.' Byford, *Literary Scholarship*, p. 94. It is also worth noting that, again, like Granovskii, Buslaev regarded the humanities as a tool for developing not only a love of truth, but also the love of goodness and beauty. Assuming the mission of enlightenment, the responsibilities of humanities scholars were therefore as much social and moral as intellectual. See Byford, p. 97, who, on this point references A. I. Kirpichnikov, 'Vospominaniia o Fedore Ivanoviche Buslaeve', in *Ocherki po novoi russkoi literature*, 2 vols (Moscow, 1903), p. 173.

13 P. Vinogradov, 'T. N. Granovskii', *Russkaia mysl'*, Vol. 4 (1893), pp. 44–66; N. Kareev, *Istoricheskoe mirosozertsanie Granovskogo* (St Petersburg, 1896); Vetrinskii, *T. N. Granovskii i ego vremiia*; D. M. Levshin, *T. N. Granovskii (opyt istoricheskogo sinteza*, 2nd edn (St Petersburg, 1902) [First pub. 1900]; Kliuchevskii 'Pamiati T. N. Granovskogo' (1905); R. Vipper, 'Obshchestvenno-istoricheskie vzgliady Granovskogo', *Mir bozhii*, Vol. 11 (1905), pp. 179–92; V. I. Ger'e, *Timofei Nikolaevich Granovskii. V pamiat' stoletnogo iubileia ego rozhdeniia* (Moscow, 1913).

14 As Priscilla Roosevelt put it: 'Between 1856 and 1917 the legendary Granovsky attributes became so confused and contradictory that by the turn of the century his real legacy had been totally divorced from his symbolic role.' P. Roosevelt, *Apostle of Liberalism*, p. 176. Roosevelt lists the main aspects of Granovskii's contribution to historical understanding, which his students inherited as: a critical approach to sources; an interest in other disciplines which might prove useful to history; efforts to combat Russia's cultural backwardness; an emphasis on the social and political role of history; the integration of Russia into European historiography; devising a specifically Russian approach to world history; his liberalism; his insistence on evolution, legality and the primacy of politics in social development, namely, 'constitutionalism and the individual as a citizen against the omnipotent autocratic state on the one hand, and against revolutionary radicalism on the other.' Ibid., p. 177.

15 Sl. (nom de plume) 'T. N. Granovskii v biograficheskom ocherke A. Stankevicha', *Vestnik Evropy*, Vol. 5 (1869), p. 425.

16 Cited in V. I. Ger'e from Granovskii's public address (1852): V. I. Ger'e, *Timofei Nikolaevich Granovskii. V pamiat'*, p. 66. Granovskii's appraisal of Abbot Suger also illustrates this point very well: For Granovskii, Abbot Suger's strengths lay in his clarity of mind, mental vision and great moral conviction, which, together, underpinned the purposefulness of his professed goals and intentions. See Roosevelt, *Apostle of Russian Liberalism*, p. 142. In short, as Levshin put it: '[H]e preached morality not with the help of abstract formulas, but through his own attitude towards people and events, by virtue of the empathy (*sostradanie*) he felt for the hapless (*obezdolennym*) of history'. Levshin, *T. N. Granovskii (opyt istoricheskogo sinteza)*, p. 137.

17 N. I. Kareev, *Istoricheskoe mirosozertsanie Granovskogo*, p. 2. Vetrinskii reiterated this comment, *T. N. Granovskii i ego vremiia*, p. 79.

18 Although referring to Kudriavtsev, Kareev's comment – 'the raison d'être of historical enquiry is to bring humanity closer to realization of the ideas of truth and the good' – was actually a paraphrase of a remark Granovskii made in his 1852 address, 'O sovremennom sostoianii i znachenii vseobshchei istorii', which, in turn, was a reference to Cicero. Kareev, ibid., p. 106.

19　Ibid., p. 81. Elsewhere, Kareev remarked: 'History was not just a scientific or philosophical matter but was integral to the moral and social upbringing of contemporaries' (ibid., p. 71).
20　Student demonstrations that occurred at the site of Granovskii's grave were significant in turning his memory into a symbol of defiance against the state (which in real life he was not). On 4 October 1861, the sixth anniversary of his death, students, who had not known him personally, staged a demonstration after which they tried to close down the university in protest over a new regulation making payment for auditing lectures obligatory. On Granovskii's funeral and as a symbol of defiance, see Roosevelt, *Apostle of Liberalism*; M. Wes, *Classics in Russia, 1700–1855. Between Two Bronze Horsemen* (Leiden and New York, 1992).
21　P. Kudriavtsev, 'Izvestie o literaturnykh trudakh', p. iii; N. Kareev, *Istoricheskoe mirosozertsanie*, p. 71.
22　'In speaking about the tasks and methods of history, Granovskii speaks in the same breath about the historian: the task of the historian mirrors the task of the historical process – the person and a society which answers her demands; the realization of the moral law on the part of the historian, his defence and development of socially fruitful ideas will be his profession of faith (*ispovedanie*). In this way, the historian – along with others – will become a social actor (*deiatel'*) by virtue of setting out his thoughts, oral and printed word for the masses.' Ch Vetrinskii, *T. N. Granovskii i ego vremiia*, 2nd edn, p. 92.
23　Granovskii, *Abbat Sugerii. Istoricheskie izsledovaniia* (Moscow, 1849), p. v.
24　Roosevelt, *Apostle of Russian Liberalism*, p. 18.
25　I. Paperno, *Chernyshevsky and the Age of Realism. A Study in the Semiotics of Behaviour* (Stanford, 1988), p. 2; pp. 60–1. See also Laura Engelstein and Stephanie Sandler (eds), *Self and Story in Russian History* (Ithaca & London, 2000) for analyses of identity and self-creation through narrative forms of diary, memoirs, tales etc.
26　Ibid., pp. 42–3.
27　L. Ginzburg, *On Psychological Prose* (Princeton, 1991), p. 66. 'The cult of tender feelings,' Ginzburg writes, 'was further catalyzed by Fichte's metaphysical concept of love as the main source and driving force of the Absolute'. Ibid. Ginzburg's analysis of 'the human document' – of memoirs, correspondence – brilliantly brings to view the various strategies of self-representation by the men of the forties. See also A.D. Nakimovsky & A. Stone Nakhimovsky (eds), *The Semiotics of Russian Cultural History*. Introduction by Boris Gasparov, pp. 13–29.
28　Ginzburg, ibid. (And so brilliantly satirized by Woody Allan in his 1976 film, *Love and Death*).
29　Ibid., p. 196ff; p. 204. As Roosevelt notes, Granovskii 'was reared on (…) romantic depictions of the age of chivalry (Gil Blas) and its precepts which exercised fascination for the romantics – loyalty to friends, tireless drive for moral self-perfection, idealization of beloved persons'. Roosevelt, *Apostle of Russian Liberalism*, p. 3.
30　Ger'e, *Timofei Nikolaevich Granovskii. V pamiat'*, p. 73; P. N. Kudriavtsev, 'Izvestie o literaturnykh trudakh Granovskogo', p. 68; Vetrinslii, *T. N. Granovskii i ego vremiia*, p. 84.
31　Roosevelt, *Apostle of Liberalism*, p. 18. See also H. White, *Metahistory*, who summarizes Hegel's views of the object of history and the historian's task: '[T]he evolution of Human life in religion and civil society, the events and destinies of the most famous individuals and peoples who have given emphasis to life in either field [that is, in religion or civil life] by their activity, all this presupposes great ends in the

compilation of such a work or the complete failure of what it implies. The historical representation of subjects and contents such as these admits of real distinction, thoroughness, and interest; and however much our historian must endeavour to reproduce actual historical fact, it is nonetheless incumbent upon him to bring before our imaginative vision this motely content of events and characters, to create anew and make vivid the same to our intelligence with his own genius.' See also Hayden White, who summarizes Hegel's views of the object of history and the historian's task which he formulated in the context of his lectures on aesthetics in the early 1820s.

32 T. Granovskii, 'Bartol'd Georg Niburg' [1847] in *Sochineniia T.N. Granovskogo*, Vol. 2, pp. 4, 36–8. On Niebuhr see, for example, R. Lovin, *Reinhold Niebuhr* (Nashville, TN, 2007).

33 Ibid., p. 2.

34 Both Stankevich and Kudriavtsev trace Granovskii's poetic/aesthetic sensibilities to his early upbringing and unstructured home education in Orel province, and the very little he gleaned from the university lectures he attended. They note his literary-imaginative cast of mind, love of fiction and thwarted ambition to become a poet in his own right.

35 Granovskii, 'Bartol'd Georg Niburg', p. 9.

36 Ibid., p. 13.

37 According to Stankevich, Granovskii's interest in history was fostered through his reading of Sir Walter Scott and the French romantic historians active during the 1820s and 1830s – Michelet, Thierry, Guizot, Barante, Thiers, Villemain and the Swiss Sismondi. But it was really during his stay in Berlin (1836–9), to complete his formation for a professorship, that he acquired the 'tools' of historical enquiry. Besides language, he recognized the importance for historical insight of other disciplines: ethnography, geography, philology, mythology and the history of law. Working mainly under Ranke on the political history of the Middle Ages (whom he admired for his 'luminous, lively, poetic view of knowledge'), Granovskii also frequented Hans Ritter's courses in historical geography, Eduard Gans and Friedrich Carl von Savigny. 'Ritter had stimulated Granovsky's interest in natural factors in history; later, he would incorporate racial factors, pre-historical evidence, and folklore into the raw material for history.' Further, 'he admired Macaulay's *History of England* and Edgar Quinet for his articles attacking historical systems, which judge events and principles on their success rather than on their intrinsic merit – Granovsky's own criterion'. Roosevelt, *Apostle of Russian Liberalism*, p. 44; p. 172.

38 Granovskii, 'Bartol'd Georg Niburg', p. 35. Granovskii was briefly employed in the Naval Ministry as secretary to the department of hydrography before taking up his post at Moscow University at the age of twenty-six. Niebuhr took up his post in the newly established University of Berlin, in 1810, at the age of thirty-four. See Vinogradov, 'T. N. Granovskii' p. 45.

39 See Gossman's account of Ranke, for whom 'God "dwells, lives, and can be known in all of history. Every deed attests to him, every moment preaches his name, and most of all the connectedness of all history. This connectedness stands before us like a holy hieroglyph." To decipher the hieroglyph is to serve God as priest and teacher.' Gossman, *Between History and Literature*, p. 307 and note 64; Leonard Krieger, *Ranke: The Meaning of History* (Chicago, 1977), p. 361. For Granovskii, the value (*pol'za*) of history resided in an 'integral and vital understanding of the past. Such an understanding (…) helps us recognize that beyond all the discoveries brought to light by the scientific laws of historical development, resides one supreme law, namely

the moral law, the realisation of which constitutes the end goal of mankind on earth. In other words, the supreme value of history is that it provides us with a reasoned conviction in the inevitable/imminent (*neminuemoe*) victory of good over evil.' Granovskii, *Sobranie sochinenii*, Vol. 2, p. 461, cited in Vetrinskii, *T. N. Granovskii i ego vremiia*, p. 84.

40 L. Gossman, ibid., p. 297. Granovskii particularly admired Augustin Thierry (the story teller par excellence) for his creative ability to retrieve from the partial remains of the past an image of man, and to resurrect the unique character of a bygone age. Granovskii, ibid., p. 427.

41 The image of the historian as a 'backward-looking prophet' comes from Friedrich Schlegel (Gossman, ibid., p. 165). On Michelet's self-image as 'poet-prophet-pedagogue', see Kelley, *Fortunes of History*, p. 171. Similarly, according to Kelley, Ranke 'fashioned his historical thinking in the context of contemporary religious and philosophical thought, in effect claiming the missionary's role for the professional historian.' Ibid., p. 133. See also White, *Metahistory*, p. 39.

42 Gossman, ibid., p. 166. Johann Gustav Droysen (1808–84) was member of the Frankfurt parliament in 1848/9. Heinrich von Treitschke (1834–96) used the university platform to overtly political ends, urging the unification of Germany. In France, Guizot served as minister of education after the Revolution of 1830 and as prime minister (1840–8). See also D. Kelley, ibid., p. 146, and p. 344, where he remarks that 'the profession of history was often an apprenticeship to entrance into the corridors of power and leadership – Guizot, Thiers, Theodore Roosevelt, Woodrow Wilson, and Jean Jaures being some of the more conspicuous examples.' In Russia, historians entered the political arena only after the 1905 revolution. A noted example is Pavel Miliukov, co-founder of the Kadets, and ill-fated minister of foreign affairs in the Provisional Government after the Revolution of February, 1917. But, it is also interesting to note that once elected to the Duma, some, such as Kareev, quickly recognized that politics in the narrow sense was not an appropriate platform for the advancement of their ideas about social justice.

43 Kelley, *Fortunes of History*, p. 171.

44 Named as such by his former pupil (and critic), Sergei Solov'ev. See V. M. Solov'ev (ed. & intro.), *Tainy istorii: M. P. Pogodin, N. I. Kostomarov, S. M. Solov'ev, V. O. Kliuchevskii o pol'ze istoricheskikh znanii* (Moscow, 1994), p. 5.

45 Pogodin was professor of Russian history from 1835 to 1844, and, in 1841, he was elected member of the Imperial Russian Academy. As a student at Moscow University (1818–21) he had studied *slovesnost'* (languages/literature/history). In 1825, he began teaching, initially offering courses in World History, then, from 1828, a course in modern and Russian history for students in the juridical faculty. Following Professor Ul'rikh's retirement in 1833, Pogodin was named ordinary professor of World History. Two years later, he was appointed to the newly created chair of Russian history. According to his biographers, the two historians who most influenced him were A. Schlözer (author of a study of the Nestor Chronicles, and, in the late-eighteenth century the recognized authority in Russian history), and Karamzin.

46 Shevyrev's expression, *gniloi zapad* (the putrid West) appeared in 'Vzgliad russkogo na obrazovanie Evropy', *Moskvitianin*, 1 (1841). In Shevyrev's reading, Germany and France were especially putrid because the Reformation and Revolution occurred on their soil; England and Italy fared slightly better thanks to a less disrupted history, and greater sense of national cohesion. See Ger'e, *Timofei Nikolaevich Granovskii*.

pp. 12–14. Pogodin's views of Russia's historical greatness found their definitive expression in his *History of Russia* (1844). Here he identified the lasting foundations of the Russian state as Byzantine Christianity and Slavic learning from the southwest, thus minimizing the legacy of the Norman–Varangian period on the grounds that it was eradicated by the arrival of the Mongol Tatars in the thirteenth century.

47 Unpublished review of Pogodin's *History of Russia up to the Mongol Yoke* [1872], in Kliuchevskii, *Neopublikovannye proizvedeniia*, p. 152. See also P. Vinogradov, who described him as 'a knowledgeable, intelligent, cunning man, but unsophisticated with no sense of decency and morally suspect views.' *Russkaia mysl'*, Vol. 4 (1893), p. 59.

48 According to Edward Thaden, Pogodin was instrumental in propagating the philosophical idealism of Schelling and romantic nationalism in Russia. Thaden, 'Historicism, N. A. Polevoi, and Rewriting Russian History', p. 303.

49 'This is why he was incapable of closing himself within the confines of the university, could not abandon the wrath of life (*zloby dnia*) for the sake of pure science.' K. Bestuzhev-Riumin, 'Mikhail Petrovich Pogodin (1800–75)', in *Biografii i kharakteristiki* (St Petersburg, 1882), p. 239. Pogodin founded and animated a number of journals: *Moskovskii vestnik*, 1827–30; *Telegraf* (1825–34); *Moskvitianin*, his platform for pan-slavism (1841–56). He also established close ties with the novelists and poets, Gogol and F. I. Tiutchev. The latter introduced him to French literature.

50 Bestuzhev-Riumin, ibid., p. 240.

51 Ibid. Bestuzhev-Riumin's remarks are actually drawn from an address given by Prince V. A. Cherkasskii on the occasion of Pogodin's seventieth birthday. The Prince's public pronouncements, cited here, stand in sharp contrast to Kliuchevskii's lacerating criticism: 'University youth crowded to his cathedra. They were drawn to his lectures, not by the eloquence of his delivery, but irrespective of the essentially scholarly worth of the course, they were attracted to his lively, uninhibited, passionate, attitude in all things. He read us Russian history using the sources, familiarized us not just with the external events of history, but with its hidden inner meaning.' Ibid. A poem dedicated to Pogodin in celebration of his jubilee captures very well the spirit of his pan-slavic project: 'Dear Friend! Today it is not only Moscow, which is joyful/cheers are raised in Belgrade/salutations arrive from the Danube, the Neva/Karkonosze, the Balkans/The Tatras, Black Mountain/glasses overflow in your honour/with exclamations of hurrah to you! Ibid.

52 M. Pogodin, *Istoricheskie aforizmy* (1836) [the book has no pagination].

53 Pogodin's dictum echoed Karamzin's famous opening phrase in his *History of the Russian State*: 'History is the sacred book of the nation.' Karamzin's lasting influence on Pogodin is evidenced in the 'hagiographical style' of the latter's two-volume study about him: *Nikolai Mikhailovich Karamzin* (Moscow, 1866).

54 Bestuzhev-Riumin, 'Mikhail Petrovich Pogodin', p. 134.

55 Kliuchevskii's comments, paraphrased here, were about Karamzin, but the point he makes applies equally to Pogodin. Kliuchevskii, *Neopublikovannye proizvedeniia*, edited by A. A. Zimin and R. A. Kireeva (Moscow, 1983), p. 133.

56 In his public address of 1852: 'O sovremennom sostoianii i znachenii vseobshchei istorii.'

57 'Nowadays, we consider it inappropriate to parade one's personal feelings in historical enquiry.' Bestuzhev-Riumin, *Biografii i kharakteristiki*, p. 220. Writing in the 1890s,

Pavel Miliukov dismissed Pogodin's possibly most famous aphorism as no longer relevant in the intellectual climate of the reform and counter reform eras. Miliukov, *Glavnye techeniia russkoi istoricheskoi mysli*, p. 3.

58 Paperno alluding to Belinskii, in *Chernyshevsky and the Age of Realism*, p. 44.
59 These proponents of the 'new science' wrote extensively on the theory of history and sociology, and contributed articles on 'historical laws' and sociology to the prestigious Brokgaus–Efron encyclopaedia.
60 A. A. Kiesewetter's portrait of the ideal historian (modelled on Kliuchevskii). Cited in Sanders (ed.), *Historiography of Imperial Russia*, p. 298.
61 Kareev, *Istoricheskoe mirosozertsanie*, p. 26. These qualities, Kareev argues, were Granovskii's ideal, but he remained a product of his age in which 'artistic and moral interests still played an important role in historical literature.' Ibid.
62 See Byrnes, 'Kliuchevskii's View of the Flow of Russian History', p. 243.
63 See Kiesewetter, *Na rubezhe dvukh stoletii. (Vospominaniia 1881–1914)* (Prague, 1929), p. 71. According to Miliukov, of all Kliuchevskii's pupils, Kiesewetter best replicated his master's style: 'His merits and talents, his scintillating wit and brilliant talent for exposition, inevitably drew him to emulate our incomparable Vasilii Osipovich.' P. Miliukov, 'Tri pokoleniia', in *Zapiski Russkogo istoricheskogo obshchestva v Prage*, bk 3 (1937) p. 16. The St Petersburg-based historian, Sergei Platonov, confirmed the reach of Kliuchevskii's authority well beyond the university auditorium, both because of the contemporary resonance of his research (for example: *Proiskhozhdenie krepostnogo prava v Rossii* [1885]; *Sostav predstavitel'stva na zemskikh soborov v drevnei Rusi* [1890–92]) and because he seemed to combine 'scholarship' with 'poetic perception.' S. F. Platonov, 'Pamiati V. O. Kliucheskogo', *Kharakteristiki i vospominaniia*, pp. 97–8.
64 Paperno, *Chernyshevsky and the Age of Realism*, p. 7.
65 Iu. Aikhenval'd, 'Kliuchevskii. Myslitel' i khudozhnik' *Kharakteristiki i vospominaniia*, p. 130. See also M. M. Bogoslovskii, who referred to Kliuchevskii as a 'historian-sociologist and artist-realist.' Ibid., cited from an offprint, p. 9. Writing in 1943, the émigré Michael Karpovich noted that Kliuchevskii 'combines a great literary skill, rivalling that of Karamzin, with profound scholarship (…), hence his simultaneous and equally powerful appeal to the general reader and the specialist.' M. Karpovich, 'Klyuchevski and Recent Trends in Russian Historiography', *Slavonic and East European Review. American Studies*, Vol. 2, No. 1 (March 1943), p. 33.
66 Kliuchevskii, *Aforizmy. Istoricheskie portrety*, pp. 367–8. Cf. Robert Byrnes suggests: 'In spite of these disclaimers, Kliuchevskii subtly advanced a philosophy of history, one that explained the past of all societies and in some detail the history of his homeland […]. He was not consistent, in part because he was so knowledgeable concerning the complications of Russia's past and in part because the massive changes affecting Russia during his last decades influenced his view of the long past. These modifications, far more evident in his essays and lectures than in the major work millions have read, suggested that individuals in modern times have played important roles and that Western influence was undermining traditional Russian values and institutions […]. They help to explain the pessimism that grew throughout his last twenty years.' Byrnes: 'Kliuchevskii's View of the Flow of Russian History', pp. 240–1.
67 According to Byrnes, Kliuchevskii is widely 'considered Russia's greatest historian.' Ibid., p. 239. Named professor in 1882, he defended his 'kandidatskaia' dissertation,

'Skazaniia inostrantsev o Moskovskom gosudarstve', in 1865. Following the defence of his Masters' dissertation, 'Drevnerusskie zhitia sviatykh kak istoricheskii istochnik' (1871), he was appointed dotsent in Russian history at the Troitsko-Sergei Posad Theological Academy (where he continued to lecture twice a week following his appointment to a professorship). In 1881, he was awarded a doctorate for his study, 'Boiarskaia duma drevnei Rusi' (which was serialized in *Russkaia mysl'* before its publication in monograph form in 1882). See A. F. Smirnov, 'V. O. Kliuchevskii i otechestvennaia slovesnost'', in Smirnov (ed.), *V. O. Kliuchevskii. Literaturnye portrety* (Moscow, 1991), p. 37.

68 'As every historian,' Karpovich wrote, 'Kliuchevskii was the child of his age. [...]. One cannot understand Kliuchevskii's approach to Russian history unless one keeps in mind that he was a contemporary of the Emancipation, and that his formative years were those of the "going to the people" movement [and that] significant for Kliuchevskii's development was the predominance in the intellectual climate of the time of [...] "realism" and "populism"'. Karpovich, 'Klyuchevski and Recent Trends in Russian Historiography', pp. 33, 34. See also S. O. Shmidt, 'Kliuchevskii i kul'tura Rossii', in *Put' istorika. Izbrannye trudy po istochnikovedeniiu i istoriografii* (Moscow, 1997), pp. 305–14. For an account by a Soviet historian, see, for example, M. Nechkina, *Vasilii Osipovich Kliuchevskii: istoriia zhizni i tvorchestva* (Moscow, 1974).

69 P. Miliukov, 'V.O. Kliuchevskii', in A. A. Kizevetter et al., *V. O. Kliuchevskii: Kharakteristiki i vospominaniia* (Moscow, 1912), p. 188.

70 G. Fedotov, 'Rossiia Kliuchevskgo' [1932], translated by Marshall S. Shatz in M. Raeff (ed.), 'Kliuchevskii's Russia: Critical Studies', *Canadian-American Slavic Studies*, Vol. 20, Nos. 3-4 (1986), p. 207.

71 Kliuchevskii entered the Seminary in 1856 where the main subjects taught were theology, Church history, ancient and modern languages, natural sciences, world history and Russian history.

72 M. Bogoslovskii, 'V.O. Kliuchevskii', in A. A. Kizevetter et al., *V. O. Kliuchevskii: Kharakteristiki i vospominaniia* (Moscow, 1912), p. 188.

73 Ibid.

74 Kliuchevskii, Notebook [1891] in *Neopublikovannye proizvedeniia*, p. 151

75 Ibid., p. 165.

76 V. O. Kliuchevskii cited in V.M. Solov'ev (ed. & intro.), *Tainy istorii*, p. 152. Other comments on the discipline include the following: 'In history, the more we know facts, the less we understand the meaning of phenomena'; 'Our history follows our calendar: every century we lag behind the world by several days.' Ibid., p. 108; p. 162.

77 Byrnes, *V. O. Klyuchevskii, Historian of Russia* (Bloomington & Indianapolis, 1995), pp. 31–2. See also A. Kirpichnikov, future professor of General Literature in Odessa (from 1885) who, as a fellow student, took courses with Kliuchevskii in the early 1860s. Kirpichnikov lists the following courses offered by Buslaev during the 1850s and 1860s: a survey course of Russian and medieval literature; comparative study of popular *slovestnost'*; legends and sagas in Scandinavia and England; Russian medieval literature and regional development; Russian *bogatyri* epics, West European literature up to the fourteenth century. Later, in the mid-1860s, Buslaev ran a three-year course on Italian literature to coincide with the 600th anniversary of Dante's birth. A. Kirpichnikov, 'Busalev, kak osnovatel' istorii vseobshchei literatury', in S. G. Smirnov (ed.), *Pamiati Fedora Ivanovicha Buslaeva* (Moscow, 1898), pp. 54–60.

78 According to Professor Arkhangel'skii, Buslaev later downplayed the importance of Grimm's view of *samobytnost'*, namely the indigenous, national (*narodnykh*) foundations of mythology, customs and legends, for a theory of 'mutual exchange among peoples (*narody*) of oral and written traditions' arising from chance borrowings from outside sources. This theory found its place in the comparative approach that Aleksandr Veselovskii later developed in his study of west European literature. As I discuss in Chapter 8 it also resonated with historians. See A. S. Arkhangel'skii, 'F. I. Buslaev v svoikh "Vospominaniiakh" i uchenykh trudakh' (Kazan, 1899), p. 70; p. 78.

79 Byrnes, *V. O. Klyuchevskii*, p. 32.

80 As a student, Kliuchevskii read Busleav's recently published *Istoricheskie ocherki russkoi narodnoi slovesnosti* (1861) in which he spoke about the correlation of history and philology, and of the significance of folklore for historical research. Byrnes, ibid.

81 V. O. Kliuchevskii, 'F. I. Buslaev, kak prepodavatel' i issledovatel'' [27 September 1897], first published in *Sochineniia* Vol. VIII (Moscow, 1959), pp. 288–94. Cited in *Literaturnye portrety*, p. 208.

82 Ibid., p. 210.

83 Kliuchevskii, *Kurs russkoi istorii* (Moscow, 1937), Pt I, p. 117, cited in Rubinshtein, *Russkaia istoriografiia*, p. 517. [1st edn: 1941].

84 The *Course in Russian History* saw several re-editions: the 1920s, 1930s and 1950s; the 1987–89 edition had a print run of 250,000 copies.

85 V. O. Kliuchevskii, 'F. I. Buslaev, kak prepodavatel' i issledovatel'', p. 207.

86 Kliuchevskii, *Pis'ma, dnevniki, aforizmy i mysli ob istorii* (Moscow, 1968), p. 343. See also Byrnes, 'Kliuchevskii's View of the Flow of Russian History', p. 240. Kliuchevskii delivered twelve lectures on the nature of history as a discipline: *Sochineniia*, Vol. VIII (Moscow, 1987–9).

87 A. Kiesewetter, 'Kliuchevskii and His Course of Russian History', *The Slavonic Review*, Vol. 1, No. 3 (March 1923), p. 512.

88 A. E. Presniakov, 'V. O. Kliuchevskii', *Russkii istoricheskii zhurnal*, Kn.8 (Petrograd, 1922), p. 220. According to Kiesewetter, Kluichevskii's seminal *Course of Russian History* was 'a rare union (…) of scientific with literary merits.' See his 'Kliuchevskii and His Course of Russian History', p. 518. Another former student, the literary specialist, Iulii Aikhenval'd, highlighted the inseparability of the form and content of Kliuchevskii's ideas: 'When you read these and other passages (…), it is hard not to express deep admiration at the finesse of words and thought, or to realize that before you is not only a scholar, but a poet.' Iu. Aikhenval'd', 'Kliuchevskii. Myslitel' i khudozhnik' in *V. O. Kliuchevskii. Kharakteristiki i vospominaniia*, p. 130.

89 Shmidt, 'Kliuchevskii i kul'tura Rossii', in *Put'* istorika, p. 314.

90 According to George Vernadsky, Miliukov found his true teachers in Kliuchevskii – for his intellectual grasp and insights – and Vinogradov, for his example as a scholar. Vernadsky, *Russian Historiography*, pp. 142–3.

91 Solov'ev pioneered the theory of the princely *udel* in the north as the personal property of the prince, distinct from practices in the southern *volost'* which was a temporary possession of the prince. See Bogoslovskii, 'V.O. Kliuchevskii, kak uchenyi', p. 32. For Solov'ev's views of history and the historical process see, for example, his 'Historical Letters', delivered on the eve of reform (1859), and *Tainy istorii*, pp. 107, 137. See also Bestuzhev–Riumin, *Biografii i kharakteristiki*, p. 267.

92 A. Lappo–Danilevskii, 'V.O. Kliuchevskii' in A. A. Kizevetter et al., *V. O. Kliuchevskii: Kharakteristiki i vospominaniia* (Moscow, 1912), p. 188; Barzun, 'Romantic Historiography as a Political Force in France', p. 326.

93 Ibid., p. 102. See also Kliuchevskii's notebook entries from the early 1900s quoted in *Tainy istorii*, p. 199. As I discuss in Chapters 3 and 4, Kliuchevskii's interest in inner, psychological factors is, indeed, as Lappo-Danilevskii and Soviet scholars after him suggested, attested by his masterfully drawn 'word portraits' of historical and invented figures, and in his sketches of *byt* and mores in post-Petrine Russia. The shift in emphasis from society and the economy towards mentalities in Kliuchevskii's later work is also noted by West European and North American scholars.

94 Accounts of Kliuchevskii's funeral, which drew huge crowds, in some ways, recaptured the spirit of Granovskii's funeral service and burial. In each case, the ceremony seemed to fix the legendary status of the professor.

95 See '*K dvadtsatipiatiletiiu ucheno–pedagogicheskoi deiatel'nosti Grevsa. Sbornik statei ego uchenikov*, p. iv, a collection of essays by Grevs' pupils commemorating his twenty-fifth anniversary as a teacher at St Petersburg University and the Higher Women's Courses (*Bestuzhevskie*).

96 I. Grevs, 'Vasilii Gregorievich Vasilevskii kak uchitel' nauki' (St Petersburg, 1899), p. 5. In stark contrast, Grevs used the occasion of a letter addressed to his friend, S. F. Oldenburg, to moan about Vasilevskii's indifference towards him: 'Vasilevskii really irritates me. He gives absolutely no help whatsoever, yet doesn't hold back with his threats [...]. It's going to end badly (*plokho budet*).' Letter dated 20 May 1891. Cited in O. B. Vakhromeeva (ed.), *Chelovek s otkrytym serdtsem*, pp. 249–50.

97 Ibid., p. 43. See also Elena Skrzhinskaia, one of Grevs's former pupils, who cites Grevs' comment that 'professorship is a supremely (*prekrasnaia*) social role'. E. Ch. Skrzhinskaia, 'Ivan Mikhailovich Grevs. Biograficheskii ocherk', in Prof. I. M. Grevs (ed.), *Tatsit* (Moscow; Leningrad, 1946), p. 241

98 Besides Grevs and Fedor Fedorovich and Sergei Fedorovich Oldenburg, other participants in the brotherhood included the natural scientist V. I. Vernadskii and Aleksandr Lappo-Danilevskii. See O. B. Vakhromeeva (ed.), *Chelovek s otkrytym serdtsem*, pp. 149–73, 175–96. In conjunction with the Fraternity, Grevs and the Oldenburg brothers ran a Student Scientific–Literary Society. Presided by the specialist in Russian literature, Professor O. F. Miller, the Society embodied, in Gary Hamburg's words: 'the best traditions of the liberal intelligentsia: commitment to truth, social equality, nonviolence and the hope for political freedom to be achieved by patient labor on behalf of the people.' G. M. Hamburg, 'A. S. Lappo-Danilevskii and the Writing of History in late Imperial Russia', in E. A. Rostovtsev *A. S. Lappo-Danilevskii i peterburgskaia istoricheskaia shkola* (Riazan', 2004), Introduction p. 13.

99 Grevs, 'Vasilii Gregorievich Vasilevskii kak uchitel' nauki', pp. 5–6. Like so many of his student peers, Grevs was initially drawn to the cause of the radical intelligentsia. Matriculating at the Historical–Philological Faculty in 1879, the year in which socio-political tensions deepened into a wave of terrorism orchestrated by a newly formed radical splinter group, the People's Will, he frequented underground populist circles where he was under police surveillance. O. B. Vakhromeeva (ed.), *Chelovek s otkrytym serdtsem*, p. 305.

100 Cited in Skrzhinskaia, 'Ivan Mikhailovich Grevs. Biograficheskii ocherk', p. 224.

101 On 'Three Meetings' (1853) in *Diary of a Superfluous Man and Other Stories*, see O. B. Vakhromeeva (ed.), *Chelovek s otkrytym serdtsem*, p. 313.

102 Ibid.

103 Stasiulevich (1826–1911) was also the founding editor of the liberal journal *European Herald* (*Vestnik Evropy*). Ibid., pp. 58–9, 302.

104 According to Skrzhinskaia, it was Grevs' Russian literature teacher, rather than his history master, who exerted the most important influence on the young Grevs. Skrzhinskaia, 'Ivan Mikhailovich Grevs. Biograficheskii ocherk', pp. 225–6.
105 Ibid. Anecdotally, it is worth mentioning that among Grevs' classmates was Chernyshevskii's son, Mikhail, who would read out in class the letters his father had sent from prison.
106 Chosen as Vasilevskii's successor in 1894, he took over his predecessor's course in medieval history, which he taught without interruption (apart from a three-year period following his suspension from the university in 1899) until 1923.
107 Grevs, 'Vasilii Gregorievich Vasilevskii kak uchitel' nauki', pp. 22–3.
108 Ibid., pp. 21–2.
109 Sveshnikov, *Peterburgskaia shkola medievistov nachala XX veka*, p. 87.
110 Ibid., p. 51; Skrzhinskaia, 'Ivan Mikhailovich Grevs. Biograficheskii ocherk', pp. 240–1.
111 Grevs' specialization in medieval France and Italy dates from his reinstatement as professor at the university in 1902 and the Bestuzhevskie the following year where he set up a 'kabinet' for medieval studies. His lecture courses at both institutions included: a social history of Italy from the end of the Middle Ages to the beginning of the Renaissance with practical studies in reading and interpretation of sources relative to the history of Florence in the thirteenth and fourteenth centuries; history of the development of urban culture in Italy from the decline of the roman world to the Renaissance ; a history of French culture in the late Middle Ages; urban culture in Italy, tenth to thirteenth centuries (society, institutions and spiritual culture); a history of culture in the late Middle Ages: Rome, Venice, Florence. Seminar topics covered: reading and interpretation of sources relative to the history of Florence; practical studies on the history of the emergence of free towns in the Middle Ages; the development of communal institutions in medieval Cologne; Francis of Assisi and early Franciscanism; Dino Compagni and Florence in the age of Dante; political theories in romance speaking regions of western Europe in the early fourteenth century. See Sveshnikov, *Peterburgskaia shkola medievistov*, p. 52.
112 G. P. Fedotov, *Sobranie sochinenii v 12 tomakk*. T 12: Pis'ma G. P. Fedotova i pis'ma raznykh lits k nemu' (Moscow, 2008) p. 119; Sveshnikov, *Peterburgskaia shkola medievistov*, p. 53.
113 Grevs, 'Vasilii Gregorievich Vasilevskii kak uchitel' nauki', p. 6.
114 See Sveshnikov, *Peterburgskaia shkola medievistov*, p. 82. In his memoirs, Nikolai Antsiferov confirmed that Grevs was indifferent when it came to publishing his work, and left a lot of unpublished material after his death: his focus was on teaching and producing the next generation of scholars. Antsiferov, *Iz dum o bylom*, p. 177.
115 Sveshnikov, *Peterburgskaia shkola medievistov*, p. 54. Grevs's standing as a 'favourite teacher' is evidenced in memoirs, correspondence, and in the prefaces to two collective volumes (1911 and 1925) compiled by his pupils in his honour. See also E. Skrzhinskaia, 'Ivan Mikhailovich Grevs. Biograficheskii ocherk', op. cit., who describes his lecturing style as both restrained yet beguiling (p. 244).
116 For a discussion of excursion history, see below, Chapter 6.
117 Sveshnikov, *Peterburgskaia shkola medievistov*, p. 85. And, indeed, it is striking to note that, just as the 'Circle' he co-founded with his student peers produced lasting friendships, even marriage (Sveshnikov mentions several – Grevs' cousins were married to F. F. Oldenburg and Lappo–Danilevskii), so, too, did his own seminar and excursions two decades later.

118 Of his students who remained in Soviet Russia, Grevs maintained closest ties with Nikolai Antsiferov and Olga Dobiash–Rozhdestvenskaia, despite her somewhat complex adherence to the new regime. Dobiash–Rozhdestvenskaia specialized in medieval Latin palaeography and the history of medieval society and culture, and in the pre-war period completed her studies under the supervision of Charles–Victor Langlois at the Sorbonne. Her Russian doctorate (1918) was on the cult of the Archangel Michael in the Middle Ages.

119 'My intention', Fedotov wrote in the introduction to his study of Christianity in Kievan Rus' 'is to describe the subjective side of religion as opposed to its objective side; that is, opposed to the complex of organized dogmas, sacraments, rites, liturgy, Canon Law, and so on. I am interested in man, religious man, and his attitude towards God, the world, and his fellow men; his attitude is not only emotional, but also rational and volitional, the attitude of the whole man. (…). I do not deny the supernatural, divine character of Christianity as a religion of revelation. But I believe its realization begins with the human response to Grace. The history of Christianity is the history of this response; its culture is the culture of this experience. History and culture are, in essence, human.' G. Fedotov, *The Russian Religious Mind*, Vol. 1 (Cambridge, MA, 1966), p. ix, pp. x–xi. Fedotov joined Grevs' seminar in 1910 where he completed his thesis on St Augustine's *Confessions*. In 1911, he contributed an essay on Augustine's Letters to the Festschrift in celebration of Grevs's twenty-five-year teaching career (*K dvadtsatipiatiletiyu ucheno-pedagogocheskoi deiatel'nosti Ivana Mikhailovicha Grevsa*, pp. 109–38).

120 See, for example, Sveshnikov, *Peterburgskaia shkola medievistov*.; B. Kaganovich, *Russkie medievisty pervoi poloviny XX veka* (St Petersburg, 2007) Grevs, himself, traced the breakdown of relations to the period, around 1912, as Karsavin embarked on his doctoral dissertation, gravitating increasingly towards mysticism with an erotic edge to it, which Grevs found distasteful. See: O. B. Vakhromeeva (ed.), *Chelovek s otkrytym serdtsem*, p. 295. On Karsavin's thought, see, for example, F. Lesourd, 'Karsavine et Likhatchev: une histoire synthetique', in Marc Weinstein (ed.), *La geste russe. Comment les Russes écrivent-ils l'histoire au XXe siècle?* (Aix-en-Provence, 2002), pp. 345–55; D. Rubin, *The Life and Thought of Lev Karsavin* (Leiden, 2013).

121 R. Markwick, 'Cultural History under Khrushchev and Brezhnev: From Social Psychology to Mentalités', *Russian* Review, Vol. 65, No. 2 (April 2006), p. 293. In his letters to Grevs, Karsavin implied use of a 'regressive' method in historical understanding, namely, that to grasp the meaning of a textual source one has to observe the contemporary landscape, architecture and artworks, thereby moving away from the familiar to the more obscure. See A. K. Klementov and S. A. Klementova (eds), *Iz epistoliarnogo naslediia L.P. Karsavina. Pis'ma I. M. Grevsu (1906–1916)* (Moscow, 1994).

122 In the Introduction to his *Osnovy srednevekovoi religioznosti v XII–XIII vv* (St Petersburg, 1915), Karsavin wrote we look at man, not in the moment when he 'constructs his worldview', but in the context of his entire life when he is not thinking about the rapport between his thoughts and feelings. The analysis is anti-genetic (i.e. not focused on causal connections and development), rather it looks at '*sostoianie*' (states/situations) and inner 'non causal' connections between them in order to capture a picture of the world. This method requires 'empathy'. (p. 36, p. 10). Cf. A. L. Iastrebitskaia, 'U Istokov kul'turno–antropologicheskoi istorii v Rossii', in A. K. Klementov and S. A. Klementova (eds), ibid., p. 13.

123 Karsavin letter to Grevs dated 24 July 1913, in Klementov and Klementova (eds), *Iz epistoliarnogo naslediia L.P. Karsavina. Pis'ma I. M. Grevsu (1906-1916)*, p. 92.
124 Grevs, 'Novyi trud po religioznoi istorii srednevekoi Italii v russkoi nauchoi literature' [offprint] (St Petersburg, 1913), p. 10.
125 M. Wachtel, 'New Scholarship on Viacheslav Ivanov', Review Article, *The Slavic and East European Journal*, Vol. 50, No. 4 (Winter 2006), p. 690.
126 Ibid.
127 Letter to Ivanov, dated 13 June 1918. Cited in O. B. Vakhromeeva (ed.), *Chelovek s otkrytym serdtsem*, p. 385. For his part, Ivanov described his impressions of his friend from student years in poetic form: chudesen pozdnii tvoi vozvrat/s privetom dal'nego bylogo,/i goloca, vse molodogo,/znakomyi zvuk, liubimy brat!/i te zhe temnye glaza,/iz lona vdrug vsia iunost' glianet,/poroi po prezhnemu tumanit/ vostorga tikhogo sleza. See his poem *Vozvrat* published in the collection 'Nord' (Baku, 1926).
128 Ibid.
129 Cited in Sveshnikov, *Peterburgskaia shkola medievistov*, p. 85.
130 Ibid., p. 83. See also *K dvadtsatipiatiletiiu ucheno-pedagogickeskoi deiatel'nosti Ivana Mikhailovicha Grevsa*, p. I; Antsiferov's obituary note published in Vakhromeeva (ed.), *Chelovek s otkrytym serdtsem*, pp. 353-5. 'I feel an affinity (*rodstvo*) with you', Karsavin wrote in a letter from France. 'You might accuse me of exaggeration, Ivan Mikhailovich, but I do not exaggerate your influence on me, or on others. The spirit of your seminars lingers with me, even today, in my own teaching.' Letter dated 16 April 1910, in Klementov and Klementova (eds), *Iz epistoliarnogo naslediia L.P. Karsavina. Pis'ma I. M. Grevsu*, pp. 56-7.
131 E. V. Fedorova, *K istorii antikovedeniia v Rossii. Vospominaniia professora, doktora istoricheskikh nauk M. E. Sergeenko*, Tr. Kafedra drevnikh iazykov. Tr. Istoricheskogo fakul'teta MGU, vyp. 15 (St Petersburg, 2000), p. 309.
132 Among these were: V. V. Bakhtin, G. P. Fedotov and E. N. Fedotova-Nechaeva (prior to their emigration in 1925), E. Ch Skrzhinskaia, A. D. and V. S. Liublinskii, M. A. Gukovskii, and N. Antsiferov.
133 See below, Chapters 6 and 7.
134 On the 'academic affair', see J. Barber, *Soviet Historians in Crisis, 1928-1932* (London, 1981).
135 Publications dating from this period consisted mostly of commentaries to edited works and translations including Dante's *Divine Comedy*, and an extensive preface and afterword to accompany the Russian translation of *Ettore Fieramosca*, a historical novel about the fifteenth-century Italian condottiero, by the statesman, Massimo D'Azeglio (1833). The last project Grevs was working on before his death in 1941, a biography of Tacitus intended for a wider readership, was published posthumously in the series 'Zhizn' zamechatel'nykh liudei' (Moscow, 1946) See Sveshnikov, *Peterburgskaia shkola medievistov*, pp. 59-60.
136 Konrad H. Jarausch differentiates between two conceptions of science in continental Europe, which throw into relief some of the distinctive features of Russian historical culture in terms of its enduring commitment to public enlightenment: 'A prerequisite of higher learning and of academic occupations was some form of general cultivation. Known variously as liberal education, *Allegemeinbildung* or *culture générale*, this generalized cultural capital functioned both as common ground for the educated and as a social divide to those below. More peculiar to tertiary institutions and professions was specialized scientific

knowledge, involving a mastery of the dynamic principles of a scholarly discipline. Such *Fachwissen* was the specific property of its initiates, providing insights beyond the grasp of the layman and thereby justifying professional prerogatives [...]. During the course of the nineteenth century, emphasis shifted from liberal education to scientific instruction.' See Ruegg, *A History of the University in Europe*, Vol. 3, pp. 365–6.

137 Granovskii, 'O sovremennom sostoianii i znachenii vseobshchei istorii', cited in Kareev, *Istoricheskoe mirosozertsanie*, p. 14. See also Sokolov (ed.), *Izbrannye sochineniia T. N. Granovskogo*, p. 24. Despite the stereotype of German scholarship, Granovskii's views of the historical process and the goal of history were, as I have argued, clearly indebted to Ranke and Hegel, and deeply romantic. According to Vetrinskii, Granovskii's immediate successors, Sergei Solov'ev, and Pavel Kudriavstev inherited his view of history as a tool for turning Russians into citizens, and, unlike Karamzin, who portrayed exemplary heroes to emulate, this next generation of historians 'tried to instil a sense of the eternal laws of historical development, respect for the past, and a pledge to improve in the future; they endeavoured to show that acquiring a sense of citizenship is a long and difficult process, that great men are, in essence, children of their society. They did not relate to the past as something irretrievably lost; rather, they sought to understand it on its own terms, and in its relationship to the present.' Ch. Vetrinskii, *T. N. Granovskii i ego vremia*, pp. 270–1.

138 In his tribute to Granovskii, Pavel Vinogradov, for example, referred to the university as a 'centre of societal life', a comment, which, possibly intentionally, echoed the medical doctor and pedagogue, Nikolai Pirogov's well-known description of the university as a 'barometer of social change'. See P. Vinogradov, 'T. N. Granovskii', p. 63. For a broader overview of this topic, see S. Kassow, *Students, Professors and the State in Tsarist Russia* (Berkeley, 1989).

139 Historical journals dating from the post-reform era also blurred the distinction between 'specialist' and 'generalist' literature: 'In order to 'increase their distribution (…) editors and publishers (…) published historical belles–lettres, secret documents, anecdotes relating to the lives of "great people" etc. The aim was to place scientific knowledge within the reach of a wider audience.' See Joseph L. Wieczynski, *The Modern Encyclopedia of Russian and Soviet History*, Vol. 14 (1979), p. 60.

140 P. Miliukov, 'V. O. Kliuchevskii', in *Kharakteristiki i vospominaniia*, p. 208.

Chapter 3

1 Kiesewetter, 'V. O. Kliuchevskii kak prepodavatel'', pp. 164–76. Cited in Sanders (ed.), p. 298.
2 Marshall Shatz (ed. & trans.), *A Course in Russian History: The Time of Catherine the Great* (Armonk, NY, 1997), p. xiv.
3 Shmidt, 'Kliuchevskii i kul'tura Rossii', in *Put' istorika*, p. 305.
4 Iu. Lotman, 'Columb russkoi istorii', in *N. M. Karamzin. Istoriia gosudarstva rossiiskogo*, Kn. iv (Moscow, 1988), pp. 16, 9–10; T. M. Bohn, 'Istorism v Rossii? O sostoianii russkoi istoricheskoi nauki v XIX stoletii', *Otechestvennaia istoriia*, Vol. 4 (2000), pp. 121–8; Derek Offord, 'Nation-Building and Nationalism in Karamzin's *History of the Russian State*', *Journal of Modern Russian History and Historiography*, Vol. 3 (2010), pp. 1–50.

5   Gossman, *Between History and Literature*, p. 244; Iu. Lotman, *Sotvorenie Karamzina*, Introduction by B. F. Egorov, (Moscow 1998) pp. 5–10.
6   Cited in K. N. Bestuzhev-Riumin, 'Karamzin, kak istorik', in *Biografii i kharakteristiki: Tatishev, Shletser, Karamzin, Pogodin, Solov'ev, Eshevskii, Gil'ferding* (St Petersburg, 1882), p. 216. In this essay, Bestuzhev-Riumin also comments on Karamzin's attitude to 'science'. If his 'scientific apparatus' (among Karamzin's models were John Gillies, Adam Ferguson and David Hume) was, for Bestuzhev-Riumin's generation, out of date, his underlying message was not: 'In Karamzin we have seen that rare combination of strengths (…). He was a scholar, but above all he was a man, and Karamzin valued the man in him more than the historian'. To this point Bestuzhev-Riumin quoted from a letter which Karamzin addressed to Turgenev: 'To live is not to write history, neither is it to write tragedy or comedy; rather, to think well, feel and act, love the good, and to be elevated (*vozvyshat'sia*) by the soul to its source. All the rest, my dear friend, is *shelukha* – including my eight or nine volumes'. Ibid., p. 229.
7   In his two-volume biography, Pogodin details Karamzin's turn to history and the approaches he made to Mikhail Murav'ev, the minister of education, tutor to the tsar and first trustee of Moscow University in order to secure the financial support he needed for his project. Judging by both his correspondence and preliminary articles published in the early 1800s (*Vestnik Evropy*), the initiative to write a history in support of autocracy and the glory of the fatherland (*slava otechestva*) came from Karamzin. M. Pogodin, *Nikolai Mikhailovich Karamzin po ego sochineniiam. Pis'mam i otzyvam sovremennikov. Materialy dlia biografii*, 2 vols (Moscow, 1866).
8   Offord, 'Nation–Building and Nationalism', p. 13; Karamzin, Foreword, *History of the Russian State* (1815). Cited from the English translation in M. Raeff (ed.), *Russian Intellectual History: An Anthology* (New Jersey, 1978), p. 122. To this point, Pogodin argued that Karamzin recognized the challenges facing historians to compete with novelists and poets by writing *krasnorechivo* (eloquently) in order to 'revive our famous ancestors from the grave'. Pogodin, *Nikolai Mikhailovich Karamzin po ego sochineniiam* Vol. 2, p. 7. Natan Eidelman argued that in his *History*, Karamzin 'combines perspectives to position himself as a dispassionate distant recorder of events, but, in the guise of an imaginary eyewitness, he occupies a good vantage point to follow the events themselves as they unfold. If this means sacrificing historical analysis, it imparts something more important (for Karamzin), namely the spirit and atmosphere'. In other words, Karamzin intended two ways of knowing the past: one, scientific, objective (…); the other, artistic, subjective: 'With his own person, spirit and gifts he brings together scattered facts, fills in the lacunae (*pustoty*), making for an important, valuable model for the general course of events (…). Thereafter, history and literature would follow their own paths, occasionally intersecting, but, in the main, separate from one another'. N. Eidelman, *Poslednii letopisets'* (Moscow, 1983), pp. 157–8.
9   S. O. Shmidt, *Put' istorika. Izbrannye trudy po istochnikovedeniiu iistoriografii* (Moscow, 1997). S. O. Shmidt, '*Istoriia gosudarstva Rossiiskogo* v kul'ture dorevoliutsionnoi Rossii' , *Put' istorika*, pp. 233–56.
10 Wachtel, *An Obsession with History*, pp. 47–8.
11 Kliuchevskii, *Neopublikovannye proizvedeniia*, p. 134.
12 Gossman, *Between History and Literature*, p. 297.
13 J. Striedter, 'Poetic Genre and the Sense of History in Pushkin', *New Literary History* (Winter 1977), p. 296.
14 The Third Section of His Imperial Majesty's Own Chancellery was set up to conduct secret police operations.

15 Lotman, 'Russkaia istoriko-filologicheskaia nauka i khudozhestvennaia literatura vtoroi poloviny XIX veka', p. 43.
16 Buslaev memoirs cited by K. Voinakhovskii, 'Znachenie trudov akademika F. I. Buslaeva v istorii nauki o russkom iazyke', in S. G. Smirnov (ed.), *Pamiati Fedora Ivanovicha Buslaeva* (Moscow, 1898), p. 96.
17 Striedter, 'Poetic Genre and the Sense of History in Pushkin', p. 300.
18 There are numerous studies of the Russian reception of Scott. See, for example, M. Al'tshuller, *Epokha Val'tera Skotta v Rossii: istoricheskii roman 1830-kh godov* (St Petersburg, 1996); also by Al'tshuller, 'The Rise and Fall of Walter Scott's Popularity in Russia', in M. Pittock (ed.), *The Reception of Sir Walter Scott in Europe* (London; New York, 2006) pp. 204–40; A. Dolinin, *Istoriia, odetaia v roman: Val'ter Skott i ego chitateli* (Moscow, 1988); E. Zhiliakova, *Shotlandskie stranitsy: ekho Val'tera Skotta v russkoi literature XIX veka: ocherki* (Tomsk, 2014).
19 Striedter, 'Poetic Genre and the Sense of History in Pushkin', pp. 300, 307.
20 Pushkin's draft of an article about Scott cited in Wachtel, in *An Obsession with History*, p. 80.
21 Striedter, 'Poetic Genre and the Sense of History in Pushkin', p. 303.
22 A point made by Kliuchevskii in an otherwise damning review of Pogodin's *Drevnaia russkaia istoriia do mongol'skogo iga* (1872). Kliuchevskii, *Neopublikovannye proizvedeniia*, p. 141.
23 Formozov, *Klassiki russkoi literatury i istoricheskaia nauka*, p. 146
24 N. P. Barsukov, *Zhizn' i trudy M. P. Pogodina*, kn. 9 (St Petersburg, 1895), p. 89; A. A. Karpov (ed.), *N.V. Gogol': Perepiska*, Vol. 1 (Moscow, 1988), p. 442.
25 See V. I. Sakharov (ed. & intro.), *Russkaia romanticheskaia povest' pisatelei 20–40godov XIX veka* (Moscow, 1992), p. 8.
26 P. Kudriavtsev, *Povesti i razskazy*, 2 vols (Moscow, 1866).
27 M. Pogodin, *Povesti. Drama* (Moscow, 1984), p. 27. Later in life, Pogodin wrote a historical play about Boris Godunuv: 'Istoriia v litsakh o tsare Borise Fedoroviche' (1868).
28 P. Kudriatsev, 'Izvestie o literaturnykh trudakh Granovskogo', in Sochineniia T. N. Granovskogo, Vol. 1 (Moscow, 1856), p. x.
29 Granovskii's poem evoked the laments of a dying youth as he gazed on his native hills at sunset. As Roosevelt notes, the poem drew on a standard set of themes found in the contemporary Russian romantic verse of Vasilii Zhukovskii and Konstantin Batiushkov, as well as in the English 'graveyard school' of Edward Young, Robert Blair and Thomas Gray, which 'Granovskii undoubtedly knew well.' P. Roosevelt, *Apostle of Russian Liberalism*, pp. 5–6.
30 Stankevich, 'Biograficheskii ocherk', p. 267.
31 Kostomarov's historical and literary output was enormous, but his *Russkaia istoriia v zhizneopisaniiakh ieio glavneishikh deiatelei*, 3 vols (1874–6) illustrates his literary-historical fusion very well. On Kostomarov, see, for example, Yu. A. Pinchuk, *Istoricheskie vzgliady N. I. Kostomarova. Kriticheskii ocherk* (Kiev, 1984); T. Prymak, *Mykola Kostomarov: A Biography* (Toronto, 1996).
32 Prymak, ibid., p. 193. Kostomarov had a deep interest in the lives of literary greats such as the eighteenth-century itinerant poet and thinker, G. S. Skovoroda, and among contemporary novelists and short story writers, he admired the work of Mar'ko Vovchok (psedonymn for Mariia Vilinska), M. P. Staritskii, Ivan Turgenev, A. N. Ostrovskii, Lev Tolstoi and, of course, his fellow Ukrainian, Taras Shevchenko.
33 D. A. Korsakov, 'Pamiati Nikolaia Ivanovicha Kostomarova', *Istoricheskii vestnik*, 7 (1885), pp. 72–86.

34 Prymak, *Mykola Kostomarov*, pp. 184, 165.
35 M. Pogodin, *Borba, ne na zhivot, a na smert', s novymi istoricheskimi eresiami* (Moscow, 1874). Kostomarov's historical novel, *Kudeiar* (1875), about the 'legendary Russian bandit' in the reign of Ivan the Terrible was also heavily criticized as an attempt to denigrate the Russian state, and for its depiction of the Tsar as evil in opposition to the 'good' Ukrainians.
36 Kliuchevskii, *Neopublikovannye proizvedeniia*, pp. 177–8.
37 The views of Herzen, cited in Gossman, *Between History and Literature*, pp. 360-1. Thierry's gifts, as Herzen recognized, lay in an ability to recall the past to life, thanks to which: 'great and wide-ranging epics (...), events and individuals (...) emerge from the tomb, shake off the dust and the dirt, take on flesh, and live again before your very eyes'. That Michelet and Thierry had set the benchmark in historical narrative is evidenced in Chernyshevskii's tribute to Granovskii: like the French historians, Granovskii's scholarship resisted 'recourse to formalistic embellishments'; the public valued the 'freshness of his thought and the absorbing way he related his points, without succumbing to scholarly foppishness'. ('tut net shchegol'stva uchenost'iu'). Chernyshevskii, 'Zametki o zhurnalakh, dek.1855 i ianv. 1856', pp. 219–22. Cited in Chernyshevskii, *Polnoe sobranie sochinenii*, edited by V. Ia Kirpotin et al., 16 vols (Moscow, 1939–53) Vol. 3, p. 632.
38 Gossman, ibid., pp. 169, 192–3.
39 Ibid., p. 97.
40 Ibid., pp. 134–5.
41 White, *Metahistory*, p. 99. Hegel elaborated his theory of historical writing (as opposed to a philosophy of history referred to in White's summary) in his lectures on aesthetics. Here he presented it as one of the verbal arts. In part III of his lectures he characterized poetic expression in general, then set out his distinction between poetry and prose in prelude to a discussion of history as one aspect of genuine artistic activity, and as the prose form closest in its immediacy to poetry in general and to the Drama in particular. As Roosevelt notes, in the intellectual hierarchy of German romantic idealism, it was, of course, 'the voice of the poet as high priest and oracle of life's highest experiences, that was privileged above all other forms'. This goes some way to explaining why, as White put it, 'Hegel poeticized and dramatized history'. Ibid., pp. 88, 85ff. See also Roosevelt, *Apostle of Liberalism*, p. 31 and G. Planty-Bonjour, *Hegel et la pensée philosophique en Russie, 1830-1917* (The Hague, 1974).
42 The word 'really' in this context is perhaps best understood as 'in essence': Ranke was a romantic and an idealist, even if, in practice, he advanced source-based critique.
43 White, *Metahistory*, pp. 187–8.
44 Granovskii's letter to Nikolai Stankevich, dated 4 March 1840 in *T. N. Granovskii i ego perepiska*, Vol. II, p. 386. The profile of the journal was conceived in terms of '*Nauka strogaia*', but in a form that would be assessable to every truly educated person. The project was aborted. As Roosevelt notes, Granovskii had nurtured an ambition to write a textbook of world history as early as 1838, since those available were condensed versions of foreign works. Commissioned in 1850, the outline he produced linked Russian and European history 'by integrating them at comparable periods'. Although Granovskii only managed to complete the introduction, the section on China with drafts of other sections on ancient history, there is enough material to access his approach and the way he faltered in his endeavour to turn history into a 'rigorous science': 'In general, the completed portions of the textbook testify to Granovskii's conviction that history, as an art but also a science, should imitate scientific methodology and utilize scientific findings. But the frequency with which Christian and philosophical presuppositions

impose themselves on the narrative show that, even had he wished to, he was constitutionally incapable of a rigidly positivist approach to history'. Roosevelt, *Apostle of Russian Liberalism*, pp. 59, 61. According to Kareev: 'Although Granovskii opposed history as a science to history as an art, this did not mean that he sought to banish artistic elements from history'. Kareev, *Istoricheskoe mirosozertsanie*, p. 9. The question of whether history is a science or an art (*istoriia-nauka/istoriia-iskusstvo* – Kareev's terms) was, as he noted, a topic of debate among romantic-era historians across Europe.

45 Granovskii, 'Bartol'd Georg Niburg', pp. 37, 39–40.
46 Granovskii, 'Sid, kak istoricheskoe litso', *Otechestvennye zapiski* (1854) in A. N. Chudinov (ed.), *Poema i izbrannye romancy o Side v perevodakh russkikh pisatelei* (St Petersburg, 1897), pp. 39–40.
47 'O sovremennom sostoianii i zhachenii vseobshchei istorii'. In this speech, Granovskii declared that historical research and writing should radically alter so that history becomes a 'true, moral preceptor of man'. See Stankevich, 'Biograficheskii ocherk', in *T.N. Granovskii i ego perepiska*, Vol. I, p. 281. See also Kareev, *Istoricheskoe mirosozertsanie*, pp. 17–18.
48 Roosevelt, *Apostle of Russian Liberalism*, p. 19.
49 See Herzen on Granovskii, cited in Miliukov, 'Universitetskii kurs Granovskogo', p. 263. See also Vinogradov, 'T. N. Granovskii', p. 54. As Kareev notes, Kudriavtsev objected to Granovskii's ambition to distance history from art, and in an open reply to Granovskii's 1852 lecture he argued that it was a violation of what Granovskii otherwise stood for and practised. P. N. Kudriavtsev, 'O sovrememmykh zadachakh istorii' in *Sochineniia*, Vol. 1 (Moscow, 1877), pp. 3–69; Kareev, *Istoricheskoe mirosozertsanie*, p. 10.
50 Stankevich, *T. N. Granovskii i ego perespiska*, Vol. I, pp. 239–40; Ch. Vetrinskii, *T. N. Granovskii i ego vremia*, pp. 291, 115.
51 Bogoslovskii 'V. O. Kliuchevskii kak uchenyi', p. 43.
52 M. Raeff, 'Kliuchevskii's Russia: Critical Studies', *Canadian–American Slavic Studies*, vol. 20, nos 3–4 (Fall–Winter, 1986), p. 202. [Special Issue on Kliuchevskii edited by M. Raeff]. The view that Kliuchevskii's narrative genius was comparable to the novels of Lev Tolstoi has become a commonplace. See, for example: S. O. Shmidt, 'Kliuchevskii i kul'tura Rossii', in *Put' istorika*, pp. 305–14; Marshall S. Shatz (trans., ed., & intro), V. O. Kliuchevsky, *A Course in Russian History. The Time of Catherine the Great* (Armonk, New York, 1997), pp. ix–xxvii; Il'ia Serman, 'Kliuchevski i russkaia literatura', *Canadian–American Slavic Studies*, vol. 20, nos 3–4, pp. 417–36. Similarly, attestations of Kliuchevskii's great artistry became a staple of commemorative literature across the revolutionary divide. See, for example, A. Kiesewetter, 'Kliuchevskii and his Course of Russian History', The *Slavonic Review*, Vol.1. No 3 (Mar., 1923), pp. 504–22. Writing in emigration, at a time when official Soviet-Stalinist historiography had firmly established its Marxist-Leninist rulebook of interpretation, Michael Karpovich reminded his readers that Kliuchevskii's 'simultaneous and equally powerful appeal to the general reader and the specialist' was down to his ability to combine 'great literary flair' with 'profound scholarship'. See: Michael Karpovich, 'Klyuchevskii and Recent Trends in Russian Historiography', *Slavonic and East European Review. American Studies*, vol.2, no 1 (Mar., 1943), p. 3. For more commentaries and obituary tributes by peers and former pupils regarding Kliuchevskii's ability to combine artistry and scholarship, see above, p. 217n. 88.
53 B. F. Egorov in Iu. Lotman, *Sotvorenie Karamzina*, Introduction, p. 8.
54 Presniakov, 'V. O. Kliuchevskii, 1911–1921', pp. 214–15;

55 Kiesewetter, 'Kliuchevskii and his *Course of Russian History*', p. 522.
56 Ibid.
57 Iu. Aikhenval'd, 'Kliuchevskii. Myslitel' i khudozhnik', p. 134; Kiesewetter, ibid., p. 519.
58 Cited from the translation by Shatz, *The Time of Catherine the Great*, p. 32. See also his Introduction, p. xiv.
59 Aikhenval'd, 'Kliuchevskii. Myslitel' i khudozhnik', pp. 130, 137.
60 Kliuchevskii, *Kurs russkoi istorii* (Moscow, 1937), Pt II, p. 117: According to Rubinshtein, more than his obvious narrative flair, his 'outer stylistic artistry', it was Kliuchevskii's 'artistry of thought' that qualified him as a 'historian-artist'. Rubinshtein, *Russkaia istoriografiia*, p. 517.
61 Bogoslovskii 'V. O. Kliuchevskii kak uchenyi', p. 42. The expression 'iazykovoe nasledie' is Rubinshtein's (ibid.).
62 Presniakov, 'V. O. Kliuchevskii', p. 220.
63 Iu. Aikhenval'd, 'Kliuchevskii. Myslitel' i khudozhnik', p. 130. As I discuss in the next chapter, these features are especially apparent in the 'word portraits', which he drew of individual historical characters.
64 Kliuchevskii, cited in P. Miliukov, 'V. O. Kliuchevskii', *Kharakteristiki i vospominaniia*, pp. 209–11. Brigadier – an allusion to Fonvizin's comedy (published in 1783), which ridiculed the contemporary fashion of aping (most often incorrectly) French manners and speech.
65 Ibid.
66 'The moral impact of serfdom', Kliuchevskii wrote, 'was broader than the juridical. It significantly lowered our level of civility (*grazhdanstvennost'*). [...]. At fault was the landowning nobility as the ruling class for distorting and defaming the direction of Russian culture in general'. Cited in ibid., p. 208. For Miliukov, Kliuchevskii's critique was deeply personal, drawn from his own experiences growing up as the son of a village priest in the Penza region: 'In this mindset (*nastroenie, vynesennom iz "byta"*) and memories, should we not look for the key to, and an explanation for, the great impression which the emancipation of the serfs had on Kliuchevskii during his student years? Did they not determine both his social antipathies and sympathies?' Ibid.
67 'And if from my outline, for all its flaws, you take away, albeit in rough broad strokes an image of the Russian nation as a historical person (*obraz russkogo naroda kak istoricheskoi lichnosti*) I will consider the scientific goal of my course accomplished'. Kliuchevskii, *Kurs*, Part I, Lecture 2 (cited from 3rd edn, Moscow–Petrograd, 1923), p. 37.
68 Aikhenval'd, 'Kliuchevskii. Myslitel' i khudozhnik', pp. 140–1.
69 Serman, 'Kliuchevskii i Russkaia literatura', p. 422. Serman also notes that 'as a special form of a nation's spiritual/cultural (*dukhovnaia*) production, Russian literature was always a part of Kliuchevskii's intellectual life (*soznanie*), and to a significant degree shaped his historical outlook'. Ibid., p. 417.
70 Rubinshtein, *Russkaia istoriografiia*, pp. 517–18. In Rubinshtein's view, Kliuchevskii subordinated his account of the oprichnina to an artificially fabricated account of Ivan the Terrible's mind.
71 Thaden, 'Historicism, N. A. Polevoi, and Rewriting Russian History', pp. 306–7; R. Byrnes, 'Kliuchevskii's View of the Flow of Russian History', pp. 240–1.
72 Il'ia Serman speaks of the moral or ideological factor. Serman, 'Kliuchevskii i Russkaia literatura', p. 436.
73 Fedotov, 'Kliuchevskii's Russia', p. 218.

74 Aikhenval'd, 'Kliuchevskii. Myslitel' i khudozhnik', p. 129. See also Platonov's remarks about Kliuchevskii's articles: 'Reading them you were not only convinced and learned something, but you also derived an aesthetic pleasure from the wealth and precision of his language, the brilliance of his eloquent expressions and the artistic qualities of his conceptions. Kliuchevskii combined strength of mind and wealth of scholarly knowledge with the talent of poetic perception and design. In this resides the secret of his charm'. S. F. Platonov, 'V. O. Kliuchevskii (1841–1911) [nekrolog]' (St Petersburg), pp. 6–7.

75 Iu. Aikhenval'd', ibid., p. 132. A. Presniakov echoed these remarks when he described Kliuchevskii as the 'undisputed master of oral and written discourse', who 'quite consciously perfected these as instruments of his thought'. Presniakov, 'V. O. Kliuchevskii', p. 220.

76 Kudriavtsev, 'Izvestie o literaturnykh trudakh Granovskogo', p. x

77 Stankevich, 'Biograficheskii ocherk', in *T. N. Granovskii i ego perepiska*, Vol. 2, p. 366.

78 Kudriavtsev, 'Izvestie o literaturnykh trudakh Granovskogo', p. xiv.

79 Shmidt, 'Kliuchevskii i kul'tura Rossii', pp. 310, 309, 312.

80 S. Solov'ev in V. O. Kliuchevskii et al., *Vospominaniia o studencheskoi zhizni* (Moscow, 1899), p. 3. See also Vinogradov, 'T. N. Granovskii', p. 61.

81 Aikhenval'd, 'Kliuchevskii. Myslitel' i khudozhnik', p. 121. The reference to 'consummate actor' is Alfred Rieber's: see his introduction to the English translation by Natalie Duddington of *A Course in Russian History: The Seventeenth Century* (Armonk, New York, 1994), p. xiv.

82 Shatz (ed. & trans.), *A Course in Russian History*, p. ix.

83 Chernyshevskii, *Polnoe sobranie sochineninii*, Vol. 3, pp. 631–2. Almost a century later, Ivan Grevs fostered a similar insouciance regarding the publication of his research: as Antsiferov recalled in his memoirs, Grevs' drawers were filled with manuscripts. Antsiferov, *Iz dum o bylom*, p. 177.

84 The reference to 'living word' is Vipper's: 'Granovskii wrote little, focusing instead on meeting the demands of the public by giving them the living word'. R. Vipper, 'Obshchestvenno-istoricheskie vzgliady Granovskogo', *Mir bozhii*, Vol. 11 (1905), p. 179. '*Pestun slova*' was the expression used by Aikenval'd in his tribute to Kliuchevskii.

85 Aikenval'd also described this as 'embedded dialogue': 'Kliuchevskii. Myslitel' i khudozhnik', p. 132. See also Shatz (ed. & trans.), *A Course in Russian History*, p. xiii.

86 Shmidt, 'Pamiatniki khudozhestvennoi literatury kak istochnik istoricheskikh znanii', pp. 40–9. Cited from the English translation by Liv Bliss *in Russian Studies in History*, Vol. 47, No. 1 (2008), pp. 14–29 (p. 19).

87 Miliukov, 'V. O. Kliuchevskii', p. 208.

88 Aikhenval'd, 'Kliuchevskii. Myslitel' i khudozhnik', p. 127.

89 Cited by Kudriavtsev from a letter addressed by Granovskii to the widow of H. G. Frolov. Kudriavtsev, 'Izvestie o literaturnykh trudakh Granovskogo', p. viii.

90 On agnostic scholarship, or 'agnostic positivists', see. L. Gossman, *Between History and Literature*, p. 155.

91 Given, as I have argued, that the historian's persona was aestheticized in accordance with the cultural conventions of the epoch, it is difficult to disentangle the 'real' Granovskii or Kliuchevskii from representations of them as scholars. Whether there is any legitimate need to do so is another question; still there are, nevertheless, moments of discernible tension/or contrast between the image of the historian

as constructed in light of contemporary literary conventions and the individual temperament of the historian himself, which is perhaps most faithfully captured in the 'authorial voice'.
92 Shmidt, 'Khudozhestvennaia literatura i iskusstvo kak istochnik formirovaniia istoricheskikh predstavleniia', in *Put' istorika*, pp. 113–15; Istoricheskie istochniki i literaturnye pamiatniki' in ibid., p. 95. Also, 'Kliuchevskii i kul'tura Rossii', ibid., pp. 305–14.
93 For views of Western scholars, see, for example, G. S. Morson (ed.), *Literature and History. Theoretical Problems and Russian Case Studies* (Stanford, 1986).
94 A. Ostrovskii, *Polnoe sobranie sochinenii, v 12 tomakh* (Moscow, 1973–80), Vol. 10, p. 554, cited in L. M. Lotman, 'Russkaia istoriko-filologicheskaia nauka i khudozhestvennaia literatura', p. 32.
95 L. Tolstoi cited in Wachtel, *An Obsession with History*, p. 89. See Chapter 7.
96 Eikhenbaum, *Skvoz' literaturu. Sbornik statei* (Leningrad, 1924), p. 38. See also M. Nechkina, 'Funktsiia khudozhestvennogo obraza v istoricheskom protsessa', in *Sodruzhestvo nauk i tainy tvorchestva* (Moscow, 1968). As I mentioned earlier (note 8, above), Natan Eidelman argued that Karamzin managed to blend two ways of knowing the past – one, scientific and objective, the other, artistic and subjective. But he went on to say that: 'in the wrong hands this subjectivity could present a major risk. But we are dealing with Karamzin, that is, with the subjectivity of a talented historian-artist (*istorik-khudozhnik*), who, as such, positions himself as the collector and interpreter of facts (viz., the historian) and as a witness to the events as they unfold'. Eidelman, *Poslednii letopisets*', pp. 157–8.
97 Karpovich, 'Klyuchevskii and Recent Trends in Russian Historiography', p. 31; Iu. Lotman, 'Puti razvitiia russkoi prozy 1800-x–1810-x gg', *Uchenye zapiski Tartuskogo universiteta*, Vol. 104 (1961), pp. 42–3. For Kliuchevskii's critique of Platonov, see his 'Otzyv ob issledovanii S. F. Platonova, *Drevnerusskie skazaniia i povesti o smutnom vremeni XVIIv* kak istoricheskii istochnik' [1888], in V. O. Kliuchevskii (ed.), *Sochineniia*. T.VII (Moscow, 1959), pp. 439–53.

Chapter 4

1 Among west European historians and thinkers, the 'great man' theory was popularized by Thomas Carlyle. However, if his study of cultural heroes and hero worship (1841) seems to have been well received in Russia during the latter part of the century, I have, to date, not found much in the sources to suggest that his ideas resonated with his immediate Russian peers. There are, of course, clear parallels, as Roosevelt suggests in her study of Granovskii (see below, note 31). I discuss Carlyle and his reception in late-nineteenth-century Russia in Chapter 8.
2 See L. Ginzburg, *On Psychological Prose* (Princeton, 1991), pp. 16–17.
3 See, for example, T. Masaryk, *The Spirit of Russia: Studies in History, Literature and Philosophy* (London, 1955); V. V. Zenkovskii, *A History of Russian Philosophy* (New York, 1953); A. Walicki, *A History of Russian Thought from the Enlightenment to Marxism* (Oxford, 1988); Walicki et al., *The Flow of Ideas: Russian Thought from the Enlightenment to the Religious–Philosophical Renaissance* (Frankfurt-am-Main, 2015);

G. Barabtarlo, *Cold Fusion: Aspects of the German Cultural Presence in Russia* (New York, 2000). See also Planty-Bonjour, *Hegel et la pensée philosophique en Russie*.
4   Byrnes, *V. O. Kliuchevskii, Historian of Russia*, pp. 53, 150. See also Chapter 8 for responses to Taine by Russian contemporaries.
5   Kliuchevskii, *Kurs*, Lecture II. 'And if you take away an image of the Russian people as a historical being (*lichnost'*) - if only in terms of a general outline - from my account with all its gaps, then I will consider the scientific objective of this *Course* accomplished'.
6   Grevs, *Ocherki iz istorii Rimskogo zemlevladeniia*. On the influence of Fustel de Coulanges, which Grevs openly acknowledged (ibid., p. xvi), see also his 'Novoe issledovanie o kolonate', *Zhurnal Ministerstva narodnogo prosveshcheniia*, vols. 11, 12 (1886), pp. 118-65, 307-54.
7   Grevs, *Ocherki iz istorii rimskogo zemlevladeniia*, pp. 450-1.
8   Ibid., pp. 423, 450.
9   Granovskii, *Chetyre istoricheskie kharakteristiki* (Publichnye lektsii, chitannye v 1851 godu. Napechatany otdel'noi knizhkoi v 1852g. Moskva, Universitetskaia tipografiia) in V. A. Sokolov (ed.), *Izbrannye sochineniia T.N. Granovskogo* (Moscow, 1905), p. 26. See also Roosevelt, *Apostle of Russian Liberalism*, pp. 153-4.
10 Ibid., p. 36.
11 Ibid., p. 56.
12 Cited in Kareev, *Istoricheskoe mirosozertsanie Granovskogo*, p. 37.
13 Granovskii, *Chetyre istoricheskie kharakteristiki*, in Sokolov (ed.), p. 71.
14 Ibid., pp. 32, 43.
15 Ibid., pp. 47, 56.
16 Ibid., pp. 89, 91. As a point of interest it is worth noting that Granovskii's portrait of Bacon was in some respects similar to T. B. Macaulay's 1837 assessment, which he published in the *Edinburgh Review* (July 1837).
17 Pogodin, 'Sovremennye izvestiia Moskovskie', *Moskvitianin*, Vol. 6 (March 1851), bk. 2, p. 83, in Roosevelt, *Apostle of Russian Liberalism*, p. 154; Vetrinskii, *T. N. Granovskii i ego vremiia*, p. 289.
18 The literary and political *publitsist*, E. M. Feoktistov, cited in Roosevelt, ibid.
19 See Stankevich, *T. N. Granovskii i ego perepiska*; Vetrinskii's summary of Granovskii's outlook as a historian, *T. N. Granovskii i ego vremia*, p. 113; Kareev, *Istoricheskoe mirosozertsanie Granovskogo*, pp. 63-5; Roosevelt, *Apostle of Russian Liberalism*, pp. 153-4.
20 Kareev, ibid., p. 65.
21 Vetrinskii, *T. N. Granovskii i ego vremia*, p. 87.
22 Granovskii was also openly critical of the Slavophiles for their faith in the people (*narod*) as an agent of history: 'You can't imagine what sort of a philosophy these people have'. Letter, dated 1839 in Stankevich, *T. N. Granovskii i ego perepiska*, pp. 369-70.
23 Granovskii, *Chetyre istoricheskie kharakeristiki*, p. 26. Granovskii equated philosophical scepticism with societal and moral breakdown, assuring his students that 'history erases in us those mistrustful, skeptical opinions which deprive us of energy and moral force'. See Roosevelt, *Apostle of Russian Liberalism*, for comments by former students confirming Granovskii's endeavours to instil a sense of the eternal laws of historical development in his audiences, pp. 39, 59.
24 Cited in Vl. Ger'e, *Timofei Nikolaevich Granovskii*. p. 83; See also Kareev, who endorsed Granovskii's contention that determinism does not fetter the creative potential of the individual (Kareev, *Istoricheskoe mirosozertsanie Granovskogo*, p. 61).

25 Granovskii, 'O sovremmenom sostoianii i znachenii vseobshchei istorii' [1852], in *Sochineniia*, Vol. 2 (1856), pp. 276-7, cited in Vetrinskii, *T. N. Granovskii i ego vremia*, pp. 87-8.
26 Roosevelt, *Apostle of Russian Liberalism*, pp. 58-9; Kareev, *Istoricheskoe mirosozertsanie Granovskogo*, p. 65.
27 The expression is Kudriavtsev's: In the French monarch, Granovskii uncovered a 'moral beauty, a pure *svetlaia dusha* and integrity'. Kudriavtsev, 'Izvestie o literaturnykh trudakh Granovskogo', p. xix; Roosevelt, ibid., p. 142.
28 Kareev, *Istoricheskoe mirosozertsanie Granovskogo*, p. 42. Roosevelt comments, 'In his lectures as well as in his dealings with his contemporaries, Granovskii extended the demand for integrity to the world at large, focusing on morality and intent as the most important criteria for judging both historical and living persons. This focus is, in Granovskii's lectures, particularly clear in his description of great historical figures'. Ibid., p. 60.
29 Cited in Roosevelt, ibid., p. 142.
30 L. Ginzburg, *On Psychological Prose*, p. 33.
31 White, *Metahistory*, p. 9; Roosevelt, *Apostle of Russian Liberalism*, p. 60. A major influence in this period was, Roosevelt notes, Thomas Carlyle's *On Heroes and Hero Worship and the Heroic in History* (1841) in which he singled out prophets, priests, poets and literati as leaders of humanity (Mohammed, Shakespeare, Dante, Rousseau, among them). In Carlyle's romantic historiosophy, as Roosevelt summarizes it, history was governed not by 'interests', but by the Spirit and the Word: 'the fate of history was dependent on the conscience of individual people,' and this, indeed, seems to have informed Granovskii's historical-literary essays.
32 Paperno, *Chernyshevsky and the Age of Realism*, p. 8.
33 *Chetyre istoricheskie kharakteristiki*, cited in Roosevelt, p. 60.
34 Vipper, 'Obshchestvenno-istoricheskie vzgliady Granovskogo', p. 191.
35 Ibid., p. 190.
36 *Chetyre istoricheskie kharakteristiki*, in Sokolov (ed.), p. 75.
37 Their findings were quite different, too: if, for Granovskii, Peter the Great was an innovator, for Kliuchevskii, his reign did not mark a radical break with the past; rather, the changes he introduced had deep roots in the past. Although Kliuchevskii did concede that Peter was 'an authoritative, intelligent, energetic, and talented individual, one of those (…) who appear from time to time', this was not because of some 'providential hand': History, in his view, recorded no miracles or miracle workers. See Byrnes, *V. O. Kliuchevskii, Historian of Russia*, pp. 240-1.
38 Kliuchevskii, cited in Aikhenvald, 'Kliuchevskii. Myslitel' i khudozhnik', p. 141. Robert Byrnes also lists a number of telling aphoristic comments that diminished the importance of individuals: 'Life is like a church procession. Those in the front ranks should not conclude that they lead the others'; 'Princes are drops of water, products of conditions, not agents of change. They represent economic and other forces that thrust them to the forefront as figureheads and symbols. Muscovy's early rulers did not enlarge the state: it grew because of factors beyond the control of such mediocrities'. Cited in Byrnes, ibid., p. 162.
39 Shatz, *The Time of Catherine the Great*, Introduction, p. xxi.
40 Kliuchevskii, *Peter the Great*. Cited from the English translation by Liliana Archibald (London, 1958), pp. 38, 43 [Henceforth: Archibald].
41 Kliuchevskii, *A Course in Russian History: The Seventeenth Century*. Cited from the translation by N. Duddington (Chicago, 1968), p. 354 [Henceforth: Duddington].
42 Ibid. See also Byrnes, *V.O. Kliuchevskii, Historian of Russia*, p. 209.

43 Archibald, p. 269.
44 Cf. Shatz, *The Time of Catherine the Great*, pp. xxi–xxii.
45 Ibid., p. 55.
46 Ibid., p. 52.
47 Duddington, p. 352.
48 Ibid., p. 383.
49 Archibald, pp. 33–4. In April 1682, Sophia Alekseievna, one of Alexis' daughters from his first marriage, led a rebellion of the Streltsy (Russia's elite military corps) in which some of Peter's relatives and friends were murdered. The ten-year-old child witnessed some of these acts of political violence.
50 Ibid., p. 32.
51 Ibid., p. 56.
52 Ibid., p. 40.
53 Ibid., p. 48
54 Cf. Byrnes, *V. O. Kliuchevskii, Historian of Russia*, p. 162.
55 Archibald, p. 269.
56 Assessing the reign of Peter the Great was a topic that entered early reform historiography and was to some degree prompted by the introduction of sociological and comparative methods. See T. Emmons, 'On the Problem of Russia's "Separate Path" in Late Imperial Historiography', in Sanders, pp. 163–87; see also Kizevetter, 'V. O. Kliuchevskii kak prepodavatel', in V. O. Kliuchevskii, *Kharakteristiki i vospominaniia*, pp. 169–70; A. S. Lappo-Danilevskii, 'Istoricheskie vzgliady V. O. Kliuchevskogo', in ibid., p. 112. As Miliukov recalled in his obituary tribute, Kliuchevskii used the comparative method, but his aim was not to stress points of similarity across national borders; rather 'to determine local variations of broader historical processes, to study the distinctiveness (*svoeobrazie*) of every local (*mestnaia*) history. From this perspective, Slavophile, Westernizer, populist and liberal interpretations of Russian history were all equally suspect. (…). We did not want to construct Russian history in terms of borrowing or of claims to uniqueness (*zaimstvovanie/samobytnost'*), rather through the prism of general scientific problems, that is, the inner organic evolution of human society' (Miliukov, ' V. O. Kliuchevskii', ibid., pp. 189, 198). Kliuchevskii, himself, characterized the Westernizers as 'a "discipline of thought, love for precision, respect for scientific knowledge," and the Slavophiles as "a broad sweep (*razmashistost'*) of ideas," cheery (*bodraia*) faith in the people's strength, with a hint of lyrical dialectic which so sweetly concealed the lapses in logic (*promakhi logiki*) and gaps (*prorekhi*) in erudition.' (Miliukov, ibid., p. 200). In the views of his immediate successors, then, Kliuchevskii occupied the middle ground between these trends, combining *svoebrazie* with comparative historical development in the fields of politics and economics. For a recent analysis of Kliuchevskii's views of Russia's relations with the West and their impact on his conception of history, see Kare Johan Mjor, 'Russian History and European Ideas: The Historical Vision of Vasilii Kliuchevskii', in *The Borders of Europe* (Aarhus, 2012), pp. 71–90.
57 Archibald, pp. 254–5.
58 'Representative typical figures aid in our study of the composition of life, which nourish and shape them. The traits and interests of their milieu are articulated in pronounced fashion in such figures'. Kliuchevskii, *Kurs*, Vol. 3 (Moscow, 1937), p. 344, cited in Rubinshtein, *Russkaia istoriografiia*, p. 518. See also Aikhenval'd, 'Kliuchevskii. Myslitel' i khudozhnik', pp. 117, 138.
59 Duddington, p. 342.

60 Ibid., p. 343.
61 Ibid., pp. 360, 365.
62 Ibid., pp. 367, 377.
63 Ibid., p. 377.
64 Ibid., p. 376.
65 Ibid., p. 390.
66 Byrnes, *V. O. Kliuchevskii, Historian of Russia*, p. 252; 'Kliuchevskii devoted seven chapters in the *Course* to individuals. The Russian editor of the most recent edition of Kliuchevskii's works called it "a gallery of portraits," and in 1990 published a volume of his essays under the general title *Historical Portraits* (with a print run of two million copies)'. Ibid., p. 163. In Marshall Shatz's view: 'The almost anthropological descriptiveness and psychological depth of his historical portraits (...) bring some of the pages of Tolstoy to mind, and his characterizations of eighteenth-century sovereigns and landowners are worthy of a Salytkov-Shchedrin or a Gogol'. Shatz, *The Time of Catherine the Great*, Introduction, p. xv.
67 Cf. Aikhenval'd, 'Kliuchevskii. Myslitel' i khudozhnik', p. 141; Byrnes, ibid., p. 150; Chumachenko, *V. O. Kliuchevskii – istochnikoved*, p. 182.
68 Fedotov, 'Kliuchevskii's Russia', pp. 218–19.
69 Kliuchevskii, *Dobrye liudi drevnei Rusi'* [v pol'zu postradavshikh ot neurozhaia] (Sergeev Posad, 1892), p. 9.
70 According to Kare Johan Mjor, this statement made Kliuchevskii more historicist (i.e. more concerned with individuality and development) than either Solov'ev or Miliukov, both of whom tended to subscribe to universal laws and universal history. It also allowed him to reformulate 'the relationship of Russia to Europe by suggesting that Russia was European because of their common cultural origin, not their common historical goal'. Mjor, 'Russian History and European Ideas', p. 84.
71 See Byrnes, 'Kliuchevskii's View of the Flow of Russian History', in Sanders, p. 242. On this point, *pace* Mjor, Kliuchevskii seemed to be following in the footsteps of his teacher, Solov'ev: 'Do not divide, carve up Russian history into discrete parts, periods; rather, unite them, trace the chain of events, the direct legacy of forms. Do not dissect original principles or causes (*nachalo*), but consider them in their interrelatedness, endeavour to uncover the inner links between each phenomenon rather than divorce them from the general chain of events (...) – this is what a historian must do at the present time as the author of the proposed study understands it'. S. M. Solov'ev, lecture delivered on 3 November 1879 in St Petersburg, cited in Bestuzhev-Riumin, *Biografii i kharakteristiki*, p. 266.
72 Kliuchevskii, 'Rech' o Pushkine' (1880), in V. A. Aleksandrov (ed.), *Kliuchevskii. V. O. Istoricheskie portrety. Deiateli istoricheskoi mysli* (Moscow, 1991), p. 398. Taine's example of the knight and courtier, cited by Lidiia Ginzburg, raised the same issue: 'Each century stages its own version of (...) pageantry and creates an ideal type: for one, it is the knight, for another, the courtier. It would be interesting to disentangle the real knight from the poetical one'. *Essais de critique et d'histoire* [Paris, 1887], p. 209, cited in Ginzburg, *On Psychological Prose*, pp. 16–17.
73 The project originated in Grevs' undergraduate dissertation (1883), a socio-politically framed analysis of the struggle between the Roman aristocracy and the emperors. Rephrasing this in socio-economic terms for his master's dissertation, Grevs project was driven by leading questions concerning: the fate of ager publicus in the imperial period, the development of imperial property, the wealth of individual emperors, the history of patrimony, the relationship between emperors and the agricultural labouring

classes, and the law of imperial landownership. See Skzhinskaia, 'Ivan Mikhailovich Grevs. Biograficheskii ocherk', p. 235. As Skzhinskaia notes, Grevs initially had plans for a second volume of case studies, but abandoned the project when he discovered that a contemporary German scholar had been working on the same topic. The third sketch was meant to explore in more general terms the question of the formation of large estates during the republican period of Roman history and the spread of major forms of ownership throughout the Roman world with the establishment of imperial rule; the final part was to describe, using the biography of Pliny the Younger, the 'organism of latifundia' as it took shape during the second century AD.

74 Sveshnikov, *Peterburgskaia shkola medievistov*, p. 69.
75 Grevs, *Ocherki iz istorii Rimskogo zemlevladeniia*, p. 59. See also N. Kareev, 'Kniga g. Grevsa o rimskom zemlevladenii', in *Russkoe bogatstvo*, t. xii (1900), p. 4. In terms of the economic themes of his dissertation, Grevs chose Horace as an example of a small landowner to contrast with his case study of the wealthy magnate, Atticus, Horace's older contemporary.
76 Cf. Sveshnikov, *Peterburgskaia shkola medievistov*, p. 69. In some respects, Grevs' approach was reminiscent of Ranke (a historian who Grevs admired). In his *History of the Latin and Teutonic Nations* [1824], Ranke included private diaries, letters, eye witness accounts and memoirs as sources in addition to official documents, a decision which Donald Kelley describes as 'a more subtle and critical historical epistemology and employment of sources (*Quellenforschung, Quellenkritik*)'. As Kelley notes, for Ranke, 'the subject of "history proper" meant politics and war, but it also involved literature, philosophy and history as evidence about "the spirit of man"' (Kelley, *Fortunes of History*, pp. 135, 140). What, however, set Grevs apart from Ranke was that he also included poetry and topographical studies. I discuss this in more detail in Chapter 5.
77 Grevs, *Ocherki iz istorii Rimskogo zemlevladeniia*, p. 64.
78 Ibid., p. 245.
79 Ibid., p. 368ff.
80 Ibid., p. 409. See also B. Kaganovich, 'Vokrug *Ocherkov iz istorii rimskogo zemlevladeniia* I. M. Grevsa', in V. I. Rutenburg and I. P. Medvedev (eds), *Politicheskie struktury epokhi feodalizma v zapadnoi Evrope (vi–xvii vv)* (Leningrad, 1990), pp. 201–2.
81 Grevs, *Ocherki iz istorii Rimskogo zemlevladeniia*, p. 247.
82 Ibid., p. 250.
83 Ibid., pp. 370–1.
84 Ibid., p. 372.
85 Ibid., p. 373.
86 Ibid., p. 399.
87 Ibid., p. 398. The name of Atticus is, of course, commonly linked with the ideals of friendship largely because of Cicero's famous treatise, and, as Grevs argued, it was only with Cicero that Atticus enjoyed a truly 'disinterested friendship' based on deep feeling and a sense of kindred spirit (pp. 412–13). It is also no coincidence that Grevs took up this theme: friendship was extremely important to Grevs in his own personal life, and, as his publications dating from the First World War and post-revolutionary period suggest, it began to feature fairly prominently as a research theme. See Chapters 6 and 7.
88 Ibid.
89 Ibid., p. 406.
90 Ibid., p. 423.

91 Sveshnikov, *Peterburgskaia shkola medievistov*, p. 71.
92 We have a fair amount of information on Grevs' development as a historian after 1900, especially concerning his views on the task of the historian, thanks to recently published correspondence between him and Karsavin, personal notes and memoirs. See Klementov and Klementova (eds), *Iz epistoliarnogo naslediia L. P. Karsavina. Pis'ma I. M. Grevsu (1906-1916)*; Vakhromeeva (ed.), *Chelovek s otkrytym serdtsem*; Antsiferov, *Iz dum o bylom. Vospominaniia*. All of them attest to his wide range of cultural interests which he brought to bear in his work as a historian – from visits to archaeological sites, the examination of early Christian and mediaeval mosaics and frescos, paintings and sculpture in museums, besides close reading of archival manuscripts.
93 Antsiferov, unpublished obituary, May 1941, printed in Vakhromeeva (ed.), *Chelovek s otkrytym serdtsem*, p. 354.
94 Grevs, *Ocherki iz istorii Rimskogo zemlevladeniia*, p. 242. As Grevs pointed out, available statistics and legal records mostly related to the period post-dating the age of transition from Republic to Empire (ibid., p. 447).
95 Cited by Kareev in his review, 'Kniga g. Grevsa o rimskom zemlevladenii', t. xi, p. 12.
96 Grevs, *Ocherki iz istorii Rimskogo zemlevladeniia*, p. 438. Again, a point cited by Kareev in his review, t. xii, p. 4.
97 Cf. Sveshnikov, *Peterburgskaia shkola medievistov*.
98 Grevs, *Ocherki iz istorii Rimskogo zemlevladeniia*, pp. 441–67.
99 Ibid., p. 464. See also 'Perepiska I. M. Grevsa i Viach. Ivanova – pamiatnik russkoi kul'tury', in Bongard-Levin, Kotrelev and Liapustina (eds. and commentary), *Istoriia i poeziia*, p. 335. In his reply, Ivanov objected to this distinction between philology and history as artificial: to his mind, philology was the 'science of classical antiquity in its entirety'. Ivanov – appendix to letter 22 (4/16 October 1894), ibid., p. 83.
100 Grevs, 'Vasilii Gregorievich Vasilevskii kak uchitel' nauki', p. 18.
101 Grevs, *Istoriia proiskhozhdeniia, razvitiia i razlozheniia feodalizma v zapadnoi Evropy* [1902–3]. Typescript of lectures read at the Higher Women's Courses, compiled by auditor, S. Svirodovaia, p. 5. The emphasis Grevs placed on events and phenomena as organic, dynamic and with a certain qualitative 'durée' (*dlitel'nost'*) may have taken its inspiration from Henri Bergson.
102 Kareev, 'Kniga g. Grevsa o rimskom zemlevladenii', t. xi, p. 19.
103 Ibid., t. xii, p. 4. See also Sveshnikov, *Peterburgskaia shkola medievistov*, pp. 64, 69–70.
104 Kareev, ibid., t. xii, p. 16.
105 Grevs, *Nauchnye progulki tsentram Italii. Ocherki florentiiskoi kul'tury* (Moscow, 1903). Cited in O. B. Vakhromeeva, *Chelovek s otkrytym* serdtsem, p. 4. The sentiment echoes a remark by the seventeenth-century French philosopher, Blaise Pascal, whom Grevs directly cited in an essay on the historical component of regional studies (*kraevedenie*): 'Vsia chreda lyudei, zhivshikh v prodolozhenie stol'kikh vekov na Zemle, dolzhna rassmatrivat'sya kak odin chelovek, kotoryi zhivet vsegda i uchitsia nepreryvno'. Grevs, 'Istoriia v kraevedenii', *Kraevedenie*, 4 (1926), pp. 487– 508. Cited from reprint in M. I. Kornalov (ed.), *Otechestvo. Kraevedcheskii al'manakh*, 2 (Moscow, 1991), p. 8.
106 Grevs' friend, the historian Aleksandr Lappo-Danilevskii, expressed a similar view in his *Metodologiia istorii* (1910–13), namely that the object of historical knowledge is 'humanity as a whole'. In Gary Hamburg's summary, 'Lappo-Danilevskii asserted that historians, as sentient beings, have the capacity to grasp at least to some degree the

past behavior of other sentient beings. Our capacity to understand others depends on our empathy for them, on our ability to associate their acts with acts of our own, or to comprehend their acts by analogy to our own. As historians, our accuracy in assessing the past deeds of others will be limited not only by our psychological acuity and by the degree of our cultural comprehension but also by the finitude and nature of the written sources available to us. Thus, for Lappo-Danilevskii, a crucial component of the historians' craft is the interpretation of historical sources as psychological–cultural constructs from another age'. Hamburg, 'A. S. Lappo-Danilevskii and the Writing of History in late Imperial Russia', pp. 15–16.
107   Kiesewetter, 'Kliuchevskii and his Course of Russian History', p. 518.
108   Rubinshtein, *Russkaia istoriografiia*, p. 518.
109   Kliuchevskii, *Neopublikovannoe*, pp. 133–4.
110   Rubinshtein, *Russkaia istoriografiia*, p. 518; Karpovich, 'Klyuchevski and Recent Trends', pp. 31–2.

Chapter 5

1   Paperno, *Chernyshevsky and the Age of Realism*, p. 8.
2   Ibid., p. 11.
3   Lidiia Ginzburg cites Herzen's observation: 'This mutual effect of people on books and books on people is a strange thing. The book takes its whole stamp from the society in which it comes into being, generalizes it, makes it more distinct and vivid, and then is overcome by reality. The originals turn their own sharply drawn portraits into caricatures, and real people grow used to their own literary shadows. […]. After 1862 almost all the young Russians who came to see me [in London] were right out of [Chernyshevskii's] *What Is to Be Done?* with the admixture of a few Bazarovian traits'. Ginzburg, *On Psychological Prose*, p. 17.
4   N. N. Strakhov, 'Ottsy i deti', cited in N. N. Strakhov, *Literaturnaia kritika* (Moscow, 1984), p. 191; D. I. Pisarev, *Issledovaniia i materialy*, Vyp. 1 (Moscow, 1995), p. 6.
5   Paperno's comments on the paradox of realist aesthetics according to which 'Beauty is life' (*Prekrasnoe est' zhizn'*) are worth quoting here: 'This thesis became a slogan of the radical school of realistic aesthetics. But if reality is viewed as a realm of the beautiful, it follows that aesthetic categories can be applied to phenomena of real life. It is, perhaps, the greatest paradox of realism that radical realistic aesthetics, in spite of its affirmation of the separateness of art and reality, inspired a wide expansion of literature into life, quite comparable to that in the ages of romanticism and symbolism with their conscious intention of merging art and life'. Paperno, *Chernyshevsky and the Age of Realism*, p. 11.
6   Grevs, *Ocherki iz istorii Rimskogo zemlevladeniia*, p. 450.
7   A. Rieber in Duddington of *A Course in Russian History*, p. xxxiv.
8   Ibid.
9   Chumachenko, *V. O. Kliuchevskii – istochnikoved*, pp. 182–3.
10   Ibid., p. 205. Kliuchevskii's love of poetry and the nation's literary classics dated from his voracious, if somewhat chaotic, childhood reading at home. In among the religious literature on his father's bookshelves he discovered works by the eighteenth-century writer and philanthropist, Nikolai Novikov, Milton's *Paradise Lost*, Pushkin, and Karamzin's almanac, *Aglaia*. Of the formative novels he studied at school, Kliuchevskii singled out *Evgenii Onegin*, Turgenev's *Nest of Gentlefolk* and

Goncharov's seminal novel, *Oblomov*. The two prose novels, as he later recalled, read like funereal incantations, one an adieu to a particular way of life and the other to the disappearance of a social type. Turgenev's image of Shchigrovskii uezd 'forced us to think about the fate of our culture [*obrazovannost'*] which had torn people away from reality and turned them into martyrs of education'.

11 See Shmidt, 'Kliuchevskii i kul'tura Rossii', p. 311.
12 A. F. Smirnov, 'V. O. Kliuchevskii i otechestvennaia slovesnost'', in *V. O. Kliuchevskii. Literaturnye portrety* (Moscow, 1991), p. 38.
13 'Nedorosl' Fonvizina. (Opyt istoricheskogo ob'iasneniia uchebnoi p'esy)' [first published in *Iskusstvo i nauka*, 1896, 1]. Quotations from V. A. Aleksandrov (ed.), *Kliuchevskii. V. O. Istoricheskie portrety. Deiateli istoricheskoi mysli*, pp. 341–63. Kliuchevskii was referring to the decree on the freedom of the nobility, 'O darovanii volnosti i svobody vsemu rossiikomu dvorianstvu', 18 February 1762.
In many respects this essay should be read as a companion piece to his essay about Fonvizin's immediate contemporary, Nikolai Novikov, 'Vospominaniia o N. I. Novikove i ego vremeni', published a year earlier (*Russkaia mysl'* 1895, I; Aleksandrov, pp. 364–91). Here, Kliuchevskii explored the life and career of Novikov as an editor and *publitsist* (*zhivopisets*) against a backdrop of the Russian Enlightenment. The growth in literature in the mid- to late eighteenth century, however, did not produce enlightened minds; instead, the Russian-reading public developed a taste for penny-farthing novels rather than science. Only a few engaged with enlightenment philosophy; the majority encountered it second hand, trading in received ideas, or philosophical 'tag lines', the purpose of which was to amuse, or to nurture sentiment, rather than to source ideas as a tool for reflecting on social and/or individual welfare. (Alexandrov, pp. 371–2). Through his work, Novikov endeavoured to stem this trend of growing ignorance and irresponsibility. For him, 'true enlightenment should consist in the combined development of the mind and moral feeling, in a concordance of European education and national specificity (*samobytnost*')' (Aleksandrov, p. 377). Novikov found a handful of like-minded friends (freemasons) who shared his ambition to foster genuine enlightenment: Ivan Gregor'evich Shvarts, (1751–84), writer and professor of German at Moscow University, and later inspector of the university-affiliated pedagogical seminar; Ivan Petrovich Turgenev (1752–1807), director of Moscow University (father of the Decembrist, Nikolai). However, recognizing that their enlightenment project fell on deaf ears, they chose to focus on their own self-improvement as individuals.
14 Shatz, *The Time of Catherine the Great*, pp. xxii–xxiii.
15 Kliuchevskii, *Kurs*, p. 282; Chumachenko, *V. O. Kliuchevskii – istochnikoved*, p. 205.
16 Kliuchevskii, 'Nedorosl' Fonvizina', p. 352.
17 Ibid., p. 351.
18 Ibid., p. 360.
19 Ibid., p. 343.
20 Ibid., pp. 346, 348.
21 Ibid., p. 360.
22 Ibid., pp. 344–5.
23 First published in *Russkaia mysl'*, 2 (1887), Kliuchevskii originally delivered this at a public session of the Society of Lovers of Russian Letters (1 February 1887). My own translated quotations are taken from Alekandrov (ed.), *Kliuchevskii. V. O. Istoricheskie portrety*, pp. 408–28. An English translation by Marshall Shatz was published in 1982 in *Revue canadienne-américaine d'études slaves*, Vol. 16, No. 2 (Summer 1982), pp. 227–46.
24 Aleksandrov, p. 413; Shatz, *The Time of Catherine the Great*, p. 235.

25 Shatz, *The Time of Catherine the Great*, p. xxiii.
26 The figure of Chatskii was modelled on Chaadaev, a Decembrist sympathizer and author of the *Philosophical Letters* (1829), which triggered the famous Slavophile controversy during the 1830s and 1840s.
27 Smirnov, 'V. O. Kliuchevskii i otechestvennaia slovesnost',' p. 37.
28 Aleksandrov, p. 425.
29 Smirnov, 'V. O. Kliuchevskii i otechestvennaia slovesnost',' p. 35.
30 Aleksandrov, p. 415.
31 Compare Kliuchevskii's comments about the seventeenth-century statesmen, Ordin-Nashchokin and Prince Golitsyn: 'Like Nashchokin, [Golitsyn] was fluent in Latin and Polish. In his spacious Moscow house, considered by foreigners to be one of the most magnificent in Europe, everything was arranged in Western fashion. Wall space between the windows was taken up with tall mirrors; the walls were hung with pictures, portraits of Russian and foreign sovereigns, and German maps in gilt frames; the planetary system was painted on the ceilings; a number of clocks and a thermometer of artistic workmanship served as accessories. Golitsyn had a large library of various printed and manuscript books in Russian, Polish, and German. In between Polish and Latin grammars stood *The Kievan Chronicles*, a German book on geometry, the *Koran* in a Polish translation, four manuscripts about the staging of plays [...]. Golitsyn's house was a meeting place for educated foreigners who happened to visit Moscow, and his hospitality to them went further than that of other Moscow xenophiles, for he received even Jesuits, which was more than the others were prepared to do'. Duddington, pp. 379-80.
32 Aleksandrov, p. 416.
33 Ibid., pp. 419-20.
34 Ibid., p. 422.
35 Ibid., p. 423.
36 Ibid.
37 An allusion to the Decembrist uprising.
38 Alexander I's ministers: the former drafted a project for a constitutional monarchy, the latter was known for his reactionary policies.
39 Ibid., p. 424.
40 Ibid., p. 425.
41 'Rech' o Pushkine', in V. A. Aleksandrov, p. 398.
42 'Nedorosl' Fonvizina', p. 355; 'Rech' o Pushkine', p. 398.
43 'Vospominaniia o N. I. Novikove i ego vremeni', in V. A. Aleksandrov, pp. 364-91; Miliukov, 'V. O. Kliuchevskii', *Kharakteristiki i vospominaniia*, pp. 183-217.
44 Serman, 'Kliuchevskii i russkaia literatura', p. 422, who confirms: 'As a special form of a nation's spiritual/cultural (*dukhovnaia*) production, Russian literature was always a part of Kliuchevskii's intellectual life (*soznanie*), and to a significant degree shaped his historical outlook'. Ibid., p. 417.
45 The expression 'Tatiana's Method' is used by Kireeva (introduction & commentary), *V. O. Kliuchevskii. O nravstvennosti i russkoi literature* (Moscow, 1998), p. 22.
46 Ibid., p. 21.
47 Iu. M. Lotman, 'Ocherk dvorianskogo byta oneginskoi pory', in *Roman A. S. Pushkina 'Evgenii Onegin'. Kommentarii* (Leningrad, 1980), pp. 35-110.
48 See, for example, Miliukov, who suggested that, in order to appreciate an instinctual populism informing his dismissive attitude towards the eighteenth-century nobility, it was important to bear in mind Kliuchevskii's upbringing and the intellectual

climate of the early 1860s when he matriculated at the university. Miliukov, 'V. O. Kliuchevskii', pp. 209–11.
49 Grevs, *Ocherki iz istorii rimskogo zemlevladeniia*, pp. 87, 68–9. See also Bongard-Levin, Kotrelev and E. V. Liapustina (eds), 'Perepiska I. M. Grevsa i Viach. Ivanova – pamiatnik russkoi kul'tury', in *Istoriia i poeziia: Perepiska I. M. Grevsa i Viach. Ivanova*, pp. 287–396.
50 Ibid., pp. 63, 69.
51 Bod, *A New History of the Humanities*, p. 318.
52 Grevs, *Ocherki iz istorii rimskogo zemlevladeniia*, pp. 70, 63–4.
53 Ibid., p. 96. The estate was located near Licenza, about 40 kilometres northeast of Rome.
54 Ibid., pp. 132–84.
55 Ibid., p. 65.
56 Ibid., pp. 69, 499. See also Sveshnikov, *Peterburgskaia shkola medievistov*, pp. 69–70.
57 Ibid., p. 133.
58 See O. B. Vakhromeeva, 'Biograficheskii metod professora I. M. Grevsa', in *I. S. Turgenev glazami Ivana Mikhailovicha Grevsa* (St Petersburg, 2014), p. 11; Grevs, *Ocherki iz istorii rimskogo zemlevladeniia*, p. 455ff.
59 Ibid., pp. 70–1.
60 Ibid. See also Sveshnikov, *Peterburgskaia shkola medievistov*, p. 74.
61 Ibid., pp. 63, 71.
62 'Disput I. M. Grevsa, 21/v/1900', in *Istoricheskii vestnik*, Vol. 7 (1900), p. 351.
63 Grevs' viva, cited in Kaganovich *Russkie medievisty pervoi poloviny XX veka*, p. 23. See also F. Zelinskii's review in *Zhurnal Ministerstva narodnogo prosveshcheniia*, Vol. 7 (1900), pp. 156–73. Zelinskii disputed Grevs' claim that Horace's estate contained woodland and a vineyard. He also argued that Grevs exaggerated the extent of Atticus' wealth.
64 Kareev, 'Kniga g. Grevsa o rimskom zemlevladenii', t. xi, pp. 16–27.
65 Ibid., p. 16.
66 See the protocol of the ninth meeting of the Historical Society (13/x/1904), in N. I. Kareev (ed.), *Istoricheskoe obozrenie. Sbornik Istoricheskogo Obshchestva pri Imperatorskom S. Peterburgskom universitete*, t. 15 (St Petersburg, 1909), pp. 97–101. (p. 98).
67 Ibid., p. 99.
68 Ibid.
69 Ibid., p. 101.
70 Grevs, *Ocherki iz istorii rimskogo zemlevladeniia*, pp. 68–9, 321.
71 Ibid., p. 32.
72 Ibid., pp. 8–9. See also Bérélowitch, 'History in Russia Comes of Age', p. 124.
73 Grevs, ibid., p. 464.
74 Ibid., p. 450.
75 For a different assessment of genetic history, see Kaganovich, *Russkie medievisty*, pp. 32–4.
76 See Kaganovich, *Russkie medievisty*; Sveshnikov, *Peterburgskaia shkola medievistov*; Beaune-Gray, 'Vers une histoire des mentalités', pp. 329–43. Also by Beaune-Gray, *I. M. Grevs. Un historien à travers les révolutions (1860–1941)* (Paris, 2017).
77 Kelley, *Fortunes of History*, p. 264.
78 Ibid., p. 266.
79 Ibid. As Kelley rightly notes, however, the term 'science' itself was confusingly multivalent: 'Few wanted to reject the idea of history as a science but there was little consensus as to its definition'. Ibid., p. 317.

80 See Bod, *A New History of the Humanities*, p. 312; H. White, *Metahistory*, p. 259, and below Chapter 6.
81 Kelley, *Fortunes of History*, pp. 304–5.
82 By 'psychology' he meant social or collective psychology (*Volkerpsychologie*) as developed by Wilhelm Wundt, and which Lamprecht argued offered the best approach to cultural history.
83 Kaganovich, 'Vokrug *Ocherkov iz istorii rimskogo zemlevladeniia* I. M. Grevsa', p. 200.
84 Grevs wrote an article on the French historian for the authoritative Brokgaus-Efron encyclopaedic dictionary, and one of his earliest publications was a review of Fustal de Coulanges' work on the Roman colonate in *Zhurnal Ministerstva narodnogo prosveshcheniia* (November–December 1886), pp. 347–53.
85 Sveshnikov – rightly, I think – detects a concurrence of influences. Grevs, he argues, followed Fustel de Coulanges in that he subscribed to interpretations in favour of links between ancient Rome and the medieval world, as opposed to the 'German view' predicated on a break with the past. Although a self-styled 'historian-realist', who expressed faith in progress, he also sought 'eternal values' in the Middle Ages, which remained present in all eras, but not at the cost of neglecting the individual specificities of any given age; he was Rankean in that he advocated the careful study of facts in order to draw a picture of the past in all its concreteness. Thus, against Fustel de Coulanges, he did not accept the view that historical processes are blind, impersonal: Grevs always sought individual traits 'the face of an epoch' (*litso epokhi*), '*litso kul'tury*', '*litso goroda*'. This goes some way to explaining his motivation to run specialist courses in historical biography at the university after 1900. Sveshnikov, *Peterburgskaia shkola medievistov*, pp. 167–8.
86 Kelley, *Fortunes of History*, p. 209.
87 Ibid., 216.
88 Unlike some of his immediate contemporaries, such as Fustel de Coulanges and Gabriel Monod, who conceived history as an 'exact science', Taine oscillated in his conception of history as 'science' or 'art'. See Patrizia Lombardo, 'Hippolyte Taine between Art and Science', *Yale French Studies*, 77, Reading the Archive: On Texts and Institutions (1990), pp. 117–33. See also R. Gordon Kelly, 'Literature and the Historian', *American Quarterly*, Vol. 26, No. 2 (May 1974), pp. 141–59.
89 Taine famously linked literary developments with *race, milieu et moment* – three notions which have now become largely synonymous with his name. It is, however, important to point out that by 'race' Taine meant the collective cultural dispositions that govern everyone, or shared inheritances, rather than cultural and ethnic differences, which we tend to associate the term with nowadays. Some critics have suggested 'nation' as a more appropriate translation. 'Milieu' referred to the environment, and 'moment' is perhaps best rendered as 'Zeitgeist'.
90 On Kareev's reading of Taine, see Chapter 8.
91 Shmidt, for example, asks whether Grevs took inspiration from Kliuchevskii. S. Shmidt 'I. M. Grevs i vospitanie istoriei', in Yu. V. Krivosheev (ed.), *Peterburgskie issledovaniia. Sbornik nauchnikh statei* (St Petersburg, 2006), p. 26.
92 Serman, 'Kliuchevskii i russkaia literatura', *Canadian–American Slavic Studies*, Vol. 20, p. 436. Similarly, Georgii Fedotov concluded that, with Kliuchevskii, 'Social history turns into the study of social character'. G. P. Fedotov, 'Rossiia Klyuchevskogo', ibid., p. 218.
93 Grevs, *Ocherki iz istorii rimskogo zemlevladeniia*, p. 39; Sveshnikov, *Peterburgskaia shkola medievistov*, p. 63.

Chapter 6

1. L. Karsavin et al., *K 25-letiiu uchebno-pedagogicheskoi deiatel'nosti Ivana Mikhailovicha Grevsa: sbornik statei ego uchenikov* (St Petersburg, 1911), pp. iv–v.
2. Grevs, *K teorii i praktike 'Ekskursii' kak orudiia nauchnogo izuchemiia istorii v universitetakh* (St Petersburg, 1910), p. 10 (first published in *Zhurnal Ministerstva narodnogo prosveshcheniia*, Vol. 7 (1910), pp. 21–64). Earlier, in his master's dissertation, Grevs had expressed much the same sentiment: 'Living under the beautiful Roman skies, amongst its magnificent monuments [...], you begin to feel the influence of a certain cultural ambience (*obstanovka*) on your state of being; then, you come to appreciate the significance of this for scientific research'. *Ocherki iz istorii rimskogo zemlevladeniia*, p. xix.
3. Grevs, *K teorii i praktike 'Ekskursii'*, p. 11
4. Ibid., p. 48.
5. Perhaps a better 'English sounding' rendering of excursionism would be local history, regional studies or urban studies. However, in historical methodology, these are established fields of enquiry and do not entirely match the nature of Grevs' project that he developed over the course of some thirty years with his students.
6. See, for example, Grevs' entry on St Augustine for the *Novyi entsiklopedicheskii slovar'* t. 1 (St Petersburg, 1911), pp. 127–49.
7. L. Karsavin, *Ocherki religioznoi zhizni Italii* (St Petersburg, 1912); also, *Osnovy srednevekoi religioznosti v XII–XIII vekakh preimushchestvenno v Italii* (Petrograd, 1915).
8. Danièle Beaune-Gray notes that: 'En effet, Grevs non seulement enseigne à ses étudients le travail préalable d'examen des sources, la cohérence entre la source choisie et l'objet de la recherche, ce qui n'exclut pas les textes narratifs ou littéraires, mais encore il leur montre comment dégager des notions fondamentales chez un auteur en les confrontant dans leurs évolution au fil du temps'. 'Vers une histoire des mentalites', p. 336.
9. Antsiferov, *Iz dum o bylom*, p. 279. Antsiferov used this method himself, both in his project to advance literary excursionism in the 1920s, and later in his 1940s' *kandidatskaia* thesis about Dostoevskii, where he explored the cultural resonances of, for example, 'earth' (*zemlia*) and 'stones' (*kamni*) in the author's lexicon. *Problemy urbanizma v russkoi khudozhestvennoi literature: Opyt postroeniia obraza goroda – Peterburga Dostoevskogo – na osnove analiza literaturnykh traditsii* [1944].
10. N. Perlina, 'Ivan Milkailovich Grevs i Nikolai Pavlovich Antsiferov: k obosnovaniiu ikh kul'turologicheskoi pozitsii', in T. B. Pritykina (ed.), *Antsiferovskie chteniia. Materialy i tezisy konferentsii* (Leningrad, 1989), p. 84.
11. Ibid. Perlina argues that as historians of culture brought up on classical positivism, Grevs and Antsiferov retained respect for the fact, but significantly rethought the general positivist picture of the world insofar as they were working at a time increasingly dominated by symbolism, neo-Kantianism and Bergsonian intuition. See also Kaganovich, *Russkie medievisty pervoi poloviny XX veka*, pp. 62–8: Sveshnikov, *Peterburgskaia shkola medievistov*, pp. 167–8. The limits, however, of Grevs' engagement with symbolist semantics were, for example, tested by the difficulty he had with Karsavin's theory of 'srednii chelovek' (the average man), which the latter developed in his thesis on St Francis of Assisi and medieval spirituality. Grevs: 'Novyi trud po religioznoi istorii srednevekoi Italii v Russkoi nauchnoi literature' (St Petersburg, 1913) [offprint], pp. 3–72. Nor, as has been pointed out, was Grevs ever drawn to the cult of Dionysius associated with his erstwhile friend, Viacheslav Ivanov.

12 This is borne out by numerous references to 'positivist' literature in Grevs' articles on urban culture. Among these was a popular study by the Belgian art historian, H. Fierens-Gevaert, *Psychologie d'une ville. Essai sur Bruges* (Paris, 1907). Kaganovich, however, places Grevs' 'urban anthropomorphism' in a lineage dating back to François Guizot (his *Histoire de la civilisation en France, 1829-32*) and the Russian romantics. See Kaganovich, *Russkie medievisty pervoi poloviny XX veka*, p. 50ff. Certainly there are grounds for this: Grevs was aware of and referenced a longstanding tendency among writers, philosophers and artists to personify the city.
13 Grevs *Zapiski* cited in Skrzhinskaia, 'Ivan Mikhailovich Grevs. Biograficheskii ocherk', p. 245.
14 Sveshnikov, *Peterburgskaia shkola medievistov*, p. 57.
15 Emily D. Johnson, *How St. Petersburg Learned to Study Itself: The Russian Idea of Kraevedenie* (Studies of the Harriman Institute, Columbia University, 2006), p. 98. Sveshnikov, *Peterburgskaia shkola medievistov*, pp. 283-309. In the 1890s, the historian, Sergei Platonov, had conducted trips with students at the Bestuzhevskie to Novgorod, Pskov and Moscow. See Grevs, *K teorii i praktike 'Ekskursii'*, p. 8.
16 Johnson, ibid., p. 100.
17 Ibid., p. 101.
18 Ibid.
19 Grevs, 'Neskol'ko teoreticheskikh zamechanii ob obshcheobrazovatel'nom znachenii ekskursii', in *Pamiatnaia knizhka Tenishevskogo uchilishcha za 1900/1*, p. 108. Cited in Johnson, ibid., p. 101.
20 Grevs, *Nauchnye progulki po istoricheskim tsentram Italii* (Moscow, 1903), pp. 3-4.
21 Antsiferov, *Iz dum o bylom*, p. 400. According to Danièle Beaune-Gray, Grevs' field trips were also inspired by the example of the French medievalist, Denis Jean Achille Luchaire (1846-1908) whom Grevs had met in the 1890s. Beaune-Gray, *I. M. Grevs*, p. 323.
22 Antisferov, ibid., p. 168.
23 A major author studied during the academic year 1906-7 was St Francis of Assisi. This included work on biographical legends about him (Tomaso di Celano *Speculum perfectionis*), religious poetry by the thirteenth-century Franciscan Jacopone da Todi, as well as the chronicles of Salimbene.
24 Johnson, *How St. Petersburg Learned to Study Itself*, p. 105.
25 Vakhromeeva (ed.), *Chelovek s otkrytym serdtsem*, pp. 286-7.
26 Ibid., pp. 282-9; Grevs, 'Ekskursiia v Italiiu, 1912', PFA RAN, f. 726, op. 1. D.188, pp. 1-21; Johnson, *How St. Petersburg Learned to Study Itself*, p. 105.
27 *Ocherki Florentiiskoi kul'tury*. vyp. 1: 'Progulki po naucho-khudozhestvennym tsentram Italii' (Moscow, 1903); 'K teorii i praktike 'ekskursii' kak orudiia nauchnogo izucheniia istorii v universitetakh (Poezdka v Italiiu so studentami v 1907g)', *Zhurnal Ministerstva narodnogo prosveshcheniia* Vol. 7 (1910), pp. 21-64; 'Ekskursiia v Italiiu, 1912' (unpublished).
28 Johnson, *How St. Petersburg Learned to Study Itself*, p. 103.
29 'Ekskursiia v Italiiu, 1912', in *Chelovek s otkrytym serdtsem*, pp. 286-7.
30 Ibid.
31 S. Fitzpatrick, *The Commissariat of Enlightenment: Soviet Organization of Education and the Arts under Lunarcharsky, October 1917-1921* (London; New York, 1970); also by Fitzpatrick: *The Cultural Front: Power and Culture in Revolutionary Russia* (Ithaca; London, 1992).

32 In his memoirs, Antsiferov described a field trip to Vologda in the summer of 1922: *Iz dum o bylom*, pp. 407–11.
33 Antsiferov, *O metodakh i tipakh istoriko-kul'turnykh ekskursii* (Petrograd, 1923). See also the appendix to his memoirs, *Iz dum o bylom*, pp. 399–410; I. I. Poliakskii, 'Opyt novoi organizatsii ekskursionnogo dela v shkolakh. Ekskursionnaia Sektsiia i ekskursionnye stantsii', *Ekskursionnoe delo*, 1 (1921), pp. 1–20. It is worth emphasizing that, although the intention was to meet the request of Narkompros to outline the practice of a new revolutionary method of schooling, Poliakskii's account of the different types of excursions – including humanities and art historical trips (pp. 12–13), together with his overview of the growing number of excursion centres in the regions – was, as he noted in his introduction, building on experiments conducted in field of natural science dating back to 1901 (ibid., p. 1).
34 I. Grevs, 'Monumental'nyi gorod i istoricheskie ekskursii (osnovnaia ideia obrazovatel'nykh puteshestvii po krupnym tsentram kul'tury)', *Ekskursionnoe delo*, Vol. 1 (1921), pp. 21–34. [my quotations are taken from a fourteen-page offprint]; 'Dal'nie gumanitarnye ekskursii i ikh vospitatel'no-obrazovatel'nyi smysl', 4–6 (1922), pp. 1–12.
35 Grevs, 'Monumental'nyi gorod', p. 1. Also: Grevs, 'Gorod kak predmet kraevedeniia', *Kraevedenie*, Vol. 1, No. 3 (1924), pp. 247–9.
36 Grevs, 'Monumental'nyi gorod', pp. 2, 8. In this connection, Grevs referenced Fierens-Gevaet, *Psychologie d'une ville*, as well as Renan (on the origins of Christianity), Taine (his travels in Italy), the German historian, Ferdinand Gregorovius (*Wanderjahre in Italien*, 1856–77) and the novels of Emile Zola as models for the study of collective psychology and cities as 'spiritual entities'.
37 Ibid., p. 8.
38 Ibid., p. 4.
39 Grevs, 'Gorod kak predmet kraevedeniia', p. 246. Grevs was also familiar with the works of Paul Vidal de la Blache (under whom Marc Bloch and Lucien Febvre, cofounders of the French *Annales* School, had studied), and Jean Bruhnes, author of *La géographie humaine* (1910).
40 Antsiferov, *Byl' i mif Peterburga* (Petrograd, 1924), p. 5.
41 Grevs, 'Monumental'nyi gorod', p. 7.
42 Ibid., p. 4. Later, in an article on literary excursionism, Antsiferov made much the same point: 'Studying "literary nests," one should not only collate material which throws light on biography and/or the degree to which an author interacted with his surroundings, more importantly, perhaps, it is a matter of studying the reflection of those surroundings in his creative writing so as to capture aspects of the creative person which, to date, have not received attention'. See 'Belletristy-kraevedy. Vopros o sviazi kraevedeniia s khudozhestvennoi literaturoi', t. 4, No. 1, *Kraevedenie* (1927), p. 46.
43 Grevs, ibid., p. 4. The book was 'in press' by 1921, but was eventually published in 1922.
44 Antsiferov graduated from the Department of History and Philology, Petrograd University in 1915. In addition to his involvement with the Excursion Institute discussed in this chapter, he taught history in a number of secondary schools and institutes of further education: Iavorskaia Gymnasium for Women, the A. S. Cherniaev Applied Training School, a boarding school for homeless children located in Krasnaia Slavianka (a district in the outskirts of Petrograd), the Nekrasov Second Pedagogical Institute (1919–26) and the College of Art History (1925–29). From 1919, he also worked at the tour section of the Museum Department of the Petrograd

Art and Scientific Institutions. In 1921, he was appointed Member of the Old Petersburg Society where he ran a seminar dedicated to the study of 'city sightseeing'. Between 1918 and 1925 he attended meetings of Aleksandr Meier's Religious and Philosophical Society, *Voskresenie* (Resurrection). On Antsiferov, see, for example, D. S. Likhachev, *Nikolai Pavlovich Antsiferov (1889-1958). Kommentarii k faksimil'noi chasti.(Dusha Peterburga)*. Part I: Introduction; Johnson, *How St. Petersburg Learned to Study Itself*, p. 180ff. On Antsiferov's involvement with the Excursion Institute and the Central Bureau for Regional Studies, see above, pp. 127–31.

45 Antsiferov, *Dusha Peterburga* (Moscow, 1991), p. 7.
46 Ibid., p. 48. See also S. Iu. Zimina, 'Problema bessoznatel'nogo v kult'turologii Antsiferova', in T. B. Pritykina (ed.), *Antsiferovskie chteniia, materialy i tezisy konferentsii* (Leningrad, 1989), pp. 88–9.
47 Antsiferov used this expression in the Preface to his kandidatskaia dissertation on Dostoevskii's Petersburg (1944), which he defended just months after the end of the Leningrad blockade, adding: 'Now, more than twenty years on, undertaking a new study on a similar theme, I hope that, although it deals with Leningrad's past, it has some bearing on the events that have assailed this great city, as tragic destiny raises this city-hero through a path of suffering to the heights of world glory'. Antsiferov, *Problemy urbanizma v russkoi khudozhestvennoi literature: opyt postroeniia obraza goroda – Peterburga Dostoevskogo – na osnove analiza literaturnykh traditsii* (Moscow, 2009), p. 16.
48 See Johnson, *How St. Petersburg Learned to Study Itself*, p. 137.
49 Ibid., p. 128. See also the review by G. Flerovskii in *The Slavonic Review*, Vol. 5, No. 13 (June 1926), pp. 193–8.
50 Grevs, 'Monumental'nyi gorod', p. 4. As Antsiferov put it: 'To a certain extent, the method of artistic intuition (*intuitivnyi metod poznaniia mira khudozhnikov*) is both germane to (*rodstvennyi*) and necessary for the regionalist'. In this connection, he referred to the writer, Mikhail Privshin. See his 'Belletristy-kraevedy', p. 32.
51 Antsiferov, *Dusha Peterburga*, p. 88
52 Antsiferov's two daughters died of cholera in 1919, thereby lending a deeply personal inflection to the sense of tragedy, which he used to frame his analysis of the city.
53 It is also worth noting that revolution, war and, later, the blockade destroyed places on the outskirts of Petersburg – Detskoe Selo, Pavlovsk, Gatchina, Tsarskaia Slavianka – all of which were closely intertwined with Antsiferov's personal and family memory. See his *Iz dum o bylom*, p. 326ff.
54 Antsiferov, *Problemy urbanizma*, p. 2.
55 Antsiferov, *O metodakh*, pp. 21–2.
56 Ibid., p. 33. See also his *Puti izucheniia goroda kak sotsial'nogo organizma: opyt kompleksnogo podkhoda* (Leningrad, 1925).
57 *O metodakh*, pp. 32–3.
58 Ibid. See also his Belletristy-kraevedy.
59 Antsiferov, *O metodakh*, p. 7.
60 Antsiferov had known Iurii Tynianov and Boris Eikhenbaum since their student days before the war, and during the 1920s, he met Bakhtin on several occasions at meetings of the Voskresenie circle. See D. Moskovskaia, 'Zhizn' skvoz' gorod: N. P. Antsiferov – avtor lokal'nogo metoda v literaturovedenii', in *Problemy urbanizma*, pp. 508–9.
61 *O metodakh*, p. 18; See also Antsiferov's memoir, *Iz dum o bylom*, p. 165ff.
62 Moskovskaia, 'Zhizn' skvoz' gorod', p. 505.

63 Antsiferov, 'Belletristi-kraevedy', pp. 31-2. Antsiferov's remark to the effect that he had elected his 'master' is cited from his memoirs, p. 165.
64 Moskovskaia, 'Zhizn' skvoz' gorod', p. 500.
65 Johnson, *How St. Petersburg Learned to Study Itself*, p. 126
66 Ibid., p. 128.
67 Antsiferov, *Dusha Peterburga*, p. 18. On 'understanding' (*Verstehen*) as a defining feature of humanities scholarship in contrast to the explanatory function of natural science (*Erklären*), see, for example, Kelley, *Fortunes of History*, pp. 212–17.
68 D. S. Likhachev, *Nikolai Pavlovich Antsiferov (1889-1958). Prilozhenie k reprintnomy vosproizvedeniiu: 1922-1924* (Moscow, 1991), p. 17 and footnote 10 with reference to V. N. Toporov, 'Peterburg i "Peterburgskii tekst russkoi literatury"', in *Semiotika goroda i gorodskoi kul'tury* (Petersburg-Tartu, 1984), pp. 4-29.
69 Antsiferov's three-part study of St Petersburg was reviewed by, among others, V. Briusov, Tynianov and L. P. Grossman. See Moskovskaia, 'Zhizn' skvoz' gorod', pp. 516-18.
70 See, for example, Pritykina (ed.), *Antsiferovskie chteniia*; Johnson, *How St. Petersburg Learned to Study Itself*.
71 Iu. Lotman and B. Uspenskii, 'Simvolika Peterburga i problema semiotiki goroda' [1984], in Iu. M. Lotman, *Izbrannye stat'i*, Vol. 2 (Tallin, 1992), p. 14.
72 Ibid., p. 14 (footnote 11).
73 Ibid., pp. 13-14.
74 Johnson, *How St. Petersburg Learned to Study Itself*, pp. 112-23, 146.
75 Ibid., p. 158.
76 Ibid., p. 155.
77 Grevs, 'Gumanitarnyi otdel Leningradskogo Ekskursionnogo instituta (ego obshchie zadachi i blizhaishii plan)', in Vakhromeeva (ed.), *Chelovek s otkrytym serdtsem*, pp. 307-10.
78 Ibid., p. 308.
79 Ibid., p. 309.
80 Antsiferov taught at the College of Art History (1925-9) and between 1925 and 1929 was, alongside Grevs, employed by the Petrograd (Leningrad) Department of the Central Regional Study Bureau.
81 Grevs, 'Gorodskie landshafty (etiud iz kul'turnoi geografii)', *Voprosy geografii v novoi shkole* (Leningrad, 1926) pp. 102-3; 'Gorod kak predmet shkolnogo kraevedeniia', *Voprosy kraevedeniia v shkole* (Leningrad, 1926); 'Istoriia v kraevedenii', *Kraevedenie*, Vol. 4 (1926) pp. 487-508. See also V. F. Kozlov, 'Ivan Mikhailovich Grevs kak teoretik i praktik kraevedeniia 1920-kh godov (po materialam zhurnala *Kraevedenie*)', in Iu. V. Krivosheev (ed.), *Peterburgskie issledovaniia. Sbornik nauchnykh statei* (St Petersburg, 2006), pp. 136-47; A. G. Smirnova, '"Rol" I. M. Grevsa v pazrabotke ekskursionnoi metodiki', in Krivosheev, *Peterburgskie issledovaniia*, pp. 148-63. Antsiferov, *Puti izucheniia goroda, kak sotsial'nogo organizma: opyt kompleksnogo podkhoda* (Leningrad, 1925); also, by Antsiferov, 'Belletristy-kraevedy' (1927).
82 Grevs, 'Gorodskie landshafty', p. 102.
83 Antsiferov, *Teoriia i praktika literaturnykh ekskursii* (Leningrad, 1926), p. 132.
84 Ibid., p. 18.
85 Ibid., p. 89.
86 Ibid., p. 79.
87 For example, *Po Lermontovskim mestam [putevoditel' - spravochnik]* (Moscow, 1940); *Moskva Pushkina* (Moscow, 1950), which had a print run of 10,000 copies.

88 *Problemy urbanizma v russkoi khudozhestvennoi literature: Opyt postroeniia obraza goroda – Peterburga Dostoevskogo – na osnove analiza literaturnykh traditsii* (Moscow, 2009), edited by Natal'ia Kornienko. Among Antsiferov's case studies for comparative purposes were Balzac's Paris and Charles Dickens' London. Antsiferov sourced a range of urban studies dating from the nineteenth and twentieth centuries, including: Jean-Jacques Ampère, *La Grèce: Rome et Dante, études littéraires d'après nature* (Paris, 1850); various writings by Gabriel Ferry; Edwin Beresford Chancellor, *The London of Charles Dickens, Being an Account of the Haunts of His Characters and the Topographical Settings of His Novels* (New York, 1924). He also drew on native Russian studies, for example, Mikhail Gershenzon *Griboedovskaia Moskva* [1914] and monographs/articles dedicated to the life and work of Dostoevskii by the Soviet scholar, Leonid Grossman. See Antsiferov, 'Materialy k issledovaniiu problemy urbanizma v khudozhestvennoi literature' in ibid., pp. 22–44: On Gershenzon, see Chapter 7.
89 Ibid., p. 16.
90 Ibid., Editorial note, p. 498.
91 Kaganovich, *I. M. Grevs*; Sveshnikov, *Peterburgskaia shkola medievistov*; Danièle Beaune-Gray, 'Vers une histoire des mentalites', in Marc Weinstein (ed.), *La Geste russe*.
92 Antsiferov, *Iz dum o bylom*, p. 170.
93 A sense of communion with the past through excursions is, as we have seen, a leitmotif in the literature.
94 L. P. Karsavin et al., *K dvadtsatipiatiletiiu uchebno-pedagogicheskoi deiatel'nosti Ivana Mikhailovicha Grevsa: sbornik statei ego uchenikov* (St Petersburg, 1911); O. Dobiash-Rozhdestvenskaia, A. I. Khomentovskaia and G. P. Fedotov (eds), *Srednevekovoi byt': Sbornik statei* (Leningrad, 1925).
95 Gukovskii, 'Turniry v Italii na iskhode srednykh vekov', pp. 50–77. In the post-Stalinist era, Gukovskii was known for his studies of Leonardo da Vinci and the Italian Renaissance.
96 Khomontovskaia, 'Lukka vremen kupecheskoi dinastii Gvinidzhi', pp. 78–112; M. Tikhanova-Klimenko, 'Parizhskii Malyi Most', pp. 113–33; Antsiferov, 'Cherty sel'skogo byta vo frantsuzskom gorode', pp. 148–61.
97 Stepanovich, 'Petukh na goticheskom sobore', pp. 272–9. I believe that A. Stepanovich was a pseudonym used by Aleksandra Liublinskaia.
98 E. Skrzhinskaia, 'Ob odnom srednevekovom "kurorte"', pp. 260–71.
99 A further example of this practice of career switch within the humanities disciplines is provided by the Odessa-based medievalist, Petr Bitsilli (1879–1953). Bitsilli defended his dissertation on the twelfth-century Italian Franciscan friar, Salimbene di Adam, in 1916 (Grevs was on the panel of examiners). After the October Revolution, he emigrated, settling in Belgrade where he taught Russian literature and literary criticism. The point to stress, however, as Boris Kaganovich does in his essay on the career of Bitsilli is that his literary critical writings were grounded in the same methodological principles and approaches that he had worked with as a historian, namely, to draw out what was individual (principium individuationis) in the creative process. Bitsilli, *Etiudy o russkoi poezii* (Prague, 1926); Kaganovich, *Russkie medievisty pervoi poloviny XX veka*, p. 197ff. See also D. I. Weber, 'The Significance of Religion in Peter Bitsilli's Research', *Vestnik Sankt-Peterburgskogo Universiteta: Filosofiia i konfliktologiia*, Vol. 34, No. 1 (2018), pp. 115–21.

Chapter 7

1. Dostoevskii, *Diary of a writer, 1873–1876*, cited in Wachtel, *An Obsession with History*, p. 13: 'I would burn all history and punish its authors', he once declared. Tolstoi's parody of textbook histories targeted the great men theory and political history dating from the mid-nineteenth century. See his epilogue to *War and Peace*, part II, chapter 1. See also I. Berlin, *The Hedgehog and the Fox* (London, 1953), pp. 21–2; Formozov, *Klassiki russkoi literatury i istoricheskaia nauka*, p. 143.
2. Wachtel lists a number of possible explanations as to why Russian writers seemingly monopolized history: 'The putative uniqueness of the Russian historical situation; the impact of censorship; the unpredictable interaction of native Russian traditions and borrowed European genres, the relative weakness of the historical profession in Russia'. Wachtel, *An Obsession with History*, p. 18. Historians, themselves, were conscious of (and lamented) the difficulties of bringing historical research into the public arena, evidenced by the low circulation of specialists journals, and, for much of the nineteenth century, were constrained by the fact that the range of topics taught in university curriculum were subject to government inspection which undermined academic freedom.
3. Kliuchevskii, 'Rech', proiznesennaia Pushkinu' v torzhestvennom sobranii Moskovskogo universiteta 6 iiunia 1880g v den' otkrytiia pamiatnika Pushkinu', in V. A. Aleksandrov, p. 392. The expression 'divinatory of historical truth' is Wachtel's, ibid., p. 18.
4. N. Kareev, 'Pushkin, kak poet evropeiskii' Rech', prof. Varshavskogo univ-a, N. I. Kareeva, proiznesennaia na pushkinskom prazdnike v Warshave, 4-go Iiunia 1880 goda', in *Filologicheskie zapiski*, vyp. V, 1880 (Voronezh), pp. 1–2.
5. Ibid., p. 5.
6. Ibid., pp. 9–10.
7. Smirnov, 'V. O. Kliuchevskii i otechestvennaia slovesnost',' p. 35.
8. Kliuchevskii, 'Pamiati o Pushkine' (1899), cited in Aleksandrov, *Kliuchevskii. V. O. Istoricheskie portrety*, p. 406.
9. Ibid., p. 404; Smirnov, 'V. O. Kliuchevskii i otechestvennaia slovesnost',' p. 34.
10. Kliuchevskii, 'Pamiati o Pushkine', p. 406.
11. Kliuchevskii, 'Rech' o Pushkine' (1880), in V. A. Aleksandrov, p. 394. This address formed part of celebrations marking the unveiling of the famous Pushkin monument on Tver'skaia Street in central Moscow.
12. In addition to Wachtel, see, for example, S. Evdokimova, *Pushkin's Historical Imagination* (New Haven and London, 1999); V. D. Skvoznikov, *Pushkin: istoricheskaia mysl' poeta* (Moscow, 1999). A little known early study by the future historian-bureaucrat in the 1920s, Mikhail Pokrovskii, examined the place of Roman historians in Pushkin's portrait of Boris Godunov. Pokrovskii argued that the individual characteristics of the tsar blended with the poet's reflections on the nature of autocracy in general, negative aspects of which Pushkin had himself experienced, and which he endeavoured to make sense of with reference to Tacitus's unflattering account of the Emperor Tiberius. M. Pokrovskii, 'Pushkin i rimskie istoriki', in *Sbornik statei posviashchennykh Vasiliiu Osipovichu Kliuchevskomu ego uchenikami, druz'iami i pochitateliami ko dniu tritsatiletiia ego professorskoi deiatel'nosti v Moskovskom Universitete* (5 dek. 1879–5 dek. 1909) (Moscow, 1909), pp. 478–86.

13 As Wachtel writes, the popularity of Karamzin's *History* meant that Pushkin was able to use Karamzin's material and transpose it to his fictionalized Boris Godunov 'secure in the knowledge that his audience would recognize and appreciate the differences between Karamzin's version and his own dramatic one'. Wachtel, *An Obsession with History*, p. 75.

14 Wachtel suggests that the fact that Karamzin did not cover the Pugachev rebellion prompted Pushkin to write his own *History* of this episode, commissioned by Tsar Nicholas.

15 Kliuchevskii, 'Rech' o Pushkine', p. 394; Smirnov, 'V. O. Kliuchevskii i otechestvennaia slovesnost',' p. 33; Striedter, 'Poetic Genre and the Sense of History in Pushkin', p. 304.

16 Kliuchevskii, ibid.

17 Ibid., p. 395. As I have argued, it was this cocktail of indigenous and Western traits, the various ways the nobility responded to Europeanization – from superficial mimicry to full assimilation – that, for Kliuchevskii, was the touchstone for understanding modern Russia.

18 Ibid., p. 398.

19 See Smirnov, 'V. O. Kliuchevskii i otechestvennaia slovesnost'.'

20 Kliuchevskii, 'Rech' o Pushkine' p. 392.

21 Striedter, 'Poetic Genre and the Sense of History in Pushkin', p. 300. See also Iu. Aikhenval'd, 'Kliuchevskii. Myslitel' i khudozhnik'.

22 Kliuchevskii, 'Rech' o Pushkine', p. 398.

23 Cited from *Polnoe sobranie sochinenii*, Vol. 12 (Moscow, 1928–53), p. 338 in Wachtel, *An Obsession with History*, p. 116.

24 Tolstoi's epilogue to *War and Peace* as summarized by I. Berlin in what still ranks as a classic study of Tolstoi's view of history, *The Hedgehog and the Fox* (New York, 1953). Berlin argued that Tolstoi's interest in history was philosophically driven by a desire to penetrate first causes, to explain the meaning of life and death, but that he was obsessed by his thesis, which he ultimately failed to resolve. Berlin summarized the two horns of the dilemma as: 'the contrast between the universal and all-important but delusive experience of free will, the feeling of responsibility, the value of private life generally, on the one hand; and on the other, the reality of inexorable historical determinism, not, indeed, experienced directly, but known to be true on irrefutable theoretical grounds' (p. 29).

25 See Wachtel, *An Obsession with History*, pp. 100–1, 116; N. Kareev, *Istoricheskaia filosofiia L.N. Tol'stogo v 'Voine i mire'* (St Petersburg, 1888), p. 37 (first published in *Vestnik Evropy*, Vol. 4 (July–August 1887), pp. 227–69).

26 In addition to the epilogue, the novel itself contained some didactic passages which interrupted the main narrative and which most critics regard as infelicitous.

27 Cited in Wachtel, *An Obsession with History*, p. 90; *Polnoe sobranie sochinenii*, Vol. 15, p. 242.

28 See Berlin, *The Hedgehog and the Fox*, pp. 5–6.

29 Kareev, *Istoricheskaia filosofiia L.N. Tol'stogo*, p. 42.

30 Ibid., p. 26.

31 Ibid., pp. 26, 28.

32 Ibid., p. 25; also, p. 8.

33 Ibid., p. 43; see also I. Berlin, *The Hedgehog and the Fox*, pp. 33–4.

34 In section two of his essay about Tolstoi's philosophy of history, Kareev explained what he meant by the terms idealism, idealization, realism and naturalism with reference to literary trends. He wrote: 'Historiography, especially the popular

variety, tends to draw on prevailing literary tastes of the age; in it we find examples of the classical style, as well as the romantic manner of idealizing historical figures and events. A sober attitude to past events without any attempt to place them on a classical pedestal of heroism or to surround them in a romantic halo of perfection is precisely what we mean by realism in historiography. Recent Russian literature developed under the influence of west European models, first in the age of pseudo-classicism followed by neo-romanticism; its first steps on the path of independence coincided with the demise of the idealization of reality. Russian realism was not thought out theoretically, but it did not go to the extremes of naturalism, which we witness in France as a reaction to idealization; rather it managed to retain a legitimate place for idealism in the novel, but to avoid the idealization commonly found in the German novel. In other words, realism opposes none other than idealization, and this we encounter both in the domain of poetry and in historiography'. Ibid., pp. 15–16.

35   Berlin, *The Hedgehog and the Fox*, p. 35.
36   Wachtel, *An Obsession with History*, p. 106.
37   Kareev, *Istoricheskaia filosofiia L.N. Tol'stogo*, p. 6.
38   Ibid., pp. 6–7.
39   Grevs, 'O vliianii Turgeneva na menia i o soprikosnovenii s nim' [unpublished, 1925], cited in Vakhromeeva (ed.), *Chelovek s otkrytym serdtsem*, pp. 313–15.
40   Grevs was referring to the Oldenburg fraternity. See Chapter 2.
41   Grevs, 'O vliianii Turgeneva na menia.' See also S. G. Serdiukova, 'I. M. Grevs i I. S. Turgenev', in Iu. V. Krivosheev (ed.), *Peterburgskie issledovaniia. Sbornik nauchnykh statei* (St Petersburg, 2006), pp. 91–8.
42   Grevs, cited in Vakhromeeva (ed.), *Chelovek s otkrytym serdtsem*, p. 302.
43   'I have started studying Turgenev with renewed intensity – his biography, ideas, his style. I am compiling a bibliography, and am working through the literature about him'. Ibid., 315.
44   Other writings on Turgenev include: 'Religioznaia drama Turgeneva' (unpublished 1927), a second edition of his study about Turgenev and Viardot in 1928. Grevs spent the summer of 1928 in the Turgenev museum (located in the village of Spasskoe-Lutovinovo, Orel region) on the basis of which he wrote an account of Turgenev's worldview. In 1931 he attempted, unsuccessfully, to publish Turgenev's correspondence. In 1936, he gave two public lectures for the Old Petersburg Society: 'Turgenev i muzyka'; 'Turgenev i Dvorianskoe gnezdo'. Grevs' archive is held in the St Petersburg affiliate of the Russian Academy of Sciences Archive (PFA RAN, F.726) which, in addition to writings about Turgenev, contains materials on Pushkin (d. 223: K zaniatiiam Pushkinym. Bibliograficheskie vypiski, nabroski lektsii. r/p. 31l), and Chekhov (d.269).
45   Grevs, *Turgenev i Italiia*, Leningrad, 1925, p. 8.
46   Such ties, as Grevs noted, were, of course, confirmed by the influence of Italian-style architecture on Russian soil. Among more recent travellers to Italy, Grevs cited F.I. Buslaev's memoirs (Moscow, 1887).
47   Grevs, *Turgenev i Italiia*, pp. 15–16.
48   Ibid., p. 45.
49   During his second trip, Turgenev read Theodore Mommsen's recently published *Romische Geschichte* for his account of Caesar and Roman authors.
50   Grevs, *Turgenev i Italiia*, pp. 45–6.
51   Ibid., pp. 52–3.
52   Ibid., pp. 38–9.

53 'We clearly see how Turgenev imbibes art – knows and experiences art in Rome. He seems to link it with Italy as a whole', although, as Grevs noted, he never described Rome as such (ibid., pp. 42, 84). In fact, Grevs argued, very few, whether scholars or creative writers, had managed to capture an image of Rome in their accounts: Zola's description was as 'mechanical and dry as a Baedeker'; in his *Voyage en Italie* (1866), Hippolyte Taine was marginally more successful, but his account of Rome paled in comparison to the vivid colours with which he painted Venice and Florence (ibid., pp. 81–2). To corroborate Turgenev's description, Grevs interpolated personal memories of his own first encounter with Rome, a practice of incorporating subjective impressions which he had first experimented with in his master's thesis, but which did not go down particularly well with his examiners.
54 Here, Grevs referred to 'Song of Triumphant Love' (1881): set in Ferrari, everything about the description, Grevs argued, suggested Florence.
55 Ibid., p. 97.
56 Ibid., pp. 63, 58. Turgenev's friends, Herzen and Bakunin, were closely linked to the revolutionary movement in Italy (p. 91).
57 Ibid., p. 92.
58 Ibid., p. 102. In this connection, Grevs referenced a letter from Turgenev to Tolstoi: 'Where there is no person (*lichnost'*), there is no man (*chelovek*), no freedom'.
59 Ibid., p. 56.
60 Ibid., p. 105.
61 Ibid., pp. 118, 112.
62 Among the few to admire Grevs' writings on Turgenev were Judge Koni and Petr Bitsilli. The latter wrote a favourable review of *Istoriia odnoi liubvi*, Grevs' follow-up monograph about the life of the novelist (*Sovremmenye zapiski*, 37 (1928), pp. 544–6), although he did suggest that Grevs had painted an idealized portrait.
63 Grevs, *Turgenev i Italiia*, p.100. In this connection, Grevs referred to Tolstoi's credo as cited by Koni, namely that in every literary work one discerns three elements, the most important of which is the content, then the author's love for his subject and finally technique. Ibid., p. 8.
64 Ibid., pp. 8, 100.
65 Ibid., p. 11.
66 Ibid., p. 85.
67 Vakhromeeva (ed.), *Chelovek s otkrytym serdtsem*, p. 315.
68 Grevs, *Istoriia odnoi liubvi. I. S. Turgenev i Polina Viardo*. Introduction to first edition, reprinted in the second revised edition (Moscow, 1928), pp. 9–10.
69 Ibid., p. 27.
70 Ibid., p. 28. Grevs was unable to access Viardot's letters: these would have afforded 'a wealth of material for a biography of the man and writer, for checking and filling in gaps in the chronology of his life, in terms of both the major and minor events within it, for clarifying relations, moods, movements, self-observation, self-evaluations, as well as his views – literary, historical, philosophical, cultural – which would have allowed us to study the process of his creativity and the history of individual works'. Ibid.
71 Antsiferov, *Iz dum o bylom*, p. 173; Vakhromeeva (ed.), *Chelovek s otkrytym serdtsem*, p. 300. In his study of Turgenev in Italy, this featured as a latent theme: here Grevs spoke about the writer's friendship with the philosopher-Westernizer, Nikolai Stankevich. ('they were inseparable') and the lasting impression that the latter, who died shortly after the 1840 trip, made on the young Turgenev. Grevs, *Turgenev i Italiia*, pp. 28–32.

72 Grevs, *Chelovek s otkrytym serdtsem*, p. 301.
73 Ibid., p. 300. The choice of author was partly motivated not only by an intellectual cum aesthetic affinity with his French contemporary (who, in 1915, was awarded the Nobel Prize for literature), but also, as Danièle Baune-Gray suggests, by a mutual association as erstwhile pupils of Gabriel Monod. Baune-Gray notes that Grevs first met Monod in 1889 and corresponded with him thereafter. Beaune-Gray, *I. M. Grevs*, p. 263.
74 Antsiferov, *Iz dum o bylom*, p. 172.
75 Grevs, *Chelovek s otkrytym serdtsem*, pp. 300–1. According to Antsiferov, the symbolism of names had not occurred to contemporary literary specialists. 'I think', he wrote, 'that Grevs made this discovery thanks to his work on Dante and the Middle Ages in general'. Grevs argued that the life trajectories of Jean Christophe and Dante complemented each other in the sense that, whereas the *Divine Comedy* takes us through inferno and purgatory, Rolland's hero grasped '*humana civilitas*. Antsiferov, *Iz dum o bylom*, p. 171.
76 Grevs, ibid. Unfortunately, Grevs did not develop his comment about the men of the forties.
77 Ibid., p. 300.
78 Ibid., p. 301.
79 Cf. Sveshnikov, *Peterburgskaia shkola medievistov*, p. 168.
80 Aikhenval'd, 'Kliuchevskii. Myslitel' i khudozhnik', pp. 141–2.
81 Ibid., p. 142.
82 Kliuchevskii, 'Evgenii Onegin i ego predki', in Aleksandrov, pp. 409, 410–11.
83 'Grust'' (Pamiati M. Yu. Lermontova, umer 15 iiulia 1841).' My quotations are taken from Aleksandrov, pp. 427–44. Aikhenval'd, ibid. See also Platonov, 'V. O. Kliuchevskii (1841–1911) [nekrolog]', p. 8.
84 A. Rieber, Introduction to the English translation by Natalie Duddington of *A Course in Russian History: The Seventeenth Century*, p. xxxvi.
85 Kliuchevskii, 'Grust',' in Aleksandrov, p. 433.
86 Ibid., p. 437.
87 Rieber, Introduction to the English translation by Natalie Duddington of *A Course in Russian History: The Seventeenth Century*, p. xxxv. See also Smirnov, 'V. O. Kliuchevskii i otechestvennaia slovesnost',' p. 42.
88 Kliuchevskii, 'Grust',' in Aleksandrov, pp. 431–2.
89 Ibid., p. 432.
90 Aikhenval'd, 'Kliuchevskii. Myslitel' i khudozhnik', pp. 143–4.
91 Smirnov, 'V. O. Kliuchevskii i otechestvennaia slovesnost',' p. 39.
92 Rieber, Introduction to the English translation by Natalie Duddington of *A Course in Russian History: The Seventeenth Century*, p. xxxv. Similarly, Smirnov notes that, as a student taking Buslaev's courses in the early 1860s, Kliuchevskii had commented on the deeply melancholic timbre of folksong, the authenticity of which was more appealing to him than the romanticized representation of the people found in the poetry of, for example, Zhukovskii, Pushkin, Lermontov, even Kol'tsov. Smirnov, ibid., p. 38.
93 Platonov, 'V. O. Kliuchevskii (1841–1911) [nekrolog]', pp. 8–9.
94 Miliukov, 'V. O. Kliuchevskii', *Kharakteristiki i vospominaniia*, pp. 210–17.
95 Kliuchevskii, 'Grust',' p. 444. See also Kireeva (Introduction), *V. O. Kliuchevskii. O nravstvennosti i russkoi literature*, pp. 22–3; Smirnov, 'V. O. Kliuchevskii i otechestvennaia slovesnost',' pp. 37–42.
96 Kliuchevskii, ibid., p. 442.

97 R. Wortman, 'Epilogue', in G. S. Morson (ed.), *Literature and History. Theoretical Problems and Russian Case Studies* (Stanford, 1986), p. 281. See also Wachtel who makes a similar observation about two modes of enquiry: 'The novel can delve into areas of character and psychology that must remain outside the objective historian's realm'. Wachtel, *An Obsession with History*, p. 78.

98 Kliuchevskii 'Otzyv ob issledovanii S. F. Platonova *Drevnerusskie skazaniia i povesti o smutnom vremeni XVIIv* kak istoricheskii istochnik [1888]', in V. O. Klyuchevskii, *Sochineniia*. T.VII (Moscow, 1959), p. 441. Of note here is that, for Kliuchevskii, literature dating from the Time of Troubles marked a major paradigm shift from *skazanie* (as a collective undertaking) to the emergence of the authorial voice of the storyteller (*povestvovatel'*) who endeavours to make sense of, and pass judgement on, the events.

99 The famous collection of essays, *Landmarks/Vekhi*, 1909.

100 V. Proskurina, *Techenie gol'fstrema: Mikhail Gershenzon, ego zhizn' i mif* (St Petersburg, 1998), p. 25.

101 Gershenzon also took courses in European history and political theory with Ger'e, but his main focus was the Ancient World. In addition to Vinogradov's lectures and seminars on the subject, Gershenzon studied the 'Ancient history in the Semitic east' (M. S. Korelin), close reading and translation exercises with Professor Korsh (e.g. Ovid's *Tristia*, Cicero's *De Amicitia*, Xenophon's historical writings).

102 Gershenzon contributed to various literary and generalist journals: *Nauchnoe slovo, Vestnik Evropy, Kriticheskoe obozrenie*. Between 1905 and 1910, he contributed to Semon Vengerov's six-volume *Collected Works of Aleksandr Sergeevich Pushkin* (1907–13), before producing his own monograph about Pushkin, *Mudrost' Pushkina* (Moscow, 1919).

103 B. Horowitz, *The Myth of A.S. Pushkin in Russia's Silver Age: M.O. Gershenzon, Pushkinist* (Evanston, Ill., 1996), pp. 16–17.

104 Gershenzon, *Istoriia molodoi Rossii* (Moscow, 1908), p. iv. Gershenzon's idiosyncratic and eclectic historical method should be paired with his philosophical worldview, which he articulated in *Vekhi* as a concern with the inner self, emotional spirit and religious will of the individual. Other studies of Russian nineteenth-century intellectual life by Gershenzon dating from the pre-war and war era include: *Istoricheskie zapiski* (Moscow, 1910); *Ocherki proshlogo* (1912); *Griboedovskaia Moskva* (Moscow, 1914); *Dekabrist Krivtsov i ego brat'ia* (Moscow, 1914), which offered a literary portrait of Russia in the age of Alexander I.

105 Gershenzon, *Istoriia molodoi Rossii*, pp. iii, v.

106 Ibid. See also Proskurina, *Techenie Gol'fstrema*, p. 29.

107 Horowitz, *M. O. Gershenzon, Pushkinist*, p. 19. As Horowitz notes, Gershenzon's account of Pushkin as an organically 'holistic', ethereal, unchanging personality, who reached maturity early and remained perfect, had important repercussions for his interpretations of the poet's works, not least in the sense that any element of progression was effectively discarded. Similarly, his study of Turgenev, *Dream and thought of Turgenev* (*Mechta i mysl' I. S. Turgeneva*) (Moscow, 1919), ignored the conventions of biography. See the introduction by Thomas G. Winner to the Brown University Slavic Reprint of *Griboedov's Moscow* (1970), pp. vii–xii. As a side note, it is worth mentioning that, like Grevs, Gershenzon's monograph was occasioned by the centenary celebrations of the novelist's birth. Whether the two men knew each other personally, I am unaware, but, in this regard, a point of interest is their shared acquaintance with Viacheslav Ivanov with whom both men corresponded. The

bulk of Grevs's letters were written during the 1890s and, briefly, in the wake of the October Revolution; Gershenzon's famously 'staged' exchanges were written while the two men shared a room as convalescents in a sanatorium in the early 1920s. See *Correspondence from Two Corners* (*Perepiska iz dvukh uglov*) (Petersburg, 1921).

108 Gershenzon, *Istoriia molodoi Rossii*, p. x. In other words, for Gershenzon, historical understanding was entirely dependent on probing the conscience of certain individual people.

109 Gershenzon, *Russkaia mysl'* 1 (1894), pp. 10, 12. Cited in Proskurina, *Techenie gol'fstrema*, pp. 22–3.

110 Horowitz, *M. O. Gershenzon, Pushkinist*, p. 26.

111 Proskurina, *Techenie gol'fstrema*, p. 23. Horowitz, ibid., pp. 13–14. Gershenzon described the deep impression that his discovery of Carlyle's work had made on him in a letter to his brother (28 February 1892). In his words: 'the best book I have ever read […] it was precisely a book like this that I was in need of now, it has become my Gospel, my good news'. M. Gershenzon, *Pis'ma k bratu* (Moscow, 1927), p. 57.

112 I have, to date, found very little in the English language on the topic of the Russian reception of Carlyle, other than a study of Tolstoi's and Carlyle's sharply opposing views of Napoleon and of history, and the passing references in Priscilla Roosevelt's monograph on Granovskii.

113 Antsiferov, *Iz dum o bylom*, p. 155.

114 Proskurina defines modernistic prose as a blend of metaphysical discourse intercepted with historical research, with the result that Gershenzon's 'historical-literary work turned into a philosophical tract, while being an example of fine prose'. Proskurina, *Techenie gol'fstrema*, p. 61. See also Irina Paperno whose remarks about modernism as a European-wide reaction against positivism allow us to locate Gershenzon squarely within this movement: 'Modernism has frequently been described as a reaction against positivism (or naturalism). Indeed, a major dynamic force behind modernist movements across Europe was a rejection of the positivistic mode of cognition that relied on the surface reality of empirical facts, subject to realistic interpretation. The notion of the empirically given, objectively existing fact was questioned in many areas of knowledge – philosophy, physics, psychology, art'. I. Paperno and J. D. Grossman (eds), *Creating Life. The Aesthetic Utopia of Russian Modernism* (Stanford, 1994), p. 3.

115 B. Horowitz, *Russian Idea – Jewish Presence* (Academic Studies Press, 2013), p. 189. *Griboedov's Moscow*, he notes, 'belongs to the same genre as *Decembrist Krivtsov* – a novelistic–historical investigation – and shares the same aim of capturing the psychology of a family during the first quarter of the nineteenth century'. Ibid.

116 A. Tyrkov, for example, reviewed *Griboedov's Moscow* as a 'first-rate' historical novel. See *Russkaia mysl'* 5 (1914), p. 167, cited in Vera Proskurina, *Techenie gol'fstrema*, p. 45. In his review of *Decembrist Krivtsov*, the historian, Alexander Kiesewetter, touched on the way Gershenzon blurred the boundaries between fact and fiction, without, it seems, subordinating one to the other: 'At first glance, it can seem that the author simply recounts documents of a family chronicle. Admittedly, thanks to his outstanding literary talent, the report turns into a full artistic painting, which one reads with vivid interest as though reading a masterfully written novel. But as one reads, it is impossible not to notice that in the form of a colourful story about life there enters a psychological and historical analysis of social types corresponding to the time, which gives shades of meaning to the reigning qualities

of society's cultural development. Thus, a scientific study goes hand-in-hand with an artistic stylization'. Kiesewetter, *Russkie vedomosti*, 76 (2 April 1914), p. 6. By contrast, for the Soviet historian, Melitsa Nechkina, Gershenzon ignored the reality of Moscow in Griboedov's time and produced one of his own invention. M. Nechkina, *Griboedov i Dekabristy* (Moscow, 1977).
117 Gershenzon, *Griboedovskaia Moskva* (The Hague – Paris: Slavistic Printings and Reprintings, 1970), pp. 3, 33; Horowitz, *Russian Idea – Jewish Presence*, pp. 190–2.
118 *Griboedovskaia Moskva*, pp. 3, 33.
119 Ibid.
120 Ibid., p. 151.
121 T. Winner, *Mechta i mysl' I. S. Turgeneva* (Brown University, 1970) [Foreword], p. x.
122 Ibid. Brian Horowitz makes the same point.
123 Horowitz, *M. O. Gershenzon, Pushkinist*, p. 23.

Chapter 8

1 C. J. Berry, *Hume, Hegel and Human Nature* (The Hague; London, 1982), p. 149.
2 A. Thierry, cited in Kelley, *Fortunes of History*, p. 157; the remark about Michelet is Saint-Beuve's, cited in Lombardo, 'Hippolyte Taine between Art and Science', vol. 77, Reading the Archive: On Texts and Institutions (1990), p. 125.
3 G. Monod, 'Avant-propos', *Revue historique*, Vol. 1 (1876), p. 2 cited in Lombardo, 'Hippolyte Taine between Art and Science', p. 121. See also Kelley, who notes that 'history not only sought causes and effects but adopted the terms and claims of modern natural science. This meant not only the collecting of data, ranging from statistics and physical geography to ethnography and linguistics, but also the study of the physical aspects of history – climate, food, soil, nature'. He adds: 'It is perhaps curious that while "literary," or "mere literature," became a term of reprobation, literary historians often brandished the epithet "scientific" to grace their work'. *Fortunes of History*, p. 240.
4 Among Taine's chief writings are: *Essai sur Tite-Live* 1856; *Les philosophes français du XIXe siècle*, 1857; *Essais de critique et d'histoire*, 1858–82 (a Russian translation was published in 1896); *Histoire de la littérature anglaise*, 1864 (a Russian translation was published in 1871).
5 Cited in the original French in A. Pypin, 'Voprosy literaturnoi istorii', *Vestnik Evropy*, Vol. 10 (1893), p. 661.
6 Ibid., footnote. Cited by Pypin in the original French.
7 There are many summaries of Taine's theory of literature. See, for example, Bod, *A New History of the Humanities*, p. 327; Kelley, *Fortunes of History*, p. 215.
8 Taine made this remark in the Introduction to his study of English literature. N. Kareev, *Literaturnaia evoliutsiia na zapade. Ocherki i nabroski iz teorii i istorii literatury s tochki zreniia nespetsialista* (Voronezh, 1886), p. 107. [First published in *Filologicheskie zapiski* in 10 parts, January 1885–May 1886.]
9 According to Patrizia Lombardo, if Taine reserved his main criticism for the German school of philology, represented by Herder, Niebuhr and Michelet, he also (seemingly contradicting himself) recognized the importance of 'passions', 'since they constitute the very causes of events, are the very substance of history'. Moreover, to do justice to the real object of history – the human soul – the historian needs to be a great

writer. For Lombardo, this concluding passage in Taine's 1856 essay on Titus Livius suggests that 'traces of Taine's past culture (...) will function in resistance to his own positivistic ideology and to the later institutionalization of positivism'. Lombardo, 'Hippolyte Taine between Art and Science', p. 133. See also Kelley, *Fortunes of History*, p. 216.

10   As Taine wrote: 'Just as astronomy is in essence the task of mechanics, and physiology the task of chemistry, so, history is, in essence, *the task of psychology*'. Cited by Pypin, 'Voprosy literaturnoi istorii', p. 662. See also N. Kareev, *Osnovnye voprosy filosofii istorii. Kritika istoriosoficheskikh idei i opyt nauchnoi teorii istoricheskogo progressa* (Moscow, 1883), 2 vols. For related modern commentary, see, for example, Gordon Kelly, 'Literature and the Historian', pp. 141–59.

11   Lotman describes nineteenth-century historical–philological scholarship as 'non-differentiated, non-specialized' (*neraschlenennyi vid*), 'Russkaia istoriko-filologicheskaia nauka', p. 42. I would add that remained true well into the late imperial era: the single most important difference between the pre- and post-reform generations of scholars was a growing professionalization of the disciplines, which most equated with 'science', a term which was used both by mainstream historians and by their peers in the department of *slovesnost'*.

12   N. Kostomarov, *Ob istoricheskom znachenii russkoi narodnoi poezii. Sochinenie N. Kostomarova* (Kharkhov, 1845), p. 10.

13   The Moscow-based professor, Nikolai Savvich Tikhonravov (1832–93), was known principally for his publication of medieval chronicles and as the editor of the first 'Complete Works' of Gogol. Afanas'ev and Pypin were not 'scholars' in the sense of being employees at an institution of higher education (Pypin, a cousin of Chernyshevskii, was barred from university teaching on political grounds in the early 1860s), but they are often mentioned in the literature for their contributions to the study of pre-Christian Slavic mythology, attitudes towards nature (especially Afanas'ev) and Russian folklore and for their ideas which they developed 'in dialogue' with figures such as Buslaev, Potebnia and Veselovskii. Most of Pypin's literary scholarship was initially published in *Vestnik Evropy* (and/or Stasiulevich's companion publishing house), where he was member of the editorial board and a regular contributor. By way of example, his four-volume, *Istoriia russkoi literatury* (St Petersburg, 1902–3), monographs on freemasonry and religious movements in the reign of Alexander I suggest the breadth of his interests and expertise. See A. L. Toporkov, *Teoriya mifa v russkoi filologicheskoi nauke XIX veka* (Moscow, 1997); J. Haney, *An Introduction to the Russian Folktale* (New York, 1999).

14   A. N. Veselovskii, 'Envisioning World Literature in 1863: From the Reports on a Mission Abroad' [1863], translated by Jennifer Flaherty in *Publications of the Modern Languages Association of America*, Vol. 128, No. 2 (2013), p. 446.

15   As a student, Grevs took O. F. Miller's courses in Russian Literature, and I. I. Sreznevskii's introduction to philology. In his memoirs, he spoke of the inspiring example of A. N. Veselovskii. See Vakhromeeva (ed.), *Chelovek s otkrytym serdtsem*, p. 151. Nina Perlina has argued for affinities in the work of Grevs (and Antsiferov) with the ideas of Veselovskii, which she summarizes as follows: 'The data of empirical experience belong to various spheres of societal life, but the interpretation of these data, i.e. understanding, is grasped through the experience of them *(ikh perezhivanie)*, through the discovery of their inner forms, through the transposition of the past into the present and a semantic transfer of one particular language into another'. Perlina contends that this informed Grevs' handling of Horace as a source

for a social history of Rome. N. M. Perlina, 'Ivan Mikhailovich Grevs i Nikolai Pavlovich Antsiferov: k obosnovaniiu ikh kul'turologicheskoi pozitsii', in T. B. Pritykina (ed.), *Antsiferovskie chteniia*, p. 84.

16   Lotman, 'Russkaia istoriko-filologicheskaia nauka i khudozhestvennaia literatura', p. 44. Among the common pool of materials for both historical and literary studies were Dante and the Norse Songs from Elder Edda – two topics worthy of further research.

17   Lotman, ibid., pp. 19, 43.

18   Andy Byford, for example, elaborates on competing conceptions of the remit of reform-era literary scholarship: 'Most accounts of literary history dating from late imperial period defined it as a component of cultural history, which was itself a subsection of general history. At other times, literary history was discussed in the context of the science of philology. The latter could sometimes be reduced only to a specialized subsection of the humanities that dealt with language and its products, but more often it was given the broadest possible sense, current in Germany at the time, which identified it with the study of virtually all the manifestations of the human spirit. These classifications were never clear-cut as both history and philology were susceptible to broader and narrow definitions'. Byford, *Literary Scholarship in Late Imperial Russia*, p. 48.

19   Gogol's letter addressed to I. I. Sreznevskii, mid-1830s, cited in Formozov, *Klassiki russkoi literatury i istoricheskaia nauka*, p. 76. As Wachtel notes, Gogol privileged folksongs because, they, more than anything else, express feelings in a raw, unrefined state. In much the same vein, Gogol's vision of history, which he set out in a programmatic statement 'On the Teaching of World History' (O prepodavanii vseobshchei istorii) (1834), reads as a paean to the romantic aestheticization of life: 'The purpose of world history', he wrote, 'is to gather as one all the peoples of the world, scattered as they are by time and happenstance, mountains and seas, and to unite them in a single elegant whole; to make of them in a single whole; to make of them a single, full, magnificent poem'. Cited in Wachtel, ibid., p. 86. See also Barsukov, *Zhizn' i trudy M. P. Pogodina*, p. 89; *Perepiska N.V. Gogolia*, t. I (Moscow, 1988), p. 442; I. Kalinin, *Nauchnye i literaturnye proizvedeniia N.V. Gogolia po istorii Malorossii* (Kiev, 1902), p. 35.

20   Lotman, 'Russkaia istoriko-filologicheskaia nauka', p. 28.

21   Kostomarov, *Ob istoricheskom znachenii russkoi narodnoi poezii*, pp. 9–10.

22   Ibid., p. 8.

23   Ibid., p. 10.

24   Ibid.

25   Ibid.

26   M. M. Maksimovich (ed.), *Malorossiiskie pesni* (1827) and *Ukrainskie narodnye pesni* (1834); I. I. Sreznevskii, *Zaporozhskaia starina* (1833–8); P. A. Lukashevich, *Malorossiiskie i chervorusskie narodnye dumy i pesni* (1836); I. Sakharov (ed.), *Pesni russkogi naroda* (1838–9). As everywhere across Europe, early work in Russia on the national literary canon dating from the 1820s and 1830s was primarily bibliographical, with historical-ethnographical analyses of the nation's cultural heritage by and large modelled on contemporary German examples, most notably: Georg Gervinus, *Geschichte der poetischen National-Literatur der Deutschen* (1835).

27   *Savva chal'ii* (1838), *Ukrainskie ballady* (1839), *Vetka – Malorusskie stikhotvoreniia* (1840), *Pereiaslavskaia noch'* (1841). See Pinchuk, *Istoricheskie vzgliady N. I. Kostomarova*, pp. 35–6. Kostomarov's upbringing, education, literary tastes, friendships contained all the formative components that were so typical of this

generation: as a child he read V. A. Zhukovskii and Pushkin; although he attended the Voronezh gymnasium, he was largely self-taught. At Khar'kov University, he studied languages (Latin, French and Italian) and became familiar with the works of Rousseau, Saint-Simon, Hugo, Goethe, Walter Scott, Shakespeare and Schiller. According to Pinchuk, two major influences on Kostomarov during this period, the mid-1830s, were M. M. Lunin, professor of World History, and the poet-Professor of Russian History, P. P. Gulak–Artemovskii, whose salon he attended. In 1838, Kostomarov moved to Moscow where he attended Pogodin's lectures. In 1869, after a period in St Petersburg, where he hosted regular 'Tuesday evening gatherings' to the city's literati and literary critics – N. A. Dobroliubov, V. V. Stasov, N. A. Ge, A. N. Pypin, O. M. Bodianskii – Kostomarov was appointed to the newly created chair of History at Kiev University. Pinchuk, ibid., pp. 32-3. See also Prymak, *Mykola Kostomarov*.

28 A point made by A. S. Arkhangel'skii in his obituary tribute to Fedor Buslaev: F. I Buslaev v svoikh 'Vospominaniiakh' i uchenykh trudakh (Kazan, 1899), p. 57.
29 Kudriavtsev cited in V. A. Sokolov (ed.), *Izbrannye sochineniia T. N. Granovskogo*, Vol. 1. p. xxii.
30 Granovskii, 'Bartol'd Georg Niburg', in ibid., Vol. 2, pp. 39-40.
31 Ibid. See also his 'Pesni Eddy o Niflungakh (1851)'.
32 Pinchuk, *Istoricheskie vzgliady*, pp. 177-8. Specifically, Pinchuk refers to Kostomarov's work with Ukrainian folksong which he took up in later life as a valuable resource for the insights they afford into the way a people perceived itself.
33 Buslaev, *O vliianii khristianstva na slavianskii yazyk* (Moscow, 1848), p. 10, cited in Lotman, 'Russkaia istoriko-filologicheskaia nauka', p. 33.
34 'The study of early epic poetry is the study of the initial, original period in the inner life of a people [...]. Poetry is the expression of national (*narodnyi*) life; epic poetry is no exception to this rule'. Buslaev, cited in A. S. Arkhangel'skii, 'F. I. Buslaev v svoikh *Vospominaniiakh* i uchenykh trudakh' (Kazan, 1899) [pamphlet], p. 70.
35 See Byford, *Literary Scholarship in Late Imperial Russia*, p. 28.
36 K. Voinakhovskii, 'Znachenie trudov akademika F. I. Buslaeva', pp. 61-116; Pypin, 'Voprosy literaturnoi istorii', p. 678.
37 Byford, *Literary Scholarship in Late Imperial Russia*, pp. 132-3.
38 V. Miller, 'Pamiati Fedora Ivanovicha Buslaeva', in S. G. Smirnov (ed.), *Pamiati Fedora Ivanovicha Buslaeva* (Moscow, 1898), p. 21.
39 K. Voinakhovskii, 'Znachenie trudov akademika F. I. Buslaeva', ibid., p. 74.
40 S. Iu. Zimina 'Problema bessoznatel'nogo v kul'turologii N.P. Antsiferova', in T. B. Pritykina (ed.), *Antsiferovskie chteniia. Materialy i tezisy konferentsii* (Leningrad, 1989), pp. 86-7.
41 Lotman, 'Russkaia istoriko–filologicheskaia nauka', p. 21.
42 Cited in Miller, *Pamiati Fedora Ivanovicha Buslaeva*, p. 36.
43 To this point, Anatolii Smirnov references a letter, dated 1861, addressed to a student friend in which Kliuchevskii expressed the view that sad folksongs were dearer to him than the songs of Zhukovskii, Pushkin, Lermontov, even Kol'tsov, because of the raw feelings/sentiments of sadness, grief they contain. Poets then took these motifs and idealized the people, colouring their sentiments with a brighter hue. Smirnov, 'V. O. Kliuchevskii i otechestvennaia slovesnost',' p. 38.
44 Kliuchevskii, 'F. I. Buslaev kak prepodavatel' i issledovatel', p. 207.
45 Ibid. See also Smirnov, 'V. O. Kliuchevskii i otechestvennaia slovesnost',' p. 33.
46 Miller, *Pamiati Fedora Ivanovicha Buslaeva*, pp. 28, 30.

47 Ibid., p. 36. See also Prof. Arkhangel'skii, 'F. I. Buslaev v svoikh *Vospominaniiakh* i uchenykh trudakh', p. 55. Buslaev's status as the 'ideal professor' drew comparisons with Granovskii, his senior by a mere five years. However, unlike Granovskii, who used the university lectern as a platform for 'social activism' and to articulate a 'progressive worldview', Buslaev was a model of scholarly dedication and erudition. Both men, though, were remarkable in their professional conduct – 'honest, free of pedantry and willing to engage with the opinions of others'. A. Kirpichnikov, 'F. I. Buslaev, kak ideal'nyi professor 60-kh godov', in S. G. Smirnov (ed.), *Pamiati Fedora Ivanovicha Buslaeva*, pp. 197–8.

48 A. N. Veselovskii, 'O metode i zadachakh istorii literatury kak nauki', *Zhurnal Ministerstva narodnogo prosveshcheniia*, Vol. 11 (1870), p. 14.

49 I. K. Gorskii, 'Ob istoricheskoi poetike Aleksandra Veselovskogo', in *A. N. Veselovskii. Istoricheskaia poetika* (Moscow, 1989), pp. 12–13.

50 See, for example, A. Byford, 'The Rhetoric of Aleksandr Veselovskii's "Historical Poetics" and the Autonomy of Academic Literary Studies in Late Imperial Russia', *Slavonica*, Vol. 11 (2005), pp. 115–32; I. Kliger and B. Maslov (eds), *Persistent Forms: Explorations in Historical Poetics* (New York, 2016); V. E. Bagno, P. R. Zaborov and A. V. Lavrov (eds), *Aleksandr Veselovskii: aktual'nye aspekty naslediia: issledovaniia i materialy* (St Petersburg, 2011); I. Shaitanov, 'Aleksandr Veselovskii's Historical Poetics: Genre in Historical Poetics', *New Literary History*, Vol. 32, No. 2, *Reexamining Critical Processing* (Spring, 2001), pp. 429–43; Michel Espagne, 'Les sources allemandes des poétiques psychologiques en Russie du XIXe siècle: Veselovski, Buslaev, Jirmounski', *Revue d'histoire des sciences humaines*, Vol. 21, No. 2 (2009), pp. 55–67.

51 Shaitanov, 'Aleksandr Veselovskii's Historical Poetics', p. 435. Veselovskii began developing ideas on the subject as early as the 1860s and the 1870s, and then brought them to fruition in some of his publications dating from the 1890s. See Byford, 'The Rhetoric of Aleksandr Veselovskii's "Historical Poetics"', p. 130, note 4.

52 After graduating in 1859 from Moscow University, Veselovskii spent most of the following decade completing his education abroad in Germany, Italy, Spain and Eastern Europe. During the 1870s, he was engaged in preparing for publication a mass of material on the Italian Renaissance, which he had collected in archives (Veselovskii, *Sobranie sochinenii* (St Petersburg, 1908), Vol. III: 'Italiia i vozrozhdenie'). Otherwise, most of his time was devoted to preparing university courses and writing academic journalism. His vast erudition soon earned him a reputation in literary history, folklore and ethnography, but when in the mid-1880s he made his first statements in the area of literary theory, it came as a surprise. Nikolai Kareev, whose 1884 book on literary evolution might have prompted Veselovskii to address these questions in his own right, welcomed this turn to theory: reviewing Veselovskii's 1886 book on the narrative form (*Iz istorii romana i povesti*) and especially its introductory theoretical chapter, he noted that it was 'written by such an eminent scholar and one who does not often raise theoretical issues in his works'. Nikolai Kareev, review *Filologicheskie zapiski*, III–IV (1887), p. 1. See also Kliger and Maslov (eds), *Persistent Forms*. Introduction.

53 Veselovskii's thesis on Villa Alberti (1870), the Tuscan hunting lodge and guest house of Leon Battista Alberti and his literary circle during the late fourteenth and early fifteenth centuries, for example, served him as a starting point to explore the Italian Renaissance in light of the cultural factors and legacies that shaped it. In particular,

Veselovskii focused on the figure of Giovanni Gherardi (1360–1445), celebrated for his public lectures about Dante, and as the author of fictional miscellany including *Il Paradiso degli Alberti*. Veselovskii's approach consisted in referencing a variety of contemporary witnesses, on the basis of which, as he put it: 'I set out to articulate their unspoken thoughts, to read between the lines to capture what they themselves did not consider necessary to express more clearly, or what they were only vaguely aware of'. Veselovskii, *Sobranie sochinenii*, p. 561.

54 The articles were originally published in the journal of the Russian Imperial Ministry of Education, *Zhurnal Ministerstva narodnogo prosveshcheniia*, Vol. 117 (February 1863), section 2, pp. 152–60, vol. 119 (September 1863), section 2, pp. 440–8 under the rubric 'Selections from the Reports of Those Sent Abroad in Preparation for Professorship'.

55 Ibid., September 1863. Cited from English translation by Boris Maslov and Jennifer Flaherty in *PMLA*, Vol. 128, No. 2 (2013), p. 450.

56 Veselovskii, 'O metode i zadachakh istorii literatury kak nauki', *Zhurnal Ministerstva narodnogo prosvecheniia*, Vol. 11 (1870), pp. 1–14.

57 Ibid., pp. 7–8. Also, Byford, *Literary Scholarship*, p. 132.

58 Ibid., p. 8.

59 Ibid.

60 Veselovskii, 'Selections from the Reports of Those Sent Abroad in Preparation for Professorship' (1863), cited in Gorskii, 'Ob istoricheskoi poetike Aleksandra Veselovskogo', p. 17.

61 Veselovkii, 'Iz vvedeniia v istoricheskuiu poetiku', *Zhurnal Ministerstva narodnogo prosveshcheniia*, Vol. 293, No. 5 (1894), section 2, pp. 21–42. Cited from the English translation in Ilya Kliger and Boris Maslov (eds), *Persistent Forms*, p. 40. As the editors note, Veselovskii considered categories of poetry to be historical ones, thereby breaking with the view, since Hegel and German idealism, that they are aesthetic. But he also broke with the 'cultural–historical approach' to literature, which, to his mind, was merely another term for history of social thought insofar as it (thought) is expressed in philosophical, religious and poetical trends. Ibid., pp. 17–18.

62 By concentrating on the specificity of poetic forms Veselovskii was positioning himself against 'literary history', the term most commonly used at that time for literary scholarship, and which, he now argued, lacked a coherent definition of its object apart from as a subcategory of the more general 'history of social thought'. In Byford's summary, Veselovskii compared the current state of literary history as a free-for-all 'hunting ground' left open to all brands of 'poachers', from social theorists and cultural historians to amateur erudites and philosophically minded aestheticians. A. Byford, 'The Rhetoric of Aleksandr Veselovskii's "Historical Poetics"', p. 119.

63 Kliger and Maslov (eds), *Persistent Forms*, p. 21.

64 Ibid.

65 Veselovskii was notably highly critical of Stepan Shevyrev.

66 Veselovskii, 'Historical Poetics' cited in Byford, 'The Rhetoric of Aleksandr Veselovskii's "Historical Poetics"', p. 116.

67 N. Kareev, 'Chto takoe istoriia literatury? (Neskol'ko slov o literature i zadache ee istorii)', *Filologicheskie zapiski*, Vols 5–6 (1883), pp. 1, 28.

68 Kareev, *Osnovnye voprosy filosofii istorii*. This publication was based on Kareev's doctoral dissertation.

69 Kareev, 'Chto takoe istoriia literatury?', p. 7.

70 Ibid., p. 4. In Kareev's words: 'If, for the historian, written sources (*pis'mennie istochniki*) are his bread and butter, for the historian of literature these traces are not the materials on which he builds historical knowledge; rather, they are of interest in their own right. For this reason he does not restrict the field of literary historical enquiry to "*pis'mennost*'", but also includes oral traditions'.
71 Ibid., p. 5.
72 Ibid., p. 10.
73 Ibid., p. 11.
74 Ibid., pp. 15, 25.
75 Cf. Pypin's comments about the German scholar, Herman Paul, in his *Grundriss der germanischen Philologie* (collective volume) who made much the same point with regard to the place of poetry in national cultures. 'Voprosy literaturnoi istorii', p. 668.
76 Kareev, 'Chto takoe istoriia literatury?', p. 16.
77 Ibid., pp. 15–16, 19.
78 Ibid., pp. 12, 21–2.
79 Ibid., p. 25.
80 Ibid., p. 12.
81 Ibid., p. 26.
82 Ibid., p. 25. Kareev's remark here is quite reminiscent of Hippolyte Taine.
83 Ibid., p. 23.
84 Ibid., p. 24. Kareev developed quite strong ties with a number of French academics in part through his friendship with the sociologist, Maxim Kovalevskii, then residing in Paris. In the 1880s, Kovalevskii introduced Kareev to Fustel de Coulanges and Alphonse Aulard, historian of the French Revolution (also the topic of Kareev's master's dissertation). Later, Kareev developed ties to Gabriel Monod, the editor-in-chief of *Revue historique*, and corresponded with him on several occasions. When Monod asked him to find a correspondent for the journal who would agree to write regular reviews of Russian historiography, Kareev proposed himself for the job. Still later, Kareev met Charles-Victor Langlois and Charles Seignobos, both leaders of the so-called *école méthodique*, encounters which did not preclude his collaboration with Henri Berr, whose agenda as editor-in-chief of the journal *La synthèse historique* was entirely different from that of Langlois and Seignobos.
85 Ibid., p. 26. An exception here would be economic history, though Grevs' handling of the subject through biography arguably fits quite well with Kareev's account of the remit of the discipline.
86 Ibid., p. 26.
87 Kareev, *Literaturnaia evoliutsiia na zapade*, p. iii.
88 Ibid., pp. 40, 65.
89 Ibid., p. 40.
90 Ibid., pp. 332–3.
91 Ibid., pp. 59–65.
92 Ibid., p. 63; also, p. 94.
93 Ibid., p. 67.
94 Ibid., p. 66; also p. 43: 'Literary evolution is grounded in an interrelationship between creativity and tradition'.
95 Although Kareev did not define the notion of pragmatism here, he certainly did not intend it in the way that Karamzin had used the term at the beginning of the century, viz., usage of the past as a form of practical or political guidance in the present. As a philosophical theory in the United States, pragmatism emerged around 1870, and, to my knowledge, became the object of discussion among Russian philosophers after 1900.

96 Kareev, *Literaturnaia evoliutsiia na zapade*, pp. 72–4.
97 Ibid., pp. 74–5, 104.
98 Ibid., pp. 46, 103–4. It is interesting to note, however, that fifteen years later, when Kareev reviewed Grevs' experiment with 'economic biography', he welcomed his colleague's attempt to bridge disciplines by using Horace's poetry as a resource for understanding the social implications of economic and political changes in the Roman Empire.
99 Ibid., pp. 105–6.
100 Ibid., pp. 78–9.
101 If Kareev was touching on a fairly obvious distinction between a literary critical and historical approach to a literary work, the problem was that the discipline of *slovesnost'* – in practice – covered both. In a sense, then, 'literary history' may be regarded as the 'successor term' to *slovesnost'*
102 Pypin, 'Voprosy literaturnoi istorii', pp. 656–88. On Pypin, see above, note 13.
103 Ibid., pp. 670–1, 687–8.
104 Ibid., p. 657.
105 Like Kareev, Pypin regarded the work of Taine as a defining moment in the development of literary–historical studies, and he cited in full Taine's famous contention that 'just as astronomy is in essence the task of mechanics, and physiology the task of chemistry, so, history is in essence the task of psychology'. Ibid., p. 662
106 Ibid., pp. 676–7.
107 Ibid., p. 659.
108 Pypin, *Istoriia russkoi etnografii*, Vol. 2 (St Petersburg, 1890–2), p. 171 cited in Lotman, 'Russkaia istoriko–filologicheskaia nauka', p. 38.
109 Kliuchevskii set out his approach to working with written and material sources in a series of lectures delivered between 1888 and 1894 under the general heading 'Istochniki russkoi istorii'. See Kashtanov, 'Istochnikovedenie', pp. 594–5; Chumachenko, *V.O. Kliuchevskii – istochnikoved*.
110 Kliuchevskii, Lecture XI in *Sochineniia*, T.VI (Moscow, 1959), pp. 73–81. As I discussed in Chapter 5, Grevs' reading of Horace's poetry as a window on to farm management in the late Roman era was, similarly, characteristic of the way historians and philologists employed 'imagistic' genres of narrative, drama and especially poetry to uncover the 'soul' of a people or their day-to-day routines on the land.
111 Kareev's critique was grounded in a commonplace about the cultural historical resonances of creative literature. He wrote: 'The fashion in science for the Middle Ages with its poetical traditions, loans, "errant tales," with its questions arising from the study of folk (*narodnaia*) poetry is producing one sided, reductionist accounts based on comparative and philological methods, overlooking the aesthetic and vital, social-cultural aspect of literature'. *Literaturnaia evoliutsiia na zapade*, p. 337.
112 Bod, *A New History of the Humanities*, p. 327.
113 Ibid., pp. 327–8.
114 Kliuchevskii, *Aforizmy. Istoricheskie portrety*, pp. 367–8.

Epilogue

1. Bagalei, *Russkaia istoriia*, p. 14. See also Vetrinskii, who cited the same remark by Taine about the ideal historian (*T. N. Granovskii i ego vremia*, p. 114). Among Russian commentators, these credentials were frequently paraphrased and, as we have seen, applied to Granovskii and Kliuchevskii. Bagalei's omission of the latter may, in part, be explained by his Ukrainian origins: Kliuchevskii was, like many Russians of his age, notoriously dismissive of Ukraine's (Little Russia) right to national self-determination, which, by the onset of war and revolution, featured prominently in the Ukrainian political agenda.
2. In addition to Hayden White (history is a linguistic and rhetorical artefact constrained by a genre rule specifying reference to conventionally agreed upon historical 'facts') and Lionel Gossman's treatment of the topic, see, for example, Suzanne Gearhart, *The Open Boundary of History and Fiction* (Princeton, 1984); Peter Burke, 'Historiography and Philosophy of History', in *History and Historians in the Twentieth Century* (Oxford, 2002), who writes: 'In the 1990s, postmodernity and postmodernism were finally discussed by some British historians, especially outside the older universities, making students of history familiar, perhaps for the first time, with the fictional elements in historical writing and the ideological cargo of all Grand Narratives, Whig or Tory, radical or conservative, feminist or 'male chauvinist' (p. 249).
3. As Iurii Lotman put it: 'Literature was summoned to play the main role in the humanization of society. In the 1790s, having broken away from the Masons, Karamzin contended that precisely belles lettres (*iziashchnaia slovesnost*') poetry and novels would perform this civilizing role. Civilization means being rid of coarse feelings and thoughts.' 'Kolumb russkoi istorii', p. 10.
4. Kareev, for example, referred to a series of lectures on Marx, Herzen and the Decembrists, which he delivered in 1923 to peasants in the Smolensk guberniia of Anosov. The lecture on the Decembrists, he recalled, was coupled with a staging of Nekrasov's 'Russian Women' and a reading from 'The Decembrists' by Merezhkovskii. N. Kareev, *Prozhitoe i perezhitoe* (Leningrad, 1990), pp. 280–1.
5. Kelley, *Fortunes of History*, p. 342.
6. On Lamprecht, see Kelley, ibid., p. 264.
7. Ibid., pp. 322–4.
8. Ibid., p. 326.
9. S. O. Shmidt, 'Khudozhestvennaia literatura i iskusstvo kak istochnik formirovaniia istoricheskikh predstavleniia', in *Put' istorika*, p. 115.
10. One major Soviet exception was, of course, Rubinshtein's 1941 study, *Russkaia istoriografiia*, although he used 'science' as a yardstick by which to expose, for example, the 'weaknesses' in Kliuchevskii's account of medieval princes. See also L. Yaresh, 'The Role of the Individual in History', in C. E. Black (ed.), *Rewriting Russian History. Soviet Interpretations of Russia's Past* (New York, 1956), pp. 78–106; M. D. Kammari, *Marksizm-Leninizm o roli lichnosti v istorii* (Moscow, 1952).
11. Michael Confino, 'The New Russian Historiography and the Old – Some Considerations', *History and Memory. Studies in Representations of the Past*. Special issue: Historical Scholarship in Post-Soviet Russia, edited by Gabriel Gorodetsky, pp. 7–33; Engelstein, 'Culture, Culture Everywhere', pp. 363–93; Markwick, 'Cultural History under Khrushchev and Brezhnev', pp. 283–301.

12 B. Ponomarev, 'The Tasks Facing Historical Scholarship and the Training of History Teachers and Researchers', in the *All-Union Conference of Historians* (18 December 1962), *Soviet Studies in History,* Vol. 2 (1964), p. 10. First published in *Voprosy istorii,* Vol. 1 (1963).
13 See, for example, A. A. Vagin (ed.), *Khudozhestvennaia literatura v prepodavanii Novoi Istorii, 1640-1917* (Moscow, 1966; 2nd edn: 1978); O. V. Volobuev and S. A. Sekirinskii (eds), *Khudozhestvenno-istoricheskaia khrestomatiia. Srednie veka* (Moscow, 1965; 2nd edn: 1977). Also, R. S. Mnukhina, *Istochnikovedenie istorii novogo i noveishego vremeni* (Moscow, 1970) and 'Rol' obraznogo poznaniia v protsesse obucheniia istorii', in A. I. Hazarets et al. (eds), *Istoriia SSSR v khudozhestvenno-istoricheskikh obrazakh. Posobie dlia uchitelei* (Moscow, 1969), pp. 334-43; M. I. Smorodin, *Znachenie i metodika istoriko-khudozhestvennogo slovesnogo obraza* (Moscow, 1965). A much earlier text, dated 1930, also highlighted the value of creative literature in historical study referencing Lenin to support the claim. See G. P. Saar, *Istochniki i metody istoricheskogo issledovaniia* (Baku, 1930), pp. 146-8.

Select Bibliography

The materials on which this study is based are divided into three sections. The first group of primary (printed) sources comprises articles and monographs by the principal historians whose writings I have discussed. The second, related, section consists of commentary by their contemporaries and pupils. Works listed in the third section are Russian and Western-language secondary literature.

PRIMARY SOURCES

Antsiferov, N. P., *Dusha Peterburga* (Petrograd, 1922) [rpt. Moscow, 1991].
Antsiferov, N. P., *O metodakh i tipakh istoriko-kul'turnykh ekskursii* (Petrograd, 1923).
Antsiferov, N. P., *Peterburg Dostoevskogo* (Petrograd, 1923).
Antsiferov, N. P., *Byl' i mif Peterburga* (Petrograd, 1924).
Antsiferov, N. P., *Puti izucheniia goroda kak sotsial'nogo organizma: opyt kompleksnogo podkhoda* (Leningrad, 1925).
Antsiferov, N. P., 'Belletristy-kraevedy. Vopros o sviazi kraevedeniia s khudozhestvennoi literaturoi', *Kraevedenie*, Vol. 4, 1 (1927), pp. 31–46.
Antsiferov, N. P., *Zhizn' goroda* (Leningrad, 1927).
Antsiferov, N. P., *Problemy urbanizma v russkoi khudozhestvennoi literature: opyt postroeniia obraza goroda – Peterburga Dostoevskogo – na osnove analiza literaturnykh traditsii* [1944] (Moscow, 2009).
Antsiferov, N. P., *Iz dum o bylom* (Moscow, 1992).
Gershenzon, M., *Istoriia molodoi Rossii* (Moscow, 1908).
Gershenzon, M., *Istoricheskie zapiski* (Moscow, 1910).
Gershenzon, M., *Pis'ma k bratu* (Moscow, 1927).
Granovskii, T. N., *Volin Iumsburg i Vineta. Istoricheskie issledovaniia* (Moscow, 1845).
Granovskii, T. N., *Abbat Sugerii. Istoricheskie izsledovaniia* (Moscow, 1849).
Granovskii, T. N., 'Sid, kak istoricheskoe litso', in A. N. Chudinov (ed.), *Poema i izbrannye romancy o Side v perevodakh russkikh pisatelei*, 2nd edn (St Petersburg, 1897), pp. 140–57.
Granovskii, T. N., *Sochineniia T. N. Granovskogo*, 2 vols (Moscow, 1856).
Granovskii, T. N., *Izbrannye sochineniia T. N. Granovskogo*, edited by V. A. Sokolov (Moscow, 1905).
Granovskii, T. N., *Granovskii. Leksii po istorii srednevekov'ia*, edited by E. V. Gutnova and S. A. Asinovskaia (Moscow, 1986).
Grevs, I. M., *Istoriia srednikh vekov: Lektsii, chitannye na Sankt-Peterburgskikh kursakh v 1892–1893g* (St Petersburg, 1893).
Grevs, I. M., *Ocherki iz istorii Rimskogo zemlevladeniia (preimushchestvenno vo vremena rannei imperii*, Vol. 1 (St Petersburg, 1899).

Grevs, I. M., *Istoriia proiskhozhdeniia, razvitiia i razlozheniia feodalizma v zapadnoi Evrope (po lektsiiam Prof. I. M. Grevsa, 1902-3)*, compiled by S. Sviridovaia (St Petersburg, 1903) [typescript].
Grevs, I. M., *Ocherki Florentiiskoi kul'tury*, vyp.1: 'Progulki po naucho-khudozhestvennym tsentram Italii' (Moscow, 1903).
Grevs, I. M., 'Zabytaia nauka i unizhennoe zvanie', *Nashi dni*, No. 10 (28 December 1904), pp. 2-3.
Grevs, I. M., *K teorii i praktike 'Ekskursii' kak orudiia nauchnogo izuchemiia istorii v universitetakh* (St Petersburg, 1910).
Grevs, I. M., 'Monumental'nyi gorod i istoricheskie ekskursii (osnovnaia ideia obrazovatel'nykh puteshestvii po krupnym tsentram kul'tury', *Ekskursionnoe delo*, Vol. 1 (1921), pp. 21-34.
Grevs, I. M., 'Dal'nie gumanitarnye ekskursii i ikh vospitatel'no-obrazovatel'nyi smysl', *Ekskursionnoe delo*, vols 4-6 (1922), pp. 1-12.
Grevs, I.M., 'Priroda ekskursionnosti i glavnye tipi ekskursii v kul'turu', in I. M. Grevs (ed.), *Ekskursii v kul'turu* (Moscow, 1925), pp. 9-34.
Grevs, I. M., *Turgenev i Italiia (kul'turno-istoricheskii etiud)* (Leningrad, 1925).
Grevs, I. M., 'Gorod kak predmet kraevedeniia', *Kraevedenie*, Vol. 3 (1924), pp. 245-58.
Grevs, I. M., 'Istoriia v kraevedenii', *Kraevedenie*, Vol. 4 (1926), pp. 487-508. [rpt in M. I. Kornalov (ed.), *Otechestvo. Kraevedcheskii al'manakh*, Vol. 2 (Moscow, 1991), pp. 5-22].
Grevs, I. M., 'Gorodskie landshafty (etiud iz kul'turnoi geografii)', in *Voprosy geografii v novoi shkole* (Leningrad, 1926), pp. 102-3.
Grevs, I. M., *Istoriia odnoi liubvi: I. S. Turgenev i Polina Viardo* (Moscow, 1927).
Grevs, I. M., *Chelovek s otkrytym serdtsem. Avtobiograficheskoe i epistoliarnoe nasledie Ivana Mikhailovicha Grevsa (1860-1941)*, compiled and edited by O. B. Vakhromeeva (St Petersburg, 2004).
Grevs, I. M., *Istoriia i poeziia: Perepiska I. M. Grevsa i Viach. Ivanova*, edited by G. M. Bongard-Levin, N. V. Kotrelev and E. V. Liapustina (Moscow, 2006).
Grevs, I. M., Zelinskii, F. F., Kareev, N. I., and Rostovtsev, M. I. (eds), *Obshchaia istoriia evropeiskoi kul'tury*, Vol. 1 (St Petersburg, 1908).
Kareev, N. I., *Krest'iane i krest'ianskii vopros vo Frantsii v poslednei chetverti XVIIIv* (Moscow, 1879).
Kareev, N. I., 'Pushkin, kak poet evropeiskii': Rech' prof. Varshavskogo univ-a, N. I. Kareeva, proiznesennaia na pushkinskom prazdnike v Warshave, 4-go Iiunia 1880 goda)', *Filologicheskie zapiski*, vyp. V (Voronezh, 1880), pp. 1-10.
Kareev, N. I., 'Chto takoe istoriia literatury?' (Neskol'ko slov o literature i zadache ee istorii), *Filologicheskie zapiski*, vols 5-6 (1883), pp. 1-28.
Kareev, N. I., *Osnovnye voprosy filosofii istorii. Kritika istoriosoficheskikh idei i opyt nauchnoi teorii istoricheskogo progressa*, 2 vols (Moscow, 1883).
Kareev, N. I., *Literaturnaia evoliutsiia na zapade. Ocherki i nabroski iz teorii i istorii literatury s tochki zreniia nespetsialista* (Voronezh, 1886).
Kareev, N. I., *Istoricheskaia filosofiia L. N. Tol'stogo v 'Voine i mire'* (St Petersburg, 1888) [first published in *Vestnik Evropy*, 4 (July-August 1887), pp. 227-69].
Kareev, N. I., 'Vseobshchaia istoriia v universitete', *Istoricheskoe Obozrenie*, Vol. 3 (1891), pp. 1-21.
Kareev, N. I., *Besedy o vyrabotke mirosozertsaniia*, 5th edn (St Petersburg, 1904).
Kareev, N. I., *Epokha Frantsuzskoi revolutsii v trudakh russkikh uchenykh za poslednie desyat' let (1902-1911)* (St Petersburg, 1912).

Kareev, N. I., *Prozhitoe i perezhitoe* [1923], edited by V. P. Zolotaev (Leningrad, 1990).
Kareev, N. I. (ed.), *Istoricheskoe obozrenie. Sbornik Istoricheskogo Obshchestva pri Imperatorskom Sankt Peterburgskom universitete*, Vol. 15 (St Petersburg, 1909).
Kliuchevskii, V. O., *Sochineniia*, 8 vols (Moscow, 1956–9).
Kliuchevskii, V. O., *Pis'ma, dnevniki, aforizmy i mysli ob istorii* (Moscow, 1968).
Kliuchevskii, V. O., *Neopublikovannye proizvedeniia* (Moscow, 1983).
Kliuchevskii, V. O., *Istoricheskie portrety. Deiateli istoricheskoi mysli*, edited by V. A. Aleksandrov (Moscow, 1991).
Kliuchevskii, V. O., *Literaturnye portrety*, edited by A. Smirnov (Moscow, 1991).
Kliuchevskii, V. O., *Aforizmy. Istoricheskie portrety i etiudy. Dnevniki* (Moscow, 1993).
Kliuchevskii, V. O., *V. O. Kliuchevskii. O nravstvennosti i russkoi literature*, edited by R. A. Kireeva (Moscow, 1998).
Kostomarov, N. I., *O Istoricheskom znachenii russkoi narodnoi poezii* (Kharkhov, 1845).
Kostomarov, N. I., 'Lichnost' tsaria Ivana Vasil'evicha Groznogo', in N. Kostomarov (ed.), *Issledovaniia. Dokumenty* (Moscow, 1988), pp. 7–61.
Kudriavtsev, P. N., *Povesti i razskazy*, 2 vols (Moscow, 1866).
Kudriavtsev, P. N., 'O sovrememmykh zadachakh istorii', *Sochineniia*, Vol. 1 (Moscow, 1877), pp. 3–69.
Pogodin, M. P., 'Chernaia nemoch', *Moskovskii vestnik* [1829] in V. I. Sakharov (ed.), *Russkaia romanticheskaia povest'* (Moscow, 1992), pp. 97–126.
Pogodin, M. P., *Istoricheskie aforizmy* (n.p., 1836).
Pogodin, M. P., *Issledovaniia, zamechaniia i leksii Mikhaila Pogodina o Russkoi istorii*, Vol. 2 (Moscow, 1846).
Pogodin, M. P., *Borba, ne na zhivot, a na smert' s novymi istoricheskimi eresiami* (Moscow, 1874).
Pogodin, M. P., *Povesti. Drama*, edited by M. N. Virolainen (Moscow, 1984).
Pokrovskii, M., 'Pushkin i rimskie istoriki', in *Sbornik statei posviashchennykh Vasiliiu Osipovichu Kliuchevskomu ego uchenikami, druz'iami i pochitateliami ko dniu tritsatiletiia ego professorskoi deiatel'nosti v Moskovskom Universitete* (Moscow, 1909), pp. 478–86.
Poliakskii, I. I., 'Opyt novoi organizatsii ekskursionnogo dela v shkolakh. Ekskursionnaia Sektsiia i ekskursionnye stantsii', *Ekskursionnoe delo*, Vol. 1 (1921), pp. 1–20.
Pypin, A., 'O sravnitel'no-istoricheskom izuchenii russkoi literatury', *Vestnik Evropy*, Vol. 10 (1875), pp. 641–77.
Pypin, A., *Kharakeristiki literaturnykh mnenii ot dvatsatykh do piatidesiatykh godov* (St Petersburg, 1890).
Pypin, A., 'Voprosy literaturnoi istorii', *Vestnik Evropy*, Vol. 10 (1893), pp. 656–88.
Pypin, A., 'Narodnaia poeziia v eia istoriko-literaturnykh otnosheniiakh', pts. 2 and 3, *Vestnik Evropy*, vols 5 and 6 (1896), pp. 220–65, 609–57.
Vasilevskii, V. G., *Lektsii po srednei istorii* (St Petersburg, 1880–1).
Veselovskii, A. N., 'O metode i zadachakh istorii literatury kak nauki', *Zhurnal Ministerstva narodnogo prosveshcheniia*, Vol. 11 (1870), pp. 1–14.
Veselovskii, A. N., 'Iz vvedeniia v istoricheskuiu poetiku', *Zhurnal Ministerstva narodnogo prosveshcheniia*, Vol. 5 (1894), pp. 21–42.
Veselovskii, A. N., *Sobranie sochinenii* (St Petersburg, 1908), Vol. 3: 'Italia i Vozrozhdenie'.
Veselovskii, A. N., 'Envisioning World Literature in 1863: From Reports on a Mission Abroad', in B. Maslov (ed.), *Publications of the Modern Language Association of America*, Vol. 128, 2 (2013), pp. 439–51.

CONTEMPORAY RUSSIAN CRITIQUE AND APPRAISALS

Anon., *Vospominaniia o Petre Nikolaeviche Kudriavtseve* (Moscow, 1858).
Arkhangel'skii, A. S., F. I. *Buslaev v svoikh 'Vospominaniia' i uchenykh trudakh* (Kazan, 1899).
Bagalei, D. I., *Russkaia istoriia*, Vol. 1 (Moscow, 1914).
Barsukov, N. P., *Zhizn' i trudy M. P. Pogodina*, Vol. 9 (St Petersburg, 1895).
Bestuzhev-Riumin, K. N., *Russkaia istoriia* (St Petersburg, 1872).
Bestuzhev-Riumin, K. N., *Biografii i kharakteristiki: Tatishev, Shletser, Karamzin, Pogodin, Solov'ev, Eshevskii, Gil'ferding* (St Petersburg, 1882).
Bitsilli, P. M., 'Istoriia odnoi liubvi' [review article], *Sovremennye zapiski*, Vol. 37 (1928), pp. 544-6.
Buslaev, F. I., 'M. P. Pogodin kak professor' [chitano v publichnom zasedanii Obshchestva Liubitelei Rossiiskoi Slovestnosti, 21 iii 1876] (Moscow, 1876).
Butenko, V. A., 'Nauki novoi istorii v Rossii', *Annaly*, Vol. 2 (1923), pp. 129-67.
Buzeskul, V. P., *Vseobshchaia istoriia i ee predstaviteli v Rossii v XIX i nachale XX veke*, 2 vols (Leningrad, 1929-31).
Dmitriev, N., 'Studencheskie vospominaniia o Moskovskom universitete', *Otechestvennye zapiski*, Vol. 119, Part 4 (August 1858), pp. 81-95.
Dobiash-Rozhdestvenskaia, O. A., Khomentovskaia, A. I. and Fedotov, G. P. (eds), *Srednevekovoi byt': Sbornik statei* (Leningrad, 1925).
Eikhenbaum, B. M., *Skvoz' literaturu. Sbornik statei* (Leningrad, 1924).
Eshevskii, S. V., *Petr Nikolaveich Kudriavtsev kak prepodavatel'* (Moscow, 1858).
Gere, V. I., *Timofei Nikolaevich Granovskii. V pamiat' stoletnogo iubileya ego rozhdeniia* (Moscow, 1913).
Glinskii, B.,'Universitetskie ustavy, 1755-1884', *Istoricheskii vestnik*, vols 1 and 2 (1900), pp. 324-51, 718-42.
Grevs, I. M., 'Novoe issledovanie o kolonate', *Zhurnal Ministerstva narodnogo prosveshcheniia*, vols 11 and 12 (1886), pp. 118-65, 307-54.
Grevs, I. M., *Vasilii Grigorevich Vasilevskii kak uchitel' nauki'. Nabrosok vospominaniia i materialy dlia kharakeristiki* (St Petersburg, 1899).
Grevs, I. M., 'Novyi trud po religioznoi istorii srednevekovoi Italii v russkoi nauchnoi literatury' (St Petersburg: Senatskaia tipografiia, 1913), pp. 3-72.
Ikonnikov, V. S., *Opyt russkoi istoriografii*, 2 vols (Kiev, 1891-1908).
Kalinin, I., *Nauchnye i literaturnye proizvedeniia N. V. Gogolia po istorii Malorossii* (Kiev, 1902).
Kareev, N., *Istoricheskoe mirosozertsanie Granovskogo* (St Petersburg, 1896).
Kareev, N., 'Kniga g. Grevsa o rimskom zemlevladenii', *Russkoe bogatstvo*, vols 11 and 12 (1900), pp. 1-27, 1-20.
Kareev, N., *Histoire et historiens depuis conquante ans. Méthodes, organisations et résultats du travail historique de 1876 a 1926* (Paris, 1927).
Karpovich, M., 'Klyuchevski and Recent Trends in Russian Historiography', *Slavonic and East European Review. American Series*, Vol. 2, 1 (March 1943), pp. 31-9.
Karsavin, L. et al., *K dvadtsatipiatiletiiu ucheno-pedagogicheskoi deiatel'nosti Ivana Mikhailovicha Greva. Sbornik statei ego uchenikov* (St Petersburg, 1911).
Khvostov, V. M., *Teoriia istoricheskogo protsessa*, 2nd edn (Moscow, 1914).
Kiesewetter, A., 'Klyuchevsky and His Course of Russian History', *The Slavonic Review*, Vol. 1, 3 (March 1923), pp. 504-22.

Kizevetter, A. A. (Kiesewetter), *Na rubezhe dvukh stoletii. Vospominaniia, 1881-1914* (Moscow, 1997).
Kizevetter, A. A. et al., *V. O. Kliuchevskii: Kharakteristiki i vospominaniia* (Moscow, 1912).
Klementov, A. K. and Klementova, S. A. (eds), *Rossiiskaia istoricheskaia mysl': Iz epistoliarnogo nalediia L. P. Karsavina. Pis'ma I. M. Grevsu (1906-1916)* (Moscow, 1994).
Kliuchevskii, V. O., 'S. M. Solov'ev, kak prepodavatel'' in V. O. Kliuchevskii et al. (eds), *Vospominaniia o studencheskoi zhizni* (Moscow, 1899), pp. 3-20.
Kliuchevskii, V. O., 'Pamiati T. N. Granovskogo', *Russkie vedomosti*, 263 (8 October 1905).
Korsakov, D. A., 'Pamiati Nikolaia Ivanovicha Kostomarova', *Istoricheskii vestnik*, Vol. xxi (1885), pp. 72-86.
Kudriavtsev, P. N., 'Izvestie o literaturnykh trudakh Granovskogo', in *Sochineniia T. N. Granovskogo*, Vol. 1 (Moscow, 1856), pp. i-xviii.
Kudriavtsev, V. (ed.), *Ukazatel' istoricheskikh statei v zhurnalakh: Vestnik Evropy, Russkaia mysl', Russkoe bogatstvo, Mir bozhii, Sovremennyi mir, Obrazovanie za 1885-1908* (St Petersburg, 1910).
Kutorga, M., 'Ocherk noveishikh istorikov Zapadnoi Evropy. Leopold Ranke', *Biblioteka dlia chteniia*, Vol. 99, pt. 2 (1850), pp. 107-11.
Levshin, D. M., *T. N. Granovskii (Opyt istoricheskogo sinteza)*, 2nd edn (St Petersburg, 1902) [First published in 1900].
Maklakov, B., 'Klyuchevsky', *Slavonic and East European Review*, Vol. 13, 38 (1935), pp. 320-9.
Miliukov, P., 'Iuridicheskaia shkola v russkoi istoriografii (Solov'ev, Kavelin, Chicherin, Sergeevich)', *Russkaia mysl'*, Vol. 12 (1886), pp. 80-92.
Miliukov, P., 'Universitet', in *Entsiklopedicheskii slovar'*, Vol. xxxiv (a) (Leipzig-St Petersburg, 1902), pp. 751-803.
Miliukov, P., 'Universitetskii kurs Granovskogo' [1845-6], in *Iz Istorii russkoi intelligentsii. Sbornik statei i etiudov*, 2nd edn (St Petersburg, 1903), pp. 212-65.
Miliukov, P., *Glavnye techeniia russkoi istoricheskoi mysli*, 3rd edn (St Petersburg, 1913).
Miliukov, P. N., Seignobos, Ch., Eisenmann, L. et al., *Histoire de Russie*, 3 vols (Paris, 1932-3).
Miller, V. et al., *Pamiati Fedora Ivanovicha Buslaeva* (Moscow, 1898).
Pogodin, M. P., *Nikolai Mikhailovich Karamzin po ego sochineniiam. Pis'mam i otzyvam sovremennikov. Materialy dlia biografii*, 2 vols (Moscow, 1866).
Presniakov, A. E., 'V. O. Kliuchevskii, 1911-1921', *Russkii istoricheskii zhurnal*, 8 (1922), pp. 203-24.
Skrzhinskaia, E. Ch., 'Ivan Mikhailovich Grevs. Biograficheskii ocherk', in Prof. I. M. Grevs (ed.), *Tatsit* (Moscow; Leningrad, 1946), pp. 223-48.
Sl. [pseudonym], 'T. N. Granovskii v biograficheskom ocherke A. Stankevicha', *Vestnik Evropy*, Vol. 5 (1869), pp. 424-40.
Smirnov, S. G. (ed.), *Pamiati Fedora Ivanovicha Buslaeva* (Moscow, 1898).
Stankevich, A., *T. N. Granovskii i ego perepiska*, 2 vols (Moscow, 1897) [first published in 1869].
Stasiulevich, M. M., *Istoriia srednikh vekov v ee pisateliakh i issledovaniiakh noveishikh uchenykh*, 3 vols (St Petersburg, 1863-5).
Storozhev, V., 'Ocherki russkoi istoriografii', *Obrazovanie*, vols 4, 5-6, 7-8, 11 and 12 (1900), pp. 36-53, 126-54, 128-36, 59-78, 28-50.
Vetrinskii, Ch., *T. N. Granovskii i ego vremiia. Istoricheskii ocherk* (Moscow, 1897). [2nd edn: Moscow, 1905].

Vinogradov, P., 'T. N. Granovskii', *Russkaia mysl'*, Vol. 4 (1893), pp. 44–66.
Vipper, R., 'Obshchestvenno-istoricheskie vzgliady Granovskogo', *Mir bozhii*, Vol. 11 (1905), pp. 179–92.
Vipper, R., 'Novye gorizonty v istoricheskoi nauke', *Sovremennyi mir*, Vol. 2 (1906), pp. 257–73.
Vorob'ev, V., 'K istorii nashikh universitetskikh ustavov', *Russkaia mysl'*, Vol. 12 (1905), pp. 1–11.

SECONDARY LITERATURE

Al'tshuller, M., *Epokha Val'tera Skotta v Rossii: istoricheskii roman 1830-kh godov* (St Petersburg, 1996).
Al'tshuller, M., 'The Rise and Fall of Walter Scott's Popularity in Russia', in M. Pittock (ed.), *The Reception of Sir Walter Scott in Europe* (London; New York, 2006), pp. 204–40.
Alevras, N. N., Grishina, N. V. and Krasnova, Iu. V. (eds), *Istoriia i istoriki v prostranstve national'noi i mirovoi kul'tury XVIII – XIX vekov* (Cheliabinsk, 2011).
Andreev, A. Iu., *Byt' russkim po dukhu i evropeitsem po obrazovaniiu. Universitety Rossiiskoi imperii v obrazovatel'nom prostrantstve Tsentral'noi i Vostochnoi Evropy XVIII–nachala XXv* (Moscow, 2009).
Bagno, V. E., Zaborov, P. R. and Lavrov, A. V. (eds), *Aleksandr Veselovskii: aktual'nye aspekty naslediia: issledovaniia i materialy* (St Petersburg, 2011).
Balzer, H. D. (ed.), *Russia's Missing Middle Class: The Professions in Russian History* (Armonk, NY, 1996).
Baron, S. H. and Pletsch, C., *Introspection in Biography. The Biographer's Quest for Self-Awareness* (New Jersey; London, 1985).
Barzun, J., 'Romantic Historiography as a Political Force in France', *Journal of the History of Ideas*, Vol. 2, 3 (June 1941), pp. 318–29.
Beaune-Gray, D., 'Vers une histoire des mentalités', in Marc Weinstein (ed.), *La Geste russe. Comment les Russes ecrivent-ils l'histoire au XXe siecle?* (Aix-en-Provence, 2002), pp. 329–43.
Beaune-Gray, D., *I. M. Grevs. Un historien russe à travers les révolutions (1860–1941)* (Paris, 2017).
Bérélowitch, W., 'History in Russia Comes of Age. Institution-Building, Cosmopolitanism, and Theoretical Debates among Historians in Late Imperial Russia', *Kritika: Explorations in Russian and Eurasian History*, Vol. 9, 1 (Winter 2008), pp. 113–34.
Berliakova, N. P., 'Literaturnyi tekst kak istoricheskii istochnik v tvorcheskom nasledii V. O. Kliuchevskogo', *Izvestiia penzenskogo gosudarstvennogo universiteta*, Vol. 27 (2012), pp. 505–8.
Berlin, I., *The Hedgehog and the Fox* (New York, 1953).
Berry, C. J., *Hume, Hegel and Human Nature* (The Hague; London, 1982).
Black, C. E. (ed.), *Rewriting Russian History. Soviet Interpretations of Russia's Past* (New York, 1956).
Black, J. L., 'The "State School" Interpretation of Russian History: A Re-Appraisal of Its Genetic Origins', *Jährbücher für Geschichte Osteuropas*, Vol. 21, 4 (1973), pp. 509–30.
Black, J. L. *Nicholas Karamzin and Russian Society in the Nineteenth Century: A Study in Russian Political and Historical Thought* (Toronto, 1975).

Black, J. L. (ed.), *Essays on Karamzin: Russian Man-of-Letters, Political Thinker, Historian, 1766-1826* (The Hague, 1975).
Bod, R., *A New History of the Humanities. The Search for Principles and Patterns from Antiquity to the Present* (Oxford, 2013).
Bohn, T., 'Istorizm v Rossii? O sostoianii russkoi istoricheskoi nauki v XIX stoletii', *Otechestvennaia istoriia*, Vol. 4 (2000), pp. 121-8.
Brachev, V. S. and Dvornichenko, A. Iu., *Kafedra russkoi istorii Sankt-Peterburgskogo universiteta (1834-2004)* (St Petersburg, 2004).
Brickman, W. and Zepper, J. T. (eds), *Russian and Soviet Education, 1731-1989: A Multilingual Annotated Bibliography* (New York, 1992).
Burke, P., 'Historiography and Philosophy of History', in Burke, P. (ed.), *History and Historians in the Twentieth Century* (Oxford, 2002), pp. 230-49.
Byford, A., 'Between Literary Education and Academic Learning: The Study of Literature at Secondary School in Late Imperial Russia (1860s-1900s)', *History of Education*, Vol. 33, 6 (November 2004), pp. 637-60.
Byford, A., 'Initiation to Scholarship: The University Seminar in Late Imperial Russia', *The Russian Review*, Vol. 64 (April 2005), pp. 299-323.
Byford, A., 'The Rhetoric of Aleksandr Veselovskii's "Historical Poetics" and the Autonomy of Academic Literary Studies in Late Imperial Russia', *Slavonica*, Vol. 11 (2005), pp. 115-32.
Byford, A., *Literary Scholarship in Late Imperial Russia: Rituals of Academic Institutionalization* (London, 2007).
Byrnes, R. F., *V. O. Klyuchevsky, Historian of Russia* (Bloomington, IN, 1995).
Cherepnin, L. V., *Istoricheskie vzgliady klassikov russkoi literatury* (Moscow, 1968).
Chesnokov, V. I., *Pravitel'stvennaia politika i istoricheskaia nauka Rossii 60-kh-70-kh godov XIX v.: issledovatel'skie ocherki* (Voronezh, 1989).
Chumachenko, E. G., *V. O. Kliuchevskii - istochnikoved* (Moscow, 1970).
Clowes, E., *Fiction's Overcoat: Russian Literary Culture and the Question of Philosophy* (Ithaca, NY; London, 2004).
Dmitriev, A. N. (ed.), *Istoricheskaia kul'tura imperskoi Rossii: formirovanie predstavlenii o proshlom* (Moscow, 2012).
Dolinin, A., *Istoriia, odetaia v roman: Val'ter Skott i ego chitateli* (Moscow, 1988).
Eidelman, N., *Poslednii letopisets'* (Moscow, 1983).
Engelstein, L., 'Culture, Culture Everywhere: Interpretations of Modern Russia, across the Revolutionary Divide', *Kritika*, Vol. 2 (Spring 2001), pp. 363-93.
Espagne, M., 'Les sources allemandes des poétiques psychologiques en Russie du XIXe siècle: Veselovski, Buslaev, Jirmounski', *Revue d'histoire des sciences humaines*, Vol. 21, 2 (2009), pp. 55-67.
Evdokimova, S., *Pushkin's Historical Imagination* (New Haven; London, 1999).
Evtuhov, C. and Kotkin, S. (eds), *The Cultural Gradient. The Transmission of Ideas in Europe, 1789-1991* (Lanham, MD; Oxford, 2002).
Fedorova, E. V., *K istorii antikovedeniia v Rossii. Vospominaniia professora, doktora istoricheskikh nauk M. E. Sergeenko* (St Petersburg, 2000).
Flynn, J., *The University Reform of Tsar Alexander I, 1802-1835* (Washington, DC, 1988).
Formozov, A. A., *Klassiki russkoi literatury i istoricheskaia nauka* (Moscow, 1995).
Gamsa, M., 'Two Million Filing Cards: The Empirical-Biographical Method of Semon Vengerov', *History of Humanities*, Vol. 1, 1 (Chicago, 2016), pp. 129-53.
Gearhart, S., *The Open Boundary of History and Fiction* (Princeton, 1984).
Ginzburg, L., *On Psychological Prose* (Princeton, 1991).

Gooch, G. P., *History and Historians in the Nineteenth Century* (London, 1952).
Gorskii, I. K., 'Ob istoricheskoi poetike Aleksandra Veselovskogo', in *A. N. Veselovskii. Istoricheskaia poetika* (Moscow, 1989), pp. 11–31.
Gossman, L., *Between History and Literature* (Cambridge, MA, 1990).
Haardt, A. and Plotnikov, N. (eds), *Diskurse der Personalitat. Die Begriffsgeschichte der 'Person' aus deutscher und russicher Perspektive* (Paderborn, 2008).
Haney, J., *An Introduction to the Russian Folktale* (New York, 1999).
Harwood, J., *Styles of Scientific Thought: The German Genetics Community, 1900–1933* (Chicago, 1993).
Hecker, H., *Russisches Universalgeschichtsschreibung. Von den 'Vierziger Jahren' des 19. Jahrhunderts bis zur sowjetischen 'Weltgeschichte' (1955–1965)* (Munich; Vienna, 1983).
Holmgren, B. (ed.), *The Russian Memoir: History and Literature* (Evanston, IL, 2003).
Horowitz, B., *The Myth of A.S. Pushkin in Russia's Silver Age. M.O. Gershenzon, Pushkinist* (Evanston, IL, 1996).
Horowitz, B., *Russian Idea – Jewish Presence* (Academic Studies Press, 2013).
Istorik i khudozhnik (2004–8), Trimonthly periodical, published in Moscow.
Johnson, E. D., *How St Petersburg Learned to Study Itself. The Russian Idea of Kraevedenie* [Studies of the Harriman Institute, Columbia University] (New York, 2006).
Kaganovich, B. S., 'Vokrug *Ocherkov iz istorii rimskogo zemlevladeniia* I. M. Grevsa', in V. I. Rutenburg and I. P. Medvedev (eds), *Politicheskie struktury epokhi feodalizma v zapadnoi Evrope (vi–xvii vv)* (Leningrad, 1990), pp. 198–216.
Kaganovich, B. S., *Russkie medievisty pervoi poloviny XX veka* (St Petersburg, 2007).
Kaganovich, B. S. and Kobak, A. V. (eds), *I. M. Grevs i Peterburgskoe kraevedenie: Sbornik k 150-iu so dnia rozhdeniia* (St Petersburg, 2010).
Kalmanovskii, E., *Dni i gody. Zhizn' T. N. Granovskogo* (Leningrad, 1975).
Kamenskii, Z. A., *Timofei Nikolaevich Granovskii* (Moscow, 1988).
Kammari, M. D., *Marksizm–Leninizm o roli lichnosti v istorii* (Moscow, 1952).
Kaplan, V., *Historians and Historical Societies in the Public Life of Imperial Russia* (Bloomington, 2017).
Karpov, A. A. (ed.), *N.V. Gogol': Perepiska*, Vol. 1 (Moscow, 1988).
Kashtanov, S. M., 'Istochnikovedenie', in *Ocherki istorii istoricheskoi nauki v SSSR*, t. II (Moscow, 1960), pp. 575–94.
Kassow, S. D., *Students, Professors, and the State in Tsarist Russia* (Berkeley, 1989).
Kelley, D., *Fortunes of History. Historical Inquiry from Herder to Huizinga* (New Haven; London, 2003).
Kelley, D., *Frontiers of History. Historical Inquiry in the Twentieth Century* (New Haven; London, 2006).
Kelly, R. Gordon, 'Literature and the Historian', *American Quarterly*, Vol. 26, 2 (May 1974), pp. 141–59.
Kliger, I. and Maslov, B. (eds), *Persistent Forms: Explorations in Historical Poetics* (New York, 2016).
Korzun, V. P., *Obrazy istoricheskoi nauki na rubezhe XIX–XXvv: Analiz otechestvennykh istoriograficheskikh kontseptsii* (Ekaterinburg; Omsk, 2000).
Kozlov, V. F., 'Ivan Mikhailovich Grevs kak teoretik i praktik kraevedeniia 1920-kh godov' (po materialam zhurnala *Kraevedenie*), in Iu. V. Krivosheev (ed.), *Peterburgskie issledovaniia. Sbornik nauchnykh statei* (St Petersburg, 2006), pp. 136–47.
Laqueur, W., 'Literature and the Historian', *Journal of Contemporary History*, Vol. 2, 2 (1967), pp. 5–14.

Likhachev, D. S., *Nikolai Pavlovich Antsiferov (1889-1958). Prilozhenie k remontnomu vosproizvedeniiu: 1922-1924* (Moscow, 1991).
Lombardo, P., 'Hippolyte Taine between Art and Science', *Yale French Studies*, 77 (1990), pp. 117-33.
Lotman, Iu. M., 'Puti razvitiia russkoi prozy 1800-x – 1810-x gg', *Uchenye zapiski Tartuskogo universiteta*, Vol. 104 (1961), pp. 3-57.
Lotman, Iu. M., 'Ocherk dvorianskogo byta oneginskoi pory', in *Roman A. S. Pushkina 'Evgenii Onegin'. Kommentarii* (Leningrad, 1980), pp. 35-110.
Lotman, Iu. M., 'Kolumb russkoi istorii', in *N. M. Karamzin: Istoriia gosudarstva rossiiskogo, kn.iv 'Kliuch P. Stroeva'* (Moscow, 1988), pp. 3-16.
Lotman, Iu. M., *Sotvorenie Karamzina* (Moscow, 1998).
Lotman, Iu. and Uspenskii, B., 'Simvolika Peterburga i problema semiotiki goroda' [1984], in Iu. M. Lotman, *Izbrannye stat'i*, Vol. 2 (Tallin, 1992), pp. 9-21.
Lotman, L. M., 'Russkaia istoriko-filologicheskaia nauka i khudozhestvennaia literatura vtoroi poloviny XIX veka (vzaimodeistvie i razvitie)', *Russkaia Literatura*, Vol. 1 (1996), pp. 19-44.
Marinovich, L. P. and Mil'skaia, L. T. (eds), *Portrety istorikov: vremia i sud'by*, 2 vols (Moscow; Jerusalem, 2000).
Markwick, R., *Rewriting History in the Soviet Era: The Politics of Revisionist Historiography* (Basingstoke; New York, 2001).
Markwick, R., 'Cultural History under Khrushchev and Brezhnev: From Social Psychology to Mentalities', *Russian Review*, Vol. 65 (April 2006), pp. 283-301.
Mazour, A., *An Outline of Modern Russian Historiography* (Berkeley, 1939).
Mazour, A., *Modern Russian Historiography* (Westport, CT, 1975).
McClelland, J. C., *Autocrats and Academics: Education, Culture, and Society in Tsarist Russia* (Chicago; London, 1979).
Miagkov, G. P., *'Russkaia istoricheskaia skhlola' – metodologicheskie i ideino-politicheskie pozitsii* (Kazan, 1988).
Miagkov, G. P., *Nauchnoe soobshchestvo v istoricheskoi nauke: opyt 'Russkoi istoricheskoi shkoly'* (Kazan, 2000).
Mironets, N. I., 'Khudozhestvennaia literatura kak istoricheskii istochnik', *Istoriia SSSR*, Vol. 1 (1976), pp. 125-41.
Mjor, K. J., *Reformulating Russia: The Cultural and Intellectual Historiography of Russian First-Wave Émigré Writers* (Leiden, 2011).
Mjor, K. J., 'Russian History and European Ideas: The Historical Vision of Vasilii Kliuchevskii', in *The Borders of Europe* (Aarhus, 2012), edited by Helge Vidar Holm, Sissel Laegreid and Torgeir Skorgen pp. 71-90.
Morson, G. S. (ed.), *Literature and History. Theoretical Problems and Russian Case Studies* (Stanford, 1986).
Nakhimovsky, A. D. and Stone Nakhimovsky, A. (eds), *The Semiotics of Russian Cultural History. Essays by Iurii M.Lotman, Lidiia Ia. Ginsburg, Boris A. Uspenskii* (Ithaca; London, 1985).
Nechkina, M. V., *Griboedov i Dekabristy*, 3rd edn (Moscow, 1977).
Nethercott, F., 'Vasilij Kljuchevskij et ses muses litteraires: l'historien-écrivain' in *Ecrire et récrire l'histoire russe d'Ivan le Terrible à Vasilij Kljuchevskij (1547-1917)*, edited by Pierre Gonneau and Ecatherina Rai (Paris, 2013), pp. 145-53.
Nethercott, F., 'The Excursionism Project and the Study of Literary Places (1921-1924)', *Revue des études slaves*, LXXXVIII/1-2 (2017), pp. 13-27.

Offord, D., 'Nation-Building and Nationalism in Karamzin's *History of the Russian State*', *Journal of Modern Russian History and Historiography*, Vol. 3 (2010), pp. 1-50.
Paperno, I., *Chernyshevsky and the Age of Realism. A Study in the Semiotics of Behaviour* (Stanford, 1988).
Paperno, I. and Grossman, J. D. (eds), *Creating Life. The Aesthetic Utopia of Russian Modernism* (Stanford, 1994).
Perlina, N. M., 'Ivan Mikhailovich Grevs i Nikolai Pavlovich Antsiferov: k obosnovaniiu ikh kul'turologicheskoi pozitsii', in T. B. Pritykina (ed.), *Antsiferovskie chteniia. Materialy i tezisy konferentsii* (Leningrad, 1989), pp. 83-5.
Pinchuk, Iu. A. *Istoricheskie vzgliady N. I. Kostomarova. Kriticheskii ocherk* (Kiev, 1984).
Planty-Bonjour G., *Hegel et la pensée philosophique en Russie, 1830-1917* (The Hague, 1974).
Pogodin, S. N., *Russkaia shkola istorikov* (St Petersburg, 1997).
Proskurina, V., *Techenie gol'fstrema: Mikhail Gershenzon, ego zhizn' i mif* (St Petersburg, 1998).
Prymak, T., *Mykola Kostomarov: A Biography* (Toronto, 1996).
Raeff, M. (ed.), 'Kliuchevskii's Russia: Critical Studies', *Canadian-American Slavic Studies*, Vol. 20, 3-4 (1986), pp. 261-484.
Reingold, N., 'The Peculiarities of the Americans, or, Are There National Styles in the Sciences?' *Science in Context*, Vol. 4 (1991), pp. 347-66.
Repina, L. P. (ed.), *Soobshchestvo istorikov vysshei shkoly Rossii: nauchnaia praktika i obrazovatel'naia missiia* (Moscow, 2009).
Riasanovsky, N., 'The Norman Theory of the Origin of the Russian State', *The Russian Review*, Vol. 7, 1 (Autumn 1947), pp. 96-110.
Roosevelt, P., *Apostle of Russian Liberalism: Timofei Granovsky* (Newtonville, MA, 1986).
Rostovtsev, E. A., *A. S. Lappo-Danilevskii i peterburgskaia istoricheskaia shkola* (Riazan, 2004).
Ruegg, W. (ed.), *A History of the University in Europe*, Vol. 3: *Universities in the Nineteenth and Early Twentieth Centuries, 1800-1945* (Cambridge, 2004).
Sanders, T. (ed.), *Historiography of Imperial Russia. The Profession and Writing History in a Multinational State* (Armonk, NY, 1999).
Schlieper, H. C. (ed.), *Eastern Europe: Historical Essays* (Toronto, 1969).
Serdiukova, S. G., 'I. M. Grevs i I. S. Turgenev', in Iu. V. Krivosheev (ed.), *Peterburgskie issledovaniia. Sbornik nauchnykh statei* (St Petersburg, 2006), pp. 91-8.
Shaitanov, I., 'Aleksandr Veselovskii's Historical Poetics: Genre in Historical Poetics', *New Literary History*, Vol. 32, 2, 'Reexamining Critical Processing' (Spring 2001), pp. 429-43.
Shakhanov, A. N., 'Neformal'nye soobshchestva uchenykh Peterburga vtoroi poloviny XIX-nachala XX', in *Russkaia istoricheskaia nauka vtoroi poloviny XIX - nachala XX veka* (Moscow, 2003), pp. 352-71.
Shmidt, S. O., *Put' istorika. Izbrannye trudy po istochnikovedeniiu iistoriografii* (Moscow, 1997).
Shmidt, S. O., 'Pamiatniki khudozhestvennoi literatury kak istochnik istoricheskikh znanii', *Otechestvennaia istoriia*, vol. 1 (2002), pp. 40-9.
Shmidt, S. O., 'I. M. Grevs i vospitanie istoriei', in Iu. V. Krivosheev (ed.), *Peterburgskie issledovaniia. Sbornik nauchnikh statei* (St Petersburg, 2006), pp. 7-32.
Skvoznikov, V. D., *Pushkin: istoricheskaia mysl' poeta* (Moscow, 1999).

Smirnova, A. G., 'Rol' I. M. Grevsa v razrabotke ekskursionnoi metodiki', in Iu. V. Krivosheev (ed.), *Peterburgskie issledovaniia. Sbornik nauchnykh statei* (St Petersburg, 2006), pp. 148–63.

Solomon, S. G., 'Circulation of Knowledge and the Russian locale', *Kritika*, Vol. 9 (Winter 2008), pp. 9–26.

Stennik, Iu. V. (ed.), *Literatura i istoriia. Istoricheskii protsess v tvorcheskom soznanii russkikh pisatelei XVIII–XX vv. Sbornik Statei* (St Petersburg, 1992–2001).

Stockdale, M., *Paul Miliukov and the Quest for a Liberal Russia, 1880–1918* (Ithaca; London, 1996).

Striedter, Jurij, 'Poetic Genre and the Sense of History in Pushkin', *New Literary History* (Winter 1977), pp. 295–309.

Sveshnikov, A. V., *Peterburgskaia shkola medievistov nachala XX veka. Popytka antropologicheskogo analiza nauchnogo soobshchestva* (Omsk, 2010).

Thaden, E., *The Rise of Historicism in Russia* (New York, 1999).

Thaden, E., 'Historicism, N. A. Polevoi, and Rewriting Russian History', *East European Quarterly*, Vol. XXXVIII, 3 (September 2004), pp. 299–329.

Todd, W. Mills (ed.), *Literature and Society in Imperial Russia, 1800–1914* (Stanford, 1978).

Todd, W. Mills, *Fiction and Society in the Age of Pushkin: Ideology, Institutions, and Narrative* (Cambridge, MA, 1986).

Toporkov, L., *Teoriia mifa v russkoi filologicheskoi nauke XIX veka* (Moscow, 1997).

Tsamutali, A. N., *Bor'ba napravlenii v russkoi istoriografii v period imperializma* (Leningrad, 1986).

Ungurianu, D., 'Fact and Fiction in the Romantic Historical Novel', *Russian Review*, Vol. 57, 3 (July 1998), pp. 380–93.

Vakhromeeva, O. B., 'Biograficheskii metod professora I. M. Grevsa', in *I. S. Turgenev glazami Ivana Mikhailovicha Grevsa* (St Petersburg, 2014), pp. 5–22.

Valk, S. N., *Izbrannye trudy po istoriografii i istochnikovedeniiu* (St Petersburg, 2000).

Vernadsky, G., *Russian Historiography: A History* (Belmont, MA, 1978).

Vlasiuk, O. A., 'Puteshestvie kak sposob formirovaniia "mental'noi karty" russkihk istorikov vtoroi poloviny XIXv', *Aktual'nye Problemy otechestvennoi istorii i istoriografii (XVIII–XX1vv)*, Vestnik Tomskogo Gosudarstvennogo Universiteta, Vol. 125 (October 2007), pp. 36–43.

Wachtel, A., *An Obsession with History: Russian Writers Confront the Past* (Stanford, 1994).

Wachtel, M., 'New Scholarship on Viacheslav Ivanov', Review Article, *The Slavic and East European Journal*, Vol. 50, 4 (Winter 2006), pp. 689–93.

White, H., *Metahistory: The Historical Imagination in Nineteenth-Century Europe* (Baltimore, 1973).

Whittaker, C., *The Origins of Modern Russian Education: An Intellectual Biography of Count Sergei Uvarov, 1786–1855* (DeKalb, IL, 1984).

Zhiliakova, E., *Shotlandskie stranitsy: ekho Val'tera Skotta v russkoi literature XIX veka: ocherki* (Tomsk, 2014).

Index

academic affair 55, 134
Aikhenval'd, Iulii 69–70, 72, 155, 157, 217 n.88
Alexander I 19, 39, 57, 103–4, 238 n.38
Alexander II 9, 27–8, 49, 151, 157, 183
Antsiferov, Nikolai 4, 18, 119, 124, 126, 130–5, 137, 161, 241 n.11, 243 n.44, 244 n.52, 244 n.53, 244 n.60, 245 n.80. *See also* excursionism; *kraevedenie*
   Byl' i mif Peterburga 126
   Dusha Peterburga 126, 130, 135, 150
   on Grevs 31, 93, 119, 121, 129–30, 152–3, 207 n.57, 209 n.9, 219 n.114
   literary excursionism, theory of 4, 12, 118, 126–9, 134, 207 n.55, 243 n.42, 246 n.88
   Peterburg Dostoevskogo 126–7
   on Pushkin 127, 131
   on Turgenev 134

Bagalei, Dmitrii 187, 203–4 n.24, 262 n.1
Belinskii, Vissarion 11, 61, 106, 182, 215 n.58
Bémont, Charles 114
Bérélowitch, Wladimir 5, 194 n.15, 195 n.24, 205 n.35, 206 n.49
Berlin, Isaiah 143–4, 146, 248 n.24
Bestuzhev-Riumin, Konstantin 9, 70, 199 n.59
   on Karamzin 223 n.6
   on Pogodin 42–3, 214 n.49, 214 n.51
Bestuzhevskie 51, 54, 122, 136, 195 n.23, 207 n.54, 207 n.57, 218 n.95, 242 n.15
Bitsilli, Petr 4, 246 n.99, 250 n.62
Bloch, Marc 136, 243 n.39
Bogoslovskii, Mikhail 47
   on Kliuchevskii 66, 157, 215 n.65
Boltin, Ivan 69
Burckhardt, Jacob 113–14, 189

Buslaev, Fedor 14, 18, 45–7, 50–60, 151, 167–8, 171–4, 193 n.11, 196 n.34, 208 n.61, 210 n.12, 216 n.77, 217 n.78, 251n.92, 255 n.13, 257 n.34, 258 n.47
Byford, Andy 3, 5, 30, 176, 193 n.8, 193 n.11, 193 n.13, 196 n.31, 196 n.34, 210 n.12, 256 n.18, 259 n.62
Byrnes, Robert 45–6, 70, 89, 215 n.66, 216 n.67, 231 n.38

Carlyle, Thomas 13, 143, 161, 229 n.1, 231 n.31, 253 n.111
Catherine the Great 27, 58, 67, 85, 103–4, 142
censorship 9, 15, 26–7, 29, 32–3, 157, 192 n.6, 203–4 n.24, 247 n.2
Chernyshevskii, Nikolai 219 n.105
   on Granovskii 37, 225 n.37
Chicherin, Boris 5, 45, 202 n.8
circles
   Oldenburg 32, 152, 218 n.98
   salon culture 7, 33, 39, 44, 208 n.62
   See also kruzhok; learned societies; seminars; *soobshchestvo*
Comte, Auguste 13, 47, 120

Dante
   in Russian scholarship 31, 54, 119, 174, 180, 216 n.77, 256 n.16, 258–9 n.53
   See also Buslaev; Veselovskii; Grevs
Dobiash-Rozhdestvenskaia, Olga 4, 124, 220 n.118
Dostoevskii, Fedor 4, 18, 126, 131, 139, 148, 208 n.2, 246 n.88

Ecole des Chartes 200 n.1. *See also* historiographical trends
educational reform 3, 8–9, 15, 21, 120, 132, 197 n.40, 208 n.61
   and counter reform 15, 23, 49, 193 n.10, 197 n.40, 205 n.36

Eshevskii, Stepan 8–9, 50
excursionism 4, 12, 52, 118–26
　institute 54, 124–6, 128, 131–4
　Italy 52, 122–3, 126
　Petrograd region 124, 133
　theory of 118, 120–5, 242 n.12, 244 n.50
　See also Antsiferov; Grevs; *kraevedenie*

Fedotov, Georgii 4, 45, 52, 70
folklore 18, 46–7, 131–2, 165, 167–75, 177, 193 n.8, 212 n.37
Fonvizin, Denis 56, 68–9, 75, 100, 106, 227 n.64
　Nedorosl' 101–2, 237 n.13
friendship 18, 39, 59, 152–4, 221 n.130, 234 n.87
　Granovskii and Stankevich 39
　Grevs and Viacheslav Ivanov 53–4, 221 n.127
　and love 147, 152, 211 n.27, 219 n.117
　as a topic of historical enquiry 93, 153, 160, 250 n.71
Fustel de Coulanges, Numa Denis 78, 93, 114, 117, 188, 193 n.9, 240 n.84, 240 n.85, 260 n.84

Ger'e, Vladimir 5–6, 30
Gershenzon, Mikhail 140, 159–63, 252 n.101, 252 n.102, 252 n.104, 252 n.107, 253 n.111, 253 n.114, 253–4 n.116
Gibbon, Edward 35, 41, 143, 187
Ginzburg, Lidiia 12, 39, 83, 191
　epochal personality 12, 39, 77, 87–9
Gogol, Nikolai 10, 126, 169–70, 198 n.46, 255 n.13, 256 n.19
　and Pogodin 61, 214 n.49
Gossman, Lionel 1, 12, 41, 64
Granovskii, Timofei 4–5, 7, 9–10, 54, 209 n.7, 210 n.14, 211 n.20
　in commemorative literature 36–8, 71, 83, 208 n.2, 208–9 n.4, 222 n.138, 228 n.84
　Four Historical Characteristics 78–84
　on Niebuhr 40–1, 65, 171
　and Stankevich, Nikolai 39–40
　view of history 14, 22–3, 40–1, 55–6, 171, 212 n.37, 212–13 n.39, 222 n.137, 226 n.47, 230 n.23

Grevs, Ivan 29, 31, 49–55, 235 n.92, 255–6 n.15
　biographical method 17, 78, 90–6, 109, 111, 116, 118, 121, 123, 125, 136, 151, 240 n.85
　on Dante 29, 31, 50, 54, 116, 118–19, 122, 129, 148, 150, 153–5, 207 n.56, 219 n.111, 221 n.135, 251 n.75
　masters dissertation 90–5, 107–11, 233 n.73
　on Rolland 54, 148, 153–5, 251 n.75
　on Turgenev 50, 54, 110, 116, 147–53, 249 n.43, 249 n.44, 250 n.53
　urban culture, medieval and renaissance 51, 96, 116–18
　on Vasilevskii 49–51, 95, 189, 218 n.96
　view of history 53, 94–6, 115–17, 152, 155, 235–6 n.106
　See also Antsiferov; excursionism; friendship; *kraevedenie*
Griboedov, Aleksandr 100, 103, 162
Grimm, Jacob 45, 165, 172, 217 n.78
Guizot, François 35, 81, 114, 212 n.37, 213 n.42, 242 n.12
Gukovskii, Matvei 136, 246 n.95

Hegel, Georg Wilhelm Friedrich 4, 17, 36, 40, 48, 64, 77, 79, 82–3, 143–5, 211–12 n.31, 222 n.137, 225 n.41, 259 n.61
Herder, Johann Gottfried 48, 59, 61–2
Herzen, Aleksandr 44, 225 n.37, 236 n.3
　and Granovskii 36, 81
historians
　moral authorities 8, 29, 44, 209–10 n.12, 211 n.22, 213 n.41
　publications, attitudes to 27, 48, 219 n.114, 228 n.83
　public enlighteners 6, 29, 37, 41, 43, 49, 55–6, 140, 177–9, 187, 189, 197 n.38, 218 n.97, 222 n.139
　as scholars 13–14, 16, 55, 196 n.28, 197 n.39
　See also scholar-artist; ideal historian; *nastavnik*
historical fiction 10–11
historical–philological science 3, 192 n.7
　developments in 4, 113, 167–76, 183–4
　Faculty 3, 28, 52, 66, 159, 208 n.61
　See also folklore; history

historiographical trends
  anthropological 90, 113, 116, 128, 182, 188
  comparative approach 3, 18, 25, 31, 46, 119, 130, 168, 171, 173, 175, 182–3, 193 n.11, 193 n.13, 207 n.51, 209 n.7, 232 n.56
  cultural history 19, 46, 50–3, 112–13, 116, 119, 151, 168, 188, 198 n.50
  historicism 25, 39–40, 52, 59
  Marxist 16, 94, 189–90, 194 n.20
  modernism 160–3
  neo-idealism 48, 235–6 n.106, 241 n.11
  positivism 1, 3, 13–14, 16, 33, 43, 52, 66, 75, 113–16, 119–20, 130, 159–60, 163, 165–8, 171, 176, 183, 188, 193 n.9, 199 n.55, 202 n.8, 225–6 n.44, 241n.11, 242 n.12
  psychological approach and study of collective mentality 17, 42, 44, 77–8, 82, 84, 91, 120, 124, 126–7, 130, 157, 166–7, 169, 172, 179, 182–3, 188–9, 218 n.93, 235–6 n.106, 240 n.82
  socio-economic 23, 27, 43–4, 53, 113
  sociological 43, 69–70, 145–6, 180–2, 207 n.51
  See also romanticism; philosophical idealism; realism; symbolism
history
  as a discipline 4–6, 14, 17, 19, 27, 40, 55, 60, 72–4, 94, 110, 136, 225–6 n.44, 226 n.49
  and politics 23–9, 41, 43, 46, 213 n.42
  popularization of 33, 37, 61, 73–4
Huizinga, Johan 188–9

ideal historian 7, 36–41, 43, 49, 51, 187, 258 n.47

Johnson, Emily 120, 122–3, 130–2

Karamzin, Nikolai 11, 223 n.8, 229 n.96, 248 n.13
  History of the Russian State 6, 16–17, 23, 42, 58–9, 75
Kareev, Nikolai 5–6, 19, 30, 43
  on Granovskii 38, 83
  on Grevs 95–6, 110–11
  on Pushkin 140–1
  and Taine 19, 114, 168, 177–82
  Tolstoi, *War and Peace*, critique 139, 144–7
  and Veselovskii 114–15, 177–82
Karpovich, Michael
  on Kliuchevskii 215 n.65, 216 n.68, 226 n.52
Karsavin, Lev 52–3, 220 n.120, 220 n.121, 220 n.122, 221 n.130
Kasso, Lev. *See* Ministry of Education
Kassow, Samuel 28–9, 33
Katkov, Mikhail 28, 173, 206 n.40
Kaufman, A. A. 32, 111, 113
Kavelin, Konstantin 5, 45, 183
Kelley, Donald 41, 113–15, 165, 188–9, 213 n.41, 213 n.42, 234 n.76, 239 n.79, 254 n.3
Khomentovskaia, Anna 136
Kiesewetter [Kizevetter], Alexander 23, 43, 47, 57
  on Gershenzon 253–4 n.116
  on Granovskii 36
  on Kliuchevskii 67, 96
Kliuchevskii, Vasilii 1–2, 10, 28
  Captain's Daughter, The (Pushkin), assessment of 141–3
  on Catherine the Great 67, 85
  early life 6, 8, 14, 44–7, 236–7 n.10
  Evgenii Onegin (Pushkin) 17, 143, 155, 236–7 n.10
  Grust' (Lermontov) 18, 155–8
  Nederosl' (Fonvizin) 17, 101–2
  nobility, assessment of 12, 56, 68–9, 90, 101–7, 227 n.66, 238–9 n.48, 248 n.17
  obituary 9, 66–8, 157, 218 n.94, 227 n.66, 228 n.74, 232 n.56, 238–9 n.48
  on Peter the Great 84–8, 101, 103
  'Pushkin Speech' 141–2
  serfdom 27, 44, 47, 69, 227 n.66
  Turgenev 68, 236–7 n.10
  view of history 12, 14, 17, 44–7, 216 n.68, 216 n.76, 227 n.67
  See also scholar-artist
Koialovich, Mikhail 23, 195 n.21
Kostomarov, Nikolai 9, 12, 18, 23, 45, 62–3, 75, 167–71, 224 n.32, 225 n.35, 256–7 n.27, 257 n.32
kraevedenie 120, 126, 132–4

Central Regional Study Bureau 134, 245 n.80
historical geography 125, 132, 134, 136, 212 n.37
kruzhok 30–1, 218 n.98. *See also* circles
Kudriavtsev, Petr 8–9, 12, 50, 54
  on Granovskii 37–8, 62, 71, 171, 197 n.41, 212 n.34, 226 n.49
  short stories 61

Lamprecht, Karl 114, 188, 240 n.82
Langlois, Charles-Victor 114, 206 n.49, 220 n.118, 260 n.84
Lappo-Danilevskii, Aleksandr 32, 47–8, 113, 218 n.98, 219 n.117, 235–6 n.106
Lapshin, I. I. 113
laws of history
  discussions of 14, 25, 42–3, 64–5, 81–2, 143, 166, 176, 202 n.17, 207 n.51, 212–13 n.39, 222 n.137, 230 n.23, 233 n.70. *See also zakonomernost'*
learned societies 6, 30, 201 n.2, 205 n.35, 206 n.49
liberalism 5, 22, 25, 27, 29, 31, 51, 73, 150, 210 n.14, 218 n.98, 218 n.103
Likhachev, Dmitrii 130
literary scholarship, developments in 2–4, 18, 46, 77, 115, 120, 129, 131, 163–8, 172–83, 193 n.11, 193 n.13, 241 n.8, 241 n.9, 256 n.18. *See also slovesnost'*
Lomonosov, Mikhail 21, 58, 87, 97, 126
Lotman, Iurii 39, 57, 131, 190, 262 n.3
Lotman, Lidiia 59, 167, 169, 184, 255 n.11
Lunacharskii, Anatolii 123–4

Macaulay, Thomas 199 n.61
Maiakovskii, Vladimir 126, 134
Markwick, Roger 52
Merezhkovskii, Dmitrii 128, 157
Michelet, Jules 41, 165, 204 n.30
  Russian responses to 13, 17, 35, 63, 114, 212 n.37, 225 n.37
Miliukov, Pavel 30, 43, 45, 73, 183, 195 n.21, 202 n.8, 205 n.35, 206 n.50, 207 n.51, 213 n.42, 215 n.63, 217 n.90, 233 n.70
Ministry of Education 15, 25–6, 174
  Delianov, Ivan 28
  Kasso, Lev 29

Tolstoi, Dmitrii 9, 28, 197 n.40, 205 n.36
Uvarov, Sergei 15, 21–3, 25, 29
See also University charters; educational reform, and counter reform
Mommsen, Theodore 50, 53, 109, 249 n.49
Monod, Gabriel 114, 165, 167, 193 n.9, 206 n.49, 240 n.88, 251 n.73, 260 n.84
Moscow-Tartu school of semiotics 19, 190. *See also* Lotman, Iurii; Paperno, Irina
Müller, Gerhard 21

nadzor 25–6, 33. *See also* censorship
Narkompros 18, 118, 124, 132, 243 n.33. *See also* Ministry of Education
nastavnik, definitions of 6–9, 32–3, 36, 38, 40, 43, 48, 51, 54–5, 95, 189
nationalism
  cultural 3, 18, 21–2, 58, 167, 170–1
  political 42, 59, 63, 223 n.7
  See also Slavophile-Westernizer controversy
nauka as scholarship 3, 30–1, 40, 55, 193 n.9, 209–10 n.12, 221–2 n.136, 225–6 n.41. *See also* true scholarship
neo-idealism 48, 120, 194 n.20
Nicholas I, reign of 9, 23–4, 26–7, 32, 41, 58–9, 81, 105–6, 120, 151, 158, 169, 248 n.14
Niebuhr, Bartold 40–1
Novikov, Nikolai 117, 237 n.13

Official Nationality doctrine 21–2, 26, 37, 41, 169. *See also* nationalism
Offord, Derek 58
Ottokar, Nikolai 122

pan-Slavism 42, 214 n.49, 214 n.51
Paperno, Irina 39, 44, 236 n.5, 253 n.114
Peter the Great
  assessments of 21, 127, 231 n.37, 232 n.56
philosophical idealism 16, 22–3, 39, 64–6, 214 n.48
Pisarev, Dmitrii 99, 107
Platonov, Sergei 47, 73, 75, 157–8, 195 n.25, 215 n.63, 228 n.74, 242 n.15
Pogodin, Mikhail 9, 12, 22, 33, 37–8, 41–3, 45, 55, 61, 63, 66, 74, 81, 151, 170, 213 n.45, 214 n.48, 214 n.51
  and Gogol 61, 214 n.49
  on Karamzin 58, 223 n.7, 223 n.8

short stories 61–2
view of history 42, 61, 201 n.4, 213–4 n.46, 214 n.51
Pokrovskii, Mikhail 48, 190, 247 n.12
Polevoi, Nikolai 59, 61, 193 n.12
Ponomarev, Boris 190
populism 28, 45, 49, 107, 218 n.99
Presniakov, A. E. 47, 68, 113
publitsistika 7, 33, 42, 45, 163, 176, 178, 189, 237 n.13
Pushkin, Aleksandr 4, 6, 10–12, 17, 31, 56, 60–2, 75, 100, 110, 121, 127, 131, 159–60, 247 n.12, 252–3 n.107, 256–7 n.27. *See also* Kareev; Kliuchevskii
Pypin, Aleksandr 33, 45, 163, 167, 182–3, 255 n.13, 261 n.105

Raeff, Marc 67
realism (literary) 11, 13–14, 17, 37, 43–5, 66, 72, 78, 84, 99, 107, 109, 111, 145–6, 150, 153, 168, 190, 215 n.65, 216 n.68, 236 n.5, 240 n.85, 248–9 n.34
Rolland, Romain 54, 116, 148, 153–5, 251 n.75
romanticism 3, 13–14, 38–42, 44, 48, 54, 58, 62–4, 66, 83, 169–71, 174, 176–7, 183, 199 n.55, 225 n.41, 248–9 n.34
Roosevelt, Priscilla 14, 22, 39, 66, 82–3, 201–2 n.7, 210 n.14, 211 n.29, 224 n.29, 225 n.41, 225–6 n.44, 231 n.28, 231 n.31, 253 n.112
Rubinshtein, Nikolai 70, 96–7, 227 n.60, 227 n.70, 262 n.10
Russian Question 22–3, 29

Samarin, Iurii 23
Schelling, Friedrich Wilhelm Joseph 22, 39–40, 43, 55, 59, 61, 214 n.48
Schiller, Friedrich 61–2, 256–7 n.27
Schleiermacher, Friedrich 7, 25, 203 n.23
Schlözer, August 21, 66, 171, 182, 213 n.45
scholar-artist 9–10, 67–8, 136, 173, 215 n.65, 217 n.88, 227 n.60, 229 n.96. *See also* true scholarship
Scott, Sir Walter 35, 49, 60, 64, 83, 110, 141, 169, 198 n.47, 212 n.37
Seignobos, Charles 114, 205 n.35, 206 n.49, 260 n.84
seminars
development of 30, 32, 48, 51, 207 n.57, 219 n.111

home (salon) 31–2, 54, 59, 113, 153, 206 n.50, 256–7 n.27
serfdom and the Emancipation Act 8, 22–3, 27, 47, 183, 227 n.66
Shatz, Marshall 84–5, 103, 233 n.66
Shcherbatov, Mikhail 21, 58, 204 n.26
Shevyrev, Stepan 22, 37, 41, 170, 213–14 n.46, 259 n.65
Shmidt, Sigurd 47, 57, 72–4, 189, 240 n.91
Silver Age 119, 130. *See also* neo-idealism; symbolism
Skrzhinskaia, Elena 137, 218 n.97, 219 n.104, 219 n.115
Slavophile–Westernizer controversy 22, 25, 81, 87, 183, 195 n.21, 230 n.22, 232 n.56. *See also* nationalism; Russian Question
slovesnost' 3, 164, 175–7, 193 n.8, 213 n.45, 255 n.11, 261 n.101, 262 n.3
Solov'ev, Sergei 5, 14, 45, 48, 67, 72, 87, 96–7, 183, 202 n.8, 217 n.91, 222 n.137, 233 n.70, 233 n.71
Solov'ev, Vladimir, 54, 157
soobshchestvo 7, 16, 30, 32, 51–2, 152–3
Stankevich, Aleksandr
on Granovskii 7, 37–8, 62, 197 n.35, 212 n.34, 212 n.37
Stankevich, Nikolai 39–40, 44, 71, 149, 160, 250 n.71
Stasiulevich, Mikhail 50, 218 n.103, 255 n.13
state
and the academic community 21, 25–9, 32, 194 n.15, 196 n.33, 203–4 n.24, 204 n.25, 204 n.30, 206 n.50
in historical interpretation 4–5, 22–3, 202 n.8, 231.38
as patron of knowledge 14, 21, 25–6
Stepanovich, A. 137, 246 n.97
Strakhov, Nikolai 99
Striedter, Jurij 59–61, 143
Sveshnikov, Anton 51–2, 116, 195–6 n.27, 240 n.85
symbolism 119–20, 130–1, 157, 236 n.5, 241 n.11. *See also* Silver Age

Taine, Hippolyte 13, 77, 166–7, 240 n.88, 240 n.89, 254–5 n.9, 255 n.10
and Russian historical enquiry 19, 77, 90, 114, 120, 140, 163, 179, 182–4, 187, 205 n.31, 243 n.36, 250 n.53

Tatishchev, Vasilii 87, 182
Thaden, Edward 70, 214 n.48
Thierry, Augustin 13, 17, 35, 41, 63–4, 165
    Russian appraisals of 114, 187, 212 n.37, 213 n.40, 225 n.37
Tikhanova–Klimenko, Maria 136
Tikhonravov, Nikolai 163, 167, 208 n.61, 255 n.13
Tolstoi, Dmitrii. *See* Ministry of Education
Tolstoi, Lev 10–11, 60, 74–5, 128, 139, 143–7, 153, 162, 197 n.41, 224 n.32, 247 n.1, 248 n.24, 250 n.63
true scholarship 7–8, 32–3, 35–6, 38, 51, 75, 178, 196 n.34, 197 n.38
Turgenev, Ivan 10, 12, 18, 39, 99, 106, 140, 144, 209 n.11, 224 n.24, 249 n.49
    See also Grevs; Kliuchevskii

University charters 2, 9, 21, 26, 28–30, 205–6 n.38
Ustrialov, Nikolai 45
Uvarov, Sergei. *See* Ministry of Education

Valk, Sigizmund 5
Vasilevskii, Vasilii 5, 9, 30, 49–51, 95, 112, 189, 218 n.96
Vengerov, Semen 9, 31, 46, 119, 207 n.54
Veselovskii, Aleksandr 18–19, 46, 115, 119, 167–8, 173–7, 179–80, 193 n.11, 255 n.15, 258 n.52, 258–9 n.53, 259 n.61, 259 n.62
Vetrinskii, Ch. (pseudonym for Vasilii Cheshikhin) 38, 81, 83, 222 n.137

Vinogradov, Pavel 23–5, 27, 30, 43, 47, 53, 159–60, 195 n.24, 202 n.12, 202 n.17, 202–3 n.18, 205 n.35, 205–6 n.38, 206 n.50, 214 n.47, 217 n.90
Violet, P. 114
Vipper, Robert 83, 206 n.50, 228 n.84
von Goethe, Johann Wolfgang 10, 62, 169, 257 n.27
von Humboldt, Wilhelm 17, 64–5, 203 n.23
von Ranke, Leopold 2, 4, 22, 40, 64–5, 83, 112, 117, 155, 188, 212 n.37, 212–13 n.39, 213 n.41, 234 n.76, 240 n.85

Wachtel, Andrew 11, 15, 146, 198 n.47, 247 n.2, 247 n.3, 248 n.14, 252 n.97, 256 n.19
Wachtel, Michael 53–4
White, Hayden 12–13, 64–5, 83, 195 n.21, 198–9 n.54, 199 n.55, 203 n.23, 204 n.30, 211–12 n.31
Women's Higher Courses. *See Bestuzhevskie*
Wortman, Richard 158, 196 n.29

Zabelin, Ivan 23, 193 n.12
zakonomernost' (law governed history) 14, 25, 42–4, 50, 64–5, 75, 81–3, 96, 112, 145, 175–6, 188, 202 n.17, 207 n.51, 212–13 n.39, 222 n.137, 233 n.70.
    See also laws of history
Zelinskii, Faddei 110–11, 124, 239 n.63
Zhukovskii, Vasilii 61, 224 n.29, 251 n.92, 256–7 n.27